In 1976 Steven F. Lawson's *Black Ballots* provided an eye-opening account of black attempts to gain voting rights in the South, from World War II to the Johnson administration. Now, in this equally engrossing sequel, Lawson continues his historical investigation into the 1980s, looking at the efforts of civil rights groups to redress grievances through U.S. government action.

Like the earlier study, *In Pursuit of Power* acknowledges the abiding faith of Afro-Americans in the ballot and chronicles the persistent attempts of an oppressed people to share its democratic promise. It examines the efforts of the federal government to broaden and protect the black suffrage since passage of the 1965 Voting Rights Act. It also analyzes the enforcement of this landmark law by Democratic and Republican administrations, and compares their performances in stimulating black political participation at the ballot box, in fostering black involvement in political party affairs, and in removing lingering barriers to enfranchisement.

Besides exploring legal and constitutional issues, Lawson deftly surveys the political pressures shaping suffrage expansion, especially those affecting

(Continued on back flap)

In Pursuit of Power: Southern Blacks and Electoral Politics, 1965–1982

CONTEMPORARY
AMERICAN HISTORY
SERIES
William E. Leuchtenburg,
General Editor

In Pursuit of Power:

Southern Blacks and Electoral Politics, 1965–1982

Steven F. Lawson

Columbia University Press
New York   1985

103928

Columbia University Press
New York   Guildford, Surrey
Copyright © 1985 Columbia University Press
All rights reserved

Printed in the United States of America

Library of Congress Cataloging in Publication Data

Lawson, Steven F., 1945–
  In pursuit of power.

  (Contemporary American history series)
  Bibliography: p.
  Includes index.
  1. Afro-Americans—Southern States—Politics and
government.   2. Afro-Americans—Southern States—
Suffrage.   3. Southern States—Politics and government—
1951–   . 4. Voting—Southern States—History—
20th century.   5. Elections—Southern States—History—
20th century.   I. Title.   II. Series.
E185.92.L37   1985   324.975′08996073   84-17036
ISBN 0-231-04626-X

Clothbound editions of Columbia University Press Books are
Smyth-sewn and printed on permanent and durable acid-free paper.

In Memory of my Mother
For my Father, Sister, and Family

Contents

Preface

S ince 1965, most election days in the South have been alive with symbolism. In one place or another throughout Dixie some black candidate has gone into the record books as the "first" member of his or her race to hold office since Reconstruction. Every triumph usually brings forth from the media a claim of the palpable transformation of the Old South of bigotry into the New South of racial justice. Each impressive victory—and there have been many—allows white Americans to congratulate themselves on finally extending the long-deferred, democratic promise of equality to Afro-Americans. Despite their noteworthy electoral gains, however, blacks still stand on the threshold of political power, waiting to participate more fully in their own governance.

Election Tuesday, November 2, 1982, fit this pattern that had developed in the South since the mid-1960s. There was much to cheer about as a large number of blacks triumphed. Blacks shattered tradition by winning elections to the state supreme court in Alabama and the state court of appeals in North Carolina. Black candidates picked up eighteen state legislative seats in the South, a gain exceeding that for any other region of the nation. North Carolina, South Carolina, and Florida led the way in boosting their number of black lawmakers sitting in statehouses, and Georgia continued to rank first in the country with its total of twenty-three black state representatives.[1] Elsewhere, black voters helped defeat white candidates unsympathetic to their plight and replaced them with moderates.

In a stunning departure, the forces of moderation included a one-time, bitter foe of racial equality who was now trying to make amends. George Wallace was running again for governor of Alabama, but this time with a difference. Once a vociferous exponent of white supremacy, Wallace now openly solicited black votes and apologized for the racist sins in his past. "I came to see," declared the former apostle of segregation, "that this society can't exist with a dual system."[2] The source of Wallace's conversion was no mystery. Always the political realist, he courted the black electorate which had expanded greatly after passage of the Voting Rights Act of 1965 and which might supply the victorious margin at the polls. Stressing the economic issues that bound impoverished whites and blacks together, Wallace easily trounced his opponent, the Republican mayor of Montgomery, who espoused the same law and order rhetoric that had been Wallace's earlier trademark. The evolution of George Wallace as a racial moderate was a vivid sign of the emerging influence of Afro-Americans in southern politics. Nevertheless, in supporting their former nemesis, black Alabamians were merely selecting the lesser of two evils. In voting for Wallace, they rejected the alternative candidate whom they viewed as a "combination of Adolf Hitler, Benito Mussolini and Tojo."[3]

On that same election day in neighboring Mississippi, black voters had better opportunity to pick a candidate of their choice to represent them. After more than fifteen years of litigation and pressure from the federal government, the Magnolia State had finally redrawn its congressional boundary lines to create in the delta a majority-black population district, though voter registration was split virtually evenly between the races. Democrat Robert Clark, the black nominee for Congress had served in the state legislature since 1967. He attempted to forge the kind of populist, interracial coalition that had swept Wallace to victory in Alabama. In contrast, his Republican adversary, Webb Franklin, eschewed black support. The GOP standardbearer campaigned for government retrenchment, but his real appeal was to the past, a past that had so conspicuously featured second-class citizenship for blacks. Speaking in front of a Confederate war memorial in Greenwood, Franklin admonished: "We welcome the new, but we must never ever forget what has gone before. We cannot forget a heritage that has been sacred through our generations."[4] Indeed, enough voters in the Second Congressional District did not forget, and by a slim margin, Clark went down to defeat. Although receiving the endorsement of prominent white Democrats in the state, Clark did not gain sufficient backing from whites in his district.[5]

The unsuccessful congressional bid of Robert Clark gave cause for concern. Race still played a significant role in determining electoral choice, and Clark lost because of the color of his skin. As long as white southerners refused to vote for blacks, the concept of a color-blind society remained a legal fiction. The suffrage might enable southern blacks to obtain more from government than they ever had before, but, as a minority, their power would nonetheless be restricted if racially polarized voting continued.

By 1984, it appeared that much was changing. Clark's chances for election had improved after his district was again redrawn under federal court order to increase the size of its black majority to 58 percent. At the same time, Reverend Jesse L. Jackson, a former aide to Martin Luther King, Jr., and a veteran of civil rights battles in both the South and North, made an impressive run for the Democratic party presidential nomination, capturing 22 percent of the popular vote in the primaries. Although his delegate total was disproportionately lower than this figure, over 450 representatives to the Democratic National Convention from Alabama, California, Georgia, Kentucky, Mississippi, New York, South Carolina, Virginia, and Washington, D.C., supported him. The political fortunes of Clark and Jackson were related. Voter registration drives during the preceding twenty years had furnished the solid block of votes upon which black candidates could build electoral victories. The campaign of the charismatic Jackson further stimulated higher black enrollment and voter turnout which boosted the prospects of candidates such as Clark on the local level.[6] In addition, Jackson had focused his presidential bid on stricter enforcement of the Voting Rights Act to challenge suffrage schemes, such as legislative gerrymandering, that diluted black voting power and reduced the opportunities of electing black candidates to public office.

It is too early to assess fully the meaning of the Jesse Jackson phenomenon, but the black minister's campaign cautions against complacency. Despite his surprising showing in the

Democratic primaries, Jackson's strength depended almost exclusively on blacks. His efforts to construct an interracial "rainbow coalition" failed to make substantial inroads into the white electorate, polarizing Democratic voters along racial lines. While Jackson brought blacks to the polls in record numbers, his campaign rhetoric heightened racial animosities among whites, including some members of the old civil rights alliance. Furthermore, Jackson's candidacy did not completely unite blacks. Though popular among the overwhelming majority of blacks, Jackson did not gain the endorsement of many prominent black politicians who identified closely with the established leadership of the national Democratic party. Following the primaries, the task remained to join Jackson's constituency with the traditional elements of the New Deal Democratic coalition.

The passage of the 1965 Voting Rights Act aroused great expectations that have yet to be fulfilled. Liberal reformers, black and white, believed that placing ballots in the hands of Afro-Americans would provide them with potent instruments to ensure and safeguard their liberation. However, amidst the euphoria of the second enfranchisement many forgot the lessons of the first. The right to cast a vote did not by itself confer power. The right to vote did not automatically eradicate political and economic inequities that left blacks double victims of both racial and class discrimination. Furthermore, while most southern jurisdictions complied with the letter of the 1965 law, many attempted to violate its spirit by grafting sophisticated forms of bias onto existing electoral institutions. Unless the underlying structural impediments blocking the franchise are removed, the considerable, but as yet limited, amount of success southern blacks have enjoyed in pursuit of political power will not go much further.

It was these considerations that have led me to write a sequel to *Black Ballots*. In that book, I traced the expansion of the suffrage from the outlawing of the white primary through the passage of the Voting Rights Act. Although I was acutely aware that the struggle was not yet over, my own faith in the curative power of the ballot, once blacks received opportunities to exercise it, made me think a follow-up volume unnecessary. Besides, the period after 1965, during which enfranchisement officially became institutionalized, lacked the high drama and sense of heroic purpose that had characterized the long, often turbulent struggle to obtain the right to vote in the first place. Unfortunately, suffrage problems have not been self-correcting, and the second phase of enfranchisement—the search for a greater share of political representation—has engendered a new round of racial conflict, especially over how far to go in remedying the effects of previous discrimination. Although conducted with more civility than during much of the 1950s and 1960s, the current debate concerning race relations is no less compelling and the stakes are no less high. For if the majority of southern blacks fell short of achieving economic and political equality in the nearly two decades since 1965, they still consider the suffrage a crucial weapon in their battle for advancement. This present volume acknowledges that abiding faith in the ballot and seeks to chronicle the persistent attempts of an oppressed people to share in its democratic promise.

This monograph, like my earlier one, closely charts the efforts of civil rights forces to redress grievances through federal action. Although the national consensus surrounding civil rights in general has eroded, the commitment to protection of the ballot has managed to survive. Despite changes in partisan control of the White House and, to a lesser extent, Congress, and shifts in the ideological orientation of the Supreme Court, the Voting Rights Act has not only remained in force but has even been broadened over the years. The federal bureaucracy, often the object of derision for its ineffectiveness, in this situation has built up considerable momentum behind guaranteeing the suffrage. The right to vote has commanded widespread appeal because conservatives as well as liberals recognize it as a cardinal principle of our democratic faith. Furthermore, it has been perceived to be the preferable option for producing social change. In fact, as southern blacks have acquired and used the ballot, they have been less inclined toward adopting disruptive tactics, such as mass demonstrations, that were so crucial to the civil rights movement during the era of disfranchisement.[7]

As southern blacks mobilized their strength at the polls,

they attempted to develop a heightened sense of racial solidarity. This held true whether they chose a strategy of building interracial coalitions or independent black parties. "Black Power" evoked a fierce and not always enlightening debate as to its definition, but its stress on awakening racial consciousness aided the cause of black southerners who struggled to shatter the debilitating notion that politics was the exclusive domain of whites. At the same time, many liberal reformers found the emphasis on racial chauvinism disturbing, coming precisely when the federal government was initiating measures to promote a color-blind society. The original quest for treatment of individuals equally without regard to race was increasingly replaced by calls for affirmative action to compensate minority groups which, on the basis of race, had suffered discrimination in the past. As this metamorphosis occurred, the issue of enfranchisement, though generating less conflict than most other aspects of civil rights, also presented tough questions about the meaning of racial justice and the methods to achieve it.

This examination of black suffrage concentrates on the enforcement of the Voting Rights Act in the South. Here the complex legal, constitutional, and political battles raised by enfranchisement during the Second Reconstruction were fought most intensely. Furthermore, the effectiveness of federal policies can best be measured by studying selected areas within this region where hostility to black political equality had been most fierce. The deplorable conditions that had brought civil rights workers to counties in Mississippi, Alabama, Louisiana, and Georgia in the early 1960s, soon led Justice Department officials to focus their efforts there. Local officials in covered jurisdictions throughout the South then assessed the likelihood of federal intervention by the vigor with which enfranchisement was pursued in the counties designated to receive examiners. The historian, too, can gauge the zeal for equality of the various presidential administrations from Johnson to Reagan by looking at those places whose racist heritage most seriously challenged the Justice Department to shape imaginative enforcement strategies. This is not to suggest that even the entire weight of federal authority could have turned the ballot into a panacea for racial ills, as some proponents of voting rights

had claimed. Nonetheless, the balance struck between full implementation of the black franchise and conciliation of southern leaders
helped determine whether the suffrage offered long strides or small
steps toward racial equality. Read as a companion to *Black Ballots*, this work traces the nation's commitment to the ideal of enfranchisement and the patient efforts of Afro-Americans to realize its potential. The fate of the Second Reconstruction hangs on
the outcome.

Acknowledgments

In writing this book I have incurred many personal and professional debts which I can never satisfactorily repay. There really is no sufficient expression of gratitude to offer the many people who helped me complete this work. If this study has any merit it is largely because of their generosity of time and energy; if it falls short, it is probably because I neglected to heed their good advice.

The preparation of this monograph took me on a research odyssey. My visits to archives throughout the country were enriched by the manuscript librarians who took an interest in my topic and attempted to furnish me with the evidence upon which this chronicle is constructed. In particular, I would like to commend the staff of the Lyndon B. Johnson Presidential Library for patiently answering my frequent requests for documents during a period of several months. A delightful summer spent in Austin at a seminar conducted by Robert A. Divine initiated this project and provided the momentum that carried it to completion. I would also like to thank Gerald Jones of the Voting Section of the Civil Rights Division of the Justice Department for making available his office's voluminous files. Marvin Wall helped me penetrate the mysteries of the federal bureaucracy in the first place and deserves special credit. The funds to travel to these and other institutions were derived in large part from grants awarded by the National Endowment for the Humanities and the American Council of Learned Societies. A year-long sabbatical from the University of South Florida allowed me the necessary time uninterrupted by teaching to write the manuscript.

Material from my article "Preserving the Second Reconstruction: Enforcement of the Voting Rights Act, 1965–1975," *Southern Studies: An Interdisciplinary Journal of the South* (Spring 1983), vol. 22, no. 1, is reprinted with permission.

My friends who are also scholars shouldered a double burden. As friends, they boosted my morale and as scholars they helped educate me. For reading and commenting on the entire manuscript, I am grateful to Mark I. Gelfand, who also supplied a newspaper clipping service, Robert P. Ingalls, my jogging partner, Darryl Paulson, my lunch companion, and John Dittmer, whose home in Mississippi was a hospitable retreat for a weary researcher. No one assisted me more than Nancy A. Hewitt. A talented historian and devoted friend, she unselfishly read and re-read successive drafts of this work, drew the charts that accompany it, and, above all, helped ease some painful moments down the home stretch.

Several other friends and colleagues sustained me in my efforts. Ira and Nancy Gouterman and Richard Pinsker know very little about the historian's craft, but they are immensely wise in the art of friendship. We have all come a long way together, and I am delighted that they can share in the completion of this project. Lou Pérez enlivened many campus walks to the library with intriguing discussions of politics, manners, and morals, and over the years he provided the strength to fight and win many good battles. The Friday afternoon group at the Cafe Don José lifted my spirits, and History Department secretaries, Peggy Cornett and Sylvia Wood, lightened my administrative duties as chairperson so that I could finish the book.

I owe a great deal to William E. Leuchtenburg. A teacher and scholar who has also become a friend, he has challenged me to live up to the highest standards of excellence throughout my career. Although it is an agonizing process to revise a manuscript under his editorial scrutiny, I have had no more rewarding intellectual experience. His open mind and breadth of knowledge have been truly inspiring.

At Columbia University Press, I would like to thank Bernard Gronert for encouraging me to write this book and Anne McCoy for applying her editorial skills to make its contents more readable. I was able to furnish her with a carefully typed copy to edit mainly due to the amazing skills of my university's word processing staff—Marian Pittman, Greg Gronlund, and Michael Copeland.

Finally, I am pleased to acknowledge my family, Murray and Belle Lawson, Lona and Jerry Mirchin, who may not always realize how deeply I appreciate them. I only hope that my mother knew.

Tampa, Florida

May 1984

In Pursuit of Power:
Southern Blacks
and Electoral Politics,
1965–1982

Part I

The Turbulent Years

1.

Ballots, Not Bullets

It was a bittersweet moment. At the National Press Club in Washington, D.C., the president faced a crowd of reporters waiting to interrogate him for the last time before he left office. Outside on this chilly seventeenth day of January in 1969, workers applied the finishing touches for the forthcoming inauguration, while antiwar demonstrators flocked to the nation's capital to picket the ceremony. Inside, Lyndon Johnson, in a relaxed mood alternating between seriousness and gaiety, fielded the questions with an obvious sense of relief and nostalgia. In three days, he would retire to his Texas ranch, out of the limelight, away from many of these same journalists who had blasted his administration for creating a credibility gap. Soon he would be free of the burden of handling issues affecting war and peace, law, order, and justice—explosive problems which sorely divided the nation and certainly figured in Johnson's decision not to run again for the presidency. Although the circumstances surrounding this final news conference were not cheerful, the president proudly reminisced about the many splended triumphs of his tenure in the White House.[1]

Nothing gave Lyndon Johnson more pleasure than recounting his role in obtaining passage of the 1965 Voting Rights Act. As a senator, he had departed from nearly all of his fellow southerners in supporting adoption of the 1957 civil rights statute strengthening the federal government's authority to challenge racially discriminatory suffrage practices. In signing the Voting Rights Act into law eight years later, President Johnson asserted: "The vote is the most powerful instrument ever devised by man for breaking down injustice and destroying the terrible walls which imprison men because they are different from other men."[2] Consequently, at his farewell news conference, the outgoing chief executive scarcely hesitated when a reporter asked: "What . . . did you regard as your greatest accomplishment as President, and what do you regard as your happiest moment while President?" The veteran of so many legislative victories picked out passage of the Voting Rights Act, explaining:

I believe if everyone has the right to vote that they [sic] can take care of their own problems pretty well. As you see, when they are electing southern sheriffs, southern mayors, and southern judges, the Negroes have been emancipated a good deal. It is going to correct an injustice of decades and centuries. I think it is going to make it possible for this Government to endure, not half slave and half free, but united.[3]

The president could take justifiable pride in the achievements brought about by his prized suffrage law. Before passage of the voting rights statute only one of four adult blacks had managed to register in the seven states covered under the act. Four years later, the proportion had leaped to three in five. These new voters generated impressive changes in the South. The presence of black officeholders, once more rare than a cool August night in the Deep South, was becoming more commonplace as over two hundred Negroes held elected positions by the time Johnson left the White House. The victories of black candidates were not the only signs of progress. Black ballots helped oust some of the most recalcitrant officials blocking the path toward civil rights and replaced them with moderates. Aware of the growing strength of the black electorate, even many of the incumbents who managed to retain office modified their old racist ways to fit the changing times. In the entire history of racial reform throughout the twentieth century there was little to rival the accomplishments gained so swiftly by passage of the landmark franchise statute. Looking over this impressive record, the NAACP commended the president for his outstanding performance. "Not only Negro Americans, but all Americans," the *Crisis* declared, "are deeply indebted to Lyndon Baines Johnson for his leadership in efforts to solve the grim and grievous problems of race which have plagued this nation since its founding nearly 200 years ago."[4]

Yet Johnson was stepping down with the nation more divided on racial issues than when he helped place the Voting Rights Act on the statute books. The coalition which had won passage of three notable civil rights laws during the Johnson years was in disarray, fractured by internal bickering over strategy. At one end of the spectrum the National Association for the Advancement of Colored People (NAACP) and the National Urban League (NUL) remained committed to desegregation and the franchise and pursued their goals in tandem with white liberals. They rarely wavered in their faith in traditional political and legal processes and viewed the Johnson administration as their most potent ally. At the opposite edge stood the Student Nonviolent Coordinating Committee (SNCC) and the Congress of Racial Equality (CORE). Their early beliefs in integration and passive resistance had given way to a growing racial nationalism and advocacy of retaliatory violence. Disappointment with white liberals during the first half of the 1960s had caused severe antagonisms, prompting them to withdraw from interracial alliances. Substituting a rhetoric of revolution for that of reform, they proclaimed black power as their clarion call and found receptive audiences in urban ghettoes of the North and the rural black belt in the South. In the middle, the Southern Christian Leadership Conference (SCLC) occupied its customary position. Led by the Reverend Martin Luther King, Jr., it refused to abandon hope for achieving the "beloved community" but became increasingly critical of the economic sources of racial inequality throughout the nation. Although viewing "black power" as too caustic a slogan, King declined to join moderate civil rights leaders in severing ties with its outspoken proponents.

The national consensus in favor of black advancement, so potent in the early 1960s, had collapsed after 1965 as racial conflicts spread northward and exploded in bloody urban riots. In the midst of these rebellions, SNCC's leadership passed to Stokely Carmichael in 1966 and to H. Rap Brown a year later. Although they were not responsible for the outburst of violence that erupted spontaneously throughout black ghettos during the mid 1960s, their bellicose rhetoric helped inflame racial animosities. After a riot in Cleveland, Carmichael remarked: "When you talk about black power, you talk of building a movement that will smash everything Western civilization has created."[5] Even more menacing, Brown shouted to a rally in Cambridge, Maryland, in 1967: "If America don't come around, we going burn it down, brother."[6] Shortly thereafter a riot broke out, thus reinforcing Brown's reputation as the nation's number one fomenter of insurrection. When the federal government attempted to prosecute Brown, he showed his unbridled contempt for President Johnson by referring to him as a "white honkey cracker, an outlaw from Texas."[7]

The ghetto violence and the stridency that accompanied it frightened whites. Convinced that the major aims of the civil rights struggle had been achieved by mid-decade, many whites failed to appreciate the sources of enduring black frustration, favored a halt to further demonstrations, and considered as ungrateful those who continued to agitate. No one played on the anxieties of whites better than did George Wallace. Having whipped up the antagonisms of southerners against desegregation, the Alabama governor carried his racist messages to the North. There he received a favorable reception from whites who feared that black advances came at their expense. Wallace exploited class as well as racial tensions. He appealed to blue collar workers and denounced "left-wing theoreticians, briefcase totin' bureaucrats, ivory tower guideline writers, bearded anarchists, smart-aleck editorial writers and pointy headed professors" for snubbing their noses at them.[8] Running in the Democratic presidential primaries in 1964, Wallace surprised his opponents by showing well in three northern states before withdrawing as a contender. Given the rising racial friction in the years after the election, Wallace grew in attraction among disgruntled whites, and he looked forward to 1968.

During that period, the more closely the Johnson administration championed the goals of the civil rights movement, even those deemed most temperate, the further it aroused the ire of whites unhappy with the accelerated pace of the black liberation struggle. In 1966, one of the president's most sensitive and thoughtful aides on the race issue, Harry McPherson, noted "that it would have been hard to pass the emancipation proclamation in the atmosphere prevailing this summer. White people are scared and some of the consensus behind improvement of the Negro's condition is running out—has run out."[9] On this point, Attorney General Nicholas Katzenbach agreed and urged Johnson to strike "a balance between denouncing those who appeal to violence and expressing support and sympathy for the evils which exist and to programs designed to overcome them."[10] Staking out this centrist position proved difficult. Although continuing to press for civil rights measures, the White House increasingly framed its responses to racial disturbances with the electoral clout of the white backlash in mind. Marvin Watson, one of the president's top political strategists, recommended: "We should emphasize that the Administration is for law and order. Looters ought to be arrested and those who resist arrest should be shot. Law abiding citizens, black and white, should have and will have the safety and protection of their government."[11]

Johnson's escalation of the war in Vietnam had not enhanced the appeal of moderation. On January 6, 1966, SNCC condemned the United States for waging a "murderous policy of aggression in Vietnam," and it urged young men to offer their services to the civil rights movement as a "valid alternative to the draft."[12] This manifesto greatly disturbed Roy Wilkins, Executive Secretary of the NAACP, and Whitney Young, Executive Director of the Urban League, who closed ranks behind the White House. They met with Johnson's civil rights advisors to map out plans "to negate the impact" of SNCC's declaration. Wilkins publicly excoriated SNCC for adhering to "doctrinaire . . . left wing theory," which he claimed was out of step with the thinking of most civil rights groups. Young scoffed that those "who criticize President Johnson over Viet Nam must realize that his domestic programs . . . mark the beginning of a new era in American life."[13] Besides sniping at SNCC and other dissenters, Johnson's black civil rights supporters aimed to increase their influence within administration councils by actively promoting and justifying the war effort. They conducted a campaign to celebrate the achievements and sacrifices of black soldiers fighting on Vietnamese battlefields. "For the first time," Simeon Booker, a widely read Negro journalist, asserted, "the U.S. has fielded a truly democratic team in Viet Nam."[14]

Pride in black heroism was not enough to hold together the civil rights movement behind the administration's foreign policy. After SNCC and CORE defected, the White House expressed confidence that blacks "on the whole do not appear to be as anti-Viet Nam as the left wing groups."[15] A more serious threat emerged when Martin Luther King launched a frontal assault against Johnson's widening of the war. Despite the FBI's surveillance of King and the attempt to uncover communist infiltration of SCLC, the president had viewed the Nobel laureate as a reasonable black spokesman. The chief executive and the minister had worked together effectively in engineering passage of civil rights acts in 1964 and 1965. Although Johnson questioned King's judgment "over the long pull," according to presidential advisor Eric Goldman, he was "aware that if King should be discredited by failure far less responsible Negroes were likely to take over the leadership of the civil rights movement."[16] Following SNCC's denunciation of the war in 1966, the administration believed that the "most difficult part of the equation is what Martin Luther King will do next."[17] During the ensuing year, the Atlanta pastor juggled his growing moral reservations concerning the war with the practical considerations for maintaining ties with the administration. This delicate balance finally snapped in April 1967 when Reverend King, speaking from the pulpit of Riverside Church in New York City, charged: "The Great Society has been shot down on the battlefields of Vietnam." Crossing the Rubicon with respect to the Johnson administration, he said passionately: "It would be very inconsistent for me to teach and preach nonviolence in this situation and then applaud when thousands and thousands of people, both adults and children, are being maimed and mutilated and many killed in this war."[18]

In response, the Johnson administration and its black allies attacked King for his apostasy. The president's disappointment with King turned vicious as the FBI fed Johnson defamatory material about his adversary's private life. Harry McPherson reflected Johnson's bitterness in dubbing King "the crown prince of the Vietniks."[19] Black supporters of the war rushed to condemn King. Carl Rowan, a columnist appointed by Johnson to direct the United States Information Agency, sniffed communist influence behind King's antiwar pronouncements. Advising the White House of his desire "to take out after King," Rowan wrote a bitter article in which he raked the clergyman over the coals for creating "doubt about the Negro's loyalty to his country,"[20] In less strident tones, the *New Pittsburgh Courier* criticized Dr. King for mixing "the matter of civil rights with the complex and confusing issue of foreign policy." Furthermore, the board of directors of the NAACP rejected King's suggestion to merge the civil rights and antiwar struggles. "Civil rights battles will have to be fought and won on their own merits irrespective of the state of war or peace in the world," it said.[21] In turn, King and his aides retorted that their black critics were "very nervous on Vietnam, afraid they're going to lose everything. . . . They're hoping the war will win them their spurs."[22]

Rallying around the president, black leaders expected that they would gain added leverage in shaping solutions to the problem of racial inequality. Whereas King had come to believe that there would not be enough butter as long as the guns roared, many of his civil rights colleagues thought the country possessed sufficient resources to treat both domestic and foreign ills. If they had doubts about the waging of the war, Johnson's civil rights allies were willing to pay the price of silence in order to obtain administration backing for their goals at home. Furthermore, they hoped to preserve the prominence of their organizations over rival groups. In the wake of the radical attacks on Johnson, the NAACP and the Urban League grasped the opportunity to persuade the White House to cease handling "so called leaders of civil rights groups with a sort of benevolent equality."[23]

This feeling was mutual. Johnson counted on respectable Negro leaders to undercut his militant opponents who were fanning the flames of discord. Troubled by urban riots and the proliferation of extremist rhetoric, the Johnson administration sought to temper the restless energies of the civil rights movement.[24] Presidential counselors suggested that Johnson meet with "responsible" Negro leaders including politicians, clergymen, union officials, and college presidents. Harry McPherson contrasted the members of this type of delegation with militants who "represent bitterness, not people," and he advised the chief executive to "ask them to use their influence and raise their voices against the riots—to appeal to their fellow Negroes to use lawful means for gaining their legitimate ends."[25] Thus, in guiding the civil rights struggle along a moderate course, both the president and his black allies would benefit: Johnson would retain the political allegiance of a vital segment of his Great Society coalition while traditional civil rights advocates improved their access to the White House.

Nevertheless, attempts to harness a volatile social movement posed serious problems. The president's conferring of approval on moderate leaders—invitations to the White House, consultations on vital issues—increased their vulnerability to criticism from militants. Close association with the administration opened leaders of the NAACP and Urban League to charges that they were being co-opted. A Johnson aide, Matthew Nimetz, admitted that the administration had "done a lot to try to bolster the moderate, responsible Negro leadership," but he acknowledged that this strategy "then has the effect of making them seem like Uncle Toms, and the younger black element becomes alienated."[26] Harry McPherson agreed that by embracing the Urban League's Whitney Young and the NAACP's Roy Wilkins, Johnson "would endanger them after a time with the Negro community."[27] Attorney General Katzenbach recognized that "one of the principal difficulties of established Negro leadership has been and will continue to be taking positions that are at the same time responsible, practical—and clearly independent of the Administration," and he realized that the chief executive "does not strengthen the leadership of Roy Wilkins or Martin Luther King when they are made to appear to be his lieutenants or apologists." The Justice Department chief suggested that the major civil rights groups establish "a militant but peaceful organization of young people which could successfully compete with SNCC."[28]

Caught in the crossfire between rising black militancy and escalating white opposition, Johnson strategists sought safer ground on which to maintain their moral commitments to the civil rights movement without demolishing the broad based political coalition which had supported the Great Society. The Voting Rights Act played a key role in their overall thinking, especially after the proliferation of riots. They counted on enfranchisement and the exercise of the ballot to provide a legitimate alternative to violence, to offer blacks a political stake in the system, and to reduce racial tensions. In 1966, a year before a fierce riot erupted in Newark, President Johnson had admonished a Democratic party rally in that troubled city: "Remember this: There is more power in the ballot than there is in the bullet, and it lasts longer." [29] At the same time, the president's associates echoed this sentiment. Louis Martin, the black deputy chairman of the Democratic National Committee and former editor of the *Chicago Defender,* noted: "With all the concern about the white backlash, the need for a big get-out-the-vote campaign is urgent." [30]

Moderate blacks agreed with the administration's assessment. With radical influence growing, established Negro leaders sought to stem an erosion in their own support. "As I look at the number of colored people who have been elected to public office," Clarence Mitchell, the astute Washington lobbyist for the NAACP, remarked two years following passage of the Voting Rights Act, "I believe that we are seeing vindication of the American dream." Encouraged by such gains, he pointed out that they gave those who believed in the Constitution of the United States a much larger "arsenal of arguments with which to defend our position." [31] Vernon Jordan, the director of the Atlanta-based Voter Education Project (VEP), a foundation-supported program of the Southern Regional Council which had helped register thousands of black southerners since 1962, worried about the growing disaffection of young blacks. To those who asked, " 'Keep WHAT faith, baby?' " Jordan replied: "The democratic political process can restore that faith and renew that hope." [32] These civil rights advocates looked to a new breed of black elected officials to restore confidence among blacks who otherwise might be tempted to follow proponents of racial chauvinism and retaliatory violence. Along these lines, Simeon Booker wrote: "Black politicians believe the democratic process must work or this nation is doomed. If the action is to leave the streets, representative government must be the answer. If votes are to replace bricks and firearms, the black man must have a rightful opportunity to participate . . . in policy-making roles in government."[33]

The franchise had particular appeal to those who viewed the continuation of the interracial liberal coalition as the most appropriate method for achieving racial equality. Bayard Rustin, a black pacifist and longtime proponent of direct mass action, endorsed the exercise of the ballot as a means of creating "a powerful realignment of democratic politics that would be an effective counterbalance both to the reactionaries on the far right and the alliance of Dixiecrats and Republicans."[34] Although few considered voting as a panacea, enfranchisement was counted on as a prerequisite to racial justice. "The ballot is not a draft on the bank of social gains," Leslie Dunbar, the director of the Southern Regional Council, remarked; however, "the empirical fact is that no steady Negro advance has been achieved in any southern community where Negroes do not vote in politically significant numbers."[35] In a similar fashion, Dr. King shared this faith in the electoral process. He did not believe "everything Negroes need will . . . like magic materialize from the use of the ballot. Yet as a lever of power . . . it will help to achieve many far-ranging changes during our lifetime."[36]

Even the most militant critics of Johnson-style liberalism embraced the vote as a potent weapon for black liberation. "The *act* of registering to vote," Stokely Carmichael and Charles V. Hamilton wrote in their espousal of black power, "marks the beginning of political modernization by broadening the base of participation," a necessary condition for the eradication of racism.[37] The organization which Carmichael chaired, SNCC, had conducted numerous voter registration drives in the Deep South and had launched independent political parties in Mississippi and Alabama. One adherent of the Mississippi Freedom Democratic Party, a SNCC offshoot, explained: "Voter registration is black power. Power is invested in the ballot and that's why the white man worked like hell to keep you away from it."[38]

Given this general agreement on suffrage, the Johnson administration emphasized the importance of enfranchisement not only because it genuinely cared about racial equality but also because it hoped to convince blacks to reject violence as a tactic and to accept the alternative of working peacefully within the system. In 1966, Katzenbach urged civil rights leaders "to devote still broader concern to the scope and speed with which Negroes can now exercise the *basic* form of democratic expression—the vote" and announced that the time had arrived "when the civil rights movement can and should turn from protest to affirmation, from force against discrimination to a major affirmative force in the life not only of the Negroes of the South but of all the South."[39] Louis Martin stressed the need to encourage political interest "as a means to achieve 'Black Power' in a constitutional, orderly manner." He intended to work hard to convince black officials "to take a more active role in community leadership and not leave the kind of vacuum which is usually filled by civil rights kooks."[40] By establishing a network of black political leaders from every level of government, the White House would have a "link to the Negro community and . . . effectively bypass the Rap Browns and Stokely Carmichaels and even the Martin Luther Kings (none of whom have been elected to anything)."[41]

Thus, for divergent and sometimes contradictory reasons, the Johnson administration and its allies and detractors shared a common desire for strengthening the ballot. Agreement on enfranchisement did not remove the friction between competing elements of the civil rights coalition or the hostility of reactionary white opponents, but it did provide a channel through which the administration could steer a moderate racial course. Seeking to navigate through the stormy seas of racial conflict, the Johnson crew embarked on a voyage to keep both southern black and white passengers on board. In doing so, the chief executive charted the route for succeeding administrations to follow.

2.

A Cautious Advance

President Johnson's signing of the Voting Rights Act on August 6, 1965, showcased the national consensus in favor of southern black enfranchisement. Enactment of the legislation climaxed a decade of struggle to empower the federal government to eliminate suffrage barriers in Dixie. Two civil rights measures enacted during the Eisenhower years and enforced under Kennedy still left the majority of southern blacks disfranchised. Experience had shown that case-by-case litigation chipped away too slowly at the structure of white supremacy built upon literacy tests, poll taxes, and intimidation. Prodded by long-suffering civil rights demonstrators, most recently in Selma, Alabama, and reinforced by the public outrage at the brutal and sometimes murderous treatment of peaceful protesters, the Johnson administration overcame opposition in Congress to pass the potent Voting Rights Act. To be sure, southern politicos attacked the suffrage measure, but their customary combativeness was missing. No match for the bipartisan, interracial coalition in defense of the right to vote, southern congressmen watched helplessly as their colleagues overwhelmingly voted to extend first-class citizenship rights to blacks.[1]

The bill Lyndon Johnson signed into law armed Washington with powerful weapons to combat racial bias. It narrowed the use of literacy tests as a suffrage qualification and established a formula to calculate which states and localities had employed them to disfranchise blacks. Section four automatically suspended the administration of literacy tests and similar devices in those places where voter registration or turnout at the polls for the 1964 presidential election dipped below fifty percent of eligible adults. To avoid cumbersome judicial enforcement, a companion section six authorized the attorney general of the United States to appoint federal examiners in the covered jurisdictions at his discretion or upon receipt and certification of twenty meritorious complaints from residents of the affected areas. Another section empowered the Justice Department to dispatch to the stipulated locations observers who would monitor the casting and counting of ballots on election day. Not only did the statute rescind current racially discriminatory practices, but it also aimed at striking out biased methods that might be adopted in the future. To this end, section five sanctioned the attorney general or the District Court for the District of Columbia to review in advance changes in "any voting qualification or prerequisite, or standard, practice, or procedure with respect to voting different from that in force or effect on November 1, 1964." Once caught by the triggering mechanism, covered jurisdictions could only bail out by proving in the District Court for the District of Columbia that they had not administered a racially objectionable test or device for the previous five years. The act did not catch every southern state which disfranchised blacks, but among the six and part of a seventh that it reached were the worst offenders: Alabama, Georgia, Louisiana, Mississippi, and South Carolina.[2]

Hardly had the ink on the new act dried when the Justice Department sprang into action. In anticipation of the bill's passage, Attorney General Nicholas Katzenbach's staff had prepared a list of unyielding counties which had hampered governmental and private attempts to remove suffrage restrictions. Within several days, nine of the most discriminatory areas had been designated to receive federal examiners, and by November 1, federal registrars were operating in thirty-two counties in Alabama, Louisiana, Mississippi, and South Carolina. By the end of the year, federal officials had added over 79,000 blacks to the registration rolls alongside the names of more than 150,000 signed up by local registrars.[3] After an inspection tour, John Macy, the chairman of the United States Civil Service Commission, the agency responsible for recruiting and training the enrollment officers, expressed his satisfaction that the "voter listing process is functioning smoothly. The individual examiners are performing with skill and efficiency. They have gained the respect and cooperation of the community leaders, white and Negro, in the counties where they are operating."[4]

The strategy for enforcement of the Voting Rights Act during the first months fixed the approach for the future. Traditionally, Justice Department officials had attempted to operate within boundaries that maintained minimum federal intervention in state registration and electoral affairs. They recognized the "normal political gravity of the American political system toward localism," as the political scientist Gary Orfield has pointed out, and intended to apply power prudently to promote change and encourage local responsibility for ultimately guaranteeing the suffrage.[5] Enactment of the voting rights law had been a response to extraordinary circumstances, and federal policymakers hoped to restore normal relations between national and local governments once southern officials came willingly to accept an unfettered black franchise. They anticipated that as blacks freely obtained the ballot, they would choose representatives who, in turn, discerned a political interest in protecting the right to vote of their nonwhite constituents. Given an initial push from Washington, southern politicos would have an incentive to take a larger role in correcting their own electoral ills. With this in mind, Justice Department lawyers had to satisfy the expectations of civil rights groups without unduly disturbing established southern political leaders.

Katzenbach directed the attempt to strike this balance. A Yale Law School graduate, Rhodes Scholar, and member of the faculty of the University of Chicago Law School, he first arrived at Justice during the Kennedy administration. After serving as Robert Kennedy's deputy, he became Lyndon Johnson's attorney general after Kennedy resigned in 1964. During that period, Katzenbach had ventured into the center of several turbulent civil rights storms. Noted for his patience and coolness under pressure, the tall, balding Katzenbach had undertaken some sensitive missions in the Deep South. On the fall day in 1962 when James Meredith's admission to the University of Mississippi sparked a riot at the Oxford campus, he was there to coordinate federal activities. A year later, he showed up at the University of Alabama and engaged in a much-publicized confrontation with Governor George Wallace before successfully shepherding two black students into the school.

These conflicts notwithstanding, Katzenbach wished to avoid such confrontations between federal and state suthorities. Like his colleagues at Justice, the attorney general shared what Victor Navasky has termed the "code of the Ivy League gentlemen." By virtue of background, training, and temperament, these department lawyers favored mediation and cooperation rather than coercion and conflict. They found negotiated settlements more desirable than lawsuits and litigation better than direct displays of armed force. Only if southern officials proved unreasonable did they sanction federal intervention in local affairs. "It is our theory," Katzenbach remarked, "that if you take over the law enforcement from [southern governors], you won't be able to maintain it and they will abdicate. From this came the attempt to preserve the federal system until we could get through the idea that local officials have an obligation to enforce the law."[6] Besides, he maintained, the national government did not have sufficient resources to furnish manpower everywhere throughout the South where civil rights were threatened.

When Katzenbach first came to the Justice Department, he found like-minded lawyers there, such as John Doar. Doar worked for the Civil Rights Division (CRD), established in 1957, which had attracted a talented band of lawyers who spent much of their time before 1965 enforcing the voting rights laws placed on the books during the previous decade. A top priority of the Kennedy civil rights policy, suffrage litigation gave division lawyers considerable expertise in challenging disfranchisement. No one had learned more than Doar, appointed to head the CRD in 1965. He was a Wisconsin Republican who had entered the CRD in the final year of the Eisenhower regime. An alumnus of Princeton and a graduate of the University of California Law School, Doar remained at his government post during the Kennedy era and served with distinction. He was a skillful trial attorney who painstakingly researched and carefully argued suffrage cases before the most hostile judges sitting on federal benches

in Dixie. Not only did Doar vigorously plead lawsuits, but he
kept in close touch with civil rights workers in the South. In many
instances, John Doar represented *the* federal presence to besieged
demonstrators. Above all, he relished his role as "peacemaker,"
and before assuming the position of CRD chief he had ample opportunity to display his talents. Following the murder of NAACP
field secretary Medgar Evers in Jackson, Mississippi, in 1963, Doar
successfully defused an explosive situation when angry mobs of
blacks cried for retribution and hostilely confronted police officers sent to disperse them. On the day of Evers' funeral, Doar
calmly walked through the middle of the raging crowd, ducked
below flying rocks and debris, and shouted: "You're not going
to win anything with bottles and bricks." His firm but sympathetic manner soothed the throng, and order was restored.[7] More
than any high-ranking official in the Justice Department, the assistant attorney general commanded respect from civil rights activists.

Despite this rapport, Doar, as the person in charge of
the CRD under Johnson, did not differ fundamentally from Katzenbach in presenting his view of federalism. Although tireless in
his devotion to broadening the right to vote, Doar insisted on
functioning within carefully defined limits of the federal system.
Two weeks after the Voting Rights Act went into effect, Assistant Attorney General Doar expressed the policy for future enforcement of the law: "Our objective [is] to obtain full compliance with the '65 Act in all states before the next election; but to
attempt to do this with a minimum amount of federal intrusion
into the registration business of the states."[8] Years later he ap-
provingly recalled the words of Burke Marshall, his Kennedy-
appointed predecessor, who articulated the position carried on by
Doar: "We . . . have a responsibility to make every effort to enforce the orders of the Court in a way that is least disruptive of
the national interest, and when we are dealing with a state, we
want to give the state every opportunity . . . to cooperate with
the Court and the Federal Government in seeing that the orders
are obeyed."[9] The prevailing viewpoint among his staff was that
there "isn't any provision whereby the Federal people will take
over the operation of an election. That illustrates how important

it is to convince our friends in these [covered] states that they should do the job themselves."[10] Thus, sensitive both to the aspirations of the suffragists and the legitimate concerns of state and local officials, Doar chose to administer the statute so "people would say that the Department of Justice . . . was fair . . . rational and objective."[11]

Federal officials felt their approach vindicated by the successful results of the act. With as little disruption of local affairs as possible, approximately one million blacks added their names to the voter registration lists from 1965 to 1969. Even more impressive, this four-year rise in enrollment was more than three times as great as the increase during the entire decade preceding it. Of the newly qualified black voters, most had been signed up by local registrars. Prohibited under the 1965 law from employing literacy exams, county officials were severely restricted in preventing blacks from enrolling. The Justice Department derived comfort from these figures, having placed its faith in the power of voluntary cooperation and the willingness of most southern officials to police their own electoral matters. When they were not susceptible to persuasion, the attorney general did exert his authority to send in federal examiners. During the Johnson era, these outside registrars added 158,000 blacks to the suffrage rolls. Indeed, many local officials displayed a readiness to obey the law knowing that by doing so they would avoid federal intervention.[12]

This conception of federalism. whether it was applied to the examiner program or the safeguarding of suffragists, preserved the boundaries between Washington and the states, generally kept the peace, and produced gains; however, it did not satisfy civil rights activists. They had looked to Washington for assistance and had received encouragement from the Kennedy and Johnson administrations to undertake voter registration drives in the South, enterprises that turned out to be extremely hazardous. Although civil rights workers demanded and expected federal protection, their requests usually went unheeded. They felt betrayed. Theories of federalism, no matter how rationally argued by Justice Department policymakers, had no appeal for those suffrage field-workers who risked their lives daily. They believed the government's moral obligation to guarantee their constitutional rights outweighed any philosophical reservations concerning the scope of federal intervention.[13] Civil rights workers had in mind the kind of incident that had occured in Selma, Alabama, back in 1963. Peaceful demonstrators led by SNCC were arrested by sheriff's deputies as they stood on the steps of the Federal Building in full view of Justice Department personnel who did little else but take photographs of the incident and jot down notes. Disappointed SNCC staffers complained bitterly that the Kennedy administration had "in effect sanctioned and perpetuated a consistent pattern on the part of law enforcement officials . . . inimical to civil rights and liberties."[14] By the mid-1960s such disenchantment was common among civil rights activists who had spent considerable time under fire in some of the most dangerous battlegrounds in the South. "There is a town in Mississippi called Liberty," read a sardonic inscription hanging on the wall of a civil rights office in the Magnolia State, "and there is a Department in Washington called Justice."[15]

Throughout the 1960s, the Justice Department and civil rights workers could not agree on the level of federal intervention that was necessary or desirable. Administration officials warned about the long-term effects of launching a massive invasion of armed troops into the South and insisted that the Justice Department did not have at its disposal a national police force since neither the FBI nor field marshals were meant to serve such a purpose. For their part, the protesters asserted that they were seeking to supplant local law enforcement only where and when it was absolutely needed, not everywhere in the South. Not only did the suffragists urge this position with respect to increased federal protection, but after 1965, they applied their criticism to the government's handling of the Voting Rights Act. In some instances, the issue of federal protection of suffragists and demands for voting examiners were linked. Following the shooting of a civil rights worker in Kosciusko, Mississippi, in February 1966, an angry John Lewis of SNCC telegraphed President Johnson: "We call for an army of 2,000 federal registrars and marshals to be sent into the black belt of the South to protect those seeking their civil rights and seeking to register voters."[16] Just how many examiners and other officials the Johnson administration could afford to dispatch into the South was debatable, but Lewis' cry for help revealed the desperation of civil rights field-workers toiling in the South.

In deciding where and when to send federal examiners, Justice Department policymakers took political factors into account in addition to its customary regard for maintaining the balance in the federal system. An associate of Katzenbach admired his "unusual combination of the professor and the practical politician."[17] Although the evidence is in good part circumstantial, it is reasonable to conclude that political pressure exerted by powerful southern lawmakers figured into the calculations of the administration. Pat Watters and Reese Cleghorn, journalists who were affiliated with the Southern Regional Council, found it more than coincidental that the attorney general initially assigned relatively few examiners to Georgia and that none were sent to Mississippi's Sunflower County until 1967. Civil rights activists contended that the Justice Department acted cautiously in deference to the position of Senator Richard Russell of Georgia, chairman of the Armed Services Committee and an influential backer of Johnson's Vietnam policies, and James Eastland, the Mississippi Senator who headed the Judiciary Committee and owned a plantation in Sunflower County. Russell was "flattered" that his critics believed "my position in Congress has helped to keep federal registrars out of Georgia"; however, he was "of the opinion that it has been the fairness of our registrars in dealing with all people of all races who present themselves for registration."[18] On the other hand, Eastland bragged: "I've objected to the sending of every Federal registrar into Mississippi. Ordinarily the Justice Department will inform me the day it plans to send a registrar into a Mississippi county, and I've been able to block some."[19]

Had the department heeded the wishes of southern congressmen it never would have authorized a single examiner to operate in the South. However, Justice did not intend to allow its belief in federal and state comity from interfering with a free black suffrage. Following enactment of the voting rights law, federal examiners sprang into action and within a year functioned in forty counties. By mid-1967, while the pace of federal efforts had slowed down—examiners were stationed in an additional fifteen political subdivisions—southern lawmakers still complained. Democratic Representative Joe Waggoner of Louisiana lambasted the attorney general for "sending voter registration people in although there are no laws being violated."[20] At the same time, civil rights advocates were also displeased and demanded more vigorous enforcement.

In trying to encourage voluntary compliance, Katzenbach and John Doar made use of the discretion given them by the 1965 act to designate selectively the counties to which federal examiners were directed. In the first few months after August 1965, the attorney general appointed examiners where there was "past evidence of discrimination." Subsequently, he based his determination on whether "obstacles of literacy, delay, and inadequate access" developed and persisted.[21] On no occasion did the CRD automatically conclude that examiners were needed when a disparity existed between the ratio of white and black registrants. Indeed, the attorney general declined to send registrars to locales "that have a substantial racial imbalance, where every other indication in the county is that the registrar is in full compliance with the Voting Rights Act and the balance is rapidly being eliminated."[22]

Justice Department lawyers negotiated with state and local officials to remedy abuses voluntarily, but that did not mean they refrained from using coercion in implementing the law. To this end, they utilized a form of affirmative action. The attempt to overcome the consequences of previous bias had led to the suspension of literacy tests, but the national government did not stop there. The department informed southern registrars: "Compliance with the Fifteenth Amendment means not only that local officials may not practice distinctions based upon race, but that they are under a duty to take *affirmative* steps to correct the effects of past discrimination" [emphasis added]. Consequently, local registration boards had to adopt procedures that insured "all persons eligible under the Act have an opportunity to become registered and to vote."[23] To reverse the disadvantageous effects of prior suffrage restrictions, registrars were instructed to keep their offices open evenings and on Saturdays, to provide for extra days of enrollment throughout the year, to employ additional clerks to conduct registration in convenient places, and to publicize registration schedules. Failure to comply with such measures resulted in the appointment of federal examiners.[24]

However, the Johnson administration's version of affirmative action reflected a desire to encourage and measure voluntary compliance rather than an urge to foster maximum black registration and political participation. Doar argued that the CRD could demand that local registrars set up additional facilities to enroll blacks who lived in outlying areas away from the county courthouse, but he maintained, "We are not in the mobile registrar business and we do not want to appear that we are."[25] The assistant attorney general contended that private civil rights organizations had to shoulder the burden of voter registration, because "when the Federal Government . . . takes over, when it leaves the whole thing caves in."[26] Civil Service Commission chairman John Macy agreed: "Nor is it the proper function of the Federal Government to conduct the organizational and educational effort to bring unregistered Negroes to either Federal or local registration offices."[27] Instead, Katzenbach encouraged leaders of the major civil rights groups to organize "at the local level because the problem is not merely the number of Negroes registered but of continuing to get these people actively participating in politics for the first time in their lives."[28]

Nor did affirmative action compel the administration actively to recruit blacks as examiners. The Civil Service Commission "did not seem particularly reluctant to use Negroes," but the Justice Department anticipated problems. Expecting that it might be difficult to find white civil servants in some localities to perform the job, a CRD attorney nevertheless suggested that hiring blacks in these instances "might aggravate the situation in such places and, indeed, create an enormous risk to the Negro involved."[29] St. John Barrett, Doar's assistant, also opposed any special treatment for black applicants. Barrett explained: "It seems to me that the recruiting of examiners must be strictly without regard to race and color. I do not think the Commission should make a conscious effort to assign Negroes as examiners in southern areas. They [sic] should, however, take steps to assure that qualified Negroes understand they can apply and their applications be treated on an equal basis. I think it would have a bad effect to give the impression that the federal government was either avoiding use of Negroes or deliberately preferring Negroes when there have been voting difficulties."[30] As a result, of the original sixty-eight examiners chosen by the Civil Service Commission, only two were black.[31]

Still, the Johnson administration favored taking affirmative steps to overcome the effects of prior racial bias. The president had made this clear in his remarks upon signing the Voting Rights Act. "For it is not enough just to give men rights," Johnson declared on that occasion. He went on:

They must be able to use those rights in their personal pursuit of happiness. The wounds and the weaknesses, the outward walls and the inward scars which diminish achievements are the work of American society. We must all now help to end them—help to end them through expanding programs already devised and through new ones to search out and forever end the special handicaps of those who are black in a Nation that happens to be mostly white.[32]

This theme sounded a note first struck by the chief executive two months earlier. In his eloquent commencement address at Howard University on June 4, 1965, President Johnson had asserted: "We seek not just freedom but opportunity—not just legal equality but human equality—not just equality as a right and a theory, but equality as a fact and a result."[33] The chief executive was aware of the magnitude of this problem, which he likened to "converting a crippled person into a four minute miler."[34]

Following the Howard speech, the White House hatched plans to convene a conference on civil rights. Originally scheduled for the fall, the meeting was conceived by the administration as a redemption of its Howard pledge and an opportunity to set an agenda on civil rights, particularly in the aftermath of urban rioting in the summer. According to Vice President Hubert Humphrey, the Johnson administration "hoped the conference will help produce a national awareness and generate a consensus to support implementation of various solutions."[35]

Even before the conference began, the administration's

initial attempts to define affirmative action had drawn fire from civil rights groups from all across the political spectrum. In mid-September 1965, representatives of the NAACP, CORE, NUL, and SCLC had complained to Humphrey that the Justice Department was not appointing suffrage examiners to all the counties that needed them. Floyd McKissick of CORE fumed: "Many of the students in the South had made personal sacrifices in order to get people out to vote. But when we did this, when we got masses to go, there were no registrars. That made us waste a whole damn summer of work."[36] In voicing his complaint, McKissick exaggerated the lack of federal activity at the time, because the government already had sent examiners to a score of counties and was planning to ship others to about a dozen more. However, the CORE leader's statement reflected the growing belief among civil rights advocates that the attorney general responded too passively in promoting voter registration. This view appeared in an agenda paper on "Voting and Citizenship Participation," prepared by Sterling Tucker of the Washington, D.C., chapter of the Urban League and Wiley Branton, formerly the director of the Voter Education Project, for the forthcoming White House Conference on Civil Rights. Recommending placement of greater stress on governmental agencies, rather than on private groups, to get citizens enrolled, the report also pointed out that the states covered under the Voting Rights Act were still engaged in delaying tactics and that physical and economic harassment served as twin deterrents to additional minority registration. In light of this situation, Tucker and Branton asked whether the federal government should undertake a more aggressive role in stimulating local voter drives as well as devise new techniques to deter reprisals against enfranchised black southerners.[37]

In November 1965 a preliminary meeting for the White House conference served as a forum for further expression of this criticism. Because of the growing furor over civil rights, the administration decided to postpone the conference until June and, in the meantime, to hold a planning session. Seated in the Satellite Room of the Hilton Hotel in Washington, D.C., on November 17 and 18, a group composed of about fifty civil rights leaders, black politicians, liberal academics, labor union executives, and government officials participated in occasionally heated discussions about the enforcement of the Voting Rights Act. In particular, critics of the administration's efforts found fault with the examiner program and complained about the Justice Department's emphasis on voluntary compliance. Arnold Aronson of the Leadership Conference on Civil Rights (LCCR), an umbrella organization which had flexed its legislative muscle behind passage of four civil rights laws during the previous decade, had learned from years of experience "that there were certain areas in the country where there was going to be continued resistance until they were to be compelled to desist." Aronson and others urged Washington to combat the evasive tactics that persisted by dispatching examiners "into every area that is covered under the terms of the act."[38] Furthermore, those registrars who were sent into the South should function with increased mobility, canvasing black neighborhoods, especially in outlying rural sections. Overall, civil rights advocates charged that the Johnson administration had not "been sufficiently aggressive in utilizing the 1965 Act."[39]

Many of the panelists wanted the federal government to intervene more directly not only in sending additional examiners but also by becoming more involved in voter registration activities customarily conducted by private organizations. Neither SNCC nor CORE, both of which had deployed their workers into some of the counties most hostile to black suffrage, could afford to bear the costs of massive enrollment drives. John Lewis, the chairman of SNCC who had his skull cracked by Alabama state troopers during the enfranchisement campaign in Selma, suggested to the gathering: "In a sense the Federal Government should be doing for civil rights what the civil rights organizations are doing. In the first place, the civil rights organizations do not have the money and the resources and the staff [whereas] . . . the Government has money, and the resources particularly."[40] Floyd McKissick, CORE's national chairman, put the matter more bluntly than did the soft-spoken Lewis:

I am the one who has to look at that budget, and I am the one who sees that that money gets there, and I am the one who has to see that this voter registration comes home under this arbitrary system. What I give a damn about is what the Constitution says. And who the hell wrote the Constitution? Not the Congress of Racial Equality, and not SCLC, and not SNCC, and not the NAACP, which has been out there longer than anybody. It is the Federal Government that has got to come in and do more.[41]

Even more financially solvent groups such as the NAACP and Urban League had "no more money available for . . . a more intensive voter and registration drive in the South."[42]

Their financial crisis notwithstanding, in making this particular demand civil rights organizations asked more than the federal government could deliver. The Justice Department had no specific budgetary authorization to underwrite voter registration drives and obtaining funds for such a purpose appeared dim. As a matter of fact, in 1967, Congress barred the administration from spending money for its war on poverty with respect to "any voting registration activity."[43] Perhaps more realistically, the suffragists called upon the Justice Department to stimulate enrollment and provide encouragement for private registration campaigns by augmenting its examiner program.

Although sympathetic to their plight, the attorney general defended administration policy. Katzenbach reiterated that the purpose of the Justice Department's policy was to ensure that blacks received every opportunity to register. "The law contemplates that a Federal examiner is to be put in any county where the state or local people are not performing their responsibilities," he reminded his audience. But he added, "I don't think I have authority to go beyond that. And I don't intend to go beyond that." He did not believe that the department should routinely assume an adversarial role under the statute. According to his conception of the proper relationship between federal and state authorities, "the general purpose should not be, let's get people turned down so we can have a Federal examiner." Furthermore, Katzenbach denied that he could legally disburse departmental funds for encouraging voter registration activities. He admitted that it was "easier to run a voting drive where there is a Federal examiner, you get a lot more cooperation." Nevertheless, he insisted federal law "did not contemplate that examiners would be sent into every county willy-nilly."[44] These differences aside, Katzenbach acknowledged that if he were a private citizen "engaged in the other aspect of voter registration drives, I would be taking the same view that you are. And I would be kicking the hell out of the Attorney General."[45]

Katzenbach's conciliatory remarks failed to soothe the audience. John Lewis remained unsure "whether the Federal Government and the Justice Department at this time is prepared to protect the right of the people to register and vote," and McKissick attacked the attorney general for "throwing all the burden right on the people to follow." While conceding "that this Administration is committed," Arnold Aronson summed up the position of the critics: "It seems to me in the area of voting we have had enough demonstration. And that was the purpose of the 1965 Act on the top of the 1957 and 1960 Acts. And to suggest that we ought to again await voluntary compliance seems to me to deny the very finding which the Attorney General has made."[46] Even the administration's friends believed that the federal government had to raise black suffrage to a higher level of priority. John P. Roche, a professor at Brandeis University and a defender of American foreign policy in Vietnam who was later appointed as a Johnson aide, urged the administration to give as much support to enfranchisement in this country "as is given to the defense of the Asian frontier."[47]

Several proposals emerged from the two days of sparring. The panelists agreed "that the Federal Government should immediately adopt a more aggressive attitude in encouraging citizens to register and vote." Specifically, they recommended that the attorney general certify more counties for examiners, station these registrars in heavily populated black areas, and authorize them to operate mobile enrollment units.[48] Suffragists still believed that the rate of registration was not proceeding swiftly enough and that the Justice Department should have shouldered more of the burden; however, they recognized the considerable gains that had occurred. Much remained to be done, but the chief problem consisted of strengthening existing enforcement procedures, rather than passage of additional franchise legislation. In looking ahead to the larger White House conference scheduled for 1966, the directors of the voting panel, Sterling Tucker and Wiley Branton, confidently expected that the suffrage would not constitute a major issue. They anticipated that the federal government would exercise this power to "advance the cause of equal opportunities in voting throughout the South . . . thus easing the need for a full-dress section on voting rights."[49] In fact, Branton had been appointed a special assistant to the attorney general, and he intended to get the administration to establish a program encouraging people to register "just as it urges farmers to use fertilizer or take advantage of federal programs."[50] By late February 1966, federal examiners had listed over 100,000 black registrants in addition to the more than 200,000 enrolled by local officials. This expansion of the right to vote had achieved sufficient progress to convince the planners not to include it as an agenda item for the upcoming assembly. Subsequently, on March 5, 1966, the advisory council for the conference dropped the topic of "Voting and Citizenship Participation." The planning group decided "that the way is clear now under the new voting rights legislation; that the problems remaining reside primarily in enforcement and getting people themselves to register and vote, and that the topic could result in discussions of Negro nationalism and block [sic] voting."[51]

Nevertheless, in the interim between the November planning sessions and the June assembly, suffragists continued to push for more vigorous implementation of the Voting Rights Act. At the end of November, Roy Wilkins met with Katzenbach and warned him of the danger of "administrative repeal" if the statute were not more strictly enforced.[52] Though civil rights leaders promised that private agencies, despite limited means, would try to continue their efforts to promote voter registration, they emphasized that they considered the deployment of federal examiners the most important stimulant to black enrollment. Annie Devine, a congressional nominee of the predominantly black Mississippi Freedom Democratic Party (FDP), requested the Justice Department to send registrars to all eighty-two counties in the Magnolia State, and then added: "As great as the need is for having federal registrars, the FDP feels that along with federal registrars, it is definitely necessary that these registrars be mobile."[53]

These pleas received substantial backing from the United

States Commission on Civil Rights (CCR). In the past, the commission had assailed the Justice Department for not using its authority more boldly and imaginatively. Both federal agencies worked closely with the civil rights movement, but the commission did not consider the borders of the federal system to be as confining as did the department. Three months after the Voting Rights Act became law, the CCR assessed the administration's role in enforcing it. At issue was not how many examiners the Justice Department had at its disposal to send to the South, for Johnson's lawyers had not claimed that they lacked sufficient manpower for the assignment. Rather the dispute revolved around differing conceptions of the proper scope of federal intervention. The commission observed that the attorney general "designated examiners only where there were flagrant violations of the Act," and discovered that in these selected counties "there has been a sharp decline in the high initial rate of Negro registration." Consequently, the commission recommended an increase in the assignment of federal examiners and the creation of an affirmative program "to encourage persons to register to vote by disseminating information . . . and by providing training and education to foster better understanding of the rights and duties of citizenship and the significance of voting."[54]

The Justice Department issued a sharp rejoinder to this critical report. The attorney general disputed the commission's findings that his agency had moved slowly in carrying out the law. "What the Report fails to recognize," Katzenbach declared, "is that until the Act was in effect and Negro applicants had sought to register, it was not possible for there to be any ground for the appointment of examiners *other* than past evidence of discrimination." In responding to the charge that subsequently he had designated too few counties to receive examiners, Katzenbach maintained: "Where local officials do not fully meet their responsibilities . . . we will meet ours—and send in examiners." He suggested that the department had not yet acted in certain counties because blacks had not mounted voter registration drives to test the willingness of registrars to comply voluntarily with the statute.[55] Still unconvinced, the CCR's staff director, William L. Taylor, retorted that even under the departmental standards of initially appointing federal personnel to counties with "past evidence of discrimination," the attorney general had failed to choose several dozen areas with a well-documented history of racial disfranchisement.[56]

Like the commission, civil rights groups remained dissatisfied with the attorney general's answers, especially when violence once again flared in the Deep South. SNCC screamed the loudest after Sammy Younge was murdered. A student at Tuskegee Institute following his discharge from the Navy, the twenty-two-year-old Younge had been associated with SNCC projects in Alabama and Mississippi. On January 3, 1966, Younge devoted some of the last hours of his life to a voter registration drive in Macon County, Alabama. Early in the day, he and his coworkers escaped injury when threatened by a local registrar wielding a knife. Later that evening at a gas station, the Tuskegee undergraduate was killed by a white attendant who resisted his attempt to use the restroom. On January 6, SNCC issued a press release condemning the federal government for not protecting "people seeking civil rights guaranteed by the Constitution," and warned that blacks would have no choice but to abandon nonviolence and protect themselves accordingly. SNCC's hostility resulted not from the belief that the federal government should have safeguarded this particular gas station, but it arose out of years of frustration with Washington for failing to protect civil rights workers. By this time, SNCC had come to view the Johnson administration as another agent of white oppression, and Younge's murder sparked the group to attack the president's policies along several fronts. It compared the killing to American policy in Vietnam, in one instance citing government neglect for the killing of southern blacks and in the other attributing the deaths of nonwhite Vietnamese peasants to United States aggression.[57]

Concerned that SNCC would turn the incident into a confrontation with white officials in Tuskegee, the federal government sought to calm the tense situation. The Johnson administration dispatched representatives from the Community Relations Service, a conciliation bureau created by the 1964 Civil Rights Act, along with CRD lawyers and FBI agents to conduct an investigation of the slaying. In addition, the Justice Department filed public accommodation litigation to desegregate restaurants in the town. President Johnson ordered the attorney general and his deputies to "follow this closely—stay on top of it," and let him know of "any action that we should take promptly."[58] This did not mollify SNCC, whose executive secretary, James Forman, ruefully observed: "Sammy's murder was one too many. There are few, if any, militant blacks today who expect the government to do much for us."[59]

Events in Birmingham provided an opportunity for Washington to mollify more moderate blacks. Four months after passage of the Voting Rights Act, thousands of eligible blacks still had not been able to sign up to register in the city derisively called "Bombingham." By the beginning of 1966, only about 35,000 of the more than 116,000 blacks of voting age had placed their names on the suffrage rolls, a slight increase over the 24,000 qualified to vote in 1964. Not more than 486 blacks had been able to register in one day, and it would have taken an additional 4,400 registrants per day to enroll the remaining number of qualified applicants before the next election. Although Jefferson County had a long history of thwarting black suffrage, the Justice Department had chosen not to designate it for federal examiners. Instead, CRD lawyers negotiated with the county board of registrars in hope of convincing its members to rectify the problem voluntarily. Running out of patience, on December 31, 1965, Doar had informed county officials that they had "a duty not only to eliminate tests and devices, but to follow the command of the Fifteenth Amendment to 'eliminate the effects of past discrimination.' " This obligation included increasing the number of registration hours and days, staying open evenings and weekends, hiring additional office staff, and providing more convenient locations for citizens living in outlying portions of Jefferson County.[60] Seeking to avoid federal examiners, county officials agreed to expand the number of voter registration days, including Saturday, from three to five and to hire extra clerks to accommodate the expected influx of applicants. However, they refused to allow evening registration or to conduct enrollment away from the county courthouse.

These concessions did not appease Birmingham's black leaders or the federal government. Civil rights protesters found the daytime hours inadequate and believed "that many of the Negroes were still afraid to go down to the courthouse"; therefore, they called on the Justice Department to furnish examiners immediately. This request took on increased weight during early January when Hosea Williams of SCLC launched street rallies against the recalcitrant board of registrars. Finally, on January 20, 1966, the attorney general sent federal examiners into Jefferson County. This decision illustrated that the federal government would act when blacks applied pressure and negotiations with local officials failed to produce satisfactory results. Furthermore, Katzenbach hoped to de-escalate the rising level of racial tensions provoked by SCLC's demonstrations.[61] In a little over one month after federal personnel arrived and worked six days and nights each week, the percentage of registered blacks leaped from 36.1 to around 50.

In defusing the crisis in Birmingham, Katzenbach sent a warning to southern officials who believed that a minimum of voluntary compliance could result in a maximum of delay. The attorney general never lost his faith in the bargaining process, but he announced that there were definite limits to his forbearance. During the negotiations in Birmingham and again three months later, he wrote all the registrars in the covered jurisdictions reminding them of their affirmative responsibilities under the Voting Rights Act. He proposed to evaluate their performances according to "what steps have been taken to correct the effects of past discrimination." He put registration boards on notice that they had to be flexible in remedying particular problems affecting black enrollment. "For example," the attorney general advised, "where there has been history of discrimination, a county with 10,000 unregistered adults has more to do to correct the effects than a county with 1,000 unregistered adults."[62] Following up on these orders, by the end of summer Katzenbach dispatched examiners to an additional eight noncompliant counties. As a result of these actions, he came under fire from southern lawmakers. Representative James Martin of Alabama called upon his colleagues "to join . . . in demanding that the attorney general be halted in creating a second reconstruction period" as he had done by sending examiners into Birmingham.[63]

At the same time, Katzenbach did not push affirmative action as far as the civil rights groups wanted. Hard pressed for funds and volunteers, civil rights forces argued that federal registrars should assume the burden of signing up blacks, especially in counties where the gap between the percentage of registered adults of each race remained wide. The attorney general declined to adopt this viewpoint. In February, he publicly challenged the assumption, voiced by the Civil Rights Commission, that the "presence or absence of federal examiners" made the crucial difference in promoting black voter registration. In an address to the Southern Regional Council, Katzenbach argued that the key to enrolling southern blacks could not be found in either local compliance or federal examiners but in registration campaigns conducted by private agencies.[64] This opinion was not shared by the council's Voter Education Project. Several months later, after conducting its own investigation, the VEP released a report that reached the opposite conclusion from the attorney general's. Taking the same items into account, the VEP ranked federal examiners at the top of the list of variables influencing black voter registration. Fortified by its own research, the SRC continued to ask the Justice Department to designate for federal examination considerably more than the forty counties it had selected by the middle of 1966.[65]

The Johnson administration's enforcement policy applied not only to the registration process but also to the conduct of elections. Under the 1965 law, the attorney general had the authority to send observers to polling places in the designated counties. The first opportunity to exercise this power came when Alabama held Democratic primary contests on May 3, 1966. The election featured the gubernatorial battle waged by Lurleen Wallace, standing in for her segregationist husband, George, against a field containing several white moderates. In the running for local posts were fifty-four black candidates. Aware that George Wallace would turn the presence of federal observers to his advantage, Katzenbach attempted "to do the least that I can safely do without upsetting civil rights groups." He explained the administration's reasoning: "We cannot afford widespread charges of fraud or intimidation of voters. Nor do I wish to 'interfere' in local elections. But the fact that observers are not going into any but the most difficult counties will . . . show we are both knowledgeable and even-handed." This cautious approach also shaped his decision to keep observers out of such problem areas as Birmingham, "so as to avoid accusations of unwarranted federal interference."[66]

On election day, approximately 300 federal observers watched the ballot boxes in six black-belt counties. Over 120,000 blacks, many casting votes for the first time in their lives, went to the polls. Their political clout was not enough to prevent the victory of Mrs. Wallace, but black ballots did succeed in sending several Negro candidates into runoffs and helped to defeat extremist white contenders. In this latter category fell Sheriff Jim Clark, the scourge of Selma, who lost his office to a more moderate challenger, Wilson Baker. Not only did black voters aid in removing Clark from office, but so did the Justice Department. Federal observers carefully scrutinized this election, and their reports came in handy when the defeated incumbent challenged the validity of the votes cast in six largely black precincts. The Justice Department brought litigation to refute Clark's claims, and its lawyers succeeded in convincing the federal district court to affirm Baker's slender triumph.[67]

However modest the gains exhibited in Alabama, they did represent significant progress during the first year of the Voting Rights Act. In the southern states caught in the triggering mechanism of the law, the number of blacks registered to vote had climbed sharply from 837,000 to 1,289,000, a proportional increase from 30 to 46 percent of those eligible. Of the more than 400,000 new registrants over one-quarter had been signed up by federal examiners. The Justice Department interpreted these figures as confirmation of the wisdom in pursuing voluntary compliance because local registrars had been responsible for most of the boost in enrollment.

Nevertheless, the federal government's task was far from completed. A majority of nonwhites remained off the voter rolls in the Deep South, and the rate of black registration had slowed markedly by mid-1966. Federal examiners still had not been dispatched to Georgia, which lagged behind its neighbors in black enrollment.[68] In light of this situation, civil rights groups continued to quarrel with the Johnson administration over its examiner policy; however, the noteworthy improvement in black suffrage lifted some of the immediacy from their complaints.

In fact, over the next few years, southern blacks labored painstakingly to extend the suffrage in a manner that generally conformed to Justice Department strategy. In doing so, they faced difficult challenges beyond the federal government's capacity to remedy. Much of the excitement surrounding the voter registration drives of the early 1960s had abated, and many of the volunteers and field workers had departed. A year after passage of the Voting Rights Act, the flood of blacks pouring out to register had dropped off to a trickle, and the federal government expected private agencies to assume responsibility for stimulating a new wave of enrollment. Left unregistered were the hardcore disfranchised, generally those most dependent on whites for their jobs or means of support. In rural areas, blacks who worked on plantations located far from the county registrar's courthouse office had difficulty getting time off and traveling to town, especially during weekday business hours. Moreover, in contemplating whether to make the journey, they had to weigh the possible benefits that the ballot might yield against the threat of reprisals from their white bosses. Against these obstacles, many of them were still unable to overcome the racist legacy that "politics was white folks' business."[69]

More than legal barriers and intimidation kept southern blacks from electoral participation. Their failure to register and turn out at the polls in greater numbers also reflected the unfavorable socioeconomic conditions in which impoverished blacks found themselves trapped. Had they acquired higher incomes and better education, southern blacks would have been more likely to sign up and cast their ballots. Victims of an enduring racial caste system, many blacks lacked the sense of political efficacy more commonly associated with individuals higher on the social and economic scale. Yet, scholars have also found "that at any given socioeconomic level blacks are more active organizational participants than whites"; consequently, the disparity between white and black rates of suffrage enrollment and voter turnout indicated the existence of an even wider separation in socioeconomic conditions between the races.[70] Thus, before black southerners could obtain more extensive political victories, they had to remove the substantial economic deficiencies that plagued them.

Not content to wait that long, civil rights groups continued to promote increased political involvement within the existing institutional framework. While voter registration activities faded from the headlines after the Mississippi freedom summers of 1964 and 1965 and the Selma to Montgomery march, they did not cease. The private campaigns suffered from the perennial lack of funds as well as the increasing disaffection of SNCC and CORE. These two groups had sent most of the shock troops into areas fiercely resistant to social change in the early 1960s, but their radicalization left southern voter registration largely to moderate civil rights organizations after 1965. Leading the field to recruit new voters after the Voting Rights Act, the NAACP eschewed "speechmaking, sloganeering, or demonstrations," and undertook "the inglorious day-to-day task of getting Negroes to register." Roy Wilkins predicted "that every 10,000 names added makes it more certain that local conditions will be forced to improve and that Negro citizens will come into some control over their own destiny."[71] Hard-pressed financially, the NAACP did not have to shoulder the burden alone. SCLC, the Urban League, and local civic associations and voter leagues also campaigned on the suffrage front. Furthermore, the void left by SNCC was partially filled by the ongoing suffrage activities of the Delta Ministry (DM). Formed by the National Council of Churches in 1964, the DM inherited the political and community organizing projects spearheaded and then abandoned by SNCC in the Mississippi delta. The "religious counterpart" of SNCC, according to its chief historian, the Delta Ministry was "basically a black power organization . . . (a la Carmichael) . . . interested in democracy based on true political pluralism for a more equal distribution of the nation's resources."[72] Whatever their ideological orientation, these diverse groups considered voter registration and related franchise programs as an integral component of black emancipation.

Helping to keep many of these campaigns solvent, as it

had done during the early 1960s, the Southern Regional Council bankrolled and monitored the renewed voter registration activities following passage of the 1965 law. Headquartered in Atlanta, for over twenty years this interracial organization had campaigned for racial equality through its research activities and its allocation of foundation grants to worthy enterprises. One such undertaking had been the creation of the Voter Education Project that functioned from 1962 to 1964. In 1966, with little else than moral encouragement from the federal government, the Council revived its VEP.[73] Directed by Vernon Jordan, a former NAACP official, the second VEP subsidized 106 suffrage programs during its first year and 122 a year later. Most of these efforts focused on voter registration, especially in locations where federal examiners operated, with the aim of enlarging the black electorate's participation in statewide and local contests throughout the South in 1966 and 1967. The Voter Education Project worked closely with local civic associations as well as national civil rights groups. For example, from January to October 1966, the VEP financed thirty NAACP registration drives, which enrolled over 31,000 blacks at a cost of $45,000.[74] As a result of their activities, the suffragists recognized the necessity for citizenship education to accompany enrollment campaigns. "It is not enough to try to register people in the South," Jordan argued, "Too many of these people have been alienated from the political process for too long a time . . . and so we have to . . . teach them what local government is, how it operates, and try to relate their votes to the things they want."[75] As black office seekers gradually won victories, the VEP expanded its efforts to include the formation of workshops and information centers to assist black candidates and incumbents.

By virtue of these endeavors, the VEP, along with the other private agencies struggling on behalf of enfranchisement, found federal aid inadequate. Suffragists argued that many counties with a low black enrollment required federal registrars, and they criticized the Johnson administration for placing too much emphasis on the good faith of local officials in complying with the Voting Rights Act. Two years after the landmark statute became law, Martin Luther King wrote: "It was proclaimed as the dawn of freedom and the open door to opportunity. What was minimally required under the law was the appointment of hundreds of registrars and thousands of marshals to inhibit Southern terror."[76] What King considered a reasonable request, the Department of Justice thought an unwise display of massive federal force. The SCLC chief would probably have settled for less than the "thousands of marshals" he suggested, but the Johnson administration, as had its predecessors, chose not to send any except in the most extraordinary circumstances where local law enforcement had completely broken down. From their perspective, civil rights leaders believed that there were ample grounds for federal protection because their followers continued to live on a daily basis under a climate of repression in many sections of the rural South. Although black leaders acknowledged the importance of socioeconomic factors in retarding the suffrage among the low income and poorly educated, they stressed that what was commonly referred to as apathy actually stemmed mostly from fear. For the civil rights workers who remained in the field hoping to convince reluctant blacks to participate in the political process, a direct connection existed between personal security and enfranchisement. Watching the progress of suffrage activities, Vernon Jordan concluded that the "protection of civil rights workers is very, very important to the implementation of the Voting Rights Act."[77]

Despite the criticism of the Johnson administration by civil rights activists from 1966 to 1968, the president stood committed to the voting rights ventures that he had initiated. During this period, the Justice Department designated another sixteen counties under the suffrage statute, bringing the total to sixty-four, and, federal registrars listed nearly 58,000 of the approximately 250,000 black voters added to the rolls in those five states to which federal personnel had been assigned. Given the long history of disfranchisement, these achievements were even more striking. In 1966, about 41 percent of adult blacks were eligible to vote in these areas; two years later the figure leaped to around 61 percent.[78] As the newly enfranchised turned out at the polls, they helped elect over 265 black public officials, an impressive gain from only a few years earlier when successful black candidates were extremely rare. Speaking to a conference in December 1968, which many of these officials attended, Attorney General Ramsey Clark, Katzenbach's successor, reminded them: "Four years ago we could have held this meeting in the telephone booth in the lobby and not interfered with anyone who wanted to make a phone call."[79]

As superb as these gains were, they fell short of the suffragists' expectations. Clearly a goal of 100 percent registration could not have been reached—even in the North where blacks could vote for generations, the figure was not nearly that high—but voting rights advocates hoped to attain for blacks a level equal to that of white enrollment in the South. After only three years the gap had closed considerably, but it still remained wide. The proportion of black registrants in the seven covered states lagged behind that of whites on the average of 24.5 percentage points.[80] Moreover, blacks worried that they would never catch up because federal enforcement was slowing down. Each year fewer counties had been designated to receive examiners, and by mid-1968 federal registrars operated in only 58 out of 185 political subdivisions in which less than 50 percent of adult blacks were enrolled. Civil rights critics believed that "apathy" alone did not keep those who remained off the registration rolls from signing up. They insisted that the enrollment gap would have closed even further had federal examiners been sent into areas that still resisted black participation or that perpetuated the effects of past discriminatory practices.

In contrast, the Justice Department contended that it had approached the limits of prudent federal intervention and stuck to its original policy of keeping federal intrusion into state electoral affairs to a minimum. Seeking to maintain "a certain neutrality," Stephen Pollak, who replaced John Doar as chief of the Civil Rights Division and shared his predecessor's thinking, denied that the Justice Department had been "given a responsibility by the law to work to promote pressures to go out and register."[81] However, events in Bolivar County, Mississippi, showed the drawbacks of this policy. In 1965, the attorney general had designated the county to receive examiners after local authorities refused to register 200 illiterate black adults. Faced with this incursion from Washington, local officials relented in their defiance, and federal examiners soon departed. This approach did not maximize black enfranchisement. Two years later, blacks in Bolivar complained that county clerks were turning "people away without being registered." They called upon the Justice Department to resume operation of federal registration, especially as a means of boosting voter enrollment activities. Their request was rejected after local officials again pledged to register previously rejected blacks, and Washington steadfastly declined to shape the examiner program as an instrument for stimulating voter registration drives.[82]

Thus, throughout the Johnson years, the Justice Department did not waver from its suffrage policy. After Katzenbach left to become under secretary of state in 1966, he was replaced by Ramsey Clark. A Texas native, a graduate of the University of Chicago Law School, and a son of a United States supreme court justice, Clark came under fire from conservatives for his defense of civil liberties and minority rights. Yet though Clark expressed a desire for the government to encourage blacks to exercise the franchise, he drew the line of federal responsibility short of directly going out and getting blacks to register and vote. Like his predecessor, he considered this an activity reserved for private civil rights agencies. Nor did he invigorate the examiner program. At first, Clark had planned to send a "big batch" of enrollment officers to "keep momentum going"; eventually, however, he dropped the idea. Because blacks did not always pour out in large numbers after federal personnel arrived in a county, the attorney general concluded that it was "just wasteful" to send examiners to a location where only "two people a day registered" and where he could not "justify keeping an office open."[83] Voter registration was usually a slow and laborious process, and civil rights workers believed that the government sometimes pulled out its examiners too soon before they had a chance to deliver the anticipated results. Each side wanted the other to become more involved. Washington preferred that private organizations have suffrage drives under way or about to begin, whereas civil rights groups called upon the Justice Department to dispatch examiners to help kick off and sustain their enrollment campaigns. As sensitive as officials like Clark were toward civil rights, the constraints of administering federal programs, including the need to make them cost effective, often limited what was possible.

Meanwhile, the Johnson administration stressed the value of the suffrage. Although blacks maintained a commitment to traditional goals of equal rights and protection, they entered a new phase of the movement emphasizing compensatory treatment for past wrongs and the building of racial solidarity. In the face of this black militancy and a resulting white backlash, the Johnson regime had underscored its faith in the ballot as a moderate instrument of social change. A year after passage of the Voting Rights Act, the chief executive fostered the view that political power should replace protest as the main weapon for eradicating discrimination. "The Molotov cocktail," the president remarked, "destroys far more than the police car or the pawn shop. It destroys the basis for civil peace and the basis for social progress." In its place, Johnson advocated "the right to vote—unchallenged, unintimidated, unblackmailed, unhandcuffed."[84] This advice would be sorely tested by the experiences of newly enfranchised black southerners.

3.

The Land of the Tree and the Home of the Grave

Civil rights advocates counted on the ballot to advance racial equality over the long run, but in the meantime, they focused attention on another demand closely related to the right to vote: the protection of civil rights workers. This issue had been a major bone of contention between Washington and suffragists who denounced the Justice Department and the FBI for not fully safeguarding their constitutional rights. Although sympathetic to their plight, the Johnson administration turned down requests for increased protection, citing limitations of federal authority and resources in dealing with local law enforcement. Several well-publicized murders of civil rights workers in the mid-1960s heightened the frustration of the activists who interpreted the administration's refusals to shield them from harm as callousness.

The problem had received a great deal of attention in November 1965 in preparation for the White House Conference on Civil Rights. At the planning session the panel concerned with the "Administration of Justice" sensed rapidly rising discontent. The conferees requested the White House to seek enactment of a statute effectively dealing with individual physical security as the top item on its legislative agenda in 1966. Until then, those in attendance resolved, federal police agencies should exercise their power "to provide protection in those instances where the states and localities are not doing so." Some participants worried that such a policy might lead to the establishment of a national police force that might threaten civil liberties, but the majority only wanted the same standard for civil rights law enforcement that currently existed for federal crimes related to vice, narcotics, bank robberies, and car thefts.[1]

The November meeting provided both an opportunity and a warning for the White House. In the wake of increased black militancy, the president reaffirmed his support for civil rights. By holding this conference, Johnson assured black leaders, especially the moderates upon whom he relied, "I have you and your problems very much in my mind."[2] Furthermore, the administration planned to introduce legislation addressing some of the unfinished business on the civil rights agenda in a manner that fostered orderly change. For some this was no longer enough. The gathering had attracted participants with diverse views, which guaranteed controversy and provided a setting for unflattering comments about their hosts. "The fact that a White House Conference took place gave the Administration a chance to prove . . . that the Administration is interested in a certain topic or concerned about solutions to a certain problem," representatives of SNCC admitted, but they found this purpose meaningless unless steps were taken "to enforce existing legislation well—and not halfheartedly." Floyd McKissick indicated how far CORE was moving away from the Great Society coalition by questioning whether a capitalistic society could secure "what we talk about . . . in the conference."[3]

These remarks did not catch White House planners by surprise. Harry McPherson declared that trying to dominate the conference with talk of our success would have backfired," because the "more militant crowd would have raised a cry about 'brainwashing' and 'Uncle Toms' that would have seriously undermined confidence in the Negro leadership."[4] However, the chief executive was not as tolerant of the way some of the participants had behaved. Johnson did not give serious thought to canceling the spring conference, but he scolded his aides: "You boys have gotten me in this controversy . . . so I've got to get somebody . . . to get me out of it."[5] The president chose Ben Heineman, chairman of the board of the Chicago and Northwestern Railway, to move the upcoming meeting onto the right track. The appointment of this influential business executive reflected a shift in the strategy that had guided the original planning sessions. The White House now wished to direct the spotlight away from its responsibilities in remedying the racial abuses that had defied correction for over one hundred years and instead to persuade private enterprise and state and local governments to become more involved. By broadening the base of attack, the administration hoped to convince white Americans "that the solution of human rights problems are in their best interest—not just for the benefit of minorities."[6]

Consequently, the White House maneuvered to orchestrate the forthcoming conference. Militant blacks were included among the two thousand invited guests, but the guest list was prepared prudently. It consisted of federal, state, and local officials, representatives of the six biggest civil rights organizations, members of human relations and public interest organizations, labor unionists, religious leaders, businessmen, and corporate executives. Greatly outnumbered among the approximately 2,500 invitees were some 150 representatives of grass roots poverty programs, potentially the most volatile critics of administration policies. The selection process exemplified the continuing attempt of President Johnson to construct a broad coalition similar to the one he had built behind passage of civil rights bills in 1964 and 1965.[7] However, on this occasion, there was a major defection. SNCC pulled out of the conference, accusing the White House of trying to shift responsibility for racism from the oppressors to the oppressed, charging that the executive branch was not serious about protecting the constitutional rights of black Americans, and attacking United States involvement in Southeast Asia as a violation of "the human rights of colored people in Vietnam."[8] The withdrawal of SNCC actually pleased administration strategists interested in preserving harmony. They considered the group's "present leadership . . . so radical that inside the conference, they could only be arch troublemakers; outside, they will provide a kind of foil that may reassure middle-ground, well meaning people that the conference is not altogether kooky."[9]

The conference program was carefully staged. Led by Heineman, an advisory council drew up a detailed and lengthy report around the theme "To Fulfill These Rights." It defined the

broad goals of racial equality and offered recommendations on how
to achieve them. The participants received a copy of this document which served as the basis of discussion; however, they were
not supposed to formulate and vote on resolutions. The report
also instructed the delegates to remember "that governmental action, however forceful and creative, cannot succeed unless it is
accompanied by mobilization of effort by private citizens and the
organizations and institutions through which they express their
will." [10]

Despite these precautions, when the invited guests convened in Washington on June 1 and 2, they engaged in heated
debates and aimed their criticism at the federal government. Although the right to vote did not appear on the agenda, panelists
debated issues of importance to suffragists. The sessions on "Administration of Justice" had special significance for voter registration workers who had risked their lives striving to encourage blacks
to enroll. Unhappy with the Justice Department's cautious deployment of federal registrars, civil rights activists clamored for
Washington to protect them from racist harm. The conferees
condemned the national government for not utilizing its existing
power to safeguard civil rights field-workers, and they singled out
the FBI for responding too slowly and hesitantly to civil rights
threats. Carl Rachlin, the general counsel of CORE, summed up
this opinion: "The problem really comes down to what . . . the
government conceives its role to be. For years . . . the federal
government and the FBI, conceived itself to be some kind of administrative body which would investigate crimes which were
brought to its attention. It has never conceived of its role as a
policeman." [11]

Delegates at these sessions demanded vigorous federal
law enforcement to ensure personal security. They denounced the
FBI for choosing not to make on-the-scene arrests in cases of harassment against civil rights workers, and asked that the bureau
hire more black agents and that its controversial director, J. Edgar Hoover, be fired. The invitees also expressed their dismay that
potential southern black registrants still encountered intimidation, violence, and economic coercion, and they recommended
that the "Department of Justice take more vigorous and affir-

mative action in enforcement and protection of voting rights."[12] Though improved implementation of the laws already on the books was their top priority, the disgruntled delegates also supported legislative proposals to strengthen federal protection of civil rights workers. They called upon Congress to penalize private persons who interfered with such constitutionally guaranteed rights as voting, jury service, and equal access to public accommodations and education. In addition, they endorsed provisions for more adequate criminal sanctions against state and local officials who interfered with the activities of civil rights workers and for furnishing monetary compensation to the victims of racial offenses. One measure that received the approval of the delegates provided for impartial selection of federal and state jurors drawn from the names on voter registration rolls. In affirming this proposal, the conference members expressed their conviction that the Voting Rights Act would result in expansion of the suffrage rolls to include a fair cross section of local community residents.[13]

The administration could not stop the delegates from raising their objections, but the two-day convocation generally proceeded the way it had hoped. Joseph Califano, a top White House advisor on domestic affairs, praised the masterful performance of two of Johnson's aides, Harry McPherson and Clifford Alexander, in handling complicated problems so "effectively and discreetly with only one overriding objective—protecting the President."[14] Another confidant of the chief executive gloated that the "White House Conference, while sitting on a number of kegs of dynamite constantly was a strong plus and the press image that came out from this was most favorable."[15] In contrast, others portrayed the administration's efforts in a less favorable light. Floyd McKissick, who failed in his attempt to obtain support for a resolution calling for the United States to pull out of Vietnam, griped that the conference was "a hoax." A representative of the Voter Education Project in South Carolina labeled the assembly "An Exercise in Futility," and Andrew Kopkind, a radical journalist, described the affair as a "strictly controlled March on Washington," which "had the effect of anesthetizing the movement."[16]

The administration did not spring to action to disprove these charges. At an address to the delegates on the evening of

June 1, Johnson had declared: "Your President may not agree with everything that you do, but he will consider everything you say."[17] Immediately after the convocation, McPherson counselled his boss: "We must consider its recommendations in a vigorous, visible and aggressive way."[18] Two months later, Johnson received the final report of the conference and appointed McPherson and Clifford Alexander to head a White House task force to advise him on which recommendations should be implemented. This advisory committee met occasionally without producing many practical results. McPherson later admitted: "The farther we got from the conference and its echoes of applause . . . the less purposeful our meetings were."[19] In fact, the conference never generated enough public enthusiasm for bold new measures on behalf of racial advancement, especially when the war in Vietnam was diverting funds away from the battle against poverty at home, and many whites were ready to call a cease-fire on the civil rights front following the outbreak of renewed urban rioting.

Although the White House Conference produced few immediate benefits, it did raise some hope for the future. The assembly spotlighted the inadequacy of federal protection of civil rights workers in the South and exerted pressure on the administration to improve the performance of the FBI in apprehending perpetrators of racial violence. Furthermore, the delegates provided strong backing to proposals pending in Congress for strengthening federal power to shield civil rights activists from intimidation and to prosecute crimes committed against them before interracial juries. Of all the recommendations endorsed at the meeting, these proposals stood the best chance of success. They focused on the activities of the civil rights movement in the South and required relatively few funds to implement, in contrast to suggestions for a nationwide equal housing law and expensive job training programs.

For many of the guests at the White House Conference the gathering had been little more than an academic exercise. The convocation lacked the stirring oratory or the morale-building camaraderie of previous civil rights celebrations. Administration efforts to manage the proceedings removed most of the drama and produced a generally dull affair. For the moment, as *New York*

Times reporter John Herbers observed, "Lyndon Johnson seemed capable of controlling even so uncertain a force as the civil rights movement."[20] However, when the show closed, one member of the audience returned home to begin his own production, which upstaged the president. Before he finished, the White House learned just how difficult it was to earn favorable civil rights reviews.

A few days after attending the conference, James H. Meredith journeyed to Mississippi, where four years earlier he had won notoriety for his successful attempt to integrate the state university. Following graduation in 1963, he had entered Columbia University Law School and had stayed out of the limelight of the raging civil rights struggle in his native Magnolia State. During those years, Meredith gained a reputation for being stubborn and fiercely independent and for being a loner. A veteran of the Air Force, he was disturbed by the attacks hurled on American foreign policy from some quarters of the civil rights movement. At the White House Conference, Meredith objected to what he considered a strident resolution connecting white bigotry with American foreign policy. Overshadowing his patriotic fervor, though, was a "divine mission" to conquer discrimination, particularly in Mississippi. "I am," he acknowledged, "a Mississippian in all respects—even the bad ones."[21]

Meredith intended to begin a 200-mile pilgrimage from Memphis, Tennessee, to Jackson, Mississippi, to encourage black voter registration. His trip reflected the sharply declining pace of Negro enrollment following the initial burst of activity after the Voting Rights Act went into operation. By the middle of 1966, the attorney general had designated about one-third of Mississippi's eighty-two counties for examiners, more than for any other state, but suffrage impediments still remained. With literacy tests suspended, the chief barriers consisted of physical and economic intimidation and the legacy of nonparticipation in politics carried over from past oppression. "The major problem," a SNCC veteran of numerous voter registration drives concluded, "is fear. The tradition of harassing Negroes through the years had built up this fear, and it requires a long time and a lot of work to break through it."[22] Consequently, Meredith mounted his crusade "to challenge this fear," and he concentrated his efforts at the local level. Mer-

edith, whose matriculation at Ole Miss had generated white rioting, approached his suffrage task in a spirit of conciliation. Acknowledging that blacks had to assume the initiative in registering
to vote, he sought to convince southern whites "that the Negro
is not out to threaten them or break up their lives."[23]

Fresh from attending the White House Conference, on
June 4, James Meredith walked southward from Memphis with
only a few close associates along the two-lane Highway 51.
Wearing a yellow pith helmet and carrying an African ebony
walking stick with an ivory head, he embarked on a personal
campaign "to fulfill these rights." In preparation, he had written
to Mississippi's governor, Paul Johnson, to the members of the
state's congressional delegation, and to the sheriffs of the counties along the route asking them to ensure his safe passage. The
chief law enforcement officer of De Soto County, the first stop
for Meredith as he entered Mississippi, pledged: "We are going
to treat James Meredith just like any other nigger chopping cotton in the fields."[24] The first day in Tennessee passed unevent-
fully. On the second, after he crossed into Mississippi, Meredith
encountered some verbal abuse from whites standing along the
sidelines. Undaunted, he urged a cluster of black onlookers to
"register and vote. And if you have any trouble, just let me know.
I'll be on the highway for several days. We'll get some federal
registrars in here. We're going to make the President do what he
said he was going to do or show that he was lying."[25]

Moments later, twenty-eight miles into the journey, as
Meredith and his companions left Hernando, the De Soto county
seat, gunfire rang out. Struck in the back, Meredith fell to the
ground, grimacing in obvious pain from the buckshot that pierced
his skin. The ambush was observed by the journalists accompanying the procession, the highway patrol, and a carload of FBI
agents taking notes. State troopers and sheriff's deputies quickly
apprehended the attacker, James Norvel, and the victim was rushed
to a Memphis hospital for emergency treatment. Having barely
penetrated the Magnolia Curtain, the march came to an abrupt
halt. However, the act of violence that delayed it also guaranteed
its resumption, this time under intense, national scrutiny. The
journalist Richard Rovere compared the consequences of the as-

sassination attempt with the impact of the recently concluded White House Conference: "Of course the presence of twenty-six hundred more or less influential people reminds the politician that they are going to be watched and judged. But two pellets in the hide of James Meredith . . . probably have had much greater effect."[26]

With Meredith recovering from his wounds in a Memphis hospital, civil rights leaders attempted to transform his personal odyssey into a fulfillment of their organizational goals. In doing so, they exposed the widening rift both within the civil rights movement and between its most militant segment and the Johnson administration. Flocking to the injured patient's bedside, the heads of the major civil rights organizations could agree on little except that the protest march should start up again while Meredith recuperated. Whitney Young of the National Urban League spoke for his colleagues in declaring that they were "united as one on man's right to walk down the highway unmolested."[27] However, they bitterly divided over other aims and the tactics to achieve them. Roy Wilkins of the NAACP wanted the reconstituted march to rally public opinion in support of pending congressional legislation to fight civil rights crimes along the lines recommended by the White House Conference. Stokely Carmichael, who had recently replaced John Lewis as chairman of SNCC, and Floyd McKissick of CORE downplayed the need for new legislative measures. Instead, they stressed the government's failure to implement adequately the current laws, and they sought to put President Johnson on the spot. Carmichael noted that "Meredith was returning from a government sponsored civil rights conference 'To Fulfill These Rights' and we find proven once again that words will not stop bullets nor will they end law enforcement committed to racism."[28] McKissick angrily derided the nation's policymakers for failing to live up to the ideals of the Statue of Liberty. "They ought to break the young lady's legs and punt her to Mississippi," CORE's spokesman snarled.[29]

SNCC leaders envisioned the march as a sharp break from those held in the past. The election of Stokely Carmichael as chairman had represented a shift in the organization away from the principles of integration and nonviolence. Carmichael wanted the trek through Mississippi to "deemphasize white participation" and to "highlight the need for independent, black political units." In stark contrast to Wilkins and Young, who sought to cool racial animosities, the SNCC leader urged Mississippi blacks to seize power for themselves and not to "beg the white man for anything [they] deserve." Moreover, he called upon the Deacons for Defense, a black self-protection group from Louisiana whose members toted guns, to patrol the march procession.[30] SNCC remained committed to Meredith's original aims of voter registration and challenging fear, but its leaders reinterpreted these goals to promote black solidarity and active resistance to oppression.

As he had done many times before, Martin Luther King stepped into the breach and tried to unite the feuding groups around a common purpose. At Meredith's bedside and in the deliberations that followed, he played the role of mediator between the two camps of the civil rights movement. King rejected the notion that white participation and nonviolence should be abandoned, but he did join SNCC and CORE in harshly criticizing the Johnson administration's execution of civil rights laws. "Scores of Negro and white civil rights workers have given their lives in our struggle to secure voting rights for an oppressed minority," Dr. King lamented, "while the Federal Government has flagrantly procrastinated in applying enforcement provisions to Federal voting rights legislation."[31] At the same time, he agreed with the position of the NAACP and the Urban League in supporting immediate enactment of congressional bills protecting civil rights workers.

The SCLC chief helped draft a manifesto which put enfranchisement at the top of the list of priorities. The document called upon the president to dispatch federal examiners to all 600 Deep South counties and to direct them to conduct mobile registration so that blacks isolated on outlying plantations could be reached. This would permit "ballots instead of buckshot [to] become the voice of the South."[32] Furthermore, the pronouncement demanded increased civil rights protection by the Justice Department, the FBI, and federal marshals, passage of legislation to improve the administration of southern justice, and adoption of a "freedom budget" to permit blacks to shape their own destinies. This negotiated declaration proved unacceptable to Wilkins and Young, who found it too critical of President Johnson, and they refused to sign it.[33] Nevertheless, the NAACP let its branches decide whether to join the march, and its Mississippi field secretary, Charles Evers, despite some reservations, did provide assistance.[34] Meanwhile, James Meredith returned to his apartment on the Morningside Heights campus of Columbia University to allow his injuries to mend and to figure out if he would return to the march that bore his name but only partially reflected his original mission.

The ambush furnished ammunition to liberal critics who assailed the federal government for not providing adequate protection for civil rights workers in the South. Joseph Rauh, the legal counsel of the Leadership Conference on Civil Rights (LCCR), succinctly stated the position: "The responsibility for the shooting of James Meredith rests squarely on the doorstep of the Federal Bureau of Investigation."[35] The editors of the *Nation* scoffed at the FBI agents who were on the scene "to witness the shooting themselves," and the editors went on to complain: "What is lacking in Washington is an honest determination at all levels, including the Presidency, to do something now, about lawlessness in Mississippi."[36]

The Johnson administration quickly dismissed these charges. A day after the incident, Attorney General Katzenbach told a panel of the Senate Judiciary Committee, which was holding hearings on proposals to strengthen federal protection for civil rights workers: "It is not possible for the FBI to provide complete protection. We try to provide deterrents when we can." After Senator Jacob Javits, a liberal Republican from New York, quizzed the attorney general about a newspaper story claiming the Justice Department had turned down a specific appeal from Meredith for help because "it was not important enough to do anything," a furious Katzenbach denied the allegation; but he affirmed the government's customary position: "We get a lot of requests from civil rights workers saying 'Send marshals to protect us.' I don't believe that one can effectively accompany around every civil rights worker, and that even if this is done, it is not necessarily going to protect them from violence when you have nuts and people of that kind." To clinch his agrument, he pointed out to the Senate committee that the attack had occurred with at least fifteen federal, state, and local law enforcement officials trailing Meredith. Unable to prevent the crime, they arrested the assailant within minutes.[37]

Before the pilgrimage recommenced, the White House made plans to avert additional bloodshed. President Johnson called the shooting "an awful act of violence that every sensible American deplores," and he ordered Katzenbach "to spare no effort in bringing the guilty . . . to justice."[38] A Justice Department task force watched the situation in Mississippi around the clock, and the FBI undertook an extensive investigation of the incident but still insisted it could not offer protection.[39] Rather than blanketing the roadway with federal agents, the attorney general accepted assurances from Governor Paul Johnson that state and local police would guarantee the safety of the marchers "provided they behave themselves, commit no acts of violence nor take a position of provocative defiance." Concerned about the effect of unfavorable publicity, the governor termed the shooting a "fool thing" and admonished Mississippians to keep their distance from the "agitators and radical politicians" when the march resumed. At the same time, he promised to prosecute the captured gunman "to the hilt." Although the federal government had jurisdiction in the case under a criminal section of the Voting Rights Act, Katzenbach had no plans to put the defendant on trial as long as Mississippi authorities moved "expeditiously under state law."[40]

Civil rights leaders refused to let the administration off the hook. Reverend Fred Shuttlesworth, King's associate in SCLC and a veteran of previous marches, urged the White House to send federal examiners to all Mississippi counties. "Such immediate registration," Shuttlesworth declared, "would also deter further injustice, further massive demonstrations with more possible violence, and erase a farcical strain from the face of America." The Justice Department declined to blitz the entire state with federal personnel, but announced that to "handle the possible increase in activity stimulated by the Meredith March, examining offices in designated Mississippi counties will be reopened for the period of the march."[41]

The next step was up to the civil rights paraders. On

June 7, the Meredith troops departed without their injured name-sake. Led by King, Carmichael, and McKissick, a procession of about 150 started southward from the spot where Meredith had been attacked two days earlier. The ranks of the crusaders swelled with blacks as they approached the towns and hamlets dotting the route. Whites also joined, but the demonstration did not command the same attraction as did the walk from Selma to Montgomery a year before. To be sure, King had won his argument on keeping the affair interracial; however, some of his companions discouraged whites from participating. Although McKissick acknowledged white support, he compared his feelings "to when you are sick and your neighbor comes in to help you. You need his assistance, but you don't want him to run your house or take your wife."[42] Stokely Carmichael carried this point further. Shortly after the trip began, he preached to a church crowd at Mr. Olive: "If you don't have power, you're begging. It's time to get power that every other group has. We've got to remove them and make sure they are gone. We're going to take over and get black sheriffs and black tax assessors."[43] Reverend Ralph David Abernathy, King's right-hand man, vigorously dissented: "If you got any notions that Negroes can solve our problems by ourselves," he warned churchgoers in Batesville, "you got another thought coming. We welcome white people."[44]

Aside from these conflicts, march leaders agreed to work on behalf of the suffrage. They chose to make forays off the highway and fan out in teams into the heart of the delta where civil rights workers had suffered the severest hardships throughout the years. The canvasers found that little had changed. In Tallahatchie County, the scene of the brutal murder of Emmett Till in 1955, local police in the town of Charleston closed all businesses and ordered people to stay off the streets. The fear that gripped blacks working on plantations, those most vulnerable to white economic reprisals, diminished only slightly. A white plantation manager commented after the marchers pulled out: "They weren't doing any good here. I told my niggers I'd run them up here on a truck, but they didn't want to come. They know they're better off right here than the ones in Chicago."[45] Nevertheless, about one hundred blacks displayed their courage by registering, prompting some optimism among the suffragists. "The main trouble is that the Negroes here are afraid," a local black leader noted, "and if nothing happens to the ones who have registered, it may help others overcome their fear."[46]

Elsewhere the results were considerably more positive. After several days off the main highway, the demonstrators returned to their original itinerary and paraded into Grenada on June 14. Their spirits were high as they celebrated Flag Day by installing an American flag on the Confederate war monument in front of the county courthouse. Surprisingly, this action did not provoke a confrontation. Rather, the white city fathers shrewdly adopted what King termed "a more sophisticated form of resistance to racial desegregation."[47] They met with the march leaders and agreed to allow six black school teachers to serve as deputy voter registrars and to extend the hours of enrollment into the evening. Underlying this conciliatory posture was a belief by city officials that the less trouble the marchers encountered the faster they would leave, which would avoid an incident that might push the federal government to send examiners.[48] Before the march, slightly less than 700 Negroes had signed up to vote, compared with nearly 6,000 whites, in a county where the population was almost equally divided between the races. When the procession departed, about 1,300 blacks had added their names in the enrollment books. However, the future did not appear quite as bright. "After they leave everything will be the same again," a deputy sheriff declared. "The nigger in this town depends on the white man for his living."[49]

More bad tidings lay ahead as the crusaders again detoured off Highway 51 into the neighboring countryside. Taking these excursions into the delta, they entered territory where SNCC had once been most active. Perhaps these familiar surroundings fanned the militancy of Stokely Carmichael and his associates, for on June 17, they were arrested in Greenwood for attempting to erect without a permit sleeping tents on the grounds of a black high school. Upon his release from jail, Carmichael addressed a rally on the Leflore County Courthouse steps: "This is the twenty-seventh time I have been arrested—and I ain't going to jail no more!" Then, he ignited the enthusiasm of the crowd and issued a clarion call for a new departure in the civil rights movement. "The only way we gonna stop them white men from whippin' us," Carmichael boomed, "is to take over. We been saying freedom for six years and we ain't got nothin'. What we gonna start saying is Black Power."[50] As soon as these rousing words poured out, Willy Ricks, a SNCC field-worker, jumped to the platform and shouted: "What do you want?" Echoing Carmichael's ringing finale, and turning the phrase into an electrifying slogan, the audience chanted, "Black Power."[51]

Not all blacks who heard Carmichael and Ricks responded so favorably. Martin Luther King believed the choice of words was unfortunate. He and his aide, Andrew Young, had spent a good deal of time in Greenwood persuading angry blacks from turning demonstrations into violent brawls. Worried that "black power" sounded too inflammatory and suggested "wrong connotations," King pleaded with Carmichael, who was supported by McKissick, to abandon the phrase. The Atlanta minister accepted Carmichael's contention that all other ethnic groups had advanced by consolidating their economic and political resources and that blacks "must work to build racial pride and refute the notion that black is evil and ugly." However, King insisted, "this must come through a program, not merely through a slogan." Fully aware of the effectiveness of battle anthems, the pastor suggested substituting "black consciousness or black equality" for "black power [which gives] the impression that we are talking about black domination rather than black equality."[52] The three leaders compromised and imposed a moratorium for the duration of the march on the use of "black power" or "freedom now," the rallying cry of past civil rights demonstrations.

This semantic struggle temporarily set aside, the civil rights activists remained in accord on the importance of the franchise as an instrument for liberation. While in Greenwood, Carmichael partially clarified his own term: "The only way we can change things in Mississippi is with the ballot. That's black power." Denying that he was antiwhite, he wanted Negroes to stop feeling ashamed of their skin color by getting "the nappiest-headed black man with the broadest nose and the thickest lips and make him sheriff!"[53] Such sentiments did not differ from those expressed by one of King's colleagues in SCLC, Hosea Williams, who urged blacks in Greenwood to "get that vote and put black faces in those uniforms. Get the vote and whip those policemen across the head with it."[54] Whatever shades of meaning the black power slogan would have in the future, it was originally understood by march leaders and their followers in Mississippi to signify that "black communities should have people running for public office so that they could control the communities."[55] At least initially, many of the blacks who lined the suffrage trail as the procession rolled by believed that the most important form of black power was electoral power.

The Meredith march not only showcased the importance of enfranchisement for black advancement, but it also accelerated the conflict between civil rights groups and Washington concerning federal protection. Following the resumption of the pilgrimage after the attack on Meredith, highway patrolmen and sheriff's deputies had generally safeguarded the travelers. However, when the marchers exited from the main road and spread out into the countryside to encourage voter registration, they lost most of their escort. As the demonstrators gathered in Greenwood, Governor Johnson ordered a reduction in the number of patrol cars from twenty to four because he refused "to wetnurse a bunch of showmen all over the country." Claiming that the march had become a typical voter registration drive, he requested local police to keep the peace.[56] The Justice Department monitored the situation closely and obtained assurances from its lawyers on the scene that following the governor's proclamation "both the state Highway Patrol and the Leflore County Sheriff's office appear in fact to be furnishing adequate protection."[57] In accordance with its traditional policy, the department was satisfied to leave law enforcement in the hands of local officials.

The suffragists appraised federal responsibility much differently. From many bloody years of experience, they had little reason to entrust their safety to Mississippi authorities. During the 1964 Freedom Summer, three of their comrades had been murdered in Neshoba County, and the sheriff and his deputy were among the eighteen people charged with the crime. Only six months before the 1966 march, Vernon Dahmer, who was busy organizing a voter registration campaign for the NAACP's branch in Hattiesburg, died after several firebombs exploded through his home at two o'clock in the morning. Such killings proved to Fannie Lou Hamer, a black activist in the Delta, that Mississippi was still "the land of the tree and the home of the grave."[58] The fact that the federal government apprehended and prosecuted the assailants in these murders only raised the expectations of the civil rights forces that the Justice Department should do more to guarantee their safety before the offenses took place.

Since the Meredith march had originated to combat the paralyzing fear that antiblack violence induced, to be successful its participants had to show their courage in the face of serious dangers. Indeed, they deliberately detoured to places where blacks had been the victims of past brutality. No stop brought more vivid memories of the savagery of racist oppression than Philadelphia, the seat of Neshoba County. Two weeks after the march had begun, the procession entered the town to hold a memorial service for the trio of civil rights workers slain two summers before. Unfortunately, not much had changed in the interim. On June 21, led by Dr. King, the demonstrators were assaulted by a mob of some 300 whites hurling rocks, bottles, firecrackers, and profanities. To add insult to injury, the local police force which failed to restrain the crowd was under the direction of Deputy Sheriff Cecil Price, one of the men charged with the murders of the three civil rights workers. Instead of shielding the marchers from attack, Price blocked them from reaching their courthouse destination. This officially sanctioned obstruction caused King to moan: "This is a terrible town, the worst I've seen. There is a complete reign of terror here."[59]

Refusing to withdraw from these hazards, the civil rights leaders planned a second march in Philadelphia, but this time they expected federal intervention. During the initial demonstration, one state highway patrol car had been on the scene along with several Justice Department lawyers and FBI agents who observed the clash. Subsequently, King, McKissick, and Carmichael wired the president to send federal marshals for their protection. On June 23, President Johnson expressed his concern over the violent incidents but informed the protesters that the Mississippi governor had assured him "law and order will be maintained . . . in Philadelphia and throughout the march and that all necessary protection will be provided."[60] The chief executive relied on Assistant Attorney General John Doar to serve as an emissary to the marchers as well as to offer advice and assistance to state and local authorities and persuade them to act responsibly. Although the Justice Department admitted that law enforcement officers in Philadelphia had failed to perform their peacekeeping duties, the White House reiterated that federal police action was inappropriate because it was "the State's primary responsibility to preserve law and order. Absent a Federal court order, or some showing that law and order have broken down completely, Federal troops or marshals are not called for."[61] The governor did beef up the contingent of state troopers in Philadelphia, and when the second march to the courthouse occurred on June 24, state police were on hand to keep unruly white bystanders away from the protesters.

The president felt vindicated by this outcome, and he was unwilling to budge from his position even after state troopers clashed with the marchers in Canton. The trouble started with a dispute between the city and the demonstrators over camping facilities. The marchers wanted to erect their tents on the campus of a black elementary school, but local officials declined to issue a permit for an activity unrelated to education. On the evening of June 23, 2,500 peaceful demonstrators gathered at the disputed campsite, in defiance of the order. State policemen arrived and routed the crowd by firing tear gas and slamming their guns into the bodies of those too incapacitated to flee. One trooper stomped on a woman who had stumbled and taunted her: "Nigger, you want your freedom? Well here it is."[62] Through a haze of noxious fumes, Martin Luther King, who was shuttling back and forth between Canton and Philadelphia, exhorted his followers to remain calm and not retaliate, and further violence was averted. The next day, King struck a compromise with Canton officials, pledging to refrain from erecting facilities on school grounds in return for permission to hold a rally on the controversial site. Notwithstanding these efforts at conciliation, the besieged minister condemned the White House for its reliance on Mississippi law enforcement agencies to maintain order. "This is the very state patrol," King scoffed, "that President Johnson said . . . would protect us. Anyone who will use gas bombs on women and children can't and won't protect anybody."[63]

King's outrage did not persuade the chief executive to change his mind and provide a federal convoy for the marchers on the remainder of their journey. The president also declined to heed the advice of Roy Wilkins, who had shunned involvement in the pilgrimage, "that it must be made clear to Mississippi that adequate protection will be furnished the marchers by federal forces during the last days of the march and rally in Jackson."[64] Instead, President Johnson utilized Justice Department attorneys such as John Doar to forestall additional violence. Doar had observed the clash in Canton but complained that he "could do nothing because neither side would give an inch."[65] Finally, the sheriff of Madison County agreed to safeguard the marchers as they paraded to the Canton city limit on the way to a stopover at Tougaloo College before they arrived in the Mississippi capital.[66] By this time, James Meredith had recuperated sufficiently from his wounds and took his position at the head of the procession. Flanked by King and Carmichael, Meredith walked unmolested the last eight miles of the crusade he had begun over three weeks earlier.

The last leg of the trip concluded on June 26, as the marchers jubilantly walked to the capitol building in Jackson. Greeted by a crowd numbering about 15,000, Meredith and his companions rejoiced in hearing Martin Luther King declare that the event "will go down in history as the greatest demonstration for freedom ever held in the state of Mississippi."[67] Amidst the nine hours of speechmaking, Stokely Carmichael delivered the one message that the marchers shared in common: "It's the vote, it's the right to control your own vote, to fire that police who uses tear gas and brutalizes you."[68] The mood was festive but tense. A SNCC member burned a Confederate flag to the delight of many black onlookers; however, the divisions that were developing within the civil rights movement surfaced at the rally. Charles Evers, the state director of the NAACP had furnished assistance to the marchers but was barred by militants from the speakers' platform. In the audience, SNCC supporters and SCLC adherents waged a battle of slogans. Chants of "Black Power" and "Freedom Now" reverberated around the capitol, drowning each other out.[69]

Despite this friction, the march qualified as a success. It resulted in an additional 3,000 to 4,000 blacks signing up to vote, proving, as Hosea Williams pointed out, "that you can rid Negroes of the deep-rooted fears that have been embedded in them for centuries."[70] With this needed boost to the pace of voter registration, suffragists made plans to conduct additional campaigns in the wake of the march. Their continued presence in Mississippi did not promise an immediate end to disfranchisement, but it did mean that attempts by local officials to revert to previous practices would be held in check. For instance, SCLC staff members who stayed behind in Grenada assured a fight if city leaders refused to honor their earlier commitment to facilitate black enrollment. When local officials had dismissed the black clerks hired during the march to handle registration and discouraged new applicants from trying to place their names on the polling lists, SCLC had mounted a series of demonstrations. Though these failed to improve the operation of Grenada's suffrage procedures, they helped convince the Justice Department to designate the county for federal examiners in mid-July.[71]

This favorable response from Washington did not indicate a significant change in enforcement of the Voting Rights Act. One of the goals of the Meredith crusaders was to convince the federal government to dispatch registrars to all 600 covered jurisdictions in the South. The Justice Department, while offering moral support, stuck with its approach of obtaining compliance through negotiations and voluntary cooperation. John Doar thought the Meredith march "has been a good thing" for encouraging "many Negroes to take a step toward independent, political assertiveness for the first time in their lives." Nevertheless, he continued to believe that civil rights groups should perform the bulk of the suffrage work. "The important thing is not statistics—the number of Federal voting examiners—but real participation by the citizen in the political life of his community," Doar declared.[72] This opinion failed to satisfy civil rights leaders. A few months after the march, Martin Luther King, appearing on "Meet the

Press," observed that "when you have Federal registrars in communities, many more Negroes go out to register because they see a different atmosphere, and they are not over-arched, under-girded with the fear of intimidation and economic reprisals as much as they do in dealing with some of the local registrars that they have dealt with so long."[73]

The administration disagreed with King over tactics, not goals. The president affirmed his faith in the ballot as a solution to ending racial inequality. "We are not interested in black power, and we are not interested in white power," the chief executive declared. "But we are interested in American democratic power with a small 'd.' We believe that the citizen ought to be armed with the power to vote."[74]

Although enfranchisement had widespread appeal within the civil rights movement, presidential rhetoric on its behalf was no longer enough to assure victory for the moderates. In some ways, the administration's handling of the Meredith situation had hampered President Johnson's own cause. During the march, the Justice Department had damaged its credibility and had helped undermine the position of Martin Luther King, the leader most capable of blending militancy with prudence. Earlier in Birmingham and Selma, King had succeeded in stemming defections from the volatile ranks of the civil rights coalition by winning support from the executive branch for the movement's legislative goals. In Mississippi, he failed to deliver federal protection at Philadelphia and Canton, thereby furnishing ammunition for the militants to attack Washington. According to King, "the federal government makes my job more difficult every day . . . to keep the Movement nonviolent."[75] Relations between the president and King cooled even further over the widening of the Vietnam War.

Coming under increasing attack from black activists, the Johnson administration also had to contend with a growing white backlash. The fragile consensus that Johnson had constructed in favor of the Civil Rights Act of 1964 and the Voting Rights Act of 1965 withered in the wake of ghetto riots and shrill shouts for black power. Concerned with maintaining the interracial, liberal-labor coalition that had advanced both civil rights and the fortunes of the Democratic party, the Johnson White House still had to calculate the political consequences of advocating measures that seemed to "reward the rioters," thereby prompting further partisan defections by whites. Harry McPherson reflected on the ambivalence of a liberal administration which took the position: "By God, there's law and order here. You can't get away with this," and followed this with, "Of course we understand why you rioted. We know you could hardly do anything else."[76] Buffeted between escalating black militancy and white reaction, the Johnson administration pushed the limits of reform to the breaking point.

The black protest movement had become too fractious for Johnson to manage, even with his legendary skills of persuasion. Increasingly bogged down in the quagmire of Vietnam after 1965, the president lacked the time and funds to lead the civil rights forces to new heights and keep dissension to a minimum. Nevertheless, the chief executive did not retreat, but instead identified with the goals of moderate black leaders and their liberal white allies. The White House wrote off the possibility of cooperating with the militant proponents of black power who, according to McPherson, "have no ideology, no program, no basic objectives. They aren't interested in politics. They're only interested in 'Black Power.' They represent a lot of genuine frustration and anger, but they don't represent many people."[77] Despite the growing urban unrest throughout the middle and late 1960s, the administration found reason to stay on its chosen course. Taking satisfaction from the victories of black mayors in Cleveland and Gary, Louis Martin exclaimed: "This was black power with a difference. These elections prove that the political ladder works for the Negro just as it has for others in our society."[78] However, Johnson's advisors realized that militants were making inroads, particularly among younger blacks, and they sought to bolster the moderate position.

Although the Johnson administration chose not to heed the call for a massive infusion of federal examiners into the South, it did respond favorably to demands for extending protection of civil rights personnel. In late August 1965, shortly after the signing of the Voting Rights Act, an interagency task force on civil rights was created with John Doar as its head. Looking to the future, the group determined that the "only area where the need for legislation seemed unanimously apparent was the area of physical security and problems of racial violence in the Southern States."[79] By the end of the year, white juries in three Alabama towns had acquitted the accused murderers of Viola Liuzzo, James Reeb, and Jon Daniels, all of whom died while participating in suffrage activities. These verdicts and the anguished outcry they brought from civil rights forces ensured that the national administration would draft proposals to remedy such injustices. In mid-December, Justice Department officials reported that they were sketching measures to guarantee an impartial jury selection system, to expand federal jurisdiction to investigate racially motivated crimes, and to enhance personal security for civil rights workers.

Katzenbach favored the introduction of these bills, but he worried more about the problems posed by supporters of civil rights than by their opponents. He believed that reform groups would demand much more than "a modest expansion" of federal authority to prosecute civil rights infractions, which he envisioned as "both appropriate and useful."[80] The Civil Rights Commission and the planners of the White House Conference on Civil Rights had already gone on record endorsing proposals for financial remuneration of civil rights victims and a vast increase of federal personnel for additional enforcement of existing statutes, recommendations which Katzenbach did not consider wise. Fearing the administration would become "the target of civil rights criticism without any compensating political advantage," the attorney general wanted to avoid a bruising battle over the specific type of legislation to support. He hoped for a lessening of pressure for a personal security measure. "To the extent that further incidents of violence do not occur, or can be successfully handled by state prosecutions," Katzenbach noted, "we will be helped."[81] He also counted on the racial climate improving as southern blacks registered and turned out to vote in large numbers in state and local elections in 1966.

These reservations did not deter the Johnson administration from placing civil rights protection as an item on its 1966 legislative agenda, in good part because Katzenbach was disappointed in his wish for a respite from racial violence in the South. Early January marked the murders of Vernon Dahmer in Mississippi and Sammy Younge in Alabama. Appalled by these slayings, the president in his State of the Union Address on January 12 proposed "legislation to strengthen authority of Federal courts to try those who murder, attack, or intimidate either civil rights workers or others exercising their constitutional rights."[82] In addition, he asked Congress to increase the penalties for civil rights crimes, to approve legislation for nondiscriminatory jury selection in federal and state courts, and to adopt a bill for equal opportunity in housing. Applauding the speech, Clarence Mitchell, the chief legislative lobbyist for the NAACP, singled out "the protection of individuals against physical violence" as the most important goal for the coming congressional session.[83]

Following Johnson's message, Justice Department lawyers undertook the delicate task of drafting legislation to implement his suggestions. They picked as their starting point statutes currently on the books. Title 18, sections 241 and 242 of the United States Criminal Code, enacted during the Reconstruction period after the Civil War, had several defects. Section 241 was a conspiracy law that concerned participation in racial crimes by two or more persons, and section 242 applied to offenses perpetrated by individuals "acting under color of law." Neither provision covered acts of violence committed solely by private persons acting without the collaboration of public officials. Moreover, the judiciary had interpreted the scope of these ordinances narrowly. The courts had ruled that to obtain conviction under the broadly worded statutes, the government had to prove that the defendant willfully intended to deprive the victim of a particular federal right. This presented a greater problem than did a typical homicide case. Not only did federal prosecutors have to demonstrate that a murder was committed, but they also had to show that the assailant had knowingly acted to keep the victim from exercising a specific constitutional right. This burden of proof was especially onerous for U.S. attorneys in southern courtrooms, where they frequently practiced before all-white juries. Making matters even more difficult, judges had limited to a few the number of federal rights protected under the laws. In addition, on those few occasions where guilty verdicts were obtained, the penalties imposed did not fit the severity of the crime. Given these circumstances, the Justice Department had employed these statutes sparingly over the years, with few resulting convictions.[84]

Throughout the first three months of 1966, attorneys in the Civil Rights Division took steps to correct the deficiencies in existing legislation. They developed a proposal that spelled out the constitutional rights subject to federal protection—voting, use of public accommodations, access to public schools, employment, jury service, and participation in or enjoyment of federally assisted programs. Also included in the coverage were persons who assisted members of minority groups in seeking to exercise these rights. These activities would be shielded from violence perpetrated by private individuals acting alone or with others and by public officials. This plan would make it easier for government prosecutors to secure convictions. They would not have to prove that a defendant had the "purpose" of interfering with the particular activity if the assailant was racially motivated and the interference took place while the victim participated in or was about to engage in the stipulated action. The penalties for violation of the proposed statute were graduated in accordance with the degree of damage inflicted on the victim.[85]

In drafting this legislation, the administration mirrored most but not all of the thinking of civil rights advocates. It rejected two critical suggestions by the Civil Rights Commission. One called for awarding an indemnity to civil rights workers injured in pursuit of their cause. The Justice Department scotched this recommendation, believing it applied too narrowly to only one category of crime. The other measure would have broadened the scope of the protection proposal by covering economic interference with the designated civil rights. In turning this down, the department argued that its experience in trying civil suits for economic intimidation demonstrated that "the facts necessary to support a successful criminal prosecution would be almost impossible to develop." Nevertheless, CRD lawyers did accept the advice of civil rights advocates for directing FBI agents to "make arrests on the spot when they observe violations of federal civil rights law."[86]

While administration draftsmen were putting the finishing touches on the proposals, the Supreme Court boosted their efforts. In companion rulings involving prosecution of civil rights crimes, the high tribunal overturned two unfavorable lower federal court decisions limiting the scope of sections 241 and 242. One case involved Lemuel Penn, a black Army reservist who was shot and killed by six private citizens as he traveled on a Georgia highway; the second concerned the notorious, triple slaying of civil rights workers by a band of Klansmen aided and abetted by a county sheriff and his deputy during the Mississippi Freedom Summer in 1964. On March 28, 1966, the Supreme Court held that sections 241 and 242 covered the violated rights, found sufficient evidence of state collaboration in the crimes, and instructed the district courts to convene new trials. However, the justices appeared unwilling in *United States v. Guest,* the Penn case, to hold section 241 applicable to strictly private conspiracies. Nevertheless, in two separate opinions, a majority of the court opened the way for passage of legislation drawn along the Justice Department's lines. Justice William Brennan summed up the position of six of his brethren: "Section 5 [of the Fourteenth Amendment] empowers Congress to enact laws punishing all conspiracies to interfere with the exercise of Fourteenth Amendment rights, whether or not state officers or others acting under the color of state law are implicated in the conspiracy."[87] Reassured by the Supreme Court's obiter dictum, Justice Department officials turned over their handiwork for final approval by the White House.

In the Oval Office, the president's aides held a generally gloomy outlook for legislative success in the coming year. Henry Wilson, Johnson's congressional liaison, suggested that not many lawmakers were "enthusiastic" about civil rights measures, and Katzenbach had agreed that the "situation in Congress is a good deal different with respect to civil rights than it was in 1964 or 1965."[88] Still, Johnson's counselors were hopeful that several items in the administration's package had a good chance of passage. The brightest prospect was for the personal security provisions, and the bleakest, for fair housing. Opposition to the latter rose with the crest of the white backlash, uniting real estate interests, southerners traditionally antagonistic toward racial equality, and northern whites, many of whom for the first time would be directly affected by civil rights legislation. Influential Republican lawmakers, including Senate Minority Leader Everett Dirksen of Illinois, upon whom Democratic strategists had depended for previous civil rights victories, withheld their approval of a fair housing bill. At the very best, administration policymakers guessed "civil rights legislation without Housing can be enacted this session."[89]

In spite of the declining level of support both inside and outside of Congress for additional civil rights measures, President Johnson decided to send an omnibus proposal up to Capitol Hill. On April 28, he met wth a delegation of civil rights leaders and, seeking to avert factionalism, urged the group to rally around "all of the package and not just for parts of it."[90] That same day, Johnson delivered a special message to Congress offering further legislation to strengthen civil rights. At a time when racial storms were brewing, the characteristically optimistic chief executive discerned a ray of hope. Noting the impressive rise in black voter registration in the Deep South, Johnson concluded: "This achievement serves to renew our faith in the ultimate triumph of a Government in which all free men can participate."[91] The president remarked upon the restorative power of the ballot to heal racial wounds and pledged that his administration would continue to assist blacks to gain "their just share in the electoral process." Worried about "the danger that recently secured rights may be violently denied by a relatively few racial fantatics," he advocated proposals for safeguarding the constitutional rights of civil rights activists and for guaranteeing racial equality in jury selection.[92] His legislative recommendations also incorporated equal housing, but the president recognized that these "legal reforms can be counted only a small part of a national program for the Negro American." The economic roots of racism remained to be overcome, and in the interim, Johnson urged blacks "to use the opportunities for orderly progress that are now becoming . . . a reality in their lives" and appealed to white Americans to work in common "to expand those opportunities."[93]

Left to deliberate on the administration's omnibus bill,

Congress did not share the enthusiasm of the chief executive. Through five months of hearings and floor debate, few features of the measure emerged unaltered. The personal security clause, Title V, did not escape without substantial attempts to blunt it. During May, the bill remained in the friendly hands of Emanuel Celler of Brooklyn, the veteran Democratic manager of civil rights bills, whose House Judiciary Committee conducted hearings on the administration's proposals. The main assault against the measure came in June, when a Senate Judiciary Subcommittee chaired by Sam Ervin held hearings. Regarded as the upper chamber's expert on constitutional law, the former Harvard Law School graduate and former North Carolina judge had been on the losing side of every major civil rights battle since 1957. "In my more pessimistic moments," Ervin quipped, "I wonder if the Senate, under its annual hypnotic spell, would not overwhelmingly defeat an amendment granting civil rights supporters eternal salvation and guaranteed access to the Kingdom of Heaven, if that amendment were offered by me to a civil rights bill."[94] The facetious North Carolinean had no intention of introducing his hypothetical provision, but he did plan to dilute the strength of Title V.

Ervin's reading of the Constitution, unlike that of the majority of the Supreme Court, convinced the senator that Title V was based on a false premise. Rejecting the advice offered by Brennan in *United States v. Guest,* he denied that the federal government possessed the authority to punish private individuals for racially motivated crimes. "No amount of intellectual sophistry, no amount of torturing of the language of the 14th Amendment," Ervin fumed, "can change the fact that a prosecution brought pursuant to its mandate requires the element of State action or action taken under color of law."[95] On June 7, Ervin pressed this reasoning on Katzenbach, who had come to testify before the subcomittee. In the course of a vigorous exchange between the two, Katzenbach insisted that the administration provision would stand the constitutional test. He agreed with the high tribunal that Congress could legislate "with respect to purely private action without State involvement, particularly where the State fails to do so, and particularly where those private actions may be the result of violations of the 14th Amendment in the past on the part of the states."[96] Still unconvinced, Ervin suggested the approach he would pursue. He acknowledged that Congress had the power to punish violations of constitutional rights, but he did "not believe that it is good policy for the Government to pick out one group of citizens and protect them and not protect all Americans."[97] In the time-honored tradition of those who opposed a specific piece of legislation, Ervin would weaken the bill by broadening its coverage. Thus, the North Carolina senator prepared to present a substitute to Title V that extended federal protection to all constitutional rights and not those solely concerning race.

However, the first successful attempt to weaken Title V came not in the Senate but in Celler's House Judiciary Committee. On June 27, the panel approved by the narrow margin of 18–16 an amendment offered by George W. Grider, a Memphis Democrat and a racial moderate. The provision stipulated that federal protection would be expanded to cover civil rights workers only if they engaged in "lawful" activities. Grider explained that his amendment was not aimed at peaceful civil rights protesters who might violate some minor ordinance, but it was directed "at the rabble-rouser who wants to incite a mob to action."[98] Administration forces worried that the Grider amendment would allow state and local governments to continue their practice of arresting civil rights activists on trivial and trumped-up charges without fear of federal prosecution.[99] Nonetheless, the amendment squeaked through, because as Senator Everett Dirksen explained, House members "have discovered that there is considerable backlash with respect to this legislation"[100]

Having cleared the House Judiciary Committee in modified form by a vote of 24–9, the omnibus bill languished in the Rules Committee, the bottleneck of liberal proposals presided over by Howard Smith of Virginia. An archfoe of racial equality, Smith believed that the chances of defeating this civil rights bill were better than they had been in a long time. He pinned his hopes especially on "the housing provision that is not so popular in the northern sections where they have voted so unanimously for anything that might affect the Southern States and help them with the Negro vote."[101] Smith could delay but not stop consideration of the bill. After three weeks of stalling by Chairman Smith, on July 25, Representative Celler brought his committee's measure to the floor under a House regulation freeing bills locked up by the Rules Committee for more than twenty-one days.[102]

The shooting of James Meredith a few weeks before the formal debate began exerted pressure on Congress to act more swiftly. The attack on Meredith and the subsequent outbreaks of violence involving the marchers en route to Jackson strengthened demands for congressional action. Following the ambush, presidential aide Clifford Alexander predicted that a bill extending security for civil rights proponents "will gain significant momentum and probably get through Congress rather quickly."[103] A Republican congressman from Michigan, Edward Hutchinson, who sat on the House Judiciary Committee, agreed with Alexander's assessment. "When it began to appear that the country might be settling down somewhat on the Civil Rights issue and the Civil Rights organizations were in disagreement among themselves," Hutchinson wrote a constituent, "some fool in Mississippi shoots another Civil Rights worker, and the drive is on again. It is quite likely that the Congress will enact legislation making such attacks a federal crime."[104] Taking advantage of the legislative fallout resulting from the Meredith shooting, moderate civil rights leaders kept up pressure. While the march took place without him, Roy Wilkins advised the Senate Judiciary Committee that the majority of blacks were feeling a "slow burning anger" and were gradually losing faith in law as an instrument of justice. Failure to pass legislation, Wilkins admonished, would further taint the democratic process in the minds of Negroes and win black converts to "the preachers of violent retaliatory action."[105] The potency of these arguments did not escape Sam Ervin's notice. Closely observing the proceedings from the upper chamber, the senator lamented that the Meredith incident "makes it much more difficult for me to protect against unconstitutional and unwise legislation when the public becomes concerned by such an outrageous act."[106]

The plight of peaceful civil rights demonstrators generated widespread sympathy, but congressmen favoring the bill gave even more emphasis to the explosive issue of ghetto violence in the North. While denouncing these outbreaks, civil rights advocates nevertheless used them in behalf of their cause. Along with the right to vote, passage of additional measures for racial equality was viewed as a means of persuading blacks to keep faith with the orderly functioning of the democratic system. By improving the administration of justice and furnishing equal access to housing nationwide, liberal lawmakers intended to show that traditional channels of redress were still open and legitimate alternatives to violence available. Congressman Celler had no illusion that the simple enactment of a bill would lessen black militancy, but he contended, "what we do in Washington is quite different from what has happened in the localities where we have had this violence, where Washington has no control."[107] William McCulloch, ranking Republican on the House Judiciary Committee and a representative from Ohio where a bloody riot had recently erupted in Cleveland, supported the pending measure as he had prior civil rights bills that had "been successful to a great degree in moving the struggle for equal rights and equal opportunities from the streets into the polling places and into the courts."[108] His Democratic colleague on the Judiciary Committee, Peter Rodino of New Jersey, also expressed this view: "Congress must . . . point the way to the only solution that can for all time set to rest the violence and upheaval on our streets and in our neighborhoods. And that is equal educational, economic, political, and social opportunity for all."[109]

As a debating weapon, violence was a double-edged sword. Civil rights opponents decried the claim that passage of the bill would promote racial accord, and they asserted that the legislative outcome should not be shaped by the fear of racial conflagration. Democratic Congressman Horace Kornegay of North Carolina suggested "that the more Civil Rights bills the Congress passes, the worse race relations become in the country. Witness the all too many examples of rioting, looting, flagrant disregard for law and order."[110] In a similar vein, Jack Edwards, an Alabama Democrat, rebutted "the notion that Federal legislation can bring about a kind of utopia. And when there was no utopia after the civil rights bills of 1960, 1964, and 1965, this fact was hard to understand. Instead of utopia we had bitterness, frustration, confusion, and then violence."[111] These sentiments were echoed by Democratic Congressman Joe Waggoner of Louisiana, who attributed the racial disturbances gripping the nation to "legislating, not equality before the law, which is every man's right, but special preference for the Negro."[112]

The southern lawmakers received a favorable hearing as their colleagues became alarmed at the escalating level of urban rioting and the inflammatory rhetoric that accompanied it. In 1966, some forty-four cities—twice as many as a year earlier—experienced violent uprisings by black ghetto dwellers. While whites recoiled from the outbreak of racial hostilities, black militants praised them. Floyd McKissick of CORE expressed his satisfaction with the riots. "Many good things," he remarked, "have occurred for blacks as a result of violence." Apparently, a large minority of Afro-Americans agreed. Forty-one percent of the black leaders responding to a Louis Harris poll shared the view that the "riots have helped."[113] Stokely Carmichael did his best to promote this idea, and his speeches that summer appeared increasingly menacing to whites. Shortly after an eruption of violence in Cleveland, Carmichael declared: "When you talk of black power, you talk of the black man doing whatever is necessary to get what he needs. . . . Last week—that wasn't no riot. That was just a get-ready party."[114]

In this tense racial situation the omnibus package passed the lower house, but not without significant alterations in Title V and the housing clause. The worker protection section was amended to include the Grider proviso guaranteeing coverage only to those engaged in "lawful" enterprises. An even more serious setback to the civil rights forces came in the adoption of an "anti-riot" rider to Title V. Introduced by Republican William Cramer of Florida, the measure made it a felony for individuals to conspire to cross state lines to incite violence. "It is high time," Cramer remarked, "that the Congress recognizes the term 'civil rights' has a broad application to all people's rights."[115] In this instance, the usual battle lines on civil rights were reversed, as opponents of the Cramer measure attacked it as an unnecessary invasion of the traditional law enforcement responsibilities of local governments. William F. Ryan, a liberal Democrat from New York City, was "intrigued" to see the foes of reform legislation, "who usually argue most vociferously for states rights, supporting the Cramer . . . amendment which would enlarge the Federal Government's role in law enforcement."[116] Nevertheless, with racial turbulence again sweeping the nation's cities, the antiriot amendment passed easily with a vote of 389–25.[117]

The real ire of civil rights opponents settled on the housing section, and to obtain sufficient support from the Republican side of the aisle, administration forces eventually agreed to a housing compromise proposed by Charles Mathias, a GOP congressman from Maryland. Although this version provided exemptions from coverage for most sales of homes, Attorney General Katzenbach persuaded the president to endorse this "husky half-a-loaf." He pointed out the practicalities of the "piecemeal approach to civil rights." "I don't think," Katzenbach contended, "we ever could have gotten the comparatively drastic 1965 voting legislation if we hadn't been able to prove by experience under the 1957 and 1961 [sic] acts that a milder approach wouldn't do the job."[118]

On August 9, following an unusually long twelve days of debate, the lawmakers approved the patched-up version of the omnibus bill. The housing compromise and the Cramer provision attracted a bipartisan coalition for the entire package. In making up his mind, GOP Representative Edward Hutchinson found it "so far watered down as to justify my joining the other members of the Michigan Delegation, both Republicans and Democrats, in voting for the final version of the bill."[119] Not only had the reformers failed to deflect assaults to weaken the bill, but they were also unsuccessful in obtaining approval for additional items. Among the proposals turned down was a plan for indemnifying victims of civil rights crimes, which the administration had opposed. In general, the legislative results attested to the waning of the consensus behind racial equality. Southern violence against civil rights workers, including James Meredith, ensured passage of Title V; however, racial disturbances in the North led to adoption of a repressive riot control proposal and a weakened housing section. In previous years, southern lawmakers had been on the defensive. This time, one liberal observed, "there almost seemed to be a reversal of roles." Arnold Aronson, a spokesman for the Leadership Conference on Civil Rights, reported on the situation in Congress: "The mood of many Northern members was one of apprehension and timidity. With the November elections coming on, their votes and speeches frequently reflected political anxiety about voter reaction to big-city riots, 'black power' slogans and the pressures of the real estate lobby."[120]

The measure survived rough treatment in the House, only to face certain death in the Senate. As it had in 1964 and 1965, the Johnson administration viewed Minority Leader Dirksen as the pivital legislative figure and sought to line up his support. The Illinois senator believed that Title V could be modified to his satisfaction, but he stood adamant in his belief that the housing title "does intrude and in fact contravene the due process clause in the Constitution."[121] Weeks of private discussions with White House counselors failed to budge him.[122] With Dirksen standing firm, the southern bloc, according to Richard Russell of Georgia, expected "to get enough Republican Senators who are not plagued with the racial problem from a political standpoint to defeat cloture."[123] This venerable leader who had battled civil rights proposals for decades counted on "the rioting outside the South [to] give us a little assistance in our fight against the new Federal Force legislation."[124]

Russell's hopes were realized. Senate liberals failed even to rally sufficient support for bringing the omnibus bill to a vote on the floor. Initially, Majority Leader Mike Mansfield succeeded in bypassing the Senate Judiciary Committee, chaired by James Eastland of Mississippi, and called up the House-passed bill directly for consideration. On September 6, the upper chamber embarked on less than two weeks of languid discussions punctuated by two votes taken to impose cloture. Although a slight majority favored terminating debate, a combination of Dirksen-led northern Republicans and southern Democrats kept the adminstration from obtaining the requisite two-thirds margin of those present and voting.[125] On this occasion, there were no Birminghams or Selmas to spark a civil rights victory, and the liberals were unable to check the negative publicity generated by urban rioting. The Georgia Democrat put it best when he declared that southern obstructionist efforts worked in this session so effectively because the rest of the country refused to be fed "some of the bitter dose that they have poured down our throat."[126]

Administration supporters worried that the legislative defeat hurt the chances of settling racial problems peacefully. Senator Philip Hart of Michigan, a leading Democratic spokesman for civil rights, whose intelligence and strength of convictions were admired by friend and foe alike, commented shortly after the failure to invoke cloture: "We do not serve the voices of moderation who counsel the aggrieved to be patient and to await the orderly course of law each day."[127] The *Pittsburgh Courier* concluded that the "temper of white Americans over the 'black power' threat was at such a fever pitch." Nevertheless, the black newspaper urged its readers to respond calmly with the "one sure 'black power' weapon. And it is the vote." It suggested that blacks had to increase their electoral strength if they were to gain victories for first-class citizenship in the future.[128]

Congress soon adjourned, and its members returned home to campaign for reelection, allowing the civil rights forces time to assess their defeat. Some blamed the Senate leadership for failing to push harder for the bill, while others condemned the president, distracted by the Vietnam War, for not waging a vigorous fight.[129] For his part, Johnson believed that he had "tried to persuade the Congress to embrace my viewpoint," and, indeed, a majority of the lawmakers had endorsed the revised bill.[130] However, the White House had failed to win over Dirksen, and the proposal came before the Senate too late to allow civil rights advocates enough time to crack the filibuster. But scapegoating probably missed the point. Quite simply, in 1966, a growing segment of white Americans gave higher priority to punishing rioters than to extending racial equality. This attitude was partially reflected at the midterm congressional elections when the Republicans increased their membership in the House by forty-seven, and some moderate southern Democrats who had voted for the bill were defeated.[131]

Undaunted, the Johnson administration decided to resubmit its civil rights omnibus bill for congressional action. For several months at the end of 1966, presidential counselors conferred with Justice Department officials to map out a legislative strategy for the coming year. They grappled with the problem of what to do about the antiriot proposal tacked onto Title V by the House. Convinced that passage of such a measure was "inevitable," the advisory group considered whether "it might be better to include an acceptably narrow anti-riot provision . . . over which we would have a degree of control . . . than to have a broader 'anti-riot' provision added by Congress." Frowning upon the bill on constitutional grounds, the panel recommended against submission of an administration antiriot measure, but suggested preparation of "a standby bill" as an alternative to harsher plans that probably would be introduced in the upcoming Congress.[132] By late February 1967, the White House had cleared the final draft of the civil rights plan and sent it to Capitol Hill.[133]

At about the same time, the president launched the opening salvo in this new legislative fight with a special message to Congress on February 15. The war abroad that drained much of his energies provided him with some ammunition to use on the home front. In Southeast Asia, Johnson declared, "the Negro American has given this nation his best—but this nation has not given him equal justice." Shortly after this address, the chief executive convened a meeting with civil rights leaders, pledged "to make every effort" to obtain enactment of the omnibus proposal, and stressed the importance of rallying public support behind these measures.[134] Arnold Aronson of the LCCR spoke for his liberal colleagues in praising Johnson for his "summons to us all. The President was clearly unimpressed by those who warned him to go slow."[135]

In contrast, Congress reacted with caution. Representative Celler expressed a "definite reluctance" to have the House consider the administration measure before the upper chamber did. Believing that support for the bill in 1966 had cost numerous congressmen at the polls, the Brooklyn Democrat remarked: "Let the Senate vote on it first this time."[136] There seemed little chance of this happening quickly, since the Senate had only recently declined to alter the cloture rule to make it easier to terminate a filibuster. To break the legislative deadlock, the White House consented to revise its omnibus package and to have each item introduced separately. This gave the Senate an opportunity to deliberate on Title V without its carrying the stigma attached to the more controversial housing section.[137]

Before that occurred, members of the lower house indicated that they were more concerned with enacting measures against inciting to riot than with protecting civil rights workers. Pressure for an antiriot bill mounted as racial insurrections flared throughout the nation and black militants continued to stir up trouble. In May 1967, H. Rap Brown had replaced Stokely Carmichael as chairman of SNCC, and his public statements were no less provocative than those of his precedessor. "Violence is very American, as American as the 4th of July," he explained and added, "It is the only way we can show the Honkies we are men."[138] The Republican congressional leadership selected an antiriot bill as one of the party's "must" pieces of legislation, and on the other side of the aisle, northern Democrats eagerly joined the bandwagon.[139] Proponents of this measure succeeded in detaching the antiriot proviso from Title V, forcing it out of the Judiciary Committee, and on July 19, approving it by an overwhelming margin of 347–70. Outflanked by this maneuvering, the administration's civil rights allies managed a month later to resurrect Title V. The influence of the riots still prevailed, however, as lawmakers amended the bill to safeguard law enforcement officers who legitimately carried out their duties to pacify racial disturbances. Supporters of Title V saw its passage as the quid pro quo for enactment of the antiriot bill. They argued that both measures together promoted law and order. Approval of Title V "in combination with the anti-riot bill," Republican Congressman Marvin Esch of Michigan declared, "would clarify the differences between our concern for legitimate civil rights activity and our opposition to exploitation of race and incitement to riot."[140] Protecting both peaceful civil rights demonstrators and antiriot police, Title V sailed to victory on August 16 by a 327–93 vote.

The House endorsed the bill in a new political climate. Not only did the escalation of rioting in the summer of 1967 put a higher premium on curtailing racial violence in urban ghettos than on protecting the diminishing contingent of civil rights workers in the rural South, but there was also evidence of progress. Southern officials had taken steps to punish the perpetrators of civil rights murders committed in 1966, and federal prosecutors obtained some convictions under existing laws. To be sure, black southerners still suffered from economic coercion and the legacy of generations of intimidation, but the use of overt physical brutality to stop civil rights activities was on the decline. Furnishing symbolic evidence of this change, in the summer of 1967 James Meredith walked along the same Mississippi route he had attempted to journey the previous year. This time, after eleven uneventful days, Meredith completed the 162-mile pilgrimage. The first black Ole Miss graduate exulted that his "walk from fear" showed "that the state and local police officers if they choose can afford protection to Negroes."[141]

Under these circumstances, the Senate felt little urgency to move swiftly on Title V. Even had the lawmakers been more inclined to act, they encountered the usual stumbling blocks. Throughout August and September, a Judiciary Subcommittee, headed by Sam Ervin, held leisurely hearings on the worker protection bill. The North Carolina senator provided opponents and supporters ample time to rehash the arguments already heard in both legislative chambers. Representative Cramer told the group that it would be "the height of naiveté to suggest that Stokely Carmichael's presence or . . . the presence of H. Rap Brown in a city preceding a riot is mere coincidence," and the police chiefs of Cambridge, Maryland, Cincinnati, and Nashville testified that the SNCC leaders had inflamed racial tensions in their cities.[142] Clarence Mitchell of the NAACP issued a different warning. He admonished Ervin and his colleagues that they had "the choice of listening to those who came to petition for civil rights in an orderly way . . . or [of listening] to the aggrieved, who come in the only way that they know how to come, and that is on a wave of emotion, leaving in their path a lot of destruction, both physical and moral."[143] Ervin persisted. He did "not understand why so much anguish is expressed about crimes of violence in Mississippi and not about crimes of violence elsewhere."[144] At his direction, in early October the subcommittee approved a substitute for the House bill, dropping the racial criterion and extending coverage to anyone victimized for exercising a constitutional right. The North Carolina senator offered this proposal as a smokescreen. Instead of dealing with the acknowledged problem of racial discrimination, his measure would have weakened Title V by extending federal jurisdiction into matters that were already adequately handled by local law enforcement. The Justice Department suspected that Ervin and other opponents of civil rights legislation would vote for this amendment and then oppose the entire bill on its merits.[145] On October 25, the Johnson administration prevailed in full committee by an 8–7 vote and restored the lower chamber's version. The decisive vote was cast by Senator Hugh Scott, a Pennsylvania Republican, whom the White House arranged to fly home from England to break the tie.[146] Disappointed by such defeats, Ervin complained bitterly: "A bill sponsored in good faith by a Southerner apparently cannot see the light of day, because it would protect all persons, regardless of race or color, rather than a single minority."[147]

Having vaulted this hurdle, administration forces decided to wait until the next legislative session to reach a final disposition of the matter. Fearing that not enough time remained to debate the proposal adequately and to mobilize sufficient strength to choke off a filibuster before adjournment, the reformers came to an agreement with Mansfield to call up the bill as the first order of business on January 15 and "to stay with it until a final vote is obtained."[148]

With the dawning of the new year, the prospect for civil rights was no brighter. The NAACP noted "the deadly silence with which members of both houses greeted President Johnson's brief reference to pending civil rights legislation in his State of the Union address on January 17," in contrast to their hearty applause for the recommendations pertaining to riot control and waging of the Vietnam War.[149] A columnist for the *New Pittsburgh Courier* warned his readers: "Don't look for any social miracles out of the 90th Congress that is currently convening in Washington. Civil Rights legislation is dead."[150] Liberal lawmakers were only slightly more optimistic. Philip Hart, who served as Democratic floor manager for the civil rights package, believed that, at the very least, the Senate would adopt a worker protection provision; however, he worried that attempts to attach an equal housing amendment to it would severely hamper efforts to curtail the expected filibuster. In that event, Hart guessed, an "Ervin-type worker protection bill and nothing else" could win approval.[151]

Nevertheless, the administration did not intend to back down from its commitment to obtain all items in the omnibus measure. On January 24, in a special message to Congress, the president stood behind his entire program and urged legislators not to let the riots interfere with their obligation to promote civil rights. Striking a balance between concerns for racial peace and justice, Johnson vowed: "Lawlessness must be punished—sternly and promptly. But the criminal conduct of some must not weaken our resolve to deal with the real grievances of all those who suffer discrimination."[152] The Republicans responded favorably only to those proposals that had passed the House. In its own "State of the Union" address, the GOP advocated "immediate enactment of legislation to protect civil rights workers from violence . . . and prompt passage of legislation to make illegal the use of interstate communication and transportation facilities to provoke violence."[153] This recommendation met with the approval of Dirksen, who remained the object of administration attentions. He had some reservations about restricting the protection bill to racially motivated crimes and remained noncommittal as to whether to support Ervin's move to broaden Title V. In discussions with the Illinois senator, the Justice Department and its legislative allies contended that the measure "does not select a single group for special benefits and protection. Rather it singles out a group which has shown a demonstrated need for federal protection because state and local law enforcement have not protected Negroes and other persons working with them."[154]

These arguments surfaced publicly on the Senate floor, as debate began on the bill narrowly reported by the Judiciary Committee the preceding October. Starting in January, Ervin resumed his attempt to garner support for his substitute measure "that applied alike to all men, under like circumstances, not have one murder punished as a Federal Crime because of the race of the accused or the race of the victim and another exempt from punishment because in that case the race of the accused and of the victim is the same."[155] Once again, civil rights adversaries switched their customary positions on the issue of federal-state authority. In this instance, liberals advocated restraint in the exercise of national power and pointed out that Ervin's offering "represents maximum federal encroachment in an area where local law enforcement has been both willing and able to handle the job."[156]

For the most part, the discussion ranged over familiar ground, and each side played the usual role. James Eastland warned that unless a meaningful antiriot bill was enacted first, "the American people will get the clear and unmistakeable message that this body is more interested in protecting the agitators and incitors to riot . . . than it is in punishing these persons for their misdeeds."[157] However, for Hugh Scott the passage of civil rights legislation was a necessary step " 'to preserve the domestic tranquility,' " and the Pennsylvania Republican further asserted: "What we do here, in these cool days of winter, may well serve to cool and to tamp down emotions which may otherwise rise with the temperature."[158]

As deliberationns entered their third week, Senate liberals won a convincing opening victory. On February 6, Senator Hart offered a motion, which carried 54–29, to table the Ervin amendment. Senator Richard Russell, who had utilized his sharp parliamentary skills against numerous civil rights measures, concluded following this vote: "We are badly outnumbered here."[159] Joining the administration camp were nine Republicans who deserted the minority leader. Instead, they followed the advice of Thruston Morton, chairman of the Senate GOP Policy Committee, "that in an election year the Republicans should not seem to align themselves with the Southern conservatives against civil rights legislation by voting for the Southern substitute."[160] By contrast, Dirksen opposed the liberals' tabling resolution, preferring to prolong debate until "we can come reasonably close to a common denominator."[161] Nevertheless, the outcome was far from certain, and the administration continued to negotiate with him in order to win his backing for a comprehensive civil rights plan.

With the worker protection bill, HR 2516, intact, the Senate shifted its attention to the controversial fair housing proposal submitted as an amendment by Walter Mondale, a Minnesota Democrat. Throughout the remainder of February, progress on the measure came to a halt as its opponents tied up the chamber with a filibuster. Two cloture votes attracted a bipartisan majority in favor of closing debate, but, with Dirksen still in the opposition, both attempts fell short of the necessary two-thirds.[162] Furthermore, the same civil rights coalition defeated a motion to table the equal housing provision. Encouraged that these votes revealed "underlying support for civil rights . . . despite riots and a sense of backlash," Johnson accelerated his efforts to fashion a compromise acceptable to Dirksen and to persuade Mansfield to keep the bill before the Senate.[163] The stakes were high. Violence against civil rights protesters had burst forth recently in Orangeburg, South Carolina, and a black lawyer in the Civil Rights Division had been shot at while traveling on an interstate highway in Mississippi. The "anger and frustration that would probably accompany a failure to enact the pending civil rights program," according to Attorney General Ramsey Clark, "might have far reaching consequences for the summer problems."[164] Weeks of intensive pressure from the administration and civil rights lobbyists, especially Clarence Mitchell of the NAACP, finally paid off. After failing a third time, the Senate voted 65–32 on March 4 to impose cloture. With a bill tailored to Dirksen's specifications, twenty-four Republicans joined forty-one Democrats, leaving not a single vote to spare.[165]

The inscrutable Dirksen, "whose heart was always with the conservatives but who reacted to political trends like litmus paper to acid," once again played a key role in this legislative triumph.[166] As he had in 1964 and 1965, the Senate minority leader reversed himself after arranging satisfactory revisions of civil rights measures without substantially detracting from their strength. In this latest instance, Dirksen had felt pressure from members of his own party to strike a bargain and to cease his objection to cloture. On three occasions over half the Senate Republicans, many of whom had been elected in 1966, supported a termination of debate despite Dirksen's disapproval. Under these circumstances, the minority leader heeded the advice of his son-in-law, Howard Baker, a freshman senator from Tennessee: "The majority of Republicans in the Senate want some kind of civil rights bill."[167]

With the stalemate broken, the Senate took only a few days to approve the civil rights package. Before doing so, the lawmakers adopted an antiriot amendment, despite administration protestations, but they refused to water down further the fair housing sections. On March 11, seventy-one senators trounced twenty of their colleagues and ratified the omnibus bill.[168] Considered hopeless only a few months earlier, the passage of this broad measure was a stunning victory for the liberals. The initially pessimistic Philip Hart was elated and "surprised that we have passed a strong housing bill."[169] HR 2516 also contained provisions for jury selection that were linked to the suffrage. Jury lists would be compiled from voter registration rolls that had become swollen with the names of blacks since enactment of the 1965 voting rights law. Troubled by racial strife, the legislators had responded both to demands for law and order and to cries for equal justice. "In an hour of contention and stress," President Johnson congratulated the senators, "those who work within the law to enlarge the liberties of all men are the true peacemakers— and they deserve the thanks of their countrymen."[170]

The revised administration package had one more steep hurdle to clear. Because the House had passed a different version consisting only of worker protection, it had the choice of agreeing either to the Senate amendments or of covening a joint conference committee to work out a compromise. The White House and its civil rights allies wanted the congressmen to acquiesce in the Senate's modifications, fearing that further protracted deliberations might result in a weakening of the crucial housing section. Since 1966, when the lower chamber had approved the original omnibus bill, including fair housing, forty-four supporters and twenty-six adversaries had left office. "In order to command a House majority," President Johnson's congressional liaison reported, "we must get a number of new Republicans and try to change some of the Democrats who opposed us in 1966."[171] A hitch in this strategy developed when Minority Leader Gerald Ford of Michigan backed the conference committee route.

Weighing the alternatives, the administration chose to fight for House concurrence largely because the "civil rights organizations would be unhappy with the . . . Democratic leadership if the Civil Rights bill was sent to conference."[172] The battle lines drawn, on March 14 HR 2516, as revised by the Senate, was sent to the House Rules Committee.

The civil rights troops lost the opening skirmish when the committee decided to delay action until April 9, the return of Congress from its Easter recess. Voting for postponement, three Democrats—chairman William Colmer of Mississippi, James Delaney of New York, and B. F. Sisk of California—joined all five Republicans to defeat seven Democrats. This scheduling decision meant that debate would resume just as a Poor People's March on Washington, led by Martin Luther King, was planned to get under way. Before the Rules Committee reconvened, King was assassinated in Memphis on April 4, igniting a spontaneous outburst of civil disorders in cities across the nation, including Washington, D.C. As buildings blazed and smoke wafted over Capitol Hill, legislators returned to discuss the fate of the omnibus civil rights measure.

It is difficult to calculate the exact impact of King's murder on the legislative outcome. Barefoot Sanders, the presidential aide responsible for rounding up votes in Congress, concluded: "King's assassination did not have much effect because yeas and nays cancelled each other out."[173] Yet, in some ways, his death strengthened the administration's position. President Johnson, whose personal relationship with the slain minister had deteriorated markedly during the past year, urged Congress to honor King's memory by enacting "legislation so long delayed and so close to fulfillment."[174] George Romney, a Republican presidential aspirant, wired the congressional delegation from his home state of Michigan, asking its members to expedite passage of the pending civil rights legislation and to fill the "vacuum in the leadership of moderate Negroes" created by King's death.[175] One GOP representative from Michigan, Edward Hutchinson, believed "that had the vote been taken in the House prior to King's murder, we could have sent it to conference where it would have taken the ordinary course of the legislative process."[176] Instead, the day of Reverend King's funeral on April 9, the Rules Committee recommended approval of the Senate's civil rights version by a 9–6 vote. In contrast to their vote on postponement a few weeks earlier, Congressmen Sisk and John B. Anderson, an Illinois Republican, joined the administration side. Anderson denied that King's assassination caused him to change his mind, but he did admit: "I seek to reward those Negroes who can become responsible leaders of our society and diminish the influence of black racists and preachers of violence."[177]

In other respects, King's killing may have hurt civil rights fortunes. The ensuing riots detracted from the outpouring of sympathy following the Memphis tragedy. Representative L. H. Fountain, a North Carolina Democrat, charged that the House was "acting on the basis of emotion instead of logic and that we are responding to threats rather than the will of the people we represent."[178] Civil rights supporters had to combat this notion that Congress was being blackmailed into taking action by the rioters. Emanuel Celler wrote a disgruntled constitutent that although the riots caused deep distress, he did not "want a whole race subjugated because a minority of that group had taken to the streets."[179]

Whatever the net effect of King's murder and the disorders that followed, passage of the omnibus statute owed a great deal to the efforts of the chief executive and civil rights lobbyists, notably Clarence Mitchell. The White House and the NAACP official worked closely together to build the necessary bipartisan approval. The president became personally involved in pressing Democrats to stand behind his program, and Mitchell devoted himself to bringing wavering Republicans in line.[180] By the time the House reassembled after Easter, the hard work had paid off. According to Senator Hart, who watched the proceedings closely, the House vote "would have been affirmative," and the King assassination merely "advanced this affirmative action" by several days."[181] Consequently, on April 10, a bipartisan majority in the lower chamber agreed to accept the Senate's modifications by a margin of 250-171.[182] The next day President Johnson signed the bill into law, proclaiming it as proof that the "only real road to progress for free people is through the process of law."[183]

This well-earned victory crowned Johnson's extraordinary accomplishments in obtaining civil rights legislation. Three times in five years he and his allies had eroded barriers to racial equality that had existed for nearly a century. The triumph in 1968 was especially remarkable because it came during a period when public support for racial reform had ebbed and the civil rights movement was torn by factionalism. Moreover, the triumph testified to the perseverance and effectiveness of the remaining elements of the interracial coalition which exerted constant pressure on the White House and Congress. The Johnson regime won a major legislative victory against considerable odds and cemented the political allegiance of moderate blacks in the Democratic coalition.

4.

Black Power, Ballot Power

Amidst the swirling currents of racial strife, black southerners plunged in to test the political waters. Across the Deep South, blacks marched peacefully to the polls to cast their votes in hopes of improving the quality of their lives. In contrast, northern blacks more frequently resorted to means other than electoral politics as instruments of social change as disillusioned black ghetto dwellers rampaged through their impoverished neighborhoods, convinced that burning did more good than balloting. In both cases, the struggle to obtain power had replaced the acquisition of basic legal rights as the main focus of concern, but in the South blacks channelled their restless energies into the mainstream of the electoral system. If their continued faith in enfranchisement as a conventional weapon of liberation was to be rewarded, the national government would have to keep the Second Reconstruction alive by breaking down the remaining barriers to political advancement.

Transformation of the civil rights movement into its militant black power phase affected the development of suffrage strategies. Following the Meredith march from which the black power slogan had emerged, Cleveland Sellers, SNCC's project director, wrote: "Everything that happened afterward was a response to that moment. More than anything, it . . . would go down in history as one of the major turning points in the black liberation struggle."[1] The march marked the last time the major civil rights groups joined together in a massive demonstration in the South. Direct action techniques did not cease, but civil rights workers increasingly turned their attention to political organizing, taking advantage of newfound opportunities in the electoral process. The march against fear heightened awareness among the people in its path that black power started with ballot power. Although SNCC's slogan took on antiwhite overtones, recently enfranchised blacks identified most readily with its political dimension and its expression of self-respect. It is also true, however, that the black power theme drove a wedge between groups in the civil rights movement and between the races. To the degree that groups such as SNCC and CORE attempted to confer an ideological rigidity on this imprecise and highly charged phrase, they isolated themselves from the very people in the South whom they had once helped enormously, and also scared off former allies. At a time when a white backlash was growing, black power rhetoric sapped the strength of the civil rights forces.

Whereas the meaning of black power in northern urban ghettos evolved throughout the late 1960s, its significance for southern blacks remained remarkably constant. The first black elected to the board of supervisors in Wilkinson County in southwestern Mississippi argued that the slogan "simply means for the people to get economic power and political power. You've really got the power when you've got that ballot."[2] Julian Bond, who had resigned as SNCC's public information director to run for the Georgia House of Representatives in 1965, viewed black power as solidly rooted within the American political tradition. "There's nothing wrong with people voting as a bloc. White people have always done it. Every other ethnic group has gotten together . . . and now it's time for the black bloc vote to rise up."[3] The disillusionment with the electoral system that northern blacks reflected in espousing their version of black power was not shared to the same degree in the South. Up North, blacks took the right to vote for granted, having learned from long experience that the ballot did not completely cure all racial ills. However, southern blacks, for whom enfranchisement had come so recently and only after a protracted struggle accompanied by considerable sacrifices, were unwilling to give up on the ballot's potential, especially when they had not yet had a real opportunity to explore its possibilities. Commenting after the Meredith march, Martin Luther King predicted: "The future shape of Southern politics will never again operate without a strong Negro electorate as a significant force."[4]

Southern Negroes varied their political approach according to circumstances, and they did not adhere to any preconceived ideological blueprint. In fact, Stokely Carmichael had derived his early conception of black power largely from his practical field work in rural Mississippi and Alabama. The harsh treatment civil rights activists had suffered at the hands of white extremists and their dissatisfaction with Kennedy-Johnson liberals convinced Carmichael that blacks had to become politically independent before freeing themselves economically. At first this process involved the rejection of interracial coalitions, and SNCC led the way in 1966 by expelling whites from its ranks. Solidarity would be forged from a consciousness of color, ultimately enabling blacks to enter into alliances with progressive whites from a position of strength. Until Afro-Americans could deal with whites on an equal foundation, Carmichael argued, "it's like asking the Jews to reform the Nazi party."[5]

This proposition drew heavy criticism from traditional civil rights activists. Bayard Rustin contended that black separatism was impractical and ill conceived. Pointing out "that southern Negroes are only in a position to win a maximum of two congressional seats and control of eighty local counties," Rustin insisted in 1966 that they "alone could not create jobs and build low cost housing; they alone could not supply quality integrated education." Rustin urged blacks to continue to align themselves with the interracial, liberal-labor wing of the Democratic party and called upon white reformers "to prove that coalition and integration are better alternatives" than black separatism.[6] King, who had benefited from Rustin's counsel during the Montgomery bus boycott in 1955 and the 1963 march on Washington, characteristically staked out a middle ground between the competing positions. Without retreating from his commitment to integration and his belief in cooperation with white liberals, he acknowledged that under certain circumstances southern blacks had no choice but to elect members of their own race to public office. In many counties in the region, especially in rural black belt areas, King agreed with SNCC that for practical reasons "there are no white liberals or moderates to cooperate with."[7] In some places, blacks were willing to extend a hand to whites, only to be rebuffed. Reverend William McKinley Branch, one of the first blacks to hold office in Greene County, Alabama, reflected: "We wanted the government to be polka dot, but the whites wouldn't cooperate, so we had to make it all chocolate."[8]

The often lively intellectual debates on the relative merits of black power versus coalition politics, usually reserved for the pages of liberal and left-wing publications, found concrete expression in the political activities of recently enfranchised blacks in the South. The practitioners of each strategy often flourished side by side, and the lines of demarcation separating them were blurred. Indeed, nowhere else in the nation was the principle of black power applied more vigorously and successfully to the political arena than in the Deep South. During the Johnson presidential years, southern black voters demonstrated their political flexibility and ingenuity. Some joined predominantly black independent parties, and others chose to unite with white moderates to capture control of the apparatus of established Democratic parties. Only a small fraction of blacks was unable to break the shackles of their past psychological bondage and to oppose traditional white candidates. Most blacks considered race an important factor in reaching political decisions and swelled with pride in electing nominees with the same color skin. In pursuing group interests, they proved that both the rival political strategies—black autonomy and interracial alliances—advanced the cause of freedom, but both, too, still left them short of their ultimate goal of racial equality.

As had happened so many times before, most recently with the Meredith march, Mississippi became the center of attention on matters concerning race and suffrage. This time, blacks and a few sympathetic whites succeeded in lifting the Magnolia Curtain that had draped the state since Reconstruction. After being released by the civil rights movement of the early 1960s, the forces of political change were boosted by passage of the Voting Rights Act. In 1964, only 6.7 percent of eligible black adults in Mississippi were signed up on the voter rolls. Five years later, the proportion of blacks enrolled to vote had leaped to 66.8. Voter registration did not automatically convert into electoral power or large numbers of black officeholders, yet with the lock on the ballot box pried open, black Mississippians seized the opportunity to devise plans for their own political advancement. Toward this end, their experiences gave some tangible meaning to the theory of black power, revealing its strengths and weaknesses.

Despite its deserved reputation as a closed society, during the early 1960s Mississippi had served as a laboratory in which the civil rights movement displayed its most creative energies. Actual successes were few as long as disfranchisement persisted; however, the foundations for change had been establshed. In 1963, groups with contrasting styles and outlooks put aside their differences to unite around the common aim of obtaining the suffrage. Spearheaded by the NAACP, SNCC, CORE, and SCLC, the Council of Federated Organizations (COFO) was formed to promote voter registration. This coalition was often an uneasy one, but it did adopt innovative tactics that attracted outside assistance to relieve the plight of blacks in Mississippi, while it also encouraged local blacks to prepare themselves for the day when enfranchisement finally became a reality. Tens of thousands of blacks punctured the myth that they were content to leave the reins of political power solely in white hands by voting in mock elections and participating in the formation of an interracial political party to combat the supremacy of the white Democratic organization. These efforts culminated in the creation of the Mississippi Freedom Democratic Party (FDP) and its challenge at the Democratic national convention in 1964. The results were mixed: the FDP faction returned home without official recognition but with the convention's pledge to approve in the future only those delegates selected without racial bias.

This flawed victory came at great expense to the civil rights movement. The FDP had split over whether to accept a compromise sponsored by the Johnson administration offering two of its members at-large seats as nonvoting guests at the convention. The decision to reject this offer brought out into the open underlying tensions existing among members of the civil rights coalition. As a result, the NAACP, whose state president, Aaron Henry, had endorsed the bargain, withdrew from COFO and the FDP the following year. Subsequently, in 1965, COFO collapsed, but the Freedom Democratic Party survived.[9]

The defection of the NAACP emphasized its commitment to building political alliances with whites and reforming the Democratic party from within. Choosing to work for Johnson's Great Society with the small segment of labor unionists and white moderates in Mississippi, the NAACP urged its followers to ignore calls for creation of separatist political parties. It viewed such arrangements as "reverse racism." Aaron Henry frowned upon "black power" because it suggested to him "that the Negro community should now begin to treat the white community as the white community has treated the Negro community all these years." Seconding Henry, Charles Evers declared: "We're going to support white as well as Negro candidates. It wouldn't be good—it would be wrong—to have all Negroes in public office down here."[10]

In contrast, the FDP did not worry about soothing whites. The party did not exclude whites from participating in its affairs; in fact, the FDP had attempted to forge an alliance with white reformers in mounting its challenge at the 1964 Democratic convention. However, after 1965 the Freedom Democrats' primary aim was to build an organization directed and controlled by blacks. The editor of the FDP newsletter asked: "Why can't the Negro people get in a party of their own dominated by Negroes? Let the white people follow us some time."[11] The chief historian of the FDP and one of its adherents, Leslie McLemore, aptly described the party's ideology as "black consciousness, a component of cultural and political pluralism, which emphasizes . . . the capturing and controlling of political offices where submissive group members predominate."[12] In other words, the FDP served as a prototype for the model of black power advocated and popularized by Stokely Carmichael.

The FDP assumed much of the style and orientation of SNCC. Putting a premium on developing participatory democracy among the poor, the Freedom Democrats scorned the NAACP for its middle-class orientation. They looked at the older group with a disdain tinged with envy of its ability to tap financial resources from its vast network, while groups such as SNCC perennially operated on the brink of insolvency. When NAACP officials in Canton collected the names and addresses of new voter registrants who had enrolled in the aftermath of the Meredith march and inscribed them on the organization's "honor roll of first class citizenship," FDP workers discouraged Madison County blacks from cooperating. They charged that the NAACP would send the voter lists "up North and say 'See what we did' and ask for more money. They're trying to get credit for our work."[13] Furthermore, the NAACP's hierarchical structure annoyed FDP leaders. The national office in New York exercised tight control over its member branches, and policy filtered down from the top of the bureaucratic pyramid. This framework allowed the NAACP to raise funds and implement programs cost effectively, but critics argued that it stifled local initiative. SNCC and FDP, in which decision-making was decentralized, interpreted the NAACP as saying that "local people in Mississippi needed someone to think for them."[14]

To the NAACP their rivals were unreliable, politically naive radicals. Recalling the Meredith march, Roy Wilkins fumed that the civil rights movement had "suffered too much already from projects and spot activity." He contrasted such sporadic efforts with those of NAACP workers in Mississippi who "have demonstrated their ability to carry through with a steady, hard, unspectacular voter registration job." Summing up his complaint, the executive secretary noted sardonically: "Our people supply the work while others contribute philosophy."[15] Wilkins took justifiable pride in his association's accomplishments. Led by Charles Evers, the NAACP achieved its greatest success in two counties in the southwestern portion of the state. Evers had participated intermittently on the Meredith trek, and he had mixed feelings about its usefulness. "I don't see how walking up and down a hot highway helps, Evers declared. "I'm for walking house to house and fence to fence to get Negroes registered."[16] Indeed, he had done just that, and in a single year following passage of the Voting Rights Act, his suffrage campaign in Claiborne and Jefferson Counties, where only thirty-two blacks were enrolled in 1965, helped black voter registrants outnumber whites by two to one. Unlike SNCC field workers, Evers organized his drives around middle-class blacks and refused to oust moderate whites from political office. A man of enormous personal magnetism and popularity among blacks from all walks of life, he emerged as the kind of ubiquitous figure that SNCC warned would endanger the development of indigenous mass movements in Mississippi. Given these fundamental differences and the conflicts they engendered on the Merdith march, the NAACP regretted "how difficult it is to have genuine cooperation, *on an equal responsibility basis,* with certain groups that do not have the same commitments and which may very well be pursuing certain goals that have nothing to do with civil rights at all."[17]

Divided by both ideology and style, Mississippi's civil rights activists had inevitablly clashed over political leadership of the state's 400,000 black adults. A year after Mississippi's regular Democrats swung their state's electoral votes behind the Republican presidential candidacy of Barry Goldwater, 125 representatives of labor, liberal white groups, and the NAACP met in Jackson to sketch plans for taking control of the Democratic party machinery. Invited in mid-July 1965 by Claude Ramsey, the state director of the AFL-CIO, and Aaron Henry, delegates created the Mississippi Democratic Conference (MDC) to construct "a Loyalist Mississippi Democratic group to restore relations with the national party."[18] Ramsey, a hard-nosed union organizer who was a descendant of a pioneer Mississippi family, attacked the policies of not only the regulars but also the FDP. He denounced the latter because it specialized "in organized confusion. More dangerous are the people in it who advocate black supremacy."[19] As a moderate alternative to both radicals and conservatives, the MDC hoped for White House endorsement for its reform efforts. However, the Johnson administration refused to become directly involved in this messy, factional dispute for fear of offending the state's two powerful United States senators, James Eastland and John Stennis. Deprived of funds and patronage from Washington, the Mississippi Democratic Conference eventually collapsed in 1966.[20]

In the meantime, followers of the coalition strategy and the FDP battled each other for control of the Young Democratic (YD) clubs. The feud that had been festering between civil rights groups erupted publically in 1965 at the YD convention in Jackson. On August 17, the contrasting styles were in evidence at the Heidelberg Hotel. Neatly attired NAACP members, labor unionists, and university students jockeyed for control of the organization with FDP, SNCC, and COFO enthusiasts dressed in "sweatshirts, tennis shoes, ban-the-bomb buttons." In a wild session, perhaps more reminiscent of traditional Democratic behavior than of a new breed of politics, the coalitionists outflanked their opponents during the morning meeting by apparently going back on a promise not to hold elections for offices. Because few representatives of the radical wing were in attendance at the time, the moderates, led by Hodding Carter, III, a white newspaper editor from Greenville, succeeded in sweeping their candidates to power. The situation soon changed. After lunch, reinforced by late arriving troops, the "freedomcrats" managed to pass a resolution censuring their rival's conduct of morning business. The meeting in shambles, Carter staged a walkout with his allies, re-elected their officers, and sniped at the FDP's antiwar pronouncements with a resolution condemning advocacy of draft evasion as "an ideology foreign to the spirit of Americanism."[21]

The skirmish at the Heidelberg Hotel behind them, the moderates won the war at the National Convention of the Young Democratic Clubs in New York City. In early October, they were granted a charter and "welcomed as the first integrated group ever to represent Mississippi." Armed with this official sanction, the Mississippi YDs set up chapters at Ole Miss, Mississippi State University, Clarksdale, and Jackson. With pride, William Silver, the club's executive secretary and son of James W. Silver, the iconoclastic history professor at Ole Miss who had supported James Meredith's admission in 1962, wrote that the YD victory made it "the only affiliated Democratic organization in Mississippi which supports the national Democratic party."[22] Along with the YDs, Hodding Carter and his labor and NAACP allies intended to reform the existing Democratic party in Mississippi "in such a way as to make it open to participation by blacks, leaving open the question of what the real ideological content of the party might be." Yet support for Johnson's Great Society was clearly what they favored, at the same time that the FDP was disenchanted with the administration's brand of liberalism at home and overseas. To Carter, the Freedom Democrats were "integrationist only to the degree that whites would go along with the objectives of the movement and would not try to upset any of their objectives in it."[23]

The YD struggle left bitter feelings between the civil rights factions, and it reinforced the FDP's distaste for coalition politics. Ed King, a white minister at Tougaloo College who had played a major role in leading the insurrection against the Carter forces, explained the gulf separating militants from moderates. "To many radicals in the movement," he asserted, "the wrong style is a most serious offense, punishable by everlasting distrust. What one does is not nearly so important as how one does it. Since Carter does everything in Southern, aristocratic fashion, all the fine editorials that he may write can never commute his sentence."[24] To the FDP, white liberals of Carter's stripe, though sympathetic to the civil rights cause, at best were guilty of paternalism and at worst were viewed as part of the ruling establishment. As such, they had not experienced the rites of passage in the hostile fields of Mississippi and suffered firsthand the harsh racist brutality faced each day by blacks and civil rights organizers. Splintered into opposing camps, each faction pursued a separate route in trying to help black Mississippians share the rewards of the electoral process.[25]

Over the next several years, both sides sought to encourage blacks to run for office. The FDP adopted a policy of nominating all-black slates, although it was not followed strictly in practice, while the coalitionists backed nominees on an integrated basis. The FDP fashioned a ticket for the regular Democratic party congressional primaries in 1966, losing overwhelmingly in every contest. Undaunted, the Freedom Democrats appeared on the November ballot as independents. Hoping to regain some of the support they had lost since the 1964 Democratic National Convention, the insurgents entered the "war for voters using every resource under the sun, with the determination that nothing is impossible."[26] However, blacks did not command a majority of the registered voters statewide or in any congressional district, and victory was hopeless. Meanwhile, the interracial coalition steered away from independent candidacies and concentrated instead on increasing black enrollment in preparation for state and local elections in 1967.

For the first time, the opposing civil rights strategies were spotlighted side by side in full public view. The 1967 election year contests showcased the efforts of the biracial alliance and the FDP to compete with the regular Democratic party for political offices. Each group concentrated on the areas of the state where it had built the strongest suffrage foundations; the FDP worked the Delta, and the coalitionists focused on Charles Evers' bailiwick in the southwestern counties. There was no specific line of demarcation, but blacks associated with the FDP admitted: "There exists an informal and unarticulated agreement among the differing political camps within the Black community to co-exist throughout the election year."[27]

Despite this truce, the elections produced mixed results for blacks. Of the twenty-five candidates supported by the NAACP, eleven won their Democratic primary contests in August, and all of them went on to triumph in the November general elections. The FDP fielded approximately sixty contestants, only six of whom won final victory. None of the twenty-three black candidates involved in primary runoffs emerged victorious, as recently enfranchised blacks failed to turn out in large numbers at the polls. The FDP achieved the single most impressive success in the election of Robert Clark of Holmes County to the state house of representatives.[28]

For the Freedom Democrats, this triumph did not compensate for the especially disappointing results of local elections in Sunflower County. Held on May 2, before the statewide primaries, contests in two small towns had great symbolic importance. A year earlier, the United States Court of Appeals for the Fifth Circuit had voided the June 1965 municipal elections in Sunflower and Moorhead, ruling that local white officials had prevented blacks from registering in time to vote. Consequently, the federal tribunal ordered the towns to conduct special elections. Since then, the Voting Rights Act had gone into effect, and although federal examiners had not been assigned to Sunflower County, where blacks comprised 70 percent of the population, the number of Negroes registered to vote in the two Delta towns was roughly equal to that of whites. Encouraged by the increase in minority enrollment, the FDP sponsored black candidates to run for almost all municipal offices. Sunflower County was the home of Senator James Eastland, the perennial foe of civil rights measures, and the Freedom Democrats believed that winning in his own backyard would "represent a way . . . of hitting back at Eastland."[29]

The FDP campaign also served to increase pressure on Washington to designate Sunflower County for federal registrars and observers. Fannie Lou Hamer, a founder of the FDP who had been fired from her job on a plantation in Eastland's county as a result of her voter registration activities, explained the need for federal intervention: "The only people registered now are the ones who have gone through a living hell to get registered. The first reaction of people when you ask them to register is fear, not only fear for their jobs or their home but fear of physical violence."[30] A National Committee For Free Elections in Sunflower, an ad hoc group led by Congressman William F. Ryan, a liberal Democrat from New York City, concurred with Hamer and urged the Justice Department to intervene. On April 26, Ryan and Bayard Rustin headed a delegation of legislators, clergymen, and civil rights lawyers who met with Attorney General Ramsey Clark and his assistant, John Doar. Their requests were only partially fulfilled. The day before, Doar had written to Sunflower County officials asking them to make "bona fide efforts to comply with the Fifteenth Amendment." This required bringing into balance the proportion of eligible blacks registered to vote with that of whites. Doar advised: "Voting should be a simple corollary of citizenship for all eligible persons, but that objective is difficult to achieve when racial discrimination has persisted in the past. In those areas it is incumbent upon local officials to take reasonable affirmative steps to overcome the effects of past discriminatory practices."[31] Three days after the conference with the Ryan delegation, the Justice Department designated Sunflower County under the Voting Rights Act; however, Clark decided only to assign observers to the May 2 election rather than send in federal registrars.[32] Apparently, local officials had satisfied the department by conducting a special enrollment period. Whether or not the long arm of Eastland had reached into the Justice Department, as civil rights advocates charged, this decision of the Johnson administration reflected its ongoing efforts to balance federal coercion with restraint.

Forced to operate without federal examiners, the FDP launched an intensive voter registration drive in Sunflower County. Freedom Democrats offered classes on the mechanics of voting, with particular attention paid to instructing functional illiterates on how to identify the names of FDP candidates on the ballot. Block captains were selected to encourage registered voters to go to the polls. In the town of Sunflower, blacks held their own primary to name a ticket when no whites could be found to participate with them. Nevertheless, the black nominee for mayor, Otis Brown, Jr., a twenty-one-year-old former SNCC field secretary, extended an olive branch to the town's white electorate. Discarding black power rhetoric, Brown pledged: "If my ticket were elected we would put white people in every department. . . . In some we would have white assistants to Negroes and in others Negro assistants to whites." In turn, the incumbent white mayor campaigned among blacks, recognizing that he needed some of their votes to win.[33]

Despite the FDP's elaborate preparations, whites closed ranks to maintain their control over local government. To accomplish this feat, they voted as a solid bloc and also obtained enough black ballots to secure the margin of victory. For generations white supremacists had raised the spectre of racial bloc voting in order to mobilize support against black enfranchisement. Ironically, this election demonstrated that whites were more likely than blacks to cast their votes as a group when the contest pitted one race against the other. This was especially true in rural, black belt areas such as Sunflower. Along with fear, the economic subservience of most blacks left them extremely vulnerable to white pressure. On the eve of the election, anonymous circulars had been distributed warning blacks against being "mislead [sic] by paid racial agitators who would promise you everything and give you nothing." The incumbent mayor of Sunflower attributed his triumph to the support he received from "good niggers."[34] Furthermore, a low level of formal education subjected blacks to manipulation at the ballot boxes. White polling officials "helped" black illiterates mark their ballots, but even without any chicanery, a significant number of votes cast by illiterates were filled out improperly and did not count.[35] On this occasion, election day irregularites were kept to a minimum, perhaps in response to the presence of federal observers. Justice Department personnel monitoring the election reported that the balloting took place "with substantial fairness and the results accurately reflect the will of the voters."[36] The final outcome suggested that as long as a racial caste system lasted, blacks could not obtain their fair share of political power unless they registered in much larger numbers. Only by building a decisive margin of enrolled blacks over whites could they offset a likely defection from their ranks on election day. The absence of federal examiners, civil rights leaders believed, made this suffrage goal more difficult to achieve.

This defeat in Sunflower County had a sobering effect on the FDP. The frustrating loss persuaded the Freedom Democrats to modify their independent stance and prodded them to join once again the interracial coalition of civil rights forces seeking to reform the Democratic party from within. The warring factions temporarily put aside their differences in late 1967 and rallied behind the candidacy of Charles Evers for Congress. With the election of Representative John Bell Williams to the governorship, Evers announced his intention to seek the vacated seat in a special election in which the candidates did not run under party labels. Given this situation, the Freedom Democrats found it easier to back the NAACP field secretary with whom they had clashed in the past. The FDP acknowledged that its differences with Evers still remained but explained that it was merely supporting his black candidacy as a demonstration of racial solidarity; in no case was it endorsing the NAACP. The radicals viewed the campaign of the popular Evers as a means of stimulating voter registration and political education among the black masses in the third congressional district.[37] The nascent alliance between the rival factions was cemented with the appointment of Lawrence Guyot, chairman of the FDP, as Evers' campaign manager.

Working together for the first time since the breakup of COFO in 1965, the FDP-NAACP-liberal white coalition managed to produce a shortlived triumph. In the February 27, 1968, election Evers led a field of six white candidates with one-third of the votes, but he fell far short of gaining the majority necessary for victory. His opponents had carved up the white electorate, while Evers received most of the black ballots that were cast. Looking toward the runoff, observers fully expected white Mississippians to rally around the candidacy of Charles Griffin, the congressional aide of John Bell Williams, in a head-to-head race with Evers. The prospects for the NAACP official looked particularly bleak because he was running without the endorsement of the state AFL-CIO. Claude Ramsey had declined to throw his group's favor behind Evers, fearing that a black candidacy would divide white moderates and ensure the election of an extreme segregationist. Embittered by labor's official stand of neutrality, Evers condemned liberal whites. "I believe they'll vote for me," he growled, "but they just haven't got the guts to come out openly and support me."[38] As expected, Evers lost the March election. With racial lines clearly drawn, whites turned out in larger numbers than they had in the first contest and helped Griffin to win a two to one margin.

Having lost the war, Evers and his boosters did conclude that they had won some battles. The *New Pittsburgh Courier* took solace from Evers' initial victory at the polls and proclaimed, somewhat prematurely, that it foreshadowed "the coming of a new generation [that] will bring the dawn of democracy closer to achievement."[39] Evers believed his candidacy would produce a sobering effect on white politicians and would improve the tone of political campaigns in the future. Shaking hands openly with the winner after the results were in, Evers commented: "That wouldn't have happened a short while ago. You know why he shook my hand? More than forty thousand votes is why."[40] Also, the black leader believed his efforts would put state Democratic leaders on notice that "they didn't have the Democratic Party to themselves anymore."[41]

The Evers candidacy paved the way for the re-formed civil rights coalition to challenge the Democratic regulars for recognition at the national convention in Chicago. Without abandoning its long-range strategy of pursuing independent political action, the FDP decided to enlist in a loyalist delegation to block the seating of the regular Democrats. In the spring of 1968, the Freedom Democrats proposed to confront "Eastland's party" by uniting with the NAACP, the Young Democrats, black professionals, and labor unionists. It was "to the advantage of all Mississippians loyal to the idea of issue-oriented politics or loyal to the platform and principles of the national Democratic Party," the FDP declared in temporarily eschewing black separatism, to coalesce with the sundry opponents of the traditional Democratic organization.[42] In practice, the FDP and the coalitionists had not been that far apart. At times the struggle for control within the movement was extremely bitter, and genuine ideological conflicts split radicals from moderates. Yet both factions agreed that blacks should exercise the suffrage as an instrument for their own liberation. Charles Evers, whose race for Congress had smoothed over some of his basic differences with the FDP, sounded very much like his former adversaries: "My advice is to control something. Control the economics of the county, control the ballot of the county, the politics of the county—in other words, control the entire county where we are predominent. We don't holler Black Power—but watch it."[43] Once again adopting a united front, civil rights activists in Mississippi struggled to convince the national Democratic party to confer upon them the official recognition that had eluded them four years earlier.

In the meantime, blacks throughout the South were exhibiting various techniques for molding black ballots into implements of power. The most exciting of these efforts occurred in Alabama, which with Mississippi had served as a bellwether for race relations in the Deep South. The treatment of Negroes in the rural black belt counties had been so repressive that SNCC had entered these locales in the early 1960s hoping to set a positive example for blacks in neighboring areas to follow—its version of the "Domino Theory."[44] Preceding SNCC's shock troops, the NAACP and the SCLC had organized blacks, especially in the larger cities of Birmingham, Montgomery, and Mobile, to mount a series of challenges against Jim Crow and disfranchisement. Out of this ferment for freedom, black Alabamians had gained valuable experience for competing in electoral politics, and they had the opportunity of choosing various political strategies developed by the civil rights groups operating across the state.

As in Mississippi, civil rights advocates divided over pursuing an independent, partisan course or entering a coalition to reform the Democratic party from within. Before black power became the cry of the Meredith march, SNCC's work in Lowndes County had foreshadowed the development of that controversial idea. In 1965, Stokely Carmichael served as a field secretary in Lowndes, and he had been deeply affected by the slaying of two white civil rights workers, Viola Liuzzo and Jonathan Daniels, during voter registration drives there. For Carmichael these murders capped a period of disillusionment with traditional civil rights approaches. Moreover, the failure of the Democratic party convention in 1964 to seat the FDP delegates profoundly influenced Carmichael and his SNCC brethren, persuading them that blacks must first organize separately and then bargain with white allies from a position of strength. They learned this lesson most powerfully in counties such as Lowndes, where blacks comprised 80 percent of the population and whites adamantly refused to deal with them on an equal footing. A local inhabitant explained that blacks had no other choice than to form an independent political party because "it didn't make sense for us to join the Democratic Party when they were the people who had done the killing in the county and had beat our heads."[45]

Determined to gain control of their government, blacks, with the assistance of SNCC formed the Lowndes County Freedom Organization (LCFO). On May 3, 1966, the party held a nominating convention as stipulated under state law, and it nominated candidates to run for five county offices in the November general elections. A year after passage of the Voting Rights Act and the presence of federal examiners, about one-half of the eligible black adults had enrolled, slightly outnumbering the white electorate.[46] Fortified by these figures, LCFO counseled blacks to boycott the regular Democratic party primaries in May and to vote exclusively for freedom candidates in the general elections. John Hulett, the chairman of LCFO and the first black in Lowndes to register to vote, reasoned this way: "To me, the Democratic primaries and the Democratic Party are something like a gambler who carries a marked card around in his pocket and every now and then has to let somebody win to keep the game going."[47] Nevertheless, the LCFO plan also involved a gamble. By refraining from participation in the Democratic contests, blacks might help defeat moderate white candidates and seal the election of rabid segregationists. Carmichael, though, believed the victory of racists would enhance the third-party strategy by revealing to blacks "the real face of the Democratic Party."[48]

In contrast, other civil rights organizations rejected the SNCC-LCFO method. Long active in challenging discriminatory suffrage restrictions, NAACP officials in Alabama preferred an attempt to reform the Democratic party. In the early 1960s, some of the association's leaders had joined in the creation of the Alabama Democratic Conference (ADC), a group dedicated to building up black voting strength to gain concessions from the regular Democratic machine. In 1966, with Negro voter registration on the upswing following the Voting Rights Act, the ADC, along with white moderates, persuaded the state Democratic executive committee to delete the white supremacy trademark from its party emblem.[49] This symbolic victory reinforced ADC thinking that blacks could achieve more from participation in a biracial coalition than from pursuit of a separatist course. The NAACP's chief architect of voter registration in Alabama, W. C. Patton, lamented: "When there are only a few Negro votes there is solidarity, but when you get a few thousand then comes a split."[50]

Steering its customary course between opposing poles of the civil rights movement, SCLC did not adhere rigidly to any one theory. Martin Luther King's group acknowledged that SNCC's strategy might work in eleven of sixty-seven Alabama counties where blacks predominated, but doubted it would succeed throughout the state because Negroes constituted a minority of the population. To obtain political leverage in the big cities, SCLC advised blacks to seek white allies within the ranks of the Democratic party. Hosea Williams asserted that SNCC followers created "a monster" in excluding themselves from participation in the Democratic primaries. "Will they treat white folks like the white folks treated them? Will they hate white folks like the white folks hated them?" he asked sadly.[51]

Most black voters ignored SNCC's call for a boycott of the primary on May 3; nevertheless, they were disappointed with the outcome. Although Negroes cast their ballots overwhelmingly against Lurleen Wallace for governor, she easily defeated a field of white moderates, including Attorney General Richmond Flowers, who had openly courted the black vote. In the rural black belt region of Wilcox and Greene Counties, white incumbents for sheriff beat their black challengers. In these contests, the alleged threat of the Negro bloc vote failed to materialize. Instead, whites stuck together, and blacks marked enough of their ballots for whites to give them victory.[52]

One notable triumph did come in Macon County, though. Led by college-educated and middle-class blacks employed at Tuskegee Institute and the Veterans Hospital, Negroes had successfully combated an array of biased suffrage practices and had registered a majority of blacks by the mid-1960s. Even before enactment of the voting rights statute, blacks had won election to public office, but under the influence of NAACP leaders Charles Gomillion and William Mitchell, they had deliberately refrained from trying to oust all the white elected officials. In a conscious effort to promote a racially balanced government, Gomillion's Macon County Democratic Club refused to endorse the black candidacy of Lucius Amerson for sheriff in 1966. Nonetheless, despite the statewide Wallace landslide, Amerson made it into a runoff which he subsequently won over the white incumbent. Macon County blacks departed from the NAACP's biracial strategy probably as a result of their disappointment in the county's large white vote for Mrs. Wallace.

However, Amerson's triumph did not vindicate SNCC. The new sheriff had explicitly declined to run on a black power platform; he advocated operating within the two-party system;

and he attributed his victory strictly to "citizens interested in becoming elected to public office and trying to do what they can to make life better in general for everybody."[53] At the same time, though, Amerson and his supporters accepted the prospects of an all black government "as long as the people are going to go on and do what is right and administer the law the way it is."[54] Thus, Macon County Negroes achieved black power as a natural stage in their political evolution and did so without a display of ideological dogmatism. Amerson and his sympathizers viewed black power as a simple extension of enfranchisement, an elementary lesson in civics.

Black political organizers in Lowndes County aimed their sights in much the same direction; however, they did so in a different manner. Generally missing from Lowndes was Tuskegee's black middle-class base, and suffragists shaped their appeals to reach the poor and badly educated. Stokely Carmichael adapted his language accordingly. "Ignorant, smelly, with our noses running, we're going to take that political power because it belongs to us," he thundered.[55] Echoing this blunt militancy, Willie Ricks of SNCC keynoted a gathering of 800 LCFO followers by telling them: "If you black and in Lowndes County, you aren't no Democrat—you black! You say you from Lowndes County, people say, 'You sure got some bad niggers down there.' Well we're the bad niggers we're gonna show Alabama how bad."[56] The desire of the freedom party to take over the courthouse was weighted in symbolism. Third parties had operated in the South before, but Dixie had not encountered one that was managed exclusively by blacks, stood up boldly to whites, and had a good chance of winning. In choosing the black panther for its insignia, LCFO proclaimed itself to be like the animal which "never bothers anything, but when you start pushing him, he moves backwards, backwards and backwards into his corner, and then he comes out to destroy everything that's before him."[57] Self-defense rather than nonviolent suffering was the freedom organization's credo. One of its members recalled the racially inspired murders that had occurred in the county, fingered some shotgun shells in his pocket, and pledged: "We gonna protect our friends this time."[58]

The outcome of the November 8 general election showed that the black panther was not yet ready to spring from its lair. All seven freedom candidates went down to defeat by margins ranging from 200 to 600 votes. The slight edge in registration that blacks in Lowndes held was not enough to produce success because their turnout lagged behind that of whites. Moreover, racial solidarity did not prevail, and some 300 to 400 blacks cast their ballots for white candidates.[59] The economic dependency of black voters helped account for their defection from LCFO-sponsored candidates. Many of those working on plantations did not support the freedom ticket for fear of losing their jobs, and some of them were transported to the polls by their white bosses. A black tenant farmer explained to a civil rights activist: "You let me work on your land, and I'll vote for your candidates."[60] The poor showing also reflected the high illiteracy rate among blacks. White polling officials failed to provide adequate assistance and sometimes marked ballots contrary to the wishes of LCFO's black supporters. Nevertheless, the leaders of the freedom organization were not crushed. For the first time, blacks had actively competed for political office under their own party banner, and despite this loss, John Hulett insisted: "We won't give up. . . . We aren't going to get discouraged and start fussing among ourselves."[61]

With this kind of determination, both coalitionist and independent forces looked ahead to the future. ADC representatives worked with anti-Wallace, white moderates to send an integrated delegation to the 1968 Democratic convention in support of the national presidential ticket. LCFO continued to concentrate on winning in Lowndes, but the standard of independent party politics was picked up by the National Democratic Party of Alabama (NDPA), with which it eventually merged. Formed in 1968 under the guidance of Dr. John Cashin, a Huntsville dentist, the NDPA contested elections on the state and county levels and launched an interracial challenge to obtain official recognition at the Democratic National Convention. Apart from this foray into national politics, it vied for public office throughout Alabama's black belt and won impressive victories. One of these came in Greene County. In 1966, Reverend Thomas Gilmore had mounted a losing campaign for sheriff against the incumbent. "The white people had been in politics so much longer than we had," Gilmore reflected, "they just figured it out to a tee how to beat us."[62] In four years, after sustained political mobilization by the NDPA, Gilmore finally captured the office of sheriff, and blacks won control of county government. At the same time, John Hulett was elected sheriff in Lowndes County, and across the black belt twenty-one of 197 NDPA candidates triumphed.[63]

As these many efforts showed, blacks throughout the South were questing for political power following passage of the Voting Rights Act. Despite some important gains, their inaugural efforts at the polls were considered disappointing, principally because their initial expectations had been so high. Blacks held only a tiny portion of elected positions in the South, and most of these officials served in small towns. By the end of the decade, blacks were included on the governing boards of twenty-eight counties, although they comprised more than 40 percent of the population in 224 counties and a majority of the voting age population in twenty-one of them.[64] Obstacles to full political participation blocked the way to greater success, and black voter registration, while increasing notably, still lagged behind that of whites, as did their turnout on election day. Not quite liberated from the suffrage restrictions of the past, blacks mapped out alternative strategies to make their emerging vote count for more. While factional disagreements were frequently acrimonious, blacks did not become demoralized. Resentment against whites did exist among black southerners, but having fought so long and hard for the right to vote, they were unwilling to abandon it too quickly as a legitimate weapon for racial advancement. In Dixie, the ballot was a vivid symbol of black pride and self-esteem, and, if painstakingly exercised, it offered Afro-Americans an opportunity to obtain a larger share of electoral power.[65]

Recognizing the moderating influence of the suffrage and concerned with justice, the Johnson administration had attempted to extend influence within the Democratic party to black southerners. Since their presidential nominating convention in 1964, the Democrats had worked on the vexing problem of creating integrated state organizations in the South that were loyal

to the national party. The Atlantic City delegates had endorsed
Johnson's plan for rejecting the challenge of the mostly black
Mississippi Freedom Democratic Party while allocating two at-
large seats to its representatives. Hobart Taylor, Jr., the black aide
closest to the president at the time, explained the rationale behind
the compromise: "What we were trying to do was to build a unified party in Mississippi. If we just simply supplanted the whites
with the Negroes . . . all we were doing was just stirring up
something that is bad socially, bad economically, bad for the
country."[66] The negotiated settlement still left Mississippi Democrats divided, but the insurgents looked forward to implementation of the convention's resolution to establish guidelines for
increased minority participation in the future.

The administration and party officials recognized that the
fate of southern blacks and the Democrats was linked. Kennedy
and Johnson had advanced the frontiers of civil rights and, in turn,
had bolstered the allegiance of blacks to the Democratic party that
had first developed under Franklin Roosevelt's New Deal. The
enfranchisement of Negroes in the South throughout the 1960s
furnished welcome recruits and offset defections to the Republican party by conservative whites who resented the egalitarian racial policies of successive Democratic regimes in Washington.
Following the 1964 presidential election in which 95 percent of
Afro-American voters cast their ballots for the Johnson-Hum-
phrey ticket, Louis Martin, in charge of minority affairs for the
Democratic National Committee, suggested that a "new registration drive among Negroes in the States of South Carolina,
Georgia, Mississippi, Alabama, and Louisiana will bring the
greatest rewards in the future."[67] Vice President Humphrey concurred that the Democratic party had "a great stake" in Negro
registration. "In a close election," Humphrey maintained, "it may
mean the difference between victory and defeat."[68] Although the
Democratic National Committee encouraged voter registration
among blacks, it preferred to follow the Johnson administration's
policy of making suffrage campaigns the prime responsibility of
private agencies.[69]

However, the Democrats did take steps to broaden minority participation in party affairs. In 1965, a Special Equal Rights

Committee (SERC) was created. Chaired by Governor David Lawrence of Pennsylvania, the panel included liberals and conservatives, northerners and southerners, blacks and whites, and men and women. Lawrence, a civil rights supporter and a Johnson loyalist who had presided over the delegate seating disputes at the 1964 convention, hoped "to prevent another battle on credentials in 1968, and it is for that reason we are trying to get to the heart of the matter early enough to develop remedial steps in ample time."[70] The designation of Joseph Rauh as associate counsel to the committee guaranteed that reform interests would be strongly represented. A dedicated civil rights lawyer, Rauh had assisted the FDP in its convention challenge in 1964. Rauh and one of his liberal allies in the group, Mildred Jeffreys of Detroit, pushed the administration to take vigorous action along all suffrage fronts. At a meeting on October 5 and 6, 1965, at which government officials and civil rights leaders testified, Rauh and Jeffreys questioned the Justice Department's implementation of the Voting Rights Act. "It seems to many of us," Jeffreys told Assistant Attorney General John Doar, "that this [voter registration] is going very very slowly." She advocated the assignment of additional federal examiners because they give "a person a sense of confidence they simply do not have in these local registrars."[71]

Following the October meeting, the committee attempted to resolve some of the civil rights complaints brought to its attention. In a conference with Attorney General Katzenbach, Lawrence expressed the conviction that voter registration was "a critical prerequisite to Party participation," and he encouraged the appointment of additional federal examiners. Following an SERC recommendation, the Democratic National Committee wielded its influence to remove the white supremacy motto on the official insignia of the Alabama Democratic Party. In addition, the SERC put all state Democratic organizations on notice "that the consequences of inaction where remedial steps are called for will . . . mean forfeiting the right to sit in the 1968 Convention."[72] However, the Democrats still had not drawn up specific blueprints to promote equal access to their party proceedings. By mid-1966, Aaron Henry, a leader of the Mississippi insurgents at Atlantic City, was complaining: "No serious efforts have come forth from this [SERC] Committee to do the job it was to do."[73] The situation worsened a few months later in November 1966 when Governor Lawrence died.

Sensitive to charges of procrastination, the Johnson administration and Democratic party leaders stepped up preparations for adjudicating challenges at the 1968 convention. Looking for "a real negotiator, who knows how to be tough but is flexible," the Democratic National Committee in early 1967 chose Governor Richard Hughes of New Jersey to replace Lawrence. An acknowledged liberal, Hughes could also be counted on as "a team player." As Johnson's top political aide confided: "Dick Hughes' loyalty is as deep as ours."[74] With the chairmanship vacancy filled, the SERC proceeded to design minimum prerequisites that each party had to meet in order to satisfy the 1964 convention mandate. The committee suggested that local Democrats conduct their meetings openly, publicize them fully, and provide an opportunity for widespread participation, all without discrimination on the basis of race or color. In addition, the group called upon the Democratic party "on all levels [to] support the broadest possible registration" without racial bias. In a letter circulating these recommendations, the special panel warned state party chairmen that failure to comply with these criteria would result in exclusion from the Chicago convention and the seating of "a delegation broadly representative of the Democrats of that State."[75] This last point was crucial to Joseph Rauh, who wanted to ensure not only that segregationist contingents were barred but also that integrated delegations took their place. This would strengthen the national Democratic party in every state and would remove the incentive for building all-Negro third parties, which Rauh and other liberals opposed.[76]

In crafting these guidelines, the committee stopped short of adopting some form of proportional representation. Rauh and Mildred Jeffrey had suggested "where Negroes constituted 20% or more of the voting age population of any state and Negroes constitute less than 10% of the delegation certified by the State Democratic Party, this shall be deemed prima facie evidence of discrimination on the grounds of race."[77] In such an instance, the challenged, regular delegation would satisfactorily have to account for the small percentage of blacks or would face expulsion. When this proposal was leaked to the press in February 1967, southern white party leaders howled over what they regarded as a quota system. State Senator Edgar A. Brown of South Carolina, a member of the SERC, called the Rauh-Jeffrey plan "obnoxious" and certain to provoke "dissension, division, and controversy" within the party.[78] To avert such a possibility, particularly when the independent presidential candidacy of George Wallace threatened to lure away traditional white Democrats, the national administration rejected the Rauh-Jeffrey recommendation. The *New York Times* best summed up Johnson's thinking: "If a hostile truce can be maintained between the White House and Southern Democrats some of these states might be salvaged for the President in 1968. [The] South may not be won by cautious, behind-the-scenes compromise, but it would certainly be lost by an act of deliberate provocation at the outset of the campaign."[79] Hence, in mid-1967, the Democratic National Committee struck a balance in fulfilling its pledge to southern blacks without unduly alienating whites in Dixie. It "agreed that a quota system for delegations is not feasible in practice, [but] it is determined to make certain that all delegations to the 1968 Democratic National Convention are broadly representative of the Democrats of the State."[80]

After the SERC promulgated its cautious guidelines, insurgents throughout the Deep South mobilized to test them. Representatives of the interracial coalition in Mississippi attended the local precinct and statewide Democratic conventions in May and June 1968. Their participation did not change the racist structure of the official party organization to any significant degree. The regulars did pick four black delegates to accompany them to the Chicago convention, but only one of them accepted the invitation to travel in this vehicle of token integration. Instead, an interracial band of "loyalists," orchestrated by the NAACP, Young Democratic Clubs, AFL-CIO, and belatedly joined by the FDP, convened their own convention in the early summer to select representatives. With each constituent group choosing members, the slate of delegates consisted of thirty-six blacks and thirty-two whites. The election of Hodding Carter and Aaron Henry as co-chairmen and Charles Evers as national committeeman indicated that the moderate element prevailed over the more militant FDP faction. "One got the impression from the composition of the various committees and delegations," a participant-historian later wrote, "that Mississippi was in the vanguard of 'biracial politics.'"[81]

Both sides pled their cases to the turbulent Windy City assembly in late August. Unlike four years before when the dispute enlivened a generally dull gathering, the seating controversy was overshadowed in 1968 by the Vietnam War and the embattled protests against it that raged outside in the streets. Within the convention hall, the credentials committee heard the Mississippi regulars argue that they had chosen their members democratically in accordance with state law and without racial discrimination. One adherent warned the panel that failure to recognize his contingent would benefit both George Wallace and the Republican party. In contrast, the loyalists contended that their rivals simply had not implemented the Hughes committee guidelines and disparaged the inclusion of a single black on the regular delegation as a "cynical gesture in mock recognition of Negro voting strength in the state."[82] After a last-ditch effort failed to work out a bargain allocating some seats to the regulars, the Hughes committee voted to recognize the loyalists and exclude their adversaries. "At a time when there are forces actively working to convince the downtrodden that the American political system has no meaning for them," Hodding Carter's *Delta Democrat-Times* commented, the loyalist victory "may be the most important, and most healthy, result of all."[83]

Interracial delegations from elsewhere in the South also triumphed. In Georgia, an insurgent group led by State Representative Julian Bond, former SNCC publicist and an outspoken critic of the Vietnam War, secured a partial triumph and was awarded half the assigned seats. In Louisiana, South Carolina, and Alabama, regular delegations won recognition because they had taken appropriate steps to satisfy the guidelines.[84]

Of these three, only Alabama faced a challenge. Democrats in the state were badly divided by the presidential bid of favorite son, George Wallace. The regular delegation to Chicago, whose members had been selected in a statewide primary, contained a large number of Wallace supporters. However, two delegates were black, and they announced their loyalty to the national party ticket. A rival group of moderate whites opposed Wallace's third-party candidacy and promised to support the convention's nominees and work for their election back home. Led by Robert Vance, the chairman of the state Democratic organization, and David Vann, a Birmingham attorney, the Alabama Independent Democrats (AID) suggested that in the future they would seek to open up the political process to increased black participation. At that point the largest portion of blacks came from yet a third delegation, one sent by the National Democratic Party of Alabama. Dr. John Cashin's NDPA, identified with the militant wing of the civil rights movement, had shunned the regular Democratic primaries and had elected its own representatives to Chicago. Convention managers took the safe path in resolving the complicated dispute. Choosing to reinforce anti-Wallace sentiment within the state party, Johnson administration strategists endorsed an arrangement allowing the regulars to take their seats if they signed a pledge to back the national ticket; however, only thirteen of fifty took the oath, and the remainder were replaced by AID loyalists. This compromise excluded the NDPA, but it did preserve unity and received the endorsement of Alabama's black moderates who expected anti-Wallace state party leaders to lower racial barriers.[85]

The Democratic convention had taken important steps to incorporate southern blacks into the party. Although blacks still held few positions of power within Democratic organizations in Dixie, their presence on integrated delegations at the national convocation signaled an historic break from the past, and national party leaders pledged that progress would continue at a faster pace in the future. Delegates in Chicago ratified the SERC guidelines and created a Commission on Party Structure to explore specific ways of enlarging minority involvement in the party. Among the suggestions for the group to ponder were the initiation of affirmative action programs for recruitment and the design of formulas for ensuring proportional representation on state committees and delegations.[86] Impressed by these deeds, a veteran black political commentator noted: "A new political movement was born, weak, kicking, protesting, and still far from maturity. A century late, black Americans moved into the mainstream of the Democratic Party, the tried champion of the poor, labor, and racial minorities."[87]

These innovative departures had the effect of undermining black support for separatist parties and advancing the cause of coalition politics. The loyalists returned to Mississippi and strengthened their hold on the biracial organization, reelecting the NAACP's Aaron Henry as chairman and Charles Evers as national committeeman. Shortly thereafter, the FDP, for all practical purposes, ceased functioning as a contender in electoral politics. The remnants of this courageous band of civil rights workers either were absorbed into the loyalist coalition or directed their attention to grass roots community organizing.[88] Much the same situation existed in Alabama. Although the NDPA continued to operate and to elect officials on the county level, its influence on statewide, partisan politics waned. In turn, blacks were brought into the ranks of the state party organization under the reform leadership of Robert Vance.[89] Thus, the Democratic party succeeded in its avowed purpose of defusing the more radical elements among blacks in the region and holding the majority of Negro southerners in the New Deal coalition.

The Democratic overtures to black southerners were more impressive when compared with the performance of the Republicans. For several years, a liberal GOP faction had urged party leaders to campaign for the newly enfranchised black electorate in Dixie. These proponents lost out to the purveyors of a "southern strategy" that sought to appeal to Democrats disaffected from their party's liberal racial views. The composition of the 1968 GOP national convention in Miami reflected the triumph of the conservatives. A handful of black representatives from the South attended, but most of the Dixie members waved their state standards from all-white delegations. A black observer from Louisiana looked around the floor and called the situation "inadequate, shameful, and intolerable," while a column in a Negro newspaper ran under the headline: "Black Role in GOP Nothing in Miami."[90] In contrast to the Democrats, the Republican party neither established a special equal rights committee nor devised guidelines for increasing minority participation in its affairs. Republican appeals to white southerners ultimately paid off when the GOP presidential ticket, led by Richard Nixon, managed to capture the electoral votes of all but six southern states, with five Deep South states lining up for George Wallace and only Texas going to Hubert Humphrey.[91]

As the nation agonized over picking his successor, Lyndon Johnson could recall his civil rights record with pride. Although his last years in the White House were marred by discord and strife, Johnson's presidency constituted the high point of the Second Reconstruction. The Great Society had extended civil and political equality to southern blacks, helping to crack a racist caste system that had endured for centuries. Throughout this stormy period, the administration stood committed to opening up greater minority participation in all aspects of American life. White House advisor Harry McPherson affirmed the credo that guided the liberal regime: "We believe in integration, we believe in reason, we believe that things are going to be fine if men of good will get together and if we put down the racists."[92] This simple faith gave Afro-Americans hope that the nation's chief executive still cared about their plight; nonetheless, they realized it did not always provide solutions to the problems confronting them. Just as one phase of the civil rights struggle reached completion, conventional reform had virtually exhausted itself. Programs of affirmative action and compensatory treatment for blacks—measures that went beyond traditional conceptions of equality—not only unleashed a backlash among moderate whites but also promoted discontent among many white liberals who felt their obligation terminated with the destruction of the legal framework of Jim Crow. Believing that without a sympathetic president like Johnson the situation would worsen, black leaders viewed the election of Richard Nixon with considerable foreboding.

Part II

Staying the Course

5.

Bring Us Together

One sign among the many that waved from the crowd caught the candidate's attention. The whistle-stop tour brought Richard Nixon to Deshler, Ohio, on October 22, 1968, and as he surveyed the group of admirers gathered before him, the Republican standardbearer noticed a young girl holding a placard bearing the inscription: "Bring Us Together Again." A few weeks later, President-elect Nixon remembered these healing words and used them as the theme of his victory statement following his narrow and bitter triumph over Hubert Humphrey. Pledging "to bring the American people together," Nixon promised "an open administration, open to new ideas, open to men and women of both parties, open to the critics as well as those who support us. We want to bridge the generation gap. We want to bridge the gap between the races."[1] These soothing sentiments offered some relief to a majority of Americans disgusted with a year of political assassinations, campus rebellions, race riots, antiwar demonstrations, and assaults on middle-class culture. However, it remained to be seen whether this "new Nixon," appearing more gracious in victory than he had ever been in defeat, was the one to unify a deeply divided nation.

Recent experience did not provide encouragement. While often taking the rhetorical high road during his campaign, Nixon had aimed his appeals at "the un-black, the un-poor and the un-young."[2] His emphasis on law and order ignored the issue of justice and exploited the fears of a considerable segment of the electorate weary of political and social strife. The GOP nominee adopted a white southern strategy, virtually conceding the black vote to his Democratic opponent. Nixon chased after conservative white Democrats in the South who were dismayed by their party's identification with racial equality and with an expansion of the welfare state. In wooing these traditional Democratic supporters, the Republicans tried to keep them out of the camp of George Wallace, the popular, segregationist Alabama governor mounting an independent bid for the presidency. Nixon undercut a good deal of the potential backing for Wallace by declaring against busing to promote school desegregation and by voicing his approval for freedom of choice plans, designed to slow down integration.[3]

This approach worked, but just barely. In a three-way contest, no candidate garnered a majority of the popular vote, and Nixon edged Humphrey by less than 1 percent. In the electoral college column, the Republicans won 301 votes, carrying six southern states. While whites who went to the polls divided their ballots nearly evenly, blacks overwhelmingly endorsed Hubert Humphrey, the long-standing advocate of civil rights. The outcome reflected and intensified racial polarization throughout the country. Outside the triumphant coalition and solidly identified with the loser, Afro-Americans interpreted the Nixon win as a vivid sign that the Second Reconstruction was over. A. Philip Randolph recalled the disturbing history of an earlier epoch. "In 1876," the civil rights leader commented, "the basic needs of all black people were sacrificed for the alleged corruption of the Reconstruction governments of the South. Today all black people are being blamed for the destructive rioting and the violent words of a few. Then as now it was charged that the black people were not ready for full equality."[4] Victims once before of a change in political climate, blacks were naturally anxious about the hostile forces that propelled Richard Nixon into the White House.

The nascent alliance between Nixon and Strom Thurmond heightened the fears of those who believed that the history of the First Reconstruction was about to be repeated. "Rutherford B. Hayes became president because the GOP nominee agreed to withdraw the troops from the South during the post Civil War era and let the South handle its own problems," a black journalist recalled. In like manner, he asserted, "In Miami Tricky Dick became the GOP Presidential nominee because of a deal with arch segregationist Strom Thurmond of South Carolina to let the South enforce the civil rights laws."[5] In fact, the South Carolina senator had lined up behind Nixon enough conservative delegates from the South to turn back the challenge of Governor Ronald Reagan of California at the Republican National Convention. After a series of discussions, Thurmond secured a pledge from Nixon to treat the South equally with respect to racial integration. "If they are going to pass a Federal voting rights law to apply to the South," Thurmond coaxed, "let it apply to the rest of the Nation."[6] Similarly, Harry Dent, a close associate of Thurmond whom Nixon tapped to serve on the White House staff, looked forward to throwing the voting rights "monkey . . . off the backs of the South."[7]

After Nixon assumed office, his appointments to key positions in the Justice Department buoyed the hopes of white southerners. With a different person in charge of civil rights in the new administration, Senator Richard Russell of Georgia was "hopeful that he will be somewhat more reasonable in his attitude toward our part of the country."[8] Indeed, Nixon's Department of Justice was prepared to be "more reasonable" than its predecessor. Concerning racial equality, neither Attorney General John Mitchell nor Jerris Leonard, Assistant Attorney General in command of the Civil Rights Division, measured up to their counterparts in the Johnson administration. Mitchell, Nixon's law partner whose specialty was municipal bonds, had managed the president's campaign and skillfully directed the southern strategy. One of his deputies, Kevin Phillips, whose *Emerging Republican Majority* became the handbook for that policy, subsequently promised southern Republicans that the administration would "change the approach" on the Voting Rights Act to please them. Leonard had only a slightly better reputation than his associates. A state representative from suburban Milwaukee, he had supported a strong open housing law in the mid-1960s. Yet, at the time of his nomination as assistant attorney general, the Wisconsin Republican belonged to a racially restricted private club from which he subsequently resigned after receiving considerable flak. On balance, a black colleague in the state assembly aptly described him: "He's not a civil rights hawk. He's a civil rights dove. But he's not chicken like a lot of his party counterparts are."[9] Not surprisingly, surveying Nixon's appointments, the Leadership Conference on Civil Rights "feared the worst" and worried that the administration was "ready to sabotage the [civil rights] program—through indifference, through insufficient effort, through ignorance of what terrible consequences can follow relaxation of enforcement."[10]

The shape of Nixon's policy soon became perfectly clear. Reversing a position nearly two deacades old, administration lawyers appeared in federal court against civil rights advocates to slow down the pace of school desegregation in Mississippi. In charting this new path, the chief executive presented a distorted view of the struggle for racial equality. "It seems to me," Nixon remarked, "that there are two extreme groups. There are those who want instant integration and those who want segregation forever. I believe that we need to have a middle course between those two extremes."[11] Fifteen years following *Brown,* it was misleading for the president to label as extremists those who demanded more than token results. The Nixon equation suggested that groups such as the NAACP were just as misguided as the recalcitrant White Citizens Councils. In effect, the "middle way" preached by the president worked to the benefit of southern white opponents of racial equality.

Neither the Supreme Court nor Congress accepted the Nixonian brand of racial neutrality. The high tribunal checked the attempt to weaken school desegregation guidelines in Mississippi and delivered to the administration and its supporters a blunt message against further stalling. "Continued operation of segregated schools under a standard of allowing 'all deliberate speed' for desegregation is no longer constitutionally possible," the court ruled in October 1969. It ordered "every school district . . . to terminate dual school systems at once and to operate now and hereafter only unitary schools."[12] At about the same time, the president nominated a conservative judge from the South to a vacancy on the Supreme Court, and Congress rebuffed him. After months of acrimonious deliberation, the Senate rejected the nomination of Clement Haynsworth of South Carolina, a federal jurist whose opinions in racial cases had aroused the suspicions of civil rights adherents.

In addition, the White House presented Congress with a proposal that damaged the cause of first-class citizenship. Unlike the battles over school desegregation and the appointment to the Supreme Court, this issue attracted less publicity and only partially involved civil rights. The tax reform measure that Nixon sent up to Capitol Hill in April 1969 contained a prohibition against private foundations "engaging in activities directly affecting political campaigns, such as voter registration drives."[13] This provision was buried among the myriad items of a bill principally aimed at closing loopholes in investment credits and oil depletion allowances. The suffrage recommendation posed a serious threat to the survival of the Voter Education Project, which disbursed foundation dollars for registration drives throughout the South. Since 1962, civil rights organizations operating in Dixie had looked to the VEP to finance a substantial share of their franchise activities. Blacks and their liberal allies charged that the suggested "voter depletion allowance" was part of the White House's southern strategy; "the Dick Nixon-Strom Thurmond scheme to cut off this money is a conspiracy to undermine the political development of black citizens," a prominent Negro columnist contended.[14]

The Nixon administration plan did reflect some dissatisfaction with the politics of black enfranchisement in the South. Although the White House had assured NAACP Executive Secretary Roy Wilkins that it "was not going to take steps which would bar foundation funds to voter registration and education projects," GOP officials were skeptical of the performance of tax-exempt suffrage organizations. A representative of the Republican National Committee doubted the nonpartisan character of such groups as the VEP and complained: "They seem to forget or ignore their responsibility to educate these people in regard to how to vote and what the two party system is. It seems that all they do is teach them how to vote for the Democrat Party."[15] The 1968 presidential election results had persuaded Republican leaders that their party's fortunes depended on appealing to traditionally Democratic southern white voters. The party of Lincoln did not write off the black electorate entirely, but it calculated few partisan gains to be derived from voter registration drives among nonwhites in Dixie.[16]

The final version of the tax reform measure passed by Congress in December 1969 softened the ban against foundation sponsorship of suffrage drives. The NAACP, the Southern Regional Council—under whose auspices the VEP operated—and the United States Commission on Civil Rights lobbied to remove this debilitating section from the bill. Placing the issue in a larger framework, Roy Wilkins argued: "The wider the use of the ballot by minority citizens and the greater their share in the decisions, responsibilities and rewards of elections, the less likelihood there is of the spread of polarization and violence."[17] Instead of an outright prohibition, Congress resolved that no more than 25 percent of the financing of voter registration drives could come from a single tax-exempt foundation, provided that the activities were nonpartisan, not confined to any one election, and conducted in at least five states.[18]

Nevertheless, the compromise hurt the VEP. The conditions imposed by the legislation forced the Voter Education Project to separate from the Southern Regional Council, because the latter received more than a quarter of its revenue from one foundation. The VEP emerged from the legislative fight and subsequent divorce from its founding agency with "the margin of survival," as its director noted, "at best slim."[19] The organization managed to continue functioning, but it never reached the same level of performance that it had before the 1969 Tax Reform Act went into effect.[20]

This blow to the VEP came at a time when black enfranchisement had slowed down considerably and new obstacles diminished electoral gains. The pace of registration had dropped off once the most highly motivated blacks had taken advantage of the Voting Rights Act. Socioeconomic factors that traditionally retarded political participation accounted for part of the inability to enroll a greater number of southern Negroes. The Delta Ministry reported on this institutional problem: "There no longer exists the larger concentration of unregistered Blacks who can be easily motivated to participate in the electoral process. The Blacks who remain unregistered represent the people who have been most victimized by the ravages of racism and segregation."[21] The registration drives of the mid-sixties, one scholar contended, had closed "the gap between an artificially low number of blacks on the voting list and the ratio customarily encountered for low income, minority group members all over the United States."[22] Many poor and ill-educated blacks had not yet overcome patterns of racial deference conditioned through generations of white supremacy. "Our biggest problem," a voter registration worker in Mississippi remarked, "is trying to encourage Negroes to go to the courthouse and register. They are still afraid, they're still frightened, and still fear that there will never be a change for them, they've always lived this life, and still think that they cannot better their condition by becoming registered voters. Some of them fear they've lived this long with things as they are and they'd prefer to live as it is until they die."[23] Thus, inhibited by a legacy of oppression and vulnerable to economic sanctions, many blacks, especially unskilled laborers and plantation field hands, held onto "the firm and self defeating belief . . . that existing political organizations will deny them admittance or help."[24]

Even without fear of reprisals, economically dependent blacks still encountered difficulty in registering. The enrollment process itself worked against them. Southern black workers often were unable to get time off during registration hours. Plantation laborers had the additional problem of finding transportation to take them from outlying rural areas to the county courthouse where enrollment usually took place. They might have to wait for a rainy day before their boss gave them permission to go into town, only to discover that they had arrived during a period when registration was not being conducted. "Voting in America," Penn Kimball accurately noted, "is enmeshed in a spider's web of prior restraints."[25]

These structural problems frequently were compounded by the personal bias of some voter registrars and election officers. Nearly all enrollment clerks were white, and many of them had changed little since they had discriminated against blacks in the early sixties. Five years after passage of the Voting Rights Act, civil rights workers in Humphreys County, Mississippi, complained to Washington that G. H. Hood, appointed registrar in 1960, was "less than cooperative" and held "grossly erratic or non existent office hours. He notifies plantation owners when their workers attempt to register. Mr. Hood's reputation is such that many people would not register to vote if he came knocking at their door."[26] Many blacks who succeeded in registering hesitated to vote because they doubted whether their ballots would be counted properly. A study of election day irregularities in Mississippi in 1969 uncovered the following abuses: black registrants were told that others had already voted in their names, black illiterates received incorrect or inadequate assistance, and white officials refused to accommodate black poll watchers and furnished faulty information to prospective black voters.[27] The process of registering and voting, although greatly simplified since 1965, was still not the routine matter for blacks that it was for white southerners.

As these examples suggest, despite the lingering barriers to voter registration, the battle over the suffrage increasingly shifted to allowing blacks to cast an effective ballot. Once a majority of blacks entered their names in the registration books, southern officials manipulated the electoral system to dilute the effect of that vote. The United States Commission on Civil Rights catalogued the second generation of franchise subterfuges developed to weaken black political power. Among the new set of injustices, the commission found schemes for gerrymandered reapportionment, for converting from single-member to multi-member districts and at-large elections, for requiring full slate instead of single shot voting, and for annexing predominantly white areas to municipalities that were majority black or about to become so. These measures had the effect, often purposeful, of diminishing the impact of black ballots while increasing the strength of the white electorate. Furthermore, as the number of Negro candidates running for office rose, so did the obstacles that confronted them. Incumbent white officeholders had their terms extended, and positions sought by blacks were abolished. The commissioners of Baker County, Georgia, where the first suffrage discrimination suit under the 1957 Civil Rights Act had been filed, voted to eliminate a vacant post for justice of the peace after a black announced his candidacy. In 1966, the Mississippi legislature switched county superintendents of education from elective to appointive jobs only in predominantly black locales. For some of the positions that were still contested, lawmakers raised qualifying fees, added requirements for getting on the ballot, and placed restrictions on independent party tickets.[28]

These ruses testified to the growing threat that whites perceived from black enfranchisement. Since 1965, several hundred Negroes had won elections to public office. The most spectacular victories had come especially where civil rights groups had broken the psychological shackles of subservience and had challenged newly installed blockades to electoral participation. By 1970, in Greene and Lowndes County, Alabama, strongholds of SNCC and its descendants, and in Hancock County, Georgia, blacks controlled the local governments. Holmes County, Mississippi, another SNCC center, elected the first black representative to sit in the state legislature since Reconstruction. In 1969, the Magnolia State also saw the triumph of Charles Evers, the indefatigable NAACP organizer, as mayor of Fayette.[29]

Yet, such victories were unlikely to multiply rapidly, not only because of new restrictive measures imposed by whites, but also because southern blacks could no longer rely on the intensive fieldwork provided by several of the leading civil rights groups active in the 1960s. SNCC and CORE, torn by ideological factionalism, had virtually abandoned the South, and the SCLC, unable to recover from the assassination of the charismatic Martin Luther King, barely survived. To be sure, other concerned organizations, such as the NAACP and the VEP, continued their suffrage activities, but they lacked the necessary resources to meet the demand for their services. Thus, the deteriorating condition of the civil rights movement heightened the dependence of suffragists on the federal government to ensure continued progress.

The Nixon administration's initial record in the field of race relations had not reassured the civil rights advocates. Added to the troubling performance of the White House on school desegregation, Supreme Court nominations, and tax-exempt foundations was its approach toward extension of the Voting Rights Act. More than any other civil rights issue, enfranchisement had acquired the broadest consensus. Aware of this, Nixon strategists prepared to retain the landmark statute while eviscerating much of its potency. In that way, they could profess their enduring support for an unfettered franchise for blacks in the South and at the same time appease Dixie's white politicians who were seeking to maintain their political power.

Without renewal of the Voting Rights Act, its toughest provisions might soon elapse. The six states and parts of a seventh that fell under the triggering formula were eligible to receive federal registrars and observers and were required to submit electoral changes for clearance by the Justice Department or the United States District Court in the nation's capital. This coverage applied for five years, and after August 6, 1970, the designated jurisdictions could petition the federal court in Washington for release from the act. Because the states had been prohibited from employing a literacy test or similar device since 1965, they could easily bail out by showing that they had been in compliance with the law for the stipulated five years.[30] In one of his last official duties before retiring from the Oval Office, President Johnson had suggested an extension of the "vital provisions of the Voting Rights Act for another five years." In conveying the administration bill to Congress, Attorney General Ramsey Clark explained the rationale for continued federal surveillance: "Affected states have taken no significant action of their own to bring Negro citizens into the election process." He claimed that they stood ready to reinstitute the discriminatory application of suffrage requirements, particularly literacy tests, in effect prior to 1965.[31]

Suffragists quickly urged Johnson's successor to work toward renewing the law well in advance of the scheduled expiration date. In doing so, they hoped to forestall the possibility that the act might lapse as a result of protracted legislative delays. On February 18, 1969, a delegation from the Leadership Conference on Civil Rights conferred with Attorney General Mitchell and his assistant, Jerris Leonard. Both officials "appeared to be for an extension of the Voting Rights Act but . . . were considering changes that they said would make the law even more effective."[32] The group cautioned Mitchell against tampering with the automatic trigger by giving judges discretion to enforce the legislation. That same day Nixon ordered the Justice Department to prepare an analysis of the statute and to recommend a legislative course of action. Acknowledging the intensive review of the voting rights law that was under way, Daniel Patrick Moynihan, one of the president's chief counselors on domestic affairs and the author of controversial studies of the Negro family and the Great Society's poverty programs, assured the chairman of the Commission on Civil Rights "that we have no intention of letting this lapse."[33]

For several months the Justice Department explored legislative options. Initially, CRD attorneys leaned toward support of extending the act for many of the same reasons President Johnson and his attorney general had offered. They strongly suspected that after August 1970 "at least some of the covered states and counties would combine restoration of the literacy test with a general requirement of registration." Staff lawyers warned that the consequence "could be disfranchisement of substantial numbers of Negroes whose registration was made possible through operation of the Act."[34] To forestall the reintroduction of racially discriminatory practices, the Civil Rights Division considered "increasing the burden which a state or county . . . must meet if it is to secure termination of . . . coverage." In order to bail out, jursidictions would have to demonstrate not only that they had ceased employing biased suffrage procedures during the prescribed period in the past, but also that they would not adopt a discriminatory registration test in the future.[35]

Increasingly, however, Leonard favored a third option that would have coupled an extension of the voting rights statute for three years with a ban on literacy tests throughout the country. This proposal suggested that the Nixon administration was following a political trail carved out to impress southern white officials. Howard "Bo" Calloway, the Republican national committeeman from Georgia, had admonished Mitchell: "I believe most southerners would feel that the Nixon Administration broke a strong commitment to the South if it allowed an extension of the present Bill. We expect [the president] to have a straight forward Bill that says what it means and means what it says and applies to all sections of the country equally."[36] The CRD's plan did not constitute a complete capitulation to the South. The measure would stop the South from restoring literacy tests and would still require it to accept a three-year extension, only two years less than the Johnson administration had suggested. However, its appeal was not really aimed at the suffragists who eyed with suspicion anything but a simple five-year renewal of the act. Rather, "by providing a relatively short extension, with . . . recommendations looking toward permanent legislation, nationwide in scope," Leonard emphasized, "I think we can show that we are not unfairly singling out one region of the country for special treatment."[37]

The Justice Department seized upon a current Supreme Court decision to reinforce its preference for eliminating literacy tests nationally. On June 2, 1969, the Court ruled that Gaston County, North Carolina, could not bail out from coverage under the Voting Rights Act, although the literacy exam it had used until 1965 was not administered in a racially biased fashion. The justices approached the issue indirectly. They concluded that the dual school system, separate and unequal, that the county operated had given blacks an inferior education and had left them at a disadvantage based on race in satisfying the voter registration qualifications. Taking into account the history of school segregation, Justice John Marshall Harlan, on behalf of his brethren, declared: " 'Impartial' administration of the literacy test today would serve only to perpetuate these inequities in a different form."[38] This opinion seemed to strengthen the argument for continued suspension of literacy requirements in states that had maintained segregated school systems, including all of the areas covered by the Voting Rights Act. Congressman Emanuel Celler scribbled this conclusion on his copy of the *Gaston* ruling: "Until it can be shown that adult Negroes have had 'Equal' Education to enable them to pass the literacy tests on a par with whites, the Voting Rights Act must prevail."[39] The Nixon administration did not exactly reject this assessment, but it did draw a different implication from it. Jerris Leonard was disturbed that in effect the Supreme Court holding prevented the application of literacy tests in the South "indefinitely," while they remained in force in fourteen northern states. The Justice Department insisted that such a situation discriminated against poorly educated southern blacks who migrated to the North and could not pass the literacy requirements there. However, the department's chief concern was not for transplanted Negroes, but for the white South. "The only course available to the President consistent with his position against regional legislation," Leonard counseled the White House, "is to propose a nationwide ban on literacy tests."[40]

Extending the scope of the literacy prohibition northward opened the way for the president to suggest a geographic expansion of other key provisions of the statute. Section five became the central object of the administration's attention. Prior to 1969, this preclearance clause had suffered from virtual neglect, for neither Justice Department attorneys nor the southern states knew precisely what types of changes in suffrage regulations had to be submitted for federal approval. In the waning days of the Johnson administration, the CRD had welcomed a clarification of the measure. Once again the Supreme Court supplied the catalyst for change. Shortly after Nixon took office, the Court discovered an untapped source of power in the little-used section, affecting much more than voter registration. On March 3, the high bench announced that the covered jurisdictions first had to clear a wide range of electoral changes either with the attorney general or with the United States District Court in Washington, D.C. The items involved comprised many of the schemes that were being implemented to dilute the strength of the newly enfranchised black electorate: shifting to at-large elections, transforming elective into appointive positions, limiting the ability of independent candidates to appear on ballots, and curtailing the ability of illiterates to vote freely. Speaking for a seven-member majority, Earl Warren read the Voting Rights Act in exceedingly broad fashion. According to the chief justice, section five "was aimed at the subtle, as well as the obvious," and he interpreted the statute as protecting "all action necessary to make a vote effective."[41] Therefore, *Allen v. State Board of Elections* affirmed the authority of the federal government to take appropriate steps to reduce the proliferation of weapons aimed at thwarting black enfranchisement.

This opinion, however, conflicted with Nixon's desire to ease federal regulation of southern electoral practices, and the administration sided with the judicial dissenters. Justice Harlan, whose ruling in the *Gaston* case for all practical purposes swept away literacy tests in the South, refused to extend federal jurisdiction over techniques that did not actually deprive blacks from registering to vote and from casting a proper ballot. The intent of the Voting Rights Act, he argued, was to grant "Negroes free access to the ballot box, [so that] state governments would then be suitably responsive to their voice, and federal intervention would not be justified."[42] In agreement on this point, Justice Hugo Black lashed out at the majority in a stinging rebuke that generally departed from the tradition of racial advancement he had championed during his distinguished career. "This is somewhat reminiscent of old Reconstruction days," the Alabamian declared referring to section five, "when soldiers controlled the South and when those states were compelled to make reports to military commanders of what they did."[43] These objections struck a responsive chord among Nixon administration policymakers unwilling to prolong the Second Reconstruction of Dixie. Hence, the *Allen* ruling stirred the Justice Department to revise section five "so that the Act would have no regional application."[44]

While the department drafted its measure, the civil rights forces moved to obtain a simple renewal of the original statute. As a practical matter, they frowned upon any design to amend the law by abolishing literacy tests nationwide. Such a proposal had some attraction for the suffragists, but they worried that its introduction "would open the door to the very real possibility of a Congressional squabble that could see the current Voting Rights Act expire by default in 1970."[45] Clarence Mitchell, the premier civil rights lobbyist, and his congressional allies suspected the intentions of the White House in raising the issue. They recognized that southern opponents of further black enfranchisement "would love to see the embarrasing situation that could result from any attempt to dictate to the 14 non-South States" which used literacy tests.[46]

To avoid this pitfall, lawmakers favoring a flat extension of the Voting Rights Act had convened public hearings in mid-May, before the administration completed its proposal. Over the next month, a procession of witness testified to the House Judiciary Committee on behalf of continuing the law for another five years. Speaking for a bipartisan majority of the panel, Representative William McCulloch, the ranking Republican on the committee, warned against tinkering with the original provisions of the act. He believed that the suspension of literacy exams was appropriately directed toward the areas in which the problem of racial disfranchisement existed, and he urged the use of section five to combat the burgeoning number of electoral devices adopted by the South to slow down "the march to political equality."[47] Most supporters acknowledged that of all the civil rights measures passed over the previous decade, "the voting rights bill is working best." Moreover, they condemned what they observed as a growing feeling of complacency "that the Voting Rights Act has solved all the problems of voter discrimination in the South."[48] Representatives of the Voter Education Project and the United States Commission on Civil Rights furnished the results of their investigations showing that black voter registration still lagged significantly behind that of whites within the covered states, as less than a majority of adult Negroes were enrolled in 176 counties. "Although voter registration may be as American as apple pie," Vernon Jordan of the VEP reported, "it still can be hazardous in much of the Deep South."[49] To deal with this ongoing problem, he called upon the federal government to step up its implementation of the law, especially the designation of voting examiners. Voicing this familiar complaint, Jordan wondered: "Much has been accomplished with only moderate and partial enforcement of the Voting Rights Act. How much more might have been accomplished if the Act had been fully enforced?"[50]

Opponents also had their say before the Judiciary Committee. Mississippi Attorney General A. F. Summer demonstrated that southern officials had reached a new stage in resisting enfranchisement. Black voter registration, perhaps because it had not caught up to the white level, no longer provided the main target for their wrath. "Illiterate voters we can abide if forced to— even though our eyes are envious of your States, exempt as they are from the act's provisions," Summer remarked to the northern members of the committee. However, he revealed that section five, as interpreted by the Supreme Court, remained unacceptable. Summer was upset that in the aftermath of *Allen,* the attorney general in Washington had objected to three legislative acts altering electoral procedures in Mississippi, one of the losing parties in the suit and, thus, specifically affected by the ruling. In this instance the Nixon administration could hardly avoid enforcing the preclearance provision, but if this became a pattern, Mississippi would lose opportunities to devise practices for diminishing the effect of the black franchise. Aware of the high stakes, Summer blasted section five for creating "an island of provinces which, if continued, will find the chief law officer of these provinces on his knees, begging and groveling for favors from the omnipotent Justice Department, or in the alternative, the Federal District Court of Washington, D.C."[51]

Throughout a month of hearings, the Judiciary Committee had not heard from the Nixon administration. Five times, Attorney General Mitchell had canceled his scheduled appearance. The committee's sixth invitation finally brought the reluctant witness. Mitchell had stalled, most likely, because the long-awaited administration bill substantially modified the existing voting rights law, and he had sought to line up greater Republican support in Congress before announcing the changes to an unsympathetic House panel dominated by civil rights supporters.[52]

On June 26, the attorney general unveiled his plan. He proposed a nationwide ban on literacy tests until January 1, 1974, removal of restrictions on state residency requirements for presidential elections, and authority for the Justice Department to send voting examiners and observers anywhere in the country. In place of the vital triggering mechanism and preclearance section of the 1965 statute, he proposed that the attorney general resort to litigation to challenge and to put a freeze on the passage of new suffrage restrictions. In defense of this drastic alteration in the law, Mitchell contended "that voting rights is not a regional issue. It is a nationwide concern for every American which must be tested on a nationwide basis."[53]

In rewriting the prescription, the administration spokesman denied that he was reducing the dosage of suffrage medicine. Mitchell couched his arguments in the language of enfranchisement. "I want to encourage our Negro citizens to take out their alienations at the ballot box, and not elsewhere," he averred, urging the Judiciary Committee "not to permit the Negro citizens outside of the South to be forgotten."[54] Mitchell asserted that the literacy tests in operation in the North resulted in a lower turnout at the polls of northern blacks than those in Dixie. Based on the reasoning in the *Gaston* case, he pointed out that many of the nonparticipating black northerners had received an inferior education in the South and should not be penalized by restrictive literacy tests. Neither would the elimination of section five harm newly enfranchised black southerners. Mitchell maintained that during the previous five years, 345 voting laws had been submitted to the Justice Department for clearance and only ten had been disallowed. Under these circumstances, he preferred to file lawsuits in a three-judge federal district court when the occasion to question local election laws arose. This approach, according to Mitchell, "properly places the burden of proof on the Government and not the States."[55]

As expected, the Mitchell bill angered civil rights proponents. For two days, liberal members of the Judiciary Committee sparred with the attorney general. Chairman Emanuel Celler wondered why the act should apply throughout the nation. "I think it is like saying," the Brooklyn Democrat groaned, "because you have a flood in Mississippi you have to build a dam in Idaho."[56] His Republican colleague William McCulloch agreed that the provisions of the Mitchell plan "sweep broadly into those areas where the need is least and retreat from those areas where the need is greatest."[57] Neither lawmaker opposed in principle the prohibition of literacy tests, but each thought that its inclusion in the bill would endanger extension of the law before the August 1970 expiration date. Celler accused Mitchell of engaging in a "delaying action, maybe not deliberately by yourself, but this is a delaying action."[58] Another witness, Clarence Mitchell, was more blunt: "This is a sophisticated, a calculated, incredible effort on the part of the chief lawyer of the Government of the United States to make it impossible for us to continue on the constitutional course that we have followed in exercising the tools . . . that we have had in protecting the right to vote."[59]

The Nixon administration clearly had challenged the liberals in a vulnerable area. In calling for the nationwide suspension of literacy tests, Mitchell occupied the position usually held by reformers. He took up the cause of enfranchisement and advocated what amounted to universal suffrage. "All adult citizens who are of sound mind and who have not been convicted of a felony," he asserted, "should be free and encouraged to participate in the political process."[60] His opponents objected on the ground that raising such complex constitutional questions could delay passage of the bill, but on this occasion their arguments sounded like special pleading. In Celler's Brooklyn district containing the heavily black populated sections of Bedford-Stuyvesant and Ocean Hill-Brownsville, residents were subject to New York's literacy test for voting. If black turnout was lower there than in parts of the South, as Mitchell contended, Celler claimed that it did not stem from racial bias. When the attorney general suggested that the literacy test as a prerequisite for voting provided a "psychological barrier for people without education," the Brooklyn congressman replied: "It is very difficult for us to legislate on the basis of indefinite psychology."[61] However, this view ignored the subtle as well as blatant dimensions of disfranchisement, an awareness that liberals usually displayed.

In contrast, white southerners gave John Mitchell's handiwork much better reviews, fueling the suspicions of the suffragists. Most opponents of the 1965 measure wished for its demise but barring that possibility found merit in the administration's attempt to expand its provisions to all fifty states. The *Clarion Ledger* of Jackson, Mississippi, commented: "If there is to be no discrimination in voting, there should be no discrimination in applying federal voting laws evenly to . . . the country."[62] Strom Thurmond, whose support of Nixon's presidential candidacy appeared to be paying off, was "pleased that this administration will not require Southern States to clear changes in their election laws with the Department of Justice here in Washington."[63] Whatever the legislative outcome, Mitchell had won the confidence of civil rights foes. Representative Joe D. Waggonner of Louisiana believed that the white South had nothing to fear "as long as John Mitchell is Attorney General, because he is at least fairminded, and you are not going to have this highhandedness under Attorney General Mitchell."[64]

With civil rights supporters in control, the House Judiciary Committee rejected the Mitchell proposal. In mid-July, a bipartisan coalition recommended, by a vote of 28–7, an extension of the 1965 Voting Rights Act with no amendments. Reporting for the majority, Peter Rodino, a New Jersey Democrat, concluded "that this Act has . . . reconfirmed the faith of many that exercise of the franchise and political participation today represent the best and most productive means of achieving social change." Consequently, the failure to renew would reverse the substantial progress achieved since 1965. In particular, Rodino contended that abandonment of section five would "restore time-consuming litigation as the principal means of assuring the equal right to vote," an approach that had worked poorly in the past.[65] The majority wanted to avoid unnecessary delays in the renewal process, and it rejected a nationwide ban on literacy tests, finding no evidence that such exams were administered on the basis of race outside the South.

The opposition in the House committee came from a combination of southern Democrats and midwestern Republicans. Impressed with the significant strides black citizens had made under the voting rights statute, these conservative lawmakers believed that the formula activating coverage of the southern jurisdictions was outdated. A law which based legal presumption of a state's racial discrimination "on election returns five years old and ignores the progress made since," Republican Richard Poff of Virginia declared, "is more a penalty than a reward."[66] A reasonable solution, according to the dissenters, was to remove the South from the special disabilities it suffered and to pursue the impartial course advocated by the Nixon administration. Although these views did not prevail, the opponents of simple renewal intended to press their case to the House Rules Committee when it took up the bill.

In the meantime, the Mitchell proposal was receiving a

warmer reception in the Senate. In early July, a Senate Judiciary
Subcommittee chaired by Sam Ervin began hearings on voting
rights. Although he claimed that the "Attorney General's bill makes
only a few small substantive changes in the 1965 Act," the North
Carolina senator appreciated that it "does eliminate the unjust and
repressive aspects which are so objectionable."[67] Rather than extend the law for another five years, Ervin suggested substituting
a triggering formula based on the 1968 presidential election and
applying the measure nationally. Thus, having been forced to
improve their voter registration performance since 1965, the
southern states would reap the benefits and escape from special
coverage.

Ervin's views did not go unchallenged. Attorney Joseph
Rauh spoke out strongly against discarding the original standard
for coverage. "What does it prove if people lived up to the 1965
law?" he asked and then answered his own question: "The 1968
situation is to a high degree an artificial situation created by a law
under which examiners went in and other methods such as abolishing tests were used to get registration."[68] But Clarence Mitchell presented the case even more strongly. Asserting that there was
no need to extend federal protection of the suffrage northward,
the ubiquitous civil rights leader frankly accused the Nixon administration of revising the law to please Strom Thurmond. A
heated exchange ensued when the South Carolina Republican, who
also sat on the subcommittee, responded: "Do you ascribe an ulterior motive to the Nixon Administration in advocating that this
bill apply . . . to all States and all people alike?" Mitchell backed
away slightly, but his anger still showed in his reply: "I would
say that regardless of whether the Nixon Administration has an
ulterior motive or not, a disastrous result would follow if the
Voting Rights Act were to expire."[69]

The remainder of the four days of hearings was not as
volatile. Most of the witnesses who had appeared before the House
Judiciary Committee reiterated their comments to the Senate
group. Attorney General Mitchell had not changed his mind, and
the probing of Birch Bayh of Indiana, a strong civil rights advocate, did not shake him from his position. Mitchell continued
to insist that black northerners needed legislative relief from the

discriminating effects of literacy tests, but Senator Bayh, whose state did not require an educational qualification for voting, remained skeptical that the evidence warranted such a modification in the existing law. The attorney general also maintained that section five should be eliminated because few submissions had been made and only a handful of them had been rejected. Besides, local officials often did not inform the attorney general when they adopted suffrage laws, forcing the Justice Department to go into federal court to challenge them. Consequently, Mitchell wanted the judiciary to handle this type of complaint. Mitchell's reasoning struck one civil rights advocate as "strange." Lawrence Speiser of the American Civil Liberties Union belittled the premise "that because a law is being ignored it should be repealed." As for the small number of measures submitted under section five, Speiser retorted that the preclearance procedure had a deterrent effect against the passage of racially restrictive suffrage proposals in most areas of the South and thus should be prolonged.[70]

With Ervin at the helm, at the end of July the Senate Subcommittee suspended indefinitely further hearings on voting rights until the House completed its deliberations. Since Celler's Judiciary Committee issued its report, the extension bill had been bottled up in the Rules Committee presided over by William Colmer of Mississippi, a foe of civil rights legislation. In late September, Celler sought the aid of John McCormack, the House Speaker, to "give the necessary push and pressure to get the Rules Committee to grant a rule."[71] A month later, Colmer relented; however, the Mississippian was in no hurry and did not convene a public hearing until November 17. On that day, Colmer playfully welcomed Celler to hear him defend "the annual civil wrongs bill." The Judiciary chairman justified his committee's recommendation for a five-year extension of the Voting Rights Act, unencumbered with administration proposals concerning literacy tests and residency requirements, both of which, Celler believed, raised serious constitutional issues. Unconvinced, as a "proud southerner," Colmer complained to Celler: "I am wondering if we are ever going to get through with the Civil War, or the War Between the States. You are going back to the days immediately following that war, the Reconstruction period."[72]

Colmer's lament was predictable, but the remarks of some other committee members sounded a warning. Two northern Democrats, James J. Delaney of New York and B. F. Sisk of California, whose ardor for civil rights measures had cooled in recent years, supported a suffrage measure that applied uniformly throughout the nation. They joined several Republicans and southern Democrats on the committee who favored adoption of a rule sending the Celler bill to the House floor as long as amendments in the form of the Nixon administration's proposals were in order. Neither Celler nor William McCulloch, who also testified at the hearing, could stem the defections. Hence, on November 18, the Colmer committee passed a resolution clearing the Judiciary bill but opening the way for the introduction of damaging amendments that otherwise might not have been ruled germane.[73]

This obvious compromise delighted the White House and breathed new life into its program. Bryce Harlow, the president's congressional liaison, exuded optimism. "There is a basic conservative cast to both Houses," he reported, "so that this Republican Administration has a power edge despite the lopsided Democratic control. Republicans plus the Southerners . . . can expect to call most signals throughout the 91st Congress, provided we are reasonably diligent in maintaining effective Congressional relations."[74] This glowing assessment notwithstanding, the liberal coalition did not appear particularly concerned about the threat to renewal of the Voting Rights Act. The bipartisan alliance had held together to enact major civil rights legislation only a year before, and despite some erosion in strength, civil rights advocates had the advantage of defending an existing law. The burden now fell on the administration's legislative allies to reverse the status quo. This dilemma became evident when the White House failed to persuade a northern Republican on the Judiciary Committee to manage its substitute bill on the floor. Indeed, Representative McCulloch, the senior GOP member of the committee, fiercely opposed the Mitchell proposal, and the task of sponsorship fell to Gerald Ford, the minority leader.[75]

When on December 10 the lower chamber agreed to consider the Judiciary Committee bill, liberals took the offensive.

Celler charged that the Mitchell substitute had no value and was full of deceit, part of "a campaign to placate and appease" the white South. Rather than enlarging the benefits of the act, he claimed, the Justice Department measure was designed to halt additional suffrage gains in the South.[76] Peter Rodino also did not want his colleagues to be misled by the label of "regionalism" that the administration had attached to the current franchise statute. Enactment of any proposal "in the guise of nationalizing voting rights protection," he argued, would "undermine the voting rights program of the past four years and threaten repetition of the practices of the past."[77] Congressman James C. Corman, a California Democrat, asked those who were uncertain as to the relative merits of the two competing proposals "to look at the players today," for they would find the traditional opponents of civil rights backing the Mitchell substitute.[78]

These assertions hit the mark. As they had a century ago, most northern Republicans were prepared to abandon newly enfranchised blacks and to make their peace with the white South. Minority Leader Ford noted the advances in voter registration in Dixie and remarked: "This is not the Reconstruction Era and neither is this 1965. Four eventful years have passed and evils and errors of another time have yielded."[79] In a similar vein, Thomas Meskill, a Connecticut Republican, desired the South restored on an equal basis within the Union. "The Civil War is over," he declared. "Let us get on with the business at hand."[80] Southern legislators eagerly concurred. Richard Poff pleaded with his northern colleagues to put "aside the old shibboleths and subdue the old passions . . . discard the old discrimination, and . . . live together as one nation—all under the same law."[81] William Colmer decried "the further efforts to divide this country" in the form of regional legislation embodied in the Celler bill.[82] However, in supporting the administration alternative, some southerners sought to eradicate eventually all protection for black suffrage. John Rarick of Louisiana favored increasing the territorial scope of the voting rights measure "in the hope that the clear and present danger of Federal intervention in the local election machinery in all parts of the country will alert members to this act's nauseating suppression of basic rights."[83]

The alliance of conservative Republicans and southern Democrats delivered a shocking defeat to the liberals. White House aides waged an intensive lobbying campaign, covering the House floor "like a carpet."[84] The civil rights coalition, perhaps over-confident and somewhat disorganized, was outmaneuvered. Nevertheless, the vote was very close. On December 11, the lower chamber approved, 208–203, an amendment sponsored by Gerald Ford to accept the administration substitute. White House pressure had brought together 129 Republicans and 69 southern Democrats, but the winning margin was supplied by a combination of 10 northern and border state Democrats. One of these crucial votes came from Representative Delaney of New York City, who defended his position as applying legislation "in simple language to every State and not just a particular few in any area."[85] Nevertheless, a majority of Democrats (154), mostly from the North, opposed the president's stand, while only 49 northern GOP lawmakers defied him. Later that same day, about half of these Republican defectors returned to the fold and approved a final version of the Mitchell bill, 234-179.[86]

The Nixon administration had gone a long way toward fulfilling its promise to Strom Thurmond and the white South. Asked what had happened to the party of Lincoln, an aide to one of the Republican congressmen who opposed the Mitchell substitute responded: "It has put on a Confederate uniform."[87] In selecting its new wardrobe, the administration was fashioning support for its southern strategy. William E. Timmons, a counselor to the chief executive, recalled the reasoning behind the legislative approach: "Our coalition in Congress . . . depended in great measure on attracting sufficient numbers of southern Demorats to join with a Republican minority. Southerners in Congress were strongly opposed to extending the Voting Rights Act without making it apply nationally."[88] The White House bill had great attraction for white southerners in states that George Wallace had won in 1968 and which Nixon loyalists hoped to swing into the president's column in 1972. Every lawmaker representing districts in the jurisdictions covered under the 1965 statute backed the administration measure.

The outcome stung the liberals. Clarence Mitchell complained that the result was "engineered by the President of the United States who was supposed to be bringing the people together, but instead has consigned Negroes to a political doghouse whose roof leaks."[89] Shocked by this initial loss, the reformers were even more determined to rescue the voting rights bill when it reached the upper chamber. The Leadership Conference on Civil Rights admitted defeat in the House but pledged to make suffrage extension "our major civil rights concern when the bill comes up in the Senate."[90] Shortly after the House action, Clarence Mitchell met with a bipartisan coalition of senators to plot strategy. They decided to accept the provisions of the administration bill banning literacy tests nationwide and providing for uniform residency requirements in national elections. Most liberals had opposed these items in the first place for tactical not philosophical reasons; however, the legislative situation now required broadening the renewal measure to attract administration supporters. The suffragists also devised a plan to overcome the hazardous potential for delay that awaited the legislation in the Senate. The bill would be assigned to Sam Ervin's Judiciary Subcommittee, and the chairman did not feel any urgency to complete his task before the August expiration deadline. The bipartisan reform coalition sought to accelerate the process while also giving Ervin reasonable time to conduct hearings on the measure. Consequently, at the end of its sesssion in mid-December, the Senate instructed the Judiciary Committee to report a suffrage bill to the floor no later than March 1. The adoption of this procedure narrowed the opportunities for launching a filibuster, because the proposal would automatically become pending business.[91]

When the Ninety-first Congress reconvened in 1970, Senate liberals found another way to minimize delay. Their opportunity arose after the president nominated G. Harrold Carswell for a vacancy on the Supreme Court. The selection of this federal judge from Florida unleashed a storm of criticism from civil rights advocates who charged him with having taken positions in the past against racial equality. The timing of the controversy worked in favor of the liberals. They received the cooperation of Democratic Majority Leader Mike Mansfield, who

scheduled a confirmation vote on Carswell to follow final disposition of the voting rights measure. In anticipation of lengthy
debate on Carswell's appointment, southern senators, who strongly
endorsed the Florida jurist, were less likely to drag out proceedings on the suffrage proposal. Indeed, Senator Ervin complained
about the pressure on his subcommittee to conduct hearings on
enfranchisement while the Carswell deliberations remained unfinished. When he requested an extension of the March deadline,
the leaders of both parties rebuffed him.[92]

The bipartisan coalition was well led by Philip Hart, a
Michigan Democrat, and Hugh Scott, the Republican Minority
Leader from Pennsylvania. Both had played active roles in previous civil rights struggles, but Scott now faced a touchy political situation. Since his days as a congressman in the early 1950s,
the Keystone State lawmaker had lined up with other moderate
Republicans in defense of racial equality. Because of his deep
convictions on the subject, the minority leader found himself at
odds with the Republican White House. Opposition to the president endangered party unity, but it did not threaten the political
fortunes of Scott in his home state. Up for reelection in 1970, the
senator counted on receiving considerable support from the black
electorate. One of his aides asked Clarence Mitchell to publicize
the senator's favorable position on the Voting Rights Act in the
state's leading Afro-American newspapers. The civil rights lobbyist gladly replied: "I will do anything Senator Scott asks me to
do and any campaigning that he feels would be in his favor because I believe that it is vital that he be reelected."[93] In addition
to Scott, Minority Whip Robert Griffin of Michigan opposed the
administration bill.[94]

Hart and Scott, along with their liberal allies, worked
on drawing up an acceptable compromise to halt the momentum
that the Nixon regime had built up in the House. They drafted a
proposal extending coverage of the 1965 statute for five years and
added separate titles incorporating literacy and residency provisions similar to those approved by the House. However, their
version did not include the section of the lower chamber's bill
authorizing nationwide appointment of examiners and observers.
Such an expansion of federal power, they claimed, would result

in a dilution of available manpower, thereby weakening enforcement efforts in the South.[95] The Scott-Hart plan received the endorsement of the suffragists. Father Theodore Hesburgh of Notre Dame University, chairman of the United States Commission on Civil Rights, argued that it retained the effective methods "to end the never-ceasing attempts of many Southern States to deny to their black citizens the right to vote," whereas the Nixon administration's proposal added "nothing to the existing powers of the Attorney General to protect voting rights."[96] The Justice Department, though, was not inclined to retreat. "If the Senate wishes to change this bill," Assistant Attorney General Leonard said, "they will do it themselves. We hold tight for [the House] passed bill."[97]

While the band of liberals operated behind the scenes to gather support for their revised measure, Senator Ervin finally got public hearings under way on February 18. Although he doubted the constitutionality of the ban on literacy tests, the North Carolina senator commended the administration bill, H. R. 4249, for repealing section five and extending the rest of its coverage nationwide. One witness from the South testified why opponents of the 1965 act found some virtue in the Mitchell plan. "Misery loves company," Lester Maddox, the segregationist governor of Georgia declared, "and the more States that are affected by this Federal encroachment upon State rights, the more voices we will hear rising in opposition to it."[98] Rather than increasing the burden uniformly throughout the country, H. R. 4249 in practice would weaken enforcement in the South. Congressman Fletcher Thompson of Georgia acknowledged that requiring fifty states to submit suffrage changes to the attorney general, with all the paperwork involved, would tax the available personnel and resources of the Justice Department.[99] To keep this from happening, civil rights advocates urged that legislation continue to be aimed at the South. Candidly admitting that the procedures of the 1965 statute were "extraordinary" and were directed at one section of the country, Senator Joseph Tydings, a Maryland Democrat who sat on the Judiciary Committee, declared that "they should be that way because the denial of the right to vote caused by racial prejudice is an extraordinary act and because this massive voting rights discrimination occurred primarily in one region."[100] Any retrenchment from federal supervision of this area, Vernon Jordan asserted, would flash "a green light from Washington" to white-dominated southern communities, "poised and ready to eliminate the burgeoning black vote in their jurisdictions."[101]

On February 26, after five days of testimony, the hearings reached a climax with the appearance of a Justice Department representative. Mitchell sent David Norman, an experienced lawyer in the CRD, who would soon succeed Jerris Leonard as assistant attorney general. A forty-six-year-old alumnus of the University of California Law School who first joined the CRD in 1957, Norman had helped to draft the Voting Rights Act of 1965; however, he no longer believed in section five. The department had received relatively few submissions during the previous five years, and most of those had been approved, he noted. In contrast to the critics of the administration bill, Norman contended that southern blacks had registered in large enough numbers to prevent their future disfranchisement. If suffrage problems did arise, he concluded that litigation was "a better way to deal with them than having the Attorney General look at every little change whether it is a stringent change or a relaxation of a voting law."[102] These arguments failed to impress the liberals who maintained that the benefits of section five should not be judged by the number of submissions but by its "deterrent effect on manipulation of election laws to disfranchise blacks."[103] They denied that southern blacks had as yet acquired an equal opportunity to participate in the electoral process and feared that the White House bill would herald a reversal to the days before 1965, when litigation had proven a cumbersome and ineffective means of protecting minority voting rights. Suggesting that the administration measure had been tailored to suit the White House's southern strategy, Birch Bayh posed a sharp question to Norman: "Do you know of any one person with a black face or brown face who has supported the Administration's position on the Voting Rights Act?" The CRD attorney's reply was as revealing as it was discouraging: "I don't know. I haven't talked to black people about this, and we don't know whether they do or not."[104]

Shortly after this exchange, time ran out for the Ervin

committee. On March 1, the Senate took up H.R. 4249 in accordance with the agreement reached back in December. Immediately, the bipartisan coalition of liberals offered the Scott-Hart version as a substitute for the House bill. The ensuing debate covered familiar ground. Most southerners expected a suffrage measure to pass, and they favored the administration proposal as the lesser of two evils. James Eastland summed up the sentiment behind accepting the lower chamber's bill: "This at least has the virtue to apply the prohibition on literacy tests to all 50 States and not to just a few carefully selected 'conquered provinces.' "[105] In response, Charles Mathias, a liberal Maryland Republican, attacked the administration bill for distorting "uniformity and equality" to mean "simply 'doing nothing nowhere.' "[106] Civil rights advocates also reminded their conservative colleagues that in maintaining intact the provisions of the 1965 law, they would help lessen the use of violence as a political weapon which had become so widespread in the latter half of the 1960s. "To deny the ballot as a means of settling disputes," warned Democratic Senator Stephen Young of Ohio, "is to *invite* settlement of those disputes in the streets."[107]

On March 5 by a vote of 47–32, the suffragists won an initial victory by blocking an attempt to table the Scott-Hart substitute. The defeated measure was sponsored by Roman Hruska who had taken up the leadership position on this issue as a result of the defection of Republican minority leaders Hugh Scott and Robert Griffin. The Nebraskan wanted to expedite a decision on the franchise so that deliberations could proceed on the nomination to the Supreme Court of Judge Harrold Carswell. "I have an idea," Hruska asserted, "that some of the important landmark cases in that Court are being held in abeyance until the full membership is qualified and ready to sit."[108] The outcome of the tabling vote indicated that although bipartisan liberals had the advantage, they did not as yet command the requisite two–thirds majority needed to choke off a possible filibuster.

Having lost the opening skirmish, the South continued to wage the war. Ervin offered a series of "compromise" amendments designed to allow some southern states to escape coverage. He proposed to change the date of the triggering formula from

the 1964 presidential election to that of 1968. Based on this criterion, the act would cease to apply to North Carolina, Virginia,
Mississippi, Louisiana, and Alabama, where the voter turnout had
exceeded the stipulated 50 percent in 1968. In defense of his
proposition, Ervin contended: "My State has been trying to get
back into the Union for 100 years. The Civil War is over. I wish
I could say the same thing about Reconstruction."[109]

However, the liberals planned to maintain federal intervention in the South for a while longer. They worried that once
"you start tinkering with the formula everyone will be tempted
to improve it slightly," opening up a "Pandorra's [sic] Box [that]
should be kept shut." In answering Ervin, Senator Hart stressed
that the original mechanism was developed merely as a method
of gauging the presence of racially discriminatory practices and
not of measuring a satisfactory level of enfranchisement. "Nor
did Congress find," according to Hart, "that this same percentage would serve as a criteria [sic] to determine when past discriminatory practices had been sufficiently eradicated to warrant
removing the safeguards which had made progress and improvement possible."[110] Besides, the Michigan senator pointed out,
southern lawmakers had recently enacted legislation to dilute the
effects of black political power, thereby justifying renewal of the
1965 law. These arguments carried. Repeating the outcome on
the tabling resolution, the Senate turned down Ervin's and other
restrictive amendments.[111]

Nevertheless, the liberals could not prevent one significant alteration. Vulnerable to the charge that the North resisted
adopting the 1968 electoral figures because it did not "want its
own ox gored," they expected trouble.[112] It came on March 10,
when Senator John Sherman Cooper offered an amendment that
retained the original formula and also added a standard for coverage based upon the 1968 presidential election. The full force of
the 1965 act would continue to be felt in the southern states, and
for the first time approximately ten counties in the North would
be subject to its special provisions. A Kentucky Republican who
had voted against Hruska's tabling motion, Cooper managed to
soften the regional orientation of the statute without sacrificing
its potency in the South. He had no desire to weaken enfran-

chisement, which "made it possible for persons to work for reforms through the ballot box rather than through demonstrations."[113] The liberals nearly blocked the Cooper measure in a tie vote, 43-43, which would have defeated the amendment. Having accepted the proposal for suspension of literacy tests nationally, they refused to yield any further and to support even a slight expansion of the designated formula. In contrast to the moratorium on educational requirements for suffrage, an enlargement of the examiner and preclearance programs would require additional enforcement machinery, thereby adding to the strain on existing resources. This victory was shortlived. Senator James Allen of Alabama, who had opposed the Cooper provision, called for its reconsideration. This time, three southern Democrats, including Allen, changed their position and supported the motion as a means of widening the application of the automatic device. Their votes provided the winning margin, and the motion carried, 47-38. This procedural hurdle cleared, the Cooper amendment passed on a 50-37 vote. Not only had it picked up support from southern Democrats and northern Republicans, but also from Democrats in the North who believed that, unlike Ervin's offerings, this modest extension of the act's geographical coverage would not endanger the voting rights of black southerners. Indeed, a few weeks earlier many of these same northern lawmakers had also backed a resolution in favor of federal enforcement of school desegregation guidelines uniformly throughout the country.[114]

The liberals bounced back from this defeat to win another round; yet, in doing so they placed renewal of the 1965 law in some jeopardy by raising the issue of reducing the voting age to eighteen. House leaders had refused to take up this proposal, and Emanuel Celler, the octogenarian civil rights advocate, believed that authorization of teenage voting required a constitutional amendment. He also doubted the practical wisdom of tacking this measure on the voting rights bill. "I frankly am fearful," he confided to Senator Edward Kennedy, a supporter of the lower voting age, "that such a provision would give opponents of civil rights another advantage." Celler viewed "a simple, unencumbered extension" of the statute as of "the highest national importance," but he weighed the possibility of calling for a joint conference committee to reconcile any discrepancies in the bills.[115] To do so, however, would hold up renewal of the act as the August deadline rapidly approached. Despite the potential threat from the House, the upper chamber overwhelmingly approved an amendment to H. R. 4249, granting eighteen to twenty-year-olds the franchise. Drafted by Kennedy and Bayh and introduced by Mansfield, the proposal passed, 64-17, reflecting a bipartisan national consensus. At a time when the military draft subjected young men to fighting in Southeast Asia and youth protests gripped the nation, legislators considered enfranchisement a way of raising morale at home and fostering allegiance to the political system.[116]

After altering the House bill, the Senate adopted it swiftly. On March 13, approximately two weeks after the measure had reached the floor, sixty-four senators voted to accept the Scott-Hart substitute. Eleven of the twelve negative votes were cast by southerners; however, six senators from the South, including William Spong of Virginia, a state covered by the 1965 act, joined the majority.[117] For the first time in three decades, Dixie lawmakers had not bothered to wage a filibuster against a civil rights bill. In this instance, delay would have interfered with the confirmation proceedings on Judge Carswell. With opposition building to the nomination, Carswell supporters wanted to consider the matter promptly. Furthermore, the base of the electorate had expanded since 1965, and southern politicos had little incentive to assume a die-hard position that would alienate black voters. Senator Ernest Hollings of South Carolina remarked privately: "Don't ask me to go out and filibuster. I'm not going back to my state and explain a filibuster against black voters."[118]

The chief stumbling block to House concurrence in the Senate version was the provision to lower the voting age. However, Representative Celler relented. The Senate measure generally resembled his original extension bill, and his ardent support for voting rights renewal overcame the reservations he had concerning the constitutionality of teenage voting.[119] The White House, though, posed a more serious challenge. On April 27, President Nixon sent a four-page letter to House leaders expressing his opposition to the Senate rider decreasing the voting age. Although he "strongly favor[ed] the 18-year-old vote [and] . . .

enactment of the Voting Rights Bill," he saw the two as separate issues. The inclusion of teenage voting as part of the renewal of the 1965 measure, Nixon declared, "represents an unconstitutional assertion of Congressional authority in an area specifically reserved to the States."[120] The president did not announce what action he would take if the lower chamber agreed to the Senate's revisions, but privately he was giving serious thought to vetoing the bill. His staff offered him contradictory advice. One group of aides counseled the president against issuing a veto, because it would encourage the belief in young people that they could not work within the system. Another set of advisors recommended rejection of the bill on the ground that "the new young voters . . . could tip several states with large electoral votes into the Democratic camp in 1972, particularly if the Democratic candidate should be a Gene McCarthy, Ted Kennedy, or other politician with appeal to youth."[121]

While Nixon was making up his mind, the House grappled with the thorny question. The lower chamber referred the Senate version to its Rules Committee where hearings did not begin for several months. Congressional lawmakers had the chief executive's wishes to consider, but they also had to take into account the possibility that their failure to approve the Senate proposal could lead to expiration of the Voting Rights Act. If the House called for a conference committee to resolve the differences in the two bills, Senator Mansfield warned, southern opponents of renewal might launch a filibuster. The Carswell nomination had been rejected in April, and the foes of the 1965 statute now had time working on their side to gain revenge. "There will either be an 18-year-old vote this year," Majority Leader Mansfield flatly predicted on May 10, "or there won't be an extension of the voting rights bill."[122] This warning failed to sway GOP leaders in the House, and they stood fast against acceptance of the bill which, they believed, lowered the voting age in an unconstitutional manner.[123] However, Republican ranks were divided on this matter. A contingent of twenty-four GOP congressmen circulated a petition to their fellow Republicans soliciting support "in our efforts to have the Senate package accepted in its entirety with the Senate's added amendments which we believe strengthen the Voting Rights Act."[124] One of the signers of this appeal, John B. Anderson of Illinois, helped tip the balance in favor of concurrence. A member of the Rules Committee, he assisted in narrowly defeating a motion on June 5 to send the bill to conference by a vote of 8-6. The committee in similar fashion immediately cleared the revised H. R. 4249 for deliberation on the floor.[125]

Six months had elapsed since the representatives voiced their preference for the administration measure over a bill like the one now before them. With the August deadline some six weeks away, the House reversed itself. On June 17, the legislators first approved a motion to take up the Rules Committee recommendation and then agreed to the Senate version of H. R. 4249. Before House concurrence, 224 members defeated 183 of their colleagues on the crucial procedural vote. In the triumphant majority were 22 Democrats and 16 Republicans who had supported the administration bill the previous December. Given the choice of extending the 1965 act in its latest form or of no bill at all, the northern Republican defectors voted for enfranchisement. The Democrats who changed their minds, nearly all of whom came from the South, favored the White House version, but they preferred the modified Senate bill to the current law.[126] Thus, in the final vote for approval 100 Republicans lined up with 172 Democrats to defeat 132 of their colleagues.

In arriving at a decision on whether to veto the legislation, Nixon had several concerns to balance. His constitutional objections and his southern strategy pulled him in the direction of rejecting the congressional proposal, but, in doing so, he would have to stand against a majority of his party's lawmakers who had voted in its favor. Then, too, there was the democratic principle of expansion of the ballot. In spite of the controversy surrounding it, the enactment of H.R. 4249 adhered to the tradition of American suffrage reform as a means of moderating social unrest through regular political channels. The propertyless, Afro-Americans, and women had all sought and obtained the right to vote as a legitimate tool for redressing their grievances, and it was difficult, if not foolish, to deny youths and the poorly educated this same opportunity, particularly at a time of great turmoil. In urging Nixon to sign the measure, Senator Marlow Cook, a Kentucky Republican, pointed out: "Two of the most alienated groups in our society, the blacks and young, have faith in this bill."[127] Representative Abner Mikva, a Chicago Democrat, agreed most eloquently that H. R. 4249 spoke "to those very groups who are so alienated from our institutions. To the poor and illiterate, it says 'yes, we want you to vote too.' To the blacks, it says 'yes, we will keep faith with you, we want you to vote too.' To the young, America's future generation, it says 'yes we welcome your participation in our system.' "[128]

This latter consideration ultimately convinced Richard Nixon. In office for over a year, his policies concerning civil rights and the Vietnam War had belied his campaign slogan to "bring us together." The gap between the races, growing larger when Nixon had campaigned for office in 1968, seemed to have widened further two years later. The escalation of the war into Cambodia in May 1970 spurred a new wave of protests on college campuses, resulting in the deaths of white and black students at Kent State and Jackson State universities. Amidst this turbulence, Nixon could offer a symbolic gesture that might please both moderates and conservatives.[129] Taking the high road and playing the role of healer, on June 22 the president signed the voting rights extension as passed by Congress. He temporarily put aside his doubts about the constitutionality of the eighteen-year-old vote and was willing to allow the courts to decide the issue as swiftly as possible.[130] To veto the entire measure for the faults of one section, Nixon ultimately concluded, would have eradicated "the basic provisions of this act [which] are of great importance." To be sure, the bill he placed into law was very different from what his administration had sought, but he could boast that the final draft submitted for his signature no longer suffered from a regional stigma. The revised statute suspended literacy test requirements for voter registration throughout the country and contained a supplementary triggering device which caught three counties in New York City and parts of Wyoming, California, and Arizona. Citing the progress made during the previous five years—close to one million new black registrants and more than 400 black elected officials in the South—the chief executive justified an extension of the legislation as evidence that "The American system works." The figures displaying the impressive rise in black voter registration, he asserted, "stand as an answer to those who claim that there is no response except to the streets."[131]

Nixon's decision to sign the 1970 bill appealed to a wide spectrum of opinion. The *New Pittsburgh Courier* stated: "Nothing Mr. Nixon has done since his advent to the White House is as reassuring to black citizens."[132] Although Dixie legislators lost the fight, they appreciated the administration's efforts, and slight success, in getting "the South out from under this sectional application."[133] As a result of Nixon's policies the GOP made some inroads with the white electorate in the South, while elsewhere Republicans could defend their record to black voters.

The president gained some praise for his action on the suffrage measure, but the civil rights coalition deserved even more credit. Initially wrong in thinking that abolition of literacy tests nationally could jeopardize the bill, they came around to supporting it. Once they reversed their tactical position against accepting alterations of the existing statute, they succeeded, over the president's protest, in extending the ballot to eighteen-year-olds. Furthermore, the liberals were correct in opposing amendments dealing with the coverage formula and preclearance that might seriously weaken the vital enforcement provisions of the 1965 act. Only five years had elapsed since enactment of the original law, and although considerable progress had been achieved, the right of blacks to vote was still not firmly established in many sections of the South. Whatever merit the creation of a national suffrage policy had would be diminished if its implementation eroded the new-found freedom of black southerners to cast their ballots. Given the long history of racial disfranchisement in the region, the reformers were justifiably concerned that it was premature to reward southern officials for good performance.

In the end, the White House practitioners of the southern strategy failed to convince Congress that it was politically or morally correct to abandon the current suffrage law. On the books for five years, the Voting Rights Act had become a valuable component of the American creed. At a time of upheaval, its revised version held out one last chance to disaffected blacks and to the young to renew their faith in the democratic process. If continuation of the popular legislation spoke to the present and the future, it also maintained an enduring link to the past.[134] The 1965 act of enfranchisement had become part of the status quo, hindering those like Richard Nixon who attempted to reverse this now entrenched policy.

6.

The Battle
Over Guidelines

During the debate on the voting rights extension bill, Senator James Allen of Alabama had appealed for a cessation of sectional hostilities. "The question," he posed, "is whether or not there remains justification in law or in fact for a continuation of Reconstruction II, and more specifically that phase of it which relates to Federal supervision of voting."[1] Congress replied by maintaining the full force of the act in the South, and a reluctant Richard Nixon acquiesced. Nevertheless, the question remained whether the law would languish on the books, as similar measures had in the years after the Civil War, because Washington failed to enforce them effectively, ultimately allowing southern whites to rescind black enfranchisement. A century later, the Nixon administration prepared to follow a course that likewise jeopardized voting rights.

When the Republicans came to power in 1969, one stage in safeguarding the black suffrage virtually had come to an end. During the Johnson era, the Justice Department had concentrated on removing barriers to registration and on providing southern blacks with an opportunity to get on the voter lists. The suspension of literacy tests, the demise of the poll tax, and the selective appointment of federal examiners all contributed to doubling the proportion of adult blacks eligible to vote in the covered states from 30 percent in 1964 to 60 percent five years later. In addition, as more blacks qualified for the franchise, the Justice Department assigned observers to check whether they were allowed to cast their ballots freely and to have them counted fairly on election day. Although black enrollment still lagged considerably behind that of whites, the Johnson regime believed that it had gone as far as it could to destroy the legal obstacles to voter registration. The department continued to monitor the scattered pockets of resistance that remained, but its lawyers expected private groups to mount the drives necessary to encourage blacks to enroll and to close the registration gap between the races. According to a Civil Rights Division staff member, "both by means of federal registration efforts and by the impetus that federal registration had given to local registrars to go ahead and register people," the agency viewed its main task as "substantially complete."[2]

During this same period, the Johnson administration had allocated limited resources to enforcing the preclearance provisions of section five. The Department of Justice received few submissions of changes in voting laws, although southern officials were quietly revising their electoral codes. Rather than restricting voter registration, they aimed their modifications at diluting the strength of black ballots. Section five had not spelled out the types of changes that required prior clearance; however, civil rights attorneys believed that the provision not only covered biased registration devices but also a broad range of practices that discriminated against black political participation. Until 1969, the federal government had initiated only a single lawsuit to explore the scope of section five. In 1966, the Justice Department challenged an Alabama statute which extended the terms of Bullock County commissioners from four to six years, thereby canceling the election scheduled for that year. This change, made in the wake of increasing black enrollment in a county where whites were outnumbered two to one, had not been cleared in advance with Washington. Consequently, a federal district court panel in the Fifth Circuit found the Alabama law in violation of section five which, it held, pertained to any kind of suffrage practice.[3]

Despite this victory, the federal government did not place a high priority on enforcement of section five, and private civil rights attorneys took the initiative in pressing litigation. For example, the National Democratic Party of Alabama contested the state's Garrett Act passed without Washington's sanction in 1967, which hampered independent candidates from getting on the ballot in general elections. In 1968, a local election official in Greene County refused to place the names of NDPA nominees on the November ballot because they had failed to meet the deadline for qualifying to run as stipulated in the recently enacted state statute. Taking its case to the federal district court, the NDPA lost its bid to obtain certification of its candidates. However, shortly before the election, the Supreme Court reversed the lower tribunal and issued a decree ordering a spot on the ballot for all NDPA candidates throughout the state. Only Greene County officials stubbornly refused, and following the election, the party again appealed to the Supreme Court to invalidate the local contest and to call a new election. The NDPA contended that its exclusion on the basis of the Garrett Act was improper because the law had not been cleared with the federal government before going into effect, as required by the Voting Rights Act.[4]

In the meantime, civil rights lawyers in Mississippi and Virginia had instituted legal proceedings with far-reaching implications for the execution of section five. Like the two Alabama cases, these suits concerned not a denial of the right to register and vote; rather, they dealt with attempts to restrict blacks from running for public office. Civil rights attorneys argued for a broad interpretation of section five, and in the waning days of the Johnson administration they were joined in their effort by the Justice Department. The suffragists reasoned that electoral changes diluting the strength of black ballots fell within the purview of the Voting Rights Act. Rebuffed in the lower courts, they received a favorable ruling from the Supreme Court in early March 1969. In the *Allen* case, a majority of seven held that section five was expansive enough to encompass rules relating to the qualifications of candidates, the switch from elective to appointive offices, and the conversion to at-large from single-member district elections. Besides giving a liberal interpretation to the practices covered by section five, the Court affirmed the right of private citizens, and not exclusively the Justice Department, to seek judicial enforcement of the preclearance provision.[5] However, the high bench refused a request to set aside the disputed elections because in this instance "the state enactments were not so clearly subject to section five that the appellees' failure to submit them for approval constituted deliberate defiance of the Act."[6] Nevertheless, three weeks later the Court did order new elections for Greene County, finding that local officials had flagrantly ignored its previous decree to place black candidates on the ballot.[7]

These judicial rulings marked a turning point in the implementation of the Voting Rights Act. They gave Justice Department lawyers who viewed their efforts in the field of voter registration as nearly finished a fresh opportunity to pursue a promising avenue of suffrage enforcement. The Court furnished a weapon for demolishing a second generation of electoral barricades—those that diluted the impact of the ballot once blacks had registered to vote. Whether Congress in 1965 had foreseen the kinds of procedural regulations that the high tribunal now declared subject to section five's jurisdiction was debatable. Clearly, the lawmakers had concentrated on preventing the South from replacing literacy tests with other devices curtailing black voter registration. Still, the legislators surely did not intend to dismantle discriminatory obstacles to enrollment only to allow southern officials to invent ways of rendering ineffective the votes of the recently enfranchised. To the framers of the statute, extension of the suffrage was the prerequisite for black advancement. Whatever their specific purpose in adopting the preclearance provision, the lawmakers understood that the ballot would have little value if blacks were not given a fair chance to make it count. Nicholas Katzenbach, the attorney general who played a leading role in shaping the original measure, later recalled: "When we drafted this legislation, we recognized that increased black voting strength might encourage a shift in tactics of discrimination. Once significant numbers of blacks could vote, communities could still throw up obstacles to discourage those voters or make it difficult for a black to win elective office."[8] By restructuring the voting process to nullify some of the effects of enfranchisement, white southerners violated the spirit, if not the letter, of the 1965 law. So the Court affirmed in *Allen,* and Congress subsequently endorsed this view in retaining section five in the 1970 extension of the statute.[9]

The judiciary had conferred on the federal government

an extraordinary remedy in section five, but it remained for the executive branch to determine how vigorously to use it. Before 1969, most of the relatively small number of submissions had been made to and approved by the attorney general rather than to the United States District Court in Washington, and this provided the pattern for the future. The covered areas preferred to deal with the Justice Department because there was less cost and time involved than in proceeding with litigation. Mailing one's submission to the attorney general was considerably less expensive than traveling to the nation's capital to present a suit before the federal judiciary. The district court in Washington was one of the most liberal in the nation and could be expected to guard vigilantly against threats to enfranchisement. Moreover, after 1969, southern politicos anticipated a better reception from John Mitchell's Justice Department.[10]

Nixon's attorney general wanted to cooperate, but he ran into problems with Congress and within his own department. The lawmakers had rejected Mitchell's attempt to eliminate section five altogether, leaving the attorney general with the obligation of enforcing the provision in light of *Allen*. Immediately following this ruling, a CRD attorney advised Jerris Leonard, the head of the division, that "our enforcement responsibilities under the Voting Rights Act compel us to make sure that no further elections are held in the covered jurisdictions pursuant to any unapproved new election procedures."[11] This opinion also prevailed among other career lawyers in the CRD, many of whom had served in the previous administration. During the first year of Nixon's presidency, most of the division's legal staff had complained about the direction of civil rights policy, especially concerning relaxation in enforcement of school desegregation in Mississippi. In the midst of this internal dissension, in September 1969 Mitchell and Leonard reorganized the CRD to "provide a more specialized and efficient method of enforcing civil rights statutes." In the past, the division had assigned personnel according to geographical regions and had handled a broad range of racial matters for designated areas. The Republican policymakers replaced this arrangement with one in which staff addressed specific issues throughout the nation. Hence, they created a Voting Rights Section and furnished an unforeseen opportunity for disgruntled attorneys to move into it. The government's suffrage lawyers soon seized the chance to enforce section five and in the process developed an expertise in recognizing various sophisticated forms of franchise discrimination. Thus, the departmental reorganization had the unanticipated consequence of producing an experienced team of attorneys dedicated to furthering compliance with section five.[12]

Unlike the cadre of CRD lawyers who sought to utilize section five as a potent instrument for blocking subtle discrimination, Nixon's top advisors wished to rein in federal interference. The *Allen* ruling and the congressional revival of the Voting Rights Act narrowed their options. Stuck with a far-ranging preclearance provision, they looked for a way of lightening the burden on their white allies in the southern states. The pressure on the Nixon administration rose as Justice Department bureaucrats pushed for compliance with section five. Following *Allen,* the CRD staff communicated with the covered jurisdictions and explained their obligations for clearing electoral changes with Washington. Within a year and a half, the number of submissions had risen to nearly 400, more than double the figure for the entire period the act had been in effect during the Johnson years.[13] The increase reflected the growing activity among white southerners as they fashioned procedures to turn back threats to their political power posed by an expanded black electorate. Having lost the battle over the Voting Rights Act in 1970, southern officials looked to the Republican regime to regain lost ground.

Events in Mississippi furnished the Nixon administration with an opportunity to signal their support for such activities. On April 6, 1970, the state legislature passed an open primary law that handicapped third party candidates. The law that it replaced mandated a runoff in a party primary if no candidate received a majority vote. In the general election, however, a contestant could win by a plurality. Under this system, a black independent candidate who received the bulk of Negro votes might pull out a victory if whites split their ballots evenly between the regular party nominees. Though unsuccessful, Charles Evers' bid for Congress in 1968 had put a scare into state lawmakers. Subsequently, Magnolia State politicos abolished party primaries and required all candidates to compete in an open, preferential contest. If no one received a majority, a second election was slated between the top two contenders. Couched as a reform to guarantee majority rule, the law had overtones of racial bias against the state's newly enfranchised black minority. Hodding Carter's *Delta Democrat-Times,* one of the leading voices of white liberalism in Mississippi, reported on the legislative deliberations leading to passage of the measure: "Backers of the open primary bill made it clear it was aimed at preventing possible election of a minority candidate through bloc voting of increased Negro voter registration."[14]

However, the Justice Department failed to discern the racial implications in the Open Primary Law. On July 23, the attorney general officially received the measure for his scrutiny, and under section five he had sixty days to respond. For nearly two months, the department investigated the circumstances surrounding enactment of the legislation. Mississippi authorities claimed that "legitimate political and economic factors" had guided their decision, while local civil rights leaders charged that there was an obvious racial motive behind the statute. Unable to resolve the conflict by the required deadline, the attorney general chose not to file an objection to the Mississippi law. On September 21, Jerris Leonard wrote the state attorney general that "the facts presently available to us do not conclusively establish that the present acts are affected with a racial purpose or that there is no other compelling reason for the State to have adopted them." Hence, Leonard was unable to conclude that "the projected effect would be to deprive Negro voters of rights under the Voting Rights Act."[15]

The Justice Department's response had enormous implications, and the decision did not go unchallenged. Howard Glickstein, the staff director of the United States Commission on Civil Rights, insisted that Mitchell had failed to interpret properly his responsibility in reviewing section five submissions. Glickstein informed the Nixon administration's chief legal officer that the law "places the burden on the State to prove that a statute or practice is not discriminatory, rather than placing it on those claiming discrimination, as had previously been the case." He scolded the Justice Department for assuming that it "must show affirmatively that the legislation under consideration is discriminatory."[16] Instead of clearing the law because he could not reach a definitive conclusion during the sixty-day time limit, Mitchell should have objected to it until Mississippi representatives convinced him of its legality. Labeling Glickstein's analysis "a gross oversimplification," Jerris Leonard answered that the department had fulfilled its obligation in a careful and thorough manner. He denied that the attorney general must "enter objections to the submitted laws of sovereign states unless he is persuaded that there is a prohibited racial purpose or effect."[17] In other words, Leonard suggested that if the Justice Department could not absolutely prove an ordinance invalid, it should rule in the state or local government's favor. However, Glickstein believed that if the department continued to enforce section five as Leonard outlined, it would result in "the *de facto* repeal" of that provision. "You appear," the CCR director lectured the assistant attorney general, "to be following procedures which impose on the Department of Justice the obligations which belong to the submitting jurisdictions."[18]

To the dismay of the suffragists, Justice Department policymakers refused to change their position. In declining to disallow the Mississippi Open Primary Law, the attorney general and his key civil rights aide were establishing a pattern of enforcement that shifted the burden of proof in the review of election measures from local authorities to Washington. This realignment of responsibility came at a time when the covered areas were engaged in reapportionment, redistricting, and in the case of Mississippi, reregistration schemes, thereby placing black southerners at a disadvantage in retaining and in possibly extending their political power. In 1970, most of the counties in the Magnolia State were redrawing their district lines as a result of population changes throughout the previous decade. Although governmental units had an obligation to act in conformity with the Supreme Court's "one person, one vote" mandate, they might turn the legal necessity of reapportionment into an opportunity for racial gerrymandering. In the guise of neutrality, states and localities might manipulate political boundaries in a manner that fragmented the black population and reduced their potential strength in choosing representatives of their own race.[19]

Required to clear electoral changes of this type, southern officials found a sympathetic arbiter in the Republican Justice Department.[20] Actually, Assistant Attorney General Leonard did not want to resolve complicated questions concerning reapportionment, preferring instead to have these matters adjudicated in the federal district court in Washington, D.C. However, he could not escape his duties under section five, because the covered areas chose to send their submissions to the Justice Department. Reluctant to become involved in such matters, he gave the benefit of the doubt to local authorities. In October 1970 Leonard informed Copiah County, Mississippi, officials, whose redistricting request he was considering, that the issue "involves a determination of purpose and statistical analysis that is extremely complex . . . and we do not have these resources available in passing on these matters in 60 days." The CRD chief, as he had in the open primary case, viewed the preclearance provision in a narrow fashion. "It is my judgment," he declared, "that Congress did not intend for the Attorney General to object to reapportionment plans . . . unless there is convincing evidence of racial purpose or effect."[21] Once again, Leonard concluded that the Justice Department and not the affected jurisdictions shouldered the burden of demonstrating that submissions were not tainted by discrimination.

The test of how Congress expected the attorney general to discharge his section five duties revolved around reregistration in Mississippi. As part of their redistricting efforts, approximately thirty of the state's eighty-two counties also wiped clean their suffrage lists and required a fresh enrollment. Mississippi Attorney General A. F. Summer explained that reregistration was necessary because "if you redistrict . . . you have to get the voters over into that district in some fashion." Besides, in some places, he asserted, "you find the [registration] books are in such a mess or have become so burdensome over a long period of years."[22] Furthermore, he pointed out, most of the twenty-one counties behind the Magnolia Curtain that contained a black voting-age population majority did not call for reregistration. Had racial disfranchisement been the main goal, counties with a high percentage of blacks would have been more likely to undertake reenrollment; but such was not the case, he maintained.[23]

However, civil rights watchdogs spied an element of bias in this procedure. They questioned why the counties had ordered reregistration when state law allowed them to make a simple administrative transfer of the names on the polling lists from one district to another. Suffragists complained that recently enfranchised black Mississippians would suffer adversely given their history and background; therefore, reregistration was discriminatory *"per se."* Howard Glickstein summed up this viewpoint: "These are people who never had registered to vote in their lives and whose parents and grandparents were never permitted to register. Participation in the political process is entirely new to this population. Reregistration provides too many opportunities to lose large numbers of this population from the voting rolls because of intimidation, confusion, or lack of knowledge about the necessity of reregistration."[24]

The Justice Department did not agree. Its leaders, like those of the Johnson administration, considered most local officials to be people of good will and favored relying on them to comply voluntarily with the 1965 act. They were not bothered by the fact that only one of thirty counties had submitted its plan for clearance prior to conducting reregistration; apparently, they were satisfied that the remaining counties complied in good faith once the omission was brought to their attention. David Norman, who succeeded Jerris Leonard as head of the CRD in mid-1971, disputed the contention that reregistration was inherently unequal for blacks in Mississippi. "I think if [it] is done in a fair, nondiscriminatory way in which everybody gets back on gets to vote, it is not a violation of section 5 or the 15th amendment."[25] To ensure that reregistration did not interfere with continued black enfranchisement, the Justice Department insisted that local officials make "affirmative efforts" to give Negroes "a fair opportunity to requalify." They might fulfill this responsibility by widely publicizing their enrollment procedures, by appearing at old precinct polling places to sign up all those unable to register at the courthouse, by staying open for business during some evenings and on Saturday, and by retaining the names of the thousands of individuals who originally had registered with federal examiners.[26] Subsequently, the CRD nullified reregistration in only one county for failing to satisfy these requirements, and given its precautions, the department concluded that the process had not resulted in a diminished level of black enrollment in the state.[27]

Nevertheless, the Nixon administration's assurances did not comfort civil rights supporters. In this instance, reregistration may not have operated substantially to disfranchise blacks, but the premise behind the Justice Department's sanctioning of it disturbed the suffragists. They doubted whether the attorney general was sensitive enough to recognize the kinds of electoral changes that impeded, however subtly, black political participation. Noting the Justice Department's recent performance in Mississippi, Congressman Don Edwards, a liberal Democrat from California, wondered whether the attorney general was "attempting to accomplish by administrative action in 1971 what he failed to accomplish in 1970 by legislative action."[28]

Indeed, rebuked by Congress over the renewal of the Voting Rights Act, the Nixon regime planned to achieve its political goals in another way. Drawing upon its experiences in reviewing suffrage submissions from Mississippi, the Civil Rights Division prepared guidelines for implementing section five. In February 1971 the department passed around a blueprint for preclearance that proposed to transfer the burden of proof in the inspection of franchise codes from local jurisdictions to the federal government.[29]

The bipartisan civil rights coalition that had been successful in 1970 once again mobilized its forces to block this latest ploy to weaken the Voting Rights Act. Led by Senators Philip Hart and Hugh Scott, the suffragists opened negotiations with the Justice Department in an effort to revise the suggested guidelines. In early March, Hart, Scott, and Jacob Javits of New York met privately with David Norman of the CRD, and they all agreed to pursue the same objective: "fair and efficient processing of submissions to the Attorney General, while guarding against any evisceration of the statutory scheme of Section 5." The lawmakers criticized the approach the department had followed in arriving at decisions concerning preclearance. They asserted that if the attorney general found himself unable to conclude within the requisite sixty-day period whether an electoral submission had a discriminatory purpose or effect, as in the open primary situation, then he should not approve it. The liberal triumvirate wanted a regulation calling for an objection unless the covered areas demonstrated that proposed changes were not racially biased. The administration took the opposite stand, and Norman reiterated that the attorney general would disallow laws only when he clearly felt they had a discriminatory purpose or effect. He rejected "any reading of Section 5 which included a presumption against validity of the local enactment."[30] The senators left the meeting convinced of the national government's reluctance to apply the full force of the preclearance provision.

The Civil Rights Commission fueled their skepticism. This federal agency had clashed with the Justice Department several times in the past decade, especially over enforcement of the suffrage. During the Eisenhower, Kennedy, and Johnson years, the CCR faulted Justice for functioning with excessive caution, but it did not question its commitment to the franchise; however, on this occasion, the commission accused the Nixon administration of taking a step backward—"*de facto* repeal of . . . Section 5." The different viewpoints of the two agencies appeared to involve a splitting of legal hairs in the interpretation of the preclearance clause of the Voting Rights Act. CCR officials understood the language of the provision to mean that "if the Attorney General is *not* persuaded that the submitted law does *not* have a prohibited racial purpose or effect, then he must enter an objection," whereas they claimed that the Justice Department "takes the position that if the Attorney General is not persuaded that the submitted law *does* have a prohibited racial purpose or effect, then he cannot enter an objection." Thus suffragists did not want the benefit of the doubt to go to local officials. This dispute concerned more than semantics; it was a fundamental difference in perspective. Howard Glickstein, who had been a member of the Civil Rights Division during the drafting of the Voting Rights Act, rephrased the issue simply: "The burden of proof must be on the submitting jurisdiction. If it cannot con-

vince the Attorney General of the innocent purpose of its enactments, the Attorney General must interpose an objection." In such
a situation, he argued, the framers of the 1965 measure obliged a
locality to assume responsibility for filing a lawsuit in the federal
district court in Washington, D.C., to win approval of its electoral changes.[31]

Reinforced by the commission, the civil rights coalition
pressed its case with the Justice Department. The liberal legislators plotted a strategy designed to keep their protests bipartisan
and to minimize publicity. They persuaded fourteen GOP senators to send letters to the attorney general voicing their objection
to the proposed guidelines, and they also advised Democrats to
quietly dispatch similar complaints. Additional support came from
the Congressional Black Caucus, the LCCR, organized labor, and
reform-minded attorneys, all of whom privately informed the
Justice Department of their opposition to the suggested section
five criteria.[32] At the same time, Senators Hart, Scott, and Javits
met again privately with David Norman. They hoped to resolve
the problem amicably but were ready "if necessary, to make another Carswell situation out of this . . . with the same broad-
based public outcry from bar groups, law schools, civil rights
groups, and probing members of the media." If the Justice Department did not retreat, the bipartisan suffragists intended to
charge Nixon with selling out black voters in the South by
"sneaking behind Congress's back less than a year after they told
him not to do what he is attempting administratively."[33] An aide
to Minority Whip Robert Griffin of Michigan advised the senator: "There is concern that, if the proposed regulation is not re-
scinded, it will be a political liability for Northern Republicans."[34] With a presidential election approaching in 1972, the
Republican regime had to decide whether to follow a course that
led to new recruits among white southerners at the expense of
established GOP lawmakers from civil rights constituencies in the
North.

Wherever the political instincts of the chief executive
might have taken him, legal constraints soon limited his choices.
On April 27, a federal district court panel in Jackson, Mississippi,
ruled that John Mitchell had acted improperly in allowing the Open

Primary Law. A group of plaintiffs headed by Charles Evers, an independent candidate for governor in 1971, contended that the attorney general had failed to decide within the sixty-day period stipulated under section five whether the submitted law had "the purpose or effect of denying or abridging the right to vote on account of race." Unable to reach a conclusion within the statutory time frame, the Justice Department had declined to object. The litigants sought an injunction to block the open primary from going into effect until the attorney general specifically approved or disapproved of it. The federal tribunal concurred, albeit in a curious manner. After asserting that section five was unconstitutional, the three judges acknowledged that they were bound to follow Supreme Court precedents to the contrary. "The problem for Mississippi in the case at bar," the judges noted tersely

is that having done what Congress humbled her to do, she did not receive a letter of approval, or a disapproval or a mere failure to interpose an objection within the statutory time. Rather, she received a lengthy, Pilate-like response in which the Attorney General recognized he had the very duty we declare the statute imposed upon him, bemoaned Congress's failure to accept his predecessor's suggestion to leave the matter to the courts, declared that he was not prepared to make the determinations required by the act, but made no literal objection.

Given this "patronizing failure" of the federal official, the court declared the open primary measure "in a state of suspended animation" and issued an injunction against its implementation. Furthermore, the ruling held that when a state presented a law to the Justice Department for clearance, it had to bear the same affirmative burden of proof as if it took the other route and submitted the plan to the District of Columbia court.[35]

In framing its opinion, the federal panel drew upon a recent Supreme Court pronouncement that had further enlarged the scope of section five. A few months earlier on January 14, the high tribunal had disposed of still another Mississippi case. The city of Canton, the scene of bloody civil rights battles during the 1960s, had conducted an election in 1969 without first clearing a series of newly adopted suffrage regulations with Washington. The changes involved the relocation of polling places, an expansion of municipal boundaries through annexation of adjacent areas that increased the number of eligible white voters, and a transfer from ward to at-large election of aldermen. The lower court held that these measures did not have the discriminatory purpose or effect of infringing upon black voting rights, but the high bench reversed this ruling on the ground that only the attorney general or the district court in Washington was authorized to make such a substantive determination. The federal court in Mississippi should merely have decided whether the state requirements were covered by section five. To this end, the Supreme Court found that each of the changes constituted a "standard, practice, or procedure with respect to voting" subject to the preclearance clause of the Voting Rights Act. With respect to the annexations, the Court read the language of the statute in a broad manner. "Section 5," Justice William Brennan wrote for the majority of seven, "was designed to cover changes having a potential for racial discrimination in voting," and such potential "inheres in a change in the composition of the electorate affected by the annexation."[36] Nevertheless, the justices declined to annul the elections conducted under the unsubmitted regulations; instead, they remanded the question for resolution to the district court in Mississippi which "is more familiar with the nuances of the local situation."[37]

In light of these judicial proclamations, the Nixon administration wavered concerning adoption of its pending guidelines. While behind the scenes negotiations with Senators Hart, Scott, and Javits progressed, Representative Don Edwards, who chaired the House Judiciary Subcommittee on Civil Rights, was preparing to convene public hearings on the enforcement of the Voting Rights Act by Mitchell's Justice Department. In tandem with quiet bargaining, this investigation, the liberals reasoned, would exert the needed "leverage of a public forum" and would serve to help "move Justice off its lethargy."[38] The bipartisan lawmakers counted public opinion on their side because, unlike attitudes toward the divisive school busing controversy, "everyone is for letting a guy have his full power to vote."[39]

A day before the Edwards committee began its probe, the Justice Department capitulated. On May 25, the attorney general promulgated guidelines almost exactly as civil rights proponents had advocated. In reviewing submissions under section five, the Civil Rights Division pledged to adopt the same standard of proof that applied in the Federal District Court for the District of Columbia, which meant "the burden in close cases is on the submitting authorities." Thus, in complicated cases such as the Mississippi Open Primary Law, "if the evidence as to the purpose or effect of the change is conflicting, and [the attorney general] is unable to resolve the conflict within the 60-day period, he shall . . . enter an objection."[40]

Having swung the Nixon administration around on the guidelines, suffragists applied pressure to ensure that they were enforced. On May 26, the day after the Justice Department issued its specifications for implementation of section five, Don Edwards gaveled his Civil Rights Oversight Committee into order. Composed of six Democrats and five Republicans, the panel was dominated by liberals. In addition to Edwards, critics of the White House's suffrage policy included John Conyers, a black representative from Detroit, Jerome Waldie of California, and Paul Sarbanes of Maryland. In contrast, the Republican administration counted on GOP stalwarts Charles Wiggins of California and Robert McClory of Illinois for a sympathetic hearing. During the three days of deliberations, the committee aimed the public spotlight on the Justice Department and attempted to illuminate its deficiencies. The panel heard the testimony of seven witnesses, five of whom represented civil rights organizations. The remaining two were the Mississippi attorney general and a spokesman for the Nixon administration. Conspicuous by his absence was John Mitchell. The committee had invited the attorney general to appear personally; instead, he sent David Norman, the acting chief of the Civil Rights Division. Over the past several months, Edwards, a former FBI special agent, had joined his liberal colleagues in the upper chamber in complaining to the Justice Department about the proposed guidelines, but the agency had chosen to confer mainly with the senators and their staffs. Feeling slighted, Edwards reacted angrily to Mitchell's refusal to testify. The congressman was appalled "not merely because of the disregard that has been shown for the Congress, but because of the apparent insensitivity that the Nation's chief law enforcement officer has shown to violation of the law affecting black and brown citizens."[41]

This charge drew an emphatic denial from Mitchell's stand-in. Norman revealed to the committee that his boss left enforcement of the law to the CRD because he "knows we are enforcing the law vigorously and he approved it."[42] Asked by Representative Waldie to compare the aggressiveness of enforcement by the current Justice Department with that of its Democratic predecessor, Norman, who had also served during the Johnson presidency, replied: "I think it is the same."[43] Like his forerunners in charge of the Civil Rights Division, Norman toed a line close to the boundaries of the federal system. Believing in the possibility of dealing with southern officials as reasonable individuals, he "implemented the law by voluntary agreements reached by the parties, because once they make these agreements you have a much better chance locally of their being carried out."[44] Although this approach did not exclude the possibility of filing lawsuits to secure compliance, Mitchell's deputy regarded that alternative mainly as a last resort. Nevertheless, he assured the committee: "We have followed a policy of trying to get people to do what it is they are supposed to do quickly, responsibly, promptly."[45] Congressman Wiggins, the most outspoken Republican on the panel, applauded the willingness of the attorney general to deal with tough suffrage problems in an evenhanded manner. For maintaining a neutral and conciliatory position, Wiggins asserted, the Mitchell Justice Department did not deserve to be called insensitive or uncommitted to effective enforcement.[46]

One area where the Nixon administration clearly carried on the program inherited from Johnson was voter registration. For all of the striking advances in black enrollment achieved between 1965 and 1969, civil rights critics had condemned the Justice Department's cautious deployment of federal examiners in the promotion of the right to vote. Not much had changed with the Republican ascendancy to the White House. Representative Edwards asked Norman if his department had "an affirmative obligation to encourage minorities who have been discriminated against to register to vote." In a replay of the answer given by Johnson's aides, the CRD chief declared: "We do not have such programs. We do not have money to support such programs from the Congress, nor do we have a mandate from Congress to do that."[47] He left this job for private groups to undertake. Neither did he find a pressing reason to send federal examiners to the South where, after the early days, "the local registrars absolutely quit applying testing devices and procedures by which blacks were having a difficult time."[48] Edwards pointed out that counties still existed with less than one-half of eligible blacks on the voter lists, and he recommended that in these instances the Justice Department should dispatch registrars automatically. Such a suggestion had already been made and rejected during the Johnson era, and Norman also adhered to this position. He did not believe that a low percentage of black registrants constituted prima facie evidence of racial discrimination. The federal government would not intervene on the basis of a fixed numerical equation but only when local officials failed to operate an "open, public, and fair" system of registration.[49]

The continuing low rate of voter registration in some places bothered liberal lawmakers, but the Justice Department's attitude toward enrollment in Mississippi troubled them even more. John Conyers argued that reregistration plans abridged the rights of voters by removing them from the suffrage lists. After finally overcoming tremendous risks and fear, many of the newly enfranchised were being placed in the difficult position of returning to register. Challenged to explain why the attorney general had not objected routinely to these practices, Norman responded: "We have not taken that position, if re-registration is done fairly, openly, and all efforts are made to get all people back on the rolls. We have not taken the position that it is *ipso facto* discriminatory."[50] Not satisfied, Conyers and his liberal colleagues wanted to know what the CRD did to the counties that had begun reregistration without first clearing it with Washington. Once more, Norman affirmed his belief in conciliation. "If I tell them to submit, and they do," he remarked, "we have accomplished the results. If I choose instead not to tell them that but to file a paper in court, it takes up the court's time."[51] According to the de-

partment spokesman, his method ultimately had resulted in convincing nearly all the counties to submit their plans.[52]

The hearings also highlighted the disagreement between
the Nixon administration and its congressional critics over mod-
ifying procedures to enforce section five. Norman worried that
reapportionment, redistricting, and annexation plans raised complex factual problems that could not be handled satisfactorily within
the prescribed sixty-day review period, and he suggested adopting a new method to resolve difficult cases. With only half of the
calendar year gone, the number of submissions had climbed to
300, the total of all of 1970. The CRD chief wanted to set up
within the department an examiner to hear testimony from the
concerned parties, to arrive at decisions, and to make recommendations based on these findings. Although liberals thought the idea
had some merit as an administrative remedy, they rejected it for
practical reasons. The proposal would have required congressional approval, and the suffragists did not want to give their legislative opponents an opportunity to gut any portion of section
five if it were considered separately from the rest of the voting
rights law. Conyers expressed this sentiment in suggesting that
the entire preclearance provision "could get knocked out when
we try to bring it through the House of Representatives and the
Senate one more time."[53] Norman denied that the administration
was really trying to amend section five for the purpose of getting
rid of it, but the reformers listened skeptically.

Nothing they heard from the remainder of the witnesses changed their minds. Howard Glickstein opposed Norman's recommendation because it created "a very time-consuming, very dragged-out administrative procedure." Taking a leaf
from the pages of the federal district court's opinion in the Mississippi Open Primary case, the CCR staff director declared that
when complicated questions arose the attorney general should offer an objection and should allow the appropriate judicial body in
Washington to handle the matter.[54] Suffragists interpreted this step
to overhaul the preclearance mechanism as a maneuver to weaken
enforcement of the statute at a time when states were manufac-
turing artful devices to dilute enfranchisement. "I think it is fair
to say," asserted John Lewis, the former chairman of SNCC who

had become director of the VEP, "that in the minds of blacks in the South, the Federal Government is no longer seen as an advocate for equal opportunity."[55] Clarence Mitchell held up the spectre of renewed racial violence if the Justice Department reneged on its obligation to implement the 1965 measure. Unless the federal government vigorously protected the right to vote, the civil rights lobbyist warned, blacks "are going to do like we have been teaching them to do in Vietnam and every place else . . . and that is to meet force with force."[56] Armand Derfner of the Lawyers' Committee for Civil Rights Under Law, an organization of attorneys with vast experience representing southern blacks in suffrage cases, charged that the Justice Department wasted too much energy trying to obtain voluntary compliance from officials in Dixie. "Negotiations work only with those who are somewhat inclined to obey the law," Derfner remarked. "With others there will be no compliance unless there is a big stick behind the negotiations."[57]

Not surprisingly, the Edwards committee sided with the civil rights activists. Its members did not take seriously the testimony offered by the lone white southern official who attended their sessions. Admitting that racial discrimination had existed prior to passage of the Voting Rights Act, Mississippi Attorney General A. F. Summer denied that any blacks in his state had been deprived of the ballot within the past five years.[58] The oversight panel found differently. It concluded that Mississippi's reregistration practices "seriously threatened to reverse past progress." Some of the blame fell on the state for conducting reregistration in a confusing manner, leaving many of its citizens uninformed about the requirements. However, the federal government was negligent in sanctioning the cumbersome procedure. Even if most blacks eventually managed to return to the registration rolls, as the administration maintained, the Justice Department could not have known that before it cleared the changes. The congressional group believed that the department relied too heavily on mediation and conciliation when it should have presumed that reregistration was objectionable unless the submitting authorities proved conclusively that their reenrollment plans did not produce a racially discriminatory effect. Furthermore, had Justice been more vigilant, it would have discovered, as the committee did, that reregistration "imposed a much greater inconvenience on blacks than whites." The lawmakers argued that Negroes tended to live in the rural areas of the Mississippi counties under review, had to travel longer distances to the courthouse, and had more trouble getting time off to register than did the white population living in town. Besides, the committee reported, county officials could have avoided the problems associated with a new enrollment by simply transferring the names of registered voters to the appropriate districts.[59]

Based on these findings, the committee recommended that Justice adopt a tougher approach in implementing section five. It urged the department to depend less on bargaining to persuade a jurisdiction to submit an electoral change and more on seeking court orders to force compliance. Once submissions were made, the panel wanted the attorney general's staff to evaluate them from a perspective more sensitive to black enfranchisement. Not only should government lawyers consider how a measure would be administered, but they should also take into account the impact it would have on minority groups "in view of the political, sociological, economic and psychological circumstances within the community proposing the change."[60] Given the lingering effects of Jim Crow and disfranchisement, this suggestion would have greatly increased the obligation of southern officials to justify any changes in electoral laws and practices. Together with the battle over the guidelines, the deliberations of the House Oversight Subcommittee benefited southern blacks by highlighting the continuing suffrage problems they encountered and by underscoring the need for prolonged federal assistance to combat racial bias in the electoral process. From deep inside Dixie, Charles Evers acknowledged that the efforts of the liberal lawmakers "have been of critical importance . . . [in] letting those who govern Mississippi know that national attention is being focused on their acts."[61]

In his campaign for governor, Evers had an opportunity to find out how far blacks had advanced politically in the Magnolia State and how much further they had to go. His candidacy also challenged the Nixon administration to show whether it would heed the message that Congress had delivered in the recent struggles over the renewal and enforcement of the Voting Rights Act. Thus far, the Justice Department's suffrage performance had confirmed the fears black Mississippians had about the Nixon administration, especially following its failure to object to reregistration plans. Aaron Henry, the NAACP official who was running as a Democrat for the state legislature in 1971, recalled how southern blacks had pinned their hopes on sympathetic administrations dating back to Eisenhower. "But," he complained, "came Brother John Mitchell, that's all down the drain now."[62] Evers shared this feeling as he undertook his gubernatorial campaign. He started out with few illusions of victory, because blacks constituted a minority of the statewide electorate. Nevertheless, he hoped his campaign would stimulate a large black enrollment drive and voter turnout which might "with hard work and sufficient resources . . . elect a sizeable number of Negroes to local office."[63]

Elected mayor of Fayette in 1969, Charles Evers carried on the faith that liberals placed in the ballot. He had picked up the fallen banner of civil rights after his brother, Medgar, was assassinated in 1963. Despite his personal tragedy, he counseled moderation when many young blacks were losing patience with traditional electoral politics. "I think," Evers remarked, "I've done more to kill Medgar's killer by registerin' 200,000 blacks across the state, by bein' elected mayor of Fayette and by runnin' for governor than if I put a bullet through him."[64] As a symbol of black enfranchisement and a charismatic figure in his own right, the black civil rights leader had succeeded in attracting outside financial support for improving the quality of life in his town of 1,600 people, located in the fourth poorest county in the United States. Suffragists considered Fayette as a showcase for the improvements that black ballots could bring through impartial law enforcement, low-cost health care, paved streets, regular sanitation services, and the creation of new jobs. Serious problems concerning housing, education, and employment remained, but the mayor and his allies portrayed Fayette as having come "truly closer to the Promised Land."[65]

Nevertheless, Fayette's "Black Moses" faced enormous difficulties in launching a statewide challenge. Branching out from a hamlet populated by a Negro majority, he had to campaign in a political arena where white voter registration outnumbered black enrollment by around three to one.[66] One of Evers' aides noted dejectedly that much of Mississippi remained unchanged for blacks in 1971. "It was the white man's power, the white man's money, and white man's police force, the white man's racism," Jason Berry observed.[67] Although approximately 60 percent of black adults had signed up to vote and over 200 blacks were running for local office—many of them with a chance of winning in majority black counties—some of the old and several new barriers thwarted increased suffrage gains. A climate of fear still prevailed among Negroes in Mississippi. A staff member of the Voter Education Project quickly experienced it as she entered the state in the summer of Evers' campaign. "If one is black," Janet Shortt reported, "the first impression of Mississippi is that of weirdness and of mysteriously deadly deeds. Past events and atrocities come back hauntingly, and a chill can be felt in the very heart and stillness of midday, even in the Delta."[68] In Tallahatchie County, the location of the brutal murder of Emmett Till in 1955, a tenant farmer could not find time to make the trip to the courthouse to register. "I'm hooked up where I can't go this evening," he explained. "I'm expecting the boss man any minute for me."[69] Dependent on whites for their livelihood, many blacks hesitated to risk the economic consequences that might result from political participation, and others who did take a chance were subject to white manipulation at the polls. Present-day dangers bolstered the legacy of fear inherited from the past. Overt acts of terror against civil rights workers had declined markedly, but the sporadic violence that still occurred, particularly around election time, made many blacks pause before taking the bold step across the political threshold.[70] Furthermore, by 1971, those who had made this leap found themselves confronted by Mississippi officials who required reregistration and who redistricted boundary lines in a way that diluted black votes.

Despite these conditions, the situation did not appear to be totally bleak. To surmount some of the hurdles associated with reregistration, the VEP conducted a two-week tour through Mississippi in late June to encourage blacks to get their names on the voter lists again and also to sign up people for the first time. Expecting to receive rough treatment from whites who became alarmed when black political activities mounted, voter registration workers, instead, generally encountered a polite reception from local and state officials. Julian Bond, one of the leaders on this excursion, noticed the difference that had taken place in Mississippi since his days as a SNCC member in the early 1960s. "We received police escorts in town where we might once have been arrested or harassed as freedom riders, outside agitators, and troublemakers," the Georgia legislator pointed out. "In one town where several black men had been killed for first attempting to register and vote, we were welcomed by the white mayor."[71] This unaccustomed extension of southern hospitality to civil rights activists did not surprise the press secretary to John Bell Williams, governor of Mississippi. "If blacks hadn't registered," he remarked, "things wouldn't have changed one iota, but now these mayors know they'll be ex-mayors if they don't look after those votes."[72] The change in attitude was not limited to white officials; blacks also were throwing off some of the psychological shackles that had bound them in the past. After hearing Bond exhort a congregation in a Hattiesburg church to cast aside the notion that "politics was white folks' business," a black woman jumped out of the crowd and shouted: "All right, I don't want nobody sitting around now. Do something."[73] Witnessing such scenes, John Lewis commented that the " 'closed society' had begun to open its doors to the knock of the black ballot."[74]

The contrasting experiences spotlighted during the summer of Evers' campaign in Mississippi reflected both the progress and the limits of suffrage policy. On the one hand, since 1965 a majority of eligible blacks had succeeded in becoming registered voters through a combination of federal pressure and voluntary cooperation by local officials. At the same time, blacks still found equal access to the franchise obstructed by whites who engaged in subtle as well as blatant discriminatory practices. By any standard, Mississippi blacks were enjoying unparalleled political freedom compared to their situation prior to enactment of the voting rights law. Yet looking at the restrictions that remained and concerned that their potential for continued electoral gains could not be achieved without more stringent federal surveillance, black Mississippians felt uncertain about the future. Given the long and bloody history of disfranchisement, they were particularly sensitive to any relaxation in enforcement, however subtle, of the statute they had worked so hard to obtain. Impressed with recent victories, nonetheless, civil rights activists were mindful of the past and worried about how fragile their successes might be.

Meanwhile, Charles Evers was trying to step even further through the suffrage portals. The candidate of the Democratic loyalists, he decided not to compete in the regular party primary after the judiciary had invalidated the open primary law. Evers reasoned that he might survive the first contest in a field of several candidates but might lose in a runoff where the white majority would rally around the single white contender against him. Under the circumstances, recently enfranchised black voters would have to show up at the polls twice, a prospect that might be more than a little confusing for new voters with scant electoral experience. Rather, the insurgents chose to concentrate their organizational efforts on getting out the vote only once at the general election in November. Having adopted this strategy, Evers hoped that the regular Democratic nominee would be unacceptable to blacks and liberal whites, thereby providing a stark contrast to his own candidacy. He did his best to secure that outcome by favoring Jimmy Swan, the most blatantly racist of the Democratic primary contestants. Questioned about this selection "after all of the pain and hardship blacks in this state have endured," Evers replied: "This ain't civil rights no more. This is politics. An' in politics you play to win. That means goin' after your greatest threat, which is all the so-called moderates."[75] He was referring to Lieutenant Governor Charles Sullivan and William Waller. Moderates on race—Waller had diligently but unsuccessfully prosecuted the accused murderer of Evers' brother—they were considered by the Fayette mayor as "middle- o'-the-roaders" who would "have 'em a few Toms and say, 'Lookit us here in old Mississippi. We sho' nuf' changin.' "[76]

Black Democrats and their white allies generally ignored Evers' suggestion. The segregationist Swan went down to defeat, leaving Waller and Sullivan in a runoff. On this occasion,

Evers advocated a boycott of the election, equating the two moderate candidates with the same forces that had been responsible for racial oppression. In making this recommendation, Evers, who really had no chance of winning in November, disregarded a practical political consideration. If blacks rallied around the one Democratic party contender who triumphed in the general election, they might command more clout with the incoming governor. By and large, black voters again dismissed Evers' advice and participated in the contest.[77] With Evers on the sidelines, Waller captured the Democratic nomination and set the stage for a direct confrontation between him and the black mayor.

This gubernatorial campaign was unusual by Mississippi standards. Although the race issue was personified in Evers' candidacy, it was generally handled differently than in the past. Considered a moderate, Waller did not wish to espouse racism. Furthermore, while no one forgot the color of Evers' skin, to make appeals on that basis no longer seemed wise. Since 1966, blacks had risen as a portion of the total electorate from 23 to 28 percent, and the presence of this sizeable minority had a sobering effect on the customary campaign bluster of Magnolia State politicos.[78] Except for Swan, the white contenders in the field behaved wih civility and eschewed race-baiting. At the same time, Evers delivered a few speeches before integrated audiences, preaching the value of interracial cooperation in solving economic problems faced by poor whites and blacks.

Still, the "New Mississippi" exhibited traces of the old. "Help Stamp Out Black Rule," screamed an ad placed in local newspapers by the White Citizens Council, as the reactionary organization urged its followers to register and vote. Moreover, in many of the predominantly black counties, white officials badgered civil rights workers, sometimes arresting them for minor traffic violations. Tensions increased as liberal lawyers and college students from the North, many of them white, descended on Mississippi to monitor the elections and to protect the interests of black candidates.[79]

To encourage the efforts of these suffrage volunteers, civil rights leaders requested reinforcements from Washington. At the end of the VEP tour in late June, despite improvements he found,

John Lewis asked the Justice Department to help dispel "in some visible and concrete way" the climate of fear that still existed in Mississippi. He called upon Mitchell to transport federal registrars and observers into the state and to extend the July 2 cutoff date for reregistration. "Since federal registrars have not been present . . . during the reregistration process," the VEP director argued, "it is doubly important that registration be allowed to continue past the deadline, with the supervision and assistance of federal registrars."[80] This suggestion was seconded by the National Committee to Elect Charles Evers Governor of Mississippi, a group that listed among its backers Hubert Humphrey, Edward Kennedy, Joseph Rauh, John Doar, and Theodore Sorensen, a former aide to John F. Kennedy. So far that summer, two blacks, Eddie McClinton and Joetha Collier, had been killed in Tallahatchee and Sunflower Counties—areas with a long history of racial violence and where voter registration drives were taking place.[81] Though the slain blacks were not franchise workers, their murders had a chilling effect on the voter registration campaigns in the counties. Alarmed by the escalating level of violence, suffragists wanted Mitchell to furnish adequate protection for the civil rights workers.

In contrast, Mississippi officials opposed federal interference. They counseled residents of their state to behave calmly and not to provide any excuse for outside governmental intervention. Senator John Stennis pleaded with his constituents to act "in such a way as [not] to create suspicions against ourselves." In addition, he lodged "a vigorous protest" with the Justice Department against deploying a swarm of poll watchers and registrars.[82] It was not unusual for southern lawmakers to try to influence Washington policymakers in their enforcement of the Voting Rights Act. The Johnson administration had minimized the number of examiners dispatched to Georgia, the home state of Richard Russell, the powerful senator whose support it needed on national defense issues. Nixon's southern strategists were even more sensitive to the wishes of Dixie authorities. In 1969, the attorney general had approved a request by the city of Belzoni, Mississippi, to change the office of marshal from an elective to an appointive post. In doing so, he overturned the recommendation of a CRD staff lawyer against allowing the conversion, choosing instead to heed the advice of Senator James Eastland, who had lobbied in favor of the proposal.[83] In matters such as this, Assistant Attorney General Jerris Leonard informed a southern congressman: "I have done my best to lean over backwards to give the benefit of the doubt to southern states and southern communities."[84]

With respect to the 1971 Mississippi gubernatorial contest, the Justice Department carved out a halfhearted middle position. In response to requests from civil rights advocates, it dispatched federal personnel to Mississippi but did so in a restrained manner without enraging white officials. Before the November election, examiners went into only three of twenty-seven counties that had conducted reregistration. Suffragists complained that even where federal registrars set up for business, they did not function aggressively. "It was not policy," a VEP aide lamented, "to promote their presence other than by posting notices on the buildings where they operate and also in the county post offices. While there were apparently articles in newspapers outside the state, little attention was given within the state so that people could be informed as to the time, place, and procedure."[85] Neither did federal examiners venture into remote areas of the counties to enroll blacks who were unable to make the trip to the center of town. Although federal registrars signed up more than 1,300 blacks in time to participate in the general election, the limited scope of their activities added to the pressure on local civil rights groups to stimulate voter registration, a responsibility for which they lacked sufficient resources.[86]

The federal government assigned more of its available manpower to supervision of the balloting on election day. In response to requests by civil rights workers, the Justice Department sent a contingent of over six hundred observers and CRD attorneys to monitor the contests in Mississippi. The suffragists had high hopes for the 200 to 300 black candidates running for state and local offices, and they wanted Washington to guarantee a fair election.

Despite federal surveillance, the results of the elections disappointed civil rights leaders. Evers lost his gubernatorial bid by a wide margin. He received 22 percent of the ballots cast, 5 percent less than the total number of black registrants. Nor did most other black candidates fare much better than the defeated Evers. Only fifty-one blacks won at the local level, and most of them captured minor posts. Although the sole black state legislator was reelected and eight Negroes triumphed as county supervisors, whites usually swept to victory even where they were outnumbered in the population. Overall, positions of power in the counties—sheriff, chancery clerk, and superintendent of education—remained in white hands.[87]

Part of this poor showing stemmed from election irregularities perpetrated by defiant whites. Civil rights workers reported a variety of troubling incidents ranging from mistreatment of poll watchers for black candidates to intimidation of illiterate voters.[88] The pressure of federal observers had not deterred these fraudulent activities from occurring; in fact, civil rights leaders charged that federal supervision was inadequate. They found fault with the program because the designated overseers had not been instructed to challenge violations committed in their presence. Unauthorized to step in and correct abuses at the ballot boxes, the observers merely were expected to detail infractions in their reports to Washington. "All I do is write it up," one federal observer admitted about spotting a possible irregularity. "I can't make judgments, really, because I'm not familiar with Mississippi voting laws."[89]

Nevertheless, most black candidates did not have victories stolen from them. To be sure, fraud tipped the election returns on the side of whites in perhaps as many as eight counties. However, in the rest of the state, the appearance of federal agents and other outside observers helped curtail traditional practices of chicanery. The Mississippi attorney general rated the election the "fairest" in the state's history, and civil rights forces concurred. "It is our belief," the Delta Ministry reported, "that white folks have learned more about citizenship education and good politics in the last four years because they were pressed to do so by the Black challenge."[90] This was especially notable because whites had been expected to offer fierce resistance to the strongest challenge to their political hegemony since Reconstruction. Blacks did not achieve greater success for other reasons.

Some of the blame fell upon Charles Evers. With no real chance to win the governorship, Evers was supposed to use his campaign to attract interest in the candidacies of hundreds of local black officeseekers. However, as the contest progressed, the Fayette mayor may have taken his own chances too seriously. By spending much of the money he raised nationwide on his own media exposure, Evers neglected to funnel enough of the funds to black candidates running on meager budgets. Obtaining much less attention and financial support, local black contestants trailed behind Evers in securing votes even in their home territories.[91]

Yet, a good deal of the difficulty could be traced not to Evers but to the failure of blacks to form a cohesive voting bloc. Too often, black communities were torn by factionalism and personal disputes, leaving them poorly united around those candidates of their own race who might best represent their concerns. Moreover, many blacks cast their ballots for Evers but switched to white candidates on the local level or did not participate at all. Habits of dependency, both economic and psychological, died hard and caused some Negroes routinely to select a white aspirant over a black.[92] However, white Mississippians viewed this situation in a more favorable light. "Perhaps blacks have shown they believe they should vote with an eye on who they think is the best qualified candidate," a local newspaper columnist commented, "not strictly along racial lines."[93]

It was not surprising that newly enfranchised black Mississippians did not display greater electoral solidarity. Only six years earlier, less than 7 percent of black adults had managed to register to vote. Acquiring the ballot merely capped one phase of the struggle; the next stage involved developing the standard techniques of political organizing. In many instances, blacks had neither selected their candidates carefully nor campaigned for them effectively. The Delta Ministry, which analyzed the election returns painstakingly, went to the heart of the problem: "We have a Civil Rights hangover. There is too great a reliance on the tools of a past era. We can't depend on leaflets and mass meetings to get out the vote. We need a strong, well balanced organization to make sure the vote gets out . . . and it votes black."[94] To forge the ballot into an instrument of liberation, blacks had to have more than morality on their side; they had to perfect the fundamental skills of practical politics.

As they prepared to come of age politically, Mississippi blacks contended with demographic changes that worked to their disadvantage. They fell short of commanding a majority of the electorate statewide, and, more significantly, in many of the counties where Negroes predominated in absolute numbers, they did not comprise a majority of the crucial voting-age population. Grinding poverty and repression had sent young black adults scurrying northward in search of jobs and personal freedom. This migration left behind in some of the most impoverished counties a black population that had a disproportionate element of the very young and the elderly—segments of the citizenry that either could not yet register to vote or showed the least inclination to participate politically. In Panola County, blacks comprised 51 percent of the residents but only 21 percent of the total electorate. One local voter registration worker attributed this disparity to the fact that black youths "of voting age generally leave while their white counterparts remain and take over family businesses to continue exploitation and suppression of black people."[95] At the same time, whites who had much greater experience than blacks in the electoral process turned out at the ballot boxes at a much higher rate. Thus, given apathy, the legacy of fear, and economic subservience, a simple black majority was a misleading indicator of potential success at the polls. Only where the black population percentage approached two-thirds of a county did the prospects for electoral victory improve substantially.

In spite of these drawbacks, the 1971 Mississippi election generated some cause for optimism. Fifty-one Negroes triumphed, double the total in the last statewide election, which gave Mississippi the lead in the number of black officeholders in the United States. No county government came under the control of blacks, but in several areas they did win important positions as supervisors, tax assessors, and circuit clerks.[96] "Black folks ain't scared anymore," Charles Evers declared, and while on the campaign trail, he asserted in front of one of the enduring monuments of white supremacy: "We all know its *our* courthouse jus' as much as it's theirs . . . and we gotta right to meet here."[97] Only a few years earlier, blacks had stood on the political sidelines as the object of white decision-making; now, due to enfranchisement, they functioned as active participants, both as voters and as candidates, in shaping the electoral system. Although the issue of race had not disappeared entirely, the inflammatory rhetoric of the past had definitely subsided. "The trumpet blew and the walls did not come tumbling down in a heap," Hodding Carter observed, "but they were breeched in many places."[98] In the process, whites as well as blacks discarded many of the customary racial shibboleths. Noting the increased willingness of lawmakers at the state capital to address bread and butter concerns instead of dwelling on segregationist issues, William Winter, elected Mississippi's lieutenant governor in 1971, explained: "Remember, that many legislators are here by the virtue of the fact they got more black votes than somebody else did."[99]

To promote additional progress, the federal government had to supervise electoral affairs while blacks continued to organize themselves. Not all the resistance to black political advancement had cracked; rather, the form it took changed as white officials tried to alter the rules of the electoral game. The enactment of the open primary and reregistration plans in Mississippi exhibited subtle but calculated techniques to dilute the power of the ballot for the newly enfranchised. At the same time, Congress and the Supreme Court handed the Justice Department a powerful weapon, section five of the voting rights law, to combat potential problems. After a faltering start, the Nixon administration succumbed to pressure and took appropriate steps to enforce the preclearance procedure.

Until Watergate forced the president's resignation, the Justice Department took its cue from the 1970–71 franchise battles and breathed new life into section five. From 1965 to 1974, of 4,226 suffrage submissions, the attorney general interposed 166 objections, 87 percent of which came after 1970. The CRD contained a dedicated and resourceful band of attorneys who became experts in the field and were able to spot sophisticated practices designed to diminish the influence of the black electorate. Its civil rights lawyers, many of them holdovers from the previous administration, generally followed the approach initiated by Johnson's attorneys. As historian William E. Leuchtenburg astutely points out, "much of the positive activity under the Nixon Administration came not because of the enterprise of Nixon and his immediate aides, but rather from momentum developed by the federal bureaucracy, a momentum which no president could easily halt."[100] While mindful of the distinctions between Democratic and Republican regimes, John Lewis of the VEP ultimately stressed the continuity of federal suffrage enforcement: "During the Johnson Administration, we did have some people we could talk with. During the Nixon-Ford years, we just haven't had anything. But for the most part it's not a vast difference."[101]

The suffrage struggles of the early seventies settled some old issues while raising new and perplexing ones. The right to vote had been strengthened despite initial attempts by President Nixon and his political allies to weaken its enforcement. Their appetite whetted by some success at the polls, Afro-Americans plunged ahead to compete more strenuously for elected office and to increase their access to political party affairs. As a result, they asked controversial questions concerning the meaning of equal opportunity and fair representation. The federal courts and the Democratic party would lead the way in furnishing innovative, if not always successful, answers to these problems.

7.

Beyond the Ballot:
The Suffrage and
Political Representation

Since 1965, Congress and the federal judiciary had shaped the Voting Rights Act into something more than a measure to guarantee the right to vote. Initially designed to clear away procedural obstacles in the electoral process, the law conceived of voter registration and going to the polls as the cardinal features of enfranchisement. However, extension of the suffrage did not automatically confer political power. One civil rights lawyer who had participated in the drafting of the original statute compared its coverage "to a protective umbrella under which a viable black political tradition could begin to grow. This umbrella must be kept in place until the roots of black political participation are deep enough to permit blacks . . . to protect themselves through the political process."[1] Southern blacks had achieved substantial electoral gains in the years following 1965, but they were still not masters of their own political fate. Influence within both major political parties remained limited, and victories at the ballot box lagged behind expectations. As the opportunity to register and to vote became more standard, black southerners turned their attention to obtaining a greater share of representation in political affairs. In doing so, they reexamined the traditional liberal view of equal opportunity and its meaning for the emancipation of an oppressed minority group.

The acquisition of the ballot had marked the opening

phase rather than the completion of the struggle for first-class citizenship. The controversy over Black Power and the attempts of its advocates to capture control over Democratic organizations in Mississippi and Alabama not only underscored this point but initiated a sharp debate concerning the direction blacks should take in entering the electoral arena. To black activists the right to vote in the abstract meant little unless it yielded tangible results and allowed Afro-Americans to represent their own constituencies. Increasingly, registration figures no longer served as the decisive yardstick of black political advancement; instead, gains were calculated by the number of black elected officials and the material benefits they bestowed on their communities. Indeed, suffragists did not consider enfranchisement merely as the ability to participate as a voter; for them, access to political power in a variety of forms became the crucial element. As the emphasis shifted from the mechanics of casting a ballot to the rewards derived from it, black southerners sought to make their voices heard throughout the entire political selection process. This included greater influence and more control than they had previously had over nomination, campaign, and election procedures. It had taken some six decades to recapture the right to vote lost around the turn of the century. To go beyond the ballot and to obtain a fair share of power without further delay required unconventional alterations in the rules of the political game.

Southern blacks had a most favorable opportunity to increase their clout within the Democratic party. As a result of the convention challenge of the Mississippi Freedom Democrats in 1964, the party had pledged to give minorities an equal opportunity to participate in its internal affairs. This made good political sense. Ninety-four percent of black ballots were cast for Lyndon Johnson, and four years later, this figure slipped only slightly as 85 percent of the black electorate supported Hubert Humphrey. More than any other bloc in the Democratic coalition, Afro-Americans remained faithful to the party; however, they had only been partially rewarded for their loyalty. In 1964, blacks composed a mere 2 percent of the delegates at the national convention, and in 1968, they constituted around 6 percent.[2] Nevertheless, making good on its promise, the Democratic convention gathered in Chicago in 1968 approved the credentials of insurgent biracial groups from Mississippi and Georgia and ratified "six basic elements" designed to remove racial discrimination from the delegate selection process for future conventions. To implement these recommendations, the Democrats established a Commission on Party Structure and Delegate Selection.

Besieged by protest in the streets of Mayor Daley's Windy City and torn by conflict over the Vietnam War, the strife-ridden convention did not detail its standard for reform. The delegates instructed the commission to develop guidelines that provided a "full, meaningful, and timely" opportunity for all constituencies to take part in the choice of delegates.[3] The task of heeding this charge fell upon the commission's twenty-eight appointees, including three blacks. Senator George McGovern of South Dakota directed the group. A leading antiwar senator and a close ally of the late Robert Kennedy, McGovern had remained a Democratic loyalist in backing Hubert Humphrey's bid for the presidency. Thus, the choice of this liberal critic of the Vietnam War who, nevertheless, maintained ties with the party leadership boded well for the eventual acceptance of reform principles.[4]

The committee began its work in earnest in March 1969. An executive committee of ten guided the deliberations and assembled a staff to prepare a report for final consideration. Among those sitting on this influential panel was Aaron Henry, the Mississippi civil rights activist who had helped the loyalist delegation gain recognition at the recent national convention and who could be counted upon to press for sweeping reforms. Because the convention had not expressed its specific views on the delegate issue, group members could interpret the mandate broadly. Rejecting "any narrow reading" of the phrase " 'full and meaningful' opportunity to participate," the staff advised the commissioners "to set reasonable standards—in much the same way the Supreme Court uses the equal protection and due process clauses of the 14th amendment—for delegate selection."[5] At the end of September, after several months of intensely investigating the sundry delegate selection procedures in operation throughout the nation, the commission staff suggested calling upon state parties to incorporate into their rules the six antidiscrimination provisions originally drawn up by Richard Hughes' Special Equal Rights Committee and approved by the national convention in 1968. More far reaching was a proposal for state parties "to overcome the effects of past discrimination by affirmative steps to encourage minority group participation."[6]

This latter recommendation sparked a great deal of controversy when the commissioners gathered the following month to write their report. During two days of discussions on November 19 and 20, the reformers hotly debated the extent to which the party should act to reverse the remnants of past bias. By a slim margin of 10–9, the panel approved a resolution sponsored by Senator Birch Bayh of Indiana requiring "affirmative steps to encourage minority group participation, including representation of minority groups on the national convention delegation *in reasonable relationship to the group's presence in the population of the State*."[7] The narrowness of this victory reflected the concern of dissident members that the language imposed a quota, anathema to the liberal belief in equality of opportunity. Traditionally, quotas had been applied to restrict minority groups socially and economically. Acknowledging that in the past race had constituted a rationale for exclusion, critics argued against its becoming a justification for present inclusion. They maintained that after obtaining the ballot, blacks should compete for partisan positions on an equal and not on a guaranteed basis. To diminish the stigma attached to proportional representation, the body unanimously amended the Bayh plan to include its "understanding . . . that this is not to be accomplished by the mandatory imposition of quotas." Thus, affirmative action did not call for proportional representation, explained LeRoy Collins, former governor of Florida, but only demanded that "a reasonable effort be made to secure better representation."[8]

However, the distinction between attempts to promote "reasonable representation" and the "imposition of quotas" remained fuzzy. How to achieve acceptable representation without devising some formula as a standard for measuring it was not fully explained when the McGovern commission issued its *Mandate for Reform* in 1970. The report drew a fine line between preferential treatment for blacks and affirmative action. According to Chairman McGovern, the failure of a state party to increase the representation of minorities in relation to their percentage of the population "would shift the burden of proof to the state party." If challenged at a convention, party regulars would "have to show that despite the composition of the delegates [they] had acted affirmatively to secure better representation."[9] McGovern rejected guaranteed representation, for his remarks indicated that a state technically could comply and could still field a disproportionately low share of black delegates. This assurance notwithstanding, in practice the Democrats interpreted the commission's guidelines as establishing a de facto quota, and in judging the performance of local party officials, they took into account whether the contingent of Negroes among the delegates approximated the black proportion of the state population. Harold Hughes, the liberal governor of Iowa and vice chairman of the McGovern commission, spoke candidly about the approach: "No matter what we call what we have done and say it isn't a quota system, in essence it does say we have to recognize certain standards that mean something that I would call a quota."[10] Moreover, in carrying out the guidelines, Donald Fraser, the Minnesota congressman who replaced McGovern as chair of the commission in 1971, and Lawrence O'Brien, who headed the Democratic National Committee, did not dispute Hughes' interpretation. They urged state delegations to encourage representation of Afro-Americans in accordance with their portion of the population.

The implementation of this version of affirmative action produced impressive results. In four years, the percentage of black representatives attending the national convention more than doubled, jumping from 6.7 to 14.6. At the 1972 convocation in Miami Beach, the delegations from the South contained the highest ratio of blacks, and all but one of these were states blanketed by the Voting Rights Act. Mississippi led the way with 56 percent, followed by Louisiana (43.2), South Carolina (34.4), Tennessee (32.7), Georgia (30.1), Virginia (28.3), and North Carolina (20.3). Although a quota based on population percentages had not been set officially by the reform commission, in five of these states the ratio of black delegates exceeded the proportion of Negroes in the population, and in a sixth, South Carolina, the figure was about the same. However, in one important sense, blacks still had not achieved proportional representation. They had cast over 85 percent of their ballots for the Democratic presidential tickets in the two previous elections, constituting a much higher share of party support than their proportion in the total population. Yet no other national convention had opened its doors so widely to participation by blacks and other traditionally underrepresented groups such as woman and youths. "I never thought I'd see the day," a delegate from Arizona jibed, "that middle-aged, white males would be our biggest minority." [11]

The impetus for reform that had begun with the Mississippi Freedom Democratic challenge in 1964 culminated in the seating of an interracial loyalist delegation from the Magnolia State in 1972. This triumph was not without serious consequences. The crusading fervor and moralistic passion of the original band of insurgents was replaced by the hard-nosed realism and conventional wisdom of practical politicians. Gone were the SNCC legions and radical sectors of the FDP which had been instrumental in orchestrating the pioneering challenge. Supplanting them were leaders of the more moderate NAACP and influential white liberals. Although Aaron Henry, a prime force behind the 1964 FDP protest, chaired the successful loyalist group, only two other Freedom Democrats accompanied him to Miami Beach. One of them, Fannie Lou Hamer, whose commitment to militancy continued unabated, "felt disgusted because the people they had pulled in with the Loyal Democrats didn't know what suffering is and don't know what politics is about." [12] In fact, the seating of the loyalists marked a victory for Henry's biracial coalition over not only the predominantly white regulars but also Hamer's black power advocates.

During the previous four years, Henry and his allies had carefully laid the groundwork for structuring the delegation and for obtaining recognition as official state representatives to the national convention. Having won the allotted seats at the 1968 convention, the loyalists then reorganized the state party machinery along liberal lines. As a member of the McGovern commission and a Democratic national committeeman, Henry helped draw up and oversee the controversial antidiscrimination guidelines. His colleagues on the reform panel cheered on the Clarksdale drugg-ist. Congressman Don Fraser wrote him: "I want you to know that I support your state party's efforts to bring true democracy to Mississippi."[13] The loyalists established a fifteen-person exec-utive committee run by Henry, his NAACP associates, and such prominent liberal whites as Hodding Carter. Excluded from power, in March 1969 the FDP splintered off and "sever[ed] all ties with any political organization" in the state.[14] By this time the withdrawal of SNCC personnel and a shortage of funds had severely hampered the Freedom Democrats, and, except in a few counties in the Delta, they failed to compete successfully at the polls.

More formidable as rivals for possession of the party standard were the regular Democrats. Although denied seating at the national convention in 1968, they still operated the Demo-cratic machinery on the state level. No longer entitled to receive the official call to attend national convocations or to elect na-tional officers, the regulars ran under their banner all the success-ful candidates elected on a statewide basis. In addition, they counted among their ranks the members of the congressional delegation. Representative Charles H. Griffin, who had defeated Charles Ev-ers in 1968, explained the confused situation: "The National Democratic Party . . . is a confederation of state parties. All laws pertaining to party primaries are state laws. I follow state laws."[15] Furthermore, as long as regular Democrats occupied every seat in Mississippi's congressional delegation, the influence of the loy-alists was diminished. "The only protection Mississippi citizens have against extremists being given patronage," Griffin argued, "is the presence of Democratic Senators and Congressmen."[16] Besides, the loyalists had little appeal to Magnolia State voters outside of black communities. Their problem, as one knowl-edgeable observer wrote, was that they were "a name in search of a massive following."[17]

Well aware of their weaknesses, the loyalists decided to attack one of the important levers of power held by the regulars. In January 1971, Aaron Henry petitioned the Democratic caucus in the House of Representatives to "consider a motion challeng-ing the right of the five Mississippi members to be treated as

Democrats and given the seniority privileges of Democrats." Accusing his rivals of running a "lily-white" organization, Henry contended that on this issue "there can be only one decision—politically, ideologically and morally." Either the caucus could choose to support his group "recognized by the national party and loyal to the principles of that party or it can stand with . . . seniority for segregationist Congressmen who are determined, as always, to wreck the national party's programs."[18] In spite of Henry's appeal, congressional Democrats voted by a two to one majority on the side of tradition to retain the seniority rights of their duly elected Mississippi colleagues.[19]

While preserving their power on Capitol Hill, the regulars still lacked official standing with the Democratic National Committee. Accordingly, their "paramount problem," Congressman Griffin said, "lies with the Democratic convention which meets every four years and our relationship to the National party in presidential election years."[20] In 1971, the regulars gave substantial thought to reaching some accord that would allow them to return to the fold at the quadrennial assembly. Before that happened, state party officials would have to demonstrate that blacks were welcome to participate freely in their affairs. Indeed, there were some positive signs pointing in that direction. Recognizing the growing influence of the black electorate, many white politicians not only abandoned conventional racist rhetoric but also campaigned openly for black votes. In triumphing over Evers, Governor William Waller demonstrated this restraint and spoke of reuniting both wings of the party. During the campaign, he had informed the loyalists: "I consider myself a National Democrat. I feel that I have contacts in both the white and black community which will facilitate the working together of both groups in building a Democratic party in Mississippi in which we can all feel comfortable."[21]

These soothing words aside, the rift persisted. Waller did not immediately seek a rapprochement with the loyalists following his election. He ignored an invitation from Aaron Henry to participate in a joint meeting of the rival factions on December 12. Henry hoped to patch up the differences between the two camps and to send a united delegation to the 1972 national con-

vention. Instead, the governor-elect announced that he intended
to work exclusively through his own wing of the party to put
together a group to gain recognition in Miami Beach.[22] Henry's
overture rejected, each side held separate meetings in early 1972
to choose presidential delegates. However, as the national nominating convention approached, Waller once again appeared to favor conciliation. Although his faction enjoyed a firm grip on the
state electoral machinery, it would have great difficulty wresting
from the loyalists the coveted national endorsement. Thus, following the regulars' state convention in March, the governor entered into negotiations with his adversaries.

This round of discussions also proved fruitless. Waller
offered the loyalists ten seats on the twenty-five member delegation. Rejecting this proposal, Henry's group called for a fifty-
fifty split of representation on both the convention delegation and
the state party executive committee. This merger was to take place
under the loyalist constitution, and regular leaders would agree
to follow national party rules and to campaign for the presidential ticket.[23] Furthermore, Waller was asked to support single-
member redistricting, a system that promoted the election of minority candidates. Although the bargaining continued, neither
faction relented. The regulars remained adamant because they had
power on the state level; the loyalists derived strength in knowing they had national recognition. Hodding Carter reflected on
this latter advantage: "It didn't make a damn if [the regulars] went
out there and did everything by the Ten Commandments, the
national party rules—they had to participate in our process. That
was all! We had the call!"[24]

In the end, Carter proved correct. At the Miami Beach
convention in late August, the credentials committee heard the
competing claims. The panel listened to Waller supporters argue
that the "Loyalist Democratic Party exists on paper only [and]
. . . that the registered Democratic Party is the only Democratic
organization in Mississippi which permits and encourages full
participation in party affairs by every Democrat."[25] Before a decision was reached, Waller made a final bid to strike a bargain
with his rivals by offering them 40 percent representation on all
party agencies. The loyalists snubbed this eleventh-hour deal,

confident they would win their case before the liberal credentials committee. Their firmness paid off when the committee reported that the loyalist group had correctly implemented party rules on delegate selection and, therefore, should be seated. The convention concurred.[26]

Other southern states sent biracial delegations which took their seats in conformity with the party's antidiscrimination criteria. Alabama, Louisiana, North Carolina, South Carolina, and Virginia had been among the earliest states to achieve compliance, and by the opening of the convention proceedings, Georgia had fallen in line.[27] Blacks served as vice chairpersons of the South Carolina and North Carolina delegations, and the makeup of the interracial slate from Louisiana constituted such a stunning departure from earlier delegations that Governor Edwin Edwards, a reformer who had campaigned for black votes, saluted the presence of "the new, the young, the idealistic—those who haven't been allowed to be involved in the past."[28]

The Alabama delegation had undergone a similar transformation. Following the 1968 election in which blacks accounted for more than half of Humphrey's votes in the state, the Democratic National Committee instructed the regulars to boost minority representation in their affairs. This was not easy because the party apparatus contained numerous supporters of Governor Wallace, whose independent presidential bid had captured the state's electoral votes. The burden of compliance fell upon Robert S. Vance, the party chairman who had split from Wallace over the governor's defection from the national Democrats. Guided by Vance and prodded by the McGovern commission, the state party instituted sufficient reforms to resist another challenge from John Cashin's National Democratic Party of Alabama. The NDPA faction had chosen to shun the regular Democratic primary elections for convention delegates, holding its own selection process instead. Ignoring this boycott and braving the hostility of the Wallacites, the Vance contingent included ten black delegates and eight black alternates. Slightly more than one-quarter of the representatives were Afro-Americans, a figure comparable to the proportion of the black population of Alabama. Recognizing this accomplishment, the credentials committee concluded that Vance's group had "taken every conceivable step to encourage the broadest possible opportunity for young, black and female citizens in Alabama to become delegates to our National Convention."[29] The subsequent seating of the Vance loyalists delivered a death blow to the chances of the NDPA for national recognition, thereby limiting its role to contesting for local offices in black belt counties. In Alabama and throughout the South, the national Democrats had incorporated blacks into their ranks, further redressing minority grievances as a means of conferring legitimacy on the prevailing political system. Thus, the transition from protest to politics had taken a great leap forward.

Just as the nomination of George McGovern for the presidency reflected the triumph of the procedural reforms he had helped institute, his overwhelming defeat at the polls spelled trouble for the progressive changes that had swept through the party. To be sure, blacks gave the Democratic contender an enormous percentage of their votes, exceeding by far that of other blocs in the New Deal coalition.[30] However, the fidelity of the black electorate did not compensate for the erosion of traditional Democrat support among whites. In the soul-searching that followed the Nixon landslide, many disillusioned Democrats attributed the loss to the "tragically wrong" efforts of the McGovern commission to guarantee extensive minority representation. Spearheaded by powerful segments of organized labor, whose influence at Miami Beach had waned greatly from previous conventions, and joined by displaced party regulars and estranged liberal intellectuals and lawmakers, critics denounced the reformers for introducing misguided de facto quotas. They objected to predetermined formulas based on race, sex, or age as a perversion of the traditional liberal notion of equal opportunity. One of the disgruntled was Congressman James G. O' Hara of Michigan. Former chairman of the liberal Democratic Study Group in the House, he had recently headed a party commission to modernize convention rules in conjunction with the McGovern task force on delegate selection.[31] After the 1972 fiasco, O'Hara led a Coalition for a Democratic Majority to forestall a repeat of the electoral calamity in 1976 by striving "toward fairness and unity." To undo the damage inflicted at the polls, O'Hara's organization recommended abandonment of the guidelines, "which require state parties to assure proportional representation of minority groups" and insisted that "no concept of 'affirmative action' should be applied . . . which requires application of minimal standards as tests of a delegation's representativeness." It rejected "democracy by demography" and accepted merely the obligation to "inform under-represented groups of their rights of participation and make them feel welcome."[32]

The Democratic leadership engaged in its own critical reassessment of the political impact of party procedures. In September 1972, a New Delegate Selection Commission was created, and the following April it formally began to reevaluate the operation of the guidelines. A badly defeated McGovern also backed away from his group's handiwork, declaring: "We need not pretend that the reforms were written in stone."[33] Presided over by Barbara Mikulski, a former social worker and Baltimore city councilwoman who would later win election to Congress, the commission contained eleven blacks among its seventy-five members. For nearly two years, it grappled with the problem of maintaining the party's commitment to minorities while winning back disaffected white supporters. In October 1973, the panel advised against a retreat from affirmative action programs. It suggested that the participation of a group should be related to its "presence in the Democratic electorate" and not merely to its portion of the population. However, at the same time, the commission expressly prohibited quotas as a means of implementing affirmative action. Moving away from the McGovern reforms, the group counseled that in credentials disputes involving allegations of racial bias, the burden of proof shift from the state party delegation, where the former guidelines had put it, to the challengers. At a mid-term party convention gathered at Kansas City in December 1974, the assembled Democrats modified the Mikulski proposals. Having endorsed the ban on quotas, they decided to reaffirm the responsibility of state parties for proving themselves free of discrimination.[34]

The Loyal Democrats from Mississippi soon discovered that national party leaders interpreted the proscription of quotas severely. A Compliance Review Commission had been formed to monitor affirmative action plans submitted by the states. In May 1975, the board rejected the proposal drawn up by the Mississippi loyalists because its language "moves beyond encouragement and is mandatory in terms." The objectionable clauses decreed that blacks *"must* be fully represented at every level of the Party organization" in proportion to "their presence in the Democratic electorate." Although denying that they had employed a quota, the loyalists altered their plan to satisfy the commission. In doing so, Aaron Henry lamented "any action within the National Democratic Party to deliberately reduce this inclusion [of minorities] . . . that make up the National Democratic Party, as a step backward."[35] This concern was not unfounded. With tight restrictions on using any formula to guarantee representation, the percentage of black delegates attending the 1976 presidential nominating convention declined from 14.6 in 1972 to 10.6.[36]

The Mississippi loyalists' experience with the new guidelines may have encouraged them to seek consolidation with their state rivals. They continued to be a minority faction within the Magnolia State, while the regulars remained outcasts from the national party. After 1972, both sides had worked for reconciliation, and in 1976 they arrived at an agreement to merge their forces. Blacks traded a commanding position in their own organization for increased access to the more powerful state party machinery run by their opponents. Aaron Henry became cochair of the unified executive committee on which blacks occupied twenty-seven of one hundred seats. This arrangement awarded Negroes representation roughly proportional to their voting-age population, but it kept them below the relative strength they exerted in support of Democratic candidates.[37] Furthermore, the compromise brought together strange political bedfellows. Henry embraced Senator James Eastland, the perennial civil rights foe, who welcomed this biracial partnership to enhance his prospects in the face of a tough challenge to his incumbency.[38]

While the Democratic party experimented with affirmative action, the federal judiciary was agonizing over issues of a similar nature. Like the Democrats, the courts considered whether some kind of proportional representation was an appropriate and constitutional means of combating the legacy of discrimination that kept blacks at a disadvantage in the electoral process. Although longstanding procedural obstacles—literacy tests, poll taxes—had been effectively eliminated, structural barriers continued to limit the effects of black suffrage. In particular, the manner of conducting elections greatly shaped the outcome for minority candidates. Both multimember districts and at-large elections reduced the possibilities of minority victory. Under such systems, representatives were chosen from the entire population. This made it difficult for minority group candidates to win office when voting broke down along racial lines. However, their chances for success improved greatly if elections were held by districts. In that event, blacks might constitute a majority of a ward and might elect a candidate of their own race to represent them. Hailed as methods of minimizing parochialism and fragmentation, multimember district and at-large election techniques operated impartially only if politics was "color blind." Instead, the extension of the right to vote to southern blacks during the 1960s had heightened rather than diminished racial polarization at the ballot box. Consequently, the newly enfranchised often entered the electoral system to find that the rules were stacked against them.[39] To make matters worse, if debilitating suffrage regulations had been adopted before November 1964, the Voting Rights Act did not provide a mechanism for eradicating them.

In addition to multimember districts and at-large elections, annexation and reapportionment schemes threatened to weaken black political strength. The need for reapportionment and redistricting of state and local legislative bodies had grown out of the constitutional revolution in which the Supreme Court affirmed the principle of equal representation for all individuals. The high tribunal's "one person, one vote" opinion triggered a redrawing of political boundary lines based on equality of population. This decree afforded state officials an unexpected opportunity to reshape electoral districts to dilute the voting potency of the black electorate. Unintentionally, the judiciary had ushered in what some observers called a "Gerrymandering Revolution."[40] The courts looked at malapportionment from the perspective of individual voters entitled to have their ballots weigh equally, thus leaving unanswered the question of what constituted fair representation for racial minorities and other insular groups. A legal scholar summed up the conundrum: "One person's vote, though it be the absolute equal of another's, cannot alone preserve anything but the status quo. Only with a collective voice can civil rights be preserved."[41] During the late 1960s, heightened group consciousness magnified the desire of Afro-Americans to choose officials of their own race with whom they proudly identified. The drive toward black power paralleled the call for reapportionment and forced the courts to confront the issue of minority group representation.

Following the landmark *Allen* ruling dealing with the preclearance section of the Voting Rights Act, federal courts adjudicated a series of cases that explored both the scope and the substance of section five. The suffrage statute did not touch discriminatory electoral practices in existence before 1964; however, it permitted the federal government to review and reject procedures, established since the mid-1960s, that appeared to function neutrally but actually worked in a racially biased fashion. In the process, the courts struggled to develop a set of standards concerning the safeguards of section five. In doing so, the judiciary redefined the obligations of national and state governments to promote effective representation for minorities.

A suit involving Georgia followed the pattern, initiated with *Allen,* of advancing the range of section five. The case clarified the attorney general's 1971 preclearance guidelines as they applied to changes in legislative apportionment. After the 1970 Census, Georgia lawmakers redrew district lines for election to the state legislature and to the United States Congress. In decreasing the number of state legislative districts from 118 to 105, the lawmakers increased slightly the number of multimember districts to forty-nine and also transferred into them residents of thirty-one counties that had previously employed the single-member system. On November 5, 1971, Georgia submitted this plan to the Justice Department in accordance with section five. At the request of Washington, the state provided additional information on January 6, 1972. Less than sixty days later, the attorney general objected to the proposal because he was "unable to conclude that the plan does not have a discriminatory racial effect on voting." In particular, the nation's chief legal officer cited the shift to multimember districts in combination with other electoral procedures that might handicap black voters in the choice of their preferred candidates.[42] In this case, John Mitchell's Justice Department interpreted the section five procedures as Congress had intended. Rebuffed by the federal government, Georgians adopted a new proposal that took into account the prior objections. They dropped the number of multimember districts from forty-nine to thirty-two and raised the number of districts from 105 to 128. On March 24, 1972, less than two weeks after receiving the submission, once again the Justice Department found it unacceptable.

This second rejection irked Georgia legislators who decided to hold statehouse elections under the 1972 scheme. They insisted belatedly that the voting rights law did not cover reapportionment, although in the first instance they had voluntarily offered their plan for federal inspection. State officials also maintained that the attorney general had not acted properly in turning down the legislation without conclusively finding that it had a discriminatory purpose or effect. Furthermore, they charged that the Justice Department's original refusal had been made after the sixty-day statutory limit for rendering judgments; the state calculated the time period as beginning with the initial receipt of the proposal.[43] But before Georgia politicos could proceed with their intention of holding elections, Justice Department lawyers obtained an injunction from a federal district court panel barring them from doing so. The state then appealed the decision to the Supreme Court.

On May 7, 1973, the high tribunal finally resolved the dispute. Speaking for a majority of six, Justice Potter Stewart upheld the lower court ruling. In deciding for the federal government, Stewart gave an expansive reading to section five. The preclearance clause, he affirmed, "is not concerned with a simple inventory of voting procedures as they affect Negro voters." *Allen* had established this precedent, and the jurist reasoned: "Had Congress disagreed with [this] interpretation of section 5 . . . . it had ample opportunity to amend the statue." Besides, Georgia lawmakers must have accepted this viewpoint because they had submitted reapportionment plans on two occasions. Further-more, Stewart left no doubt that replacing single-member with multimember districts had a "potential for diluting the value of the vote" and, therefore, was subject to prior federal scrutiny.[44]

Having disposed of the question of whether Georgia should have submitted the changes, Stewart turned his attention to whether the attorney general had properly performed his pre-clearance duties. The letter turning down Georgia's submission did not specifically state that the legislation was racially biased; however, the court found that Mitchell had acted reasonably in concluding that Georgia had not proven satisfactorily the absence of bias in its proposed changes. Although Stewart did not con-sider the Justice Department's "choice of language" in commu-nicating with Peach State officials "a model of precision," he held that the attorney general conveyed the message "in the context of the promulgated [1971] guidelines . . . with sufficient clar-ity." Concerning Washington's failure to reach a decision within sixty days of first receiving the submission, Stewart ruled that it was "consistent" with the intent of the Voting Rights Act for the attorney general to extend the deadline by requesting additional information.[45]

The Supreme Court had upheld the broad scope of sec-tion five, but it had not yet ruled on how much leeway the at-torney general had in using his discretionary authority. Litigation on this point arose when South Carolina passed a reapportion-ment statute in 1971. While several private parties filed federal suits challenging the act's validity under the Fourteenth and Fifteenth Amendments, the Justice Department rejected the plan in March 1972. In the meantime, a state court also voided the redistricting law and gave officials thirty days to come up with a revised one. Consequently, on May 6, South Carolina lawmakers enacted a measure that met with judicial approval at the state level. After the Justice Department received this new proposal for clearance, it bowed to the opinion of the state court and refused to object. In August, civil rights plaintiffs challenged the attorney general's decision in the United States District Court in Washington, and nearly a year later, on May 16, 1973, the jurists ruled in their fa-vor, ordering the attorney general to consider the reapportionment statute in conformity with his section five authority. Finally, on July 20, "unable to conclude that [the] act . . . does not have the effect of abridging voting rights on account of race," the Justice Department blocked the plan. Armed with this ruling, two South Carolina voters sought to halt implementation of the disputed apportionment law A state court dismissed their claim and, contrary to the verdict of the federal bench in the nation's capital, held instead that the attorney general had fulfilled his preclearance obligations when he originally failed to disallow the submission.[46]

On appeal, the Supreme Court agreed with the state court. In a 6–3 decision, the high tribunal concluded that the final determination of the attorney general in section five hearings was not subject by law to judicial review in the District of Columbia court. Writing for the majority, Lewis Powell, a strict constructionist from Virginia appointed by Richard Nixon, contended that Congress had meant to provide covered jurisdictions with an expeditious administrative process for clearing their suffrage regulations. In this instance, Mitchell had complied with the provisions of the Voting Rights Act "solely by the *absence* for whatever reason, of a timely objection on [his] part." To permit judicial review of the Justice Department's action, Powell reasoned, would have postponed the implementation of legitimate state legislation beyond a reasonable period. Although excluding section five rulings from judicial scrutiny, the court reminded the civil rights petitioners that they could challenge the discriminatory character of the law "in traditional constitutional litigation."[47]

Not satisfied with this alternative judicial route, Thurgood Marshall delivered a stinging rebuke to his brethren. The former chief counsel of the NAACP denied that Congress had intended to shelter the attorney general's rulings under section five from judicial oversight. He understood the opinion in *Georgia v. United States* to "impose on the Attorney General a duty to review submitted statutes and disapprove them unless he is satisfied that they meet standards established by the [Voting Rights] Act." According to Marshall, the Justice Department had shirked its responsibility to examine the substance of a suffrage law, choosing instead to defer to the judgment of the state tribunal.

Unfortunately, Marshall's opinion noted, the majority's reasoning had been more concerned with the form that the section five process took than with guaranteeing that the nation's top lawyer adequately reviewed the discriminatory contents of laws. Reflecting his dismay that the court had allowed the plan to stand, Marshall protested: "South Carolina, which was a leader of the movement to deprive the former slaves of their federally guaranteed right to vote is allowed to remain as one of the last successful members of that movement."[48]

In general, this opinion marked the exception to the rule of Supreme Court judgments expanding the reach of section five and the attorney general's responsibilities for enforcing it. The justices demonstrated this in decisions relating to the type of jurisdictions subject to coverage under the voting rights statute. In one such suit, the federal government complained that the municipality of Sheffield, Alabama, had not satisfactorily complied with the preclearance procedure. In 1975, the city proposed to switch its form of government from a commission to a mayor-council. Local officials alerted the Justice Department of their aim to hold a referendum on the plan, and the attorney general did not object to conducting the election; however, he reserved final judgment pending the outcome. After the voters approved the proposal, the attorney general informed the city that although he accepted the new governmental design, he objected to the feature that called for at-large elections of councilmembers. Disregarding this ruling, Sheffield officials scheduled an at-large election for August 10, 1976. A day before the balloting, Justice Department lawyers obtained a temporary restraining order blocking the voting. This victory was shortlived as the federal district court dismissed the national government's suit. It decreed that municipalities such as Sheffield were exempt from section five coverage because they did not fit the statutory definition of a political subdivision—a unit conducting voter registration. Furthermore, the lower court concluded that in sanctioning the referendum the attorney general had implicitly accepted its results.[49]

The Supreme Court thought otherwise. By a 6-3 vote the high tribunal reversed the judgment. In reaching this verdict, the spokesman for the court, William Brennan, rebutted the ar-

gument that section five applied only to governing bodies that
enrolled voters. Examining the legislative history of the Voting
Rights Act and its renewal, Brennan asserted that Congress desired the preclearance section to cover all political bodies "having
power over any aspect of the electoral process within designated
jurisdictions." A finding to the contrary, according to the justice,
would be "irrational" because it "would permit the precise evil
that section 5 was designed to eliminate." Under these circumstances, Brennan maintained, political entities such as Sheffield
would be free to respond to local pressure to limit the political
power of minorities and to take steps that would, temporarily at
least, dilute or entirely defeat the voting rights of minorities."[50]
The question of coverage decided, Justice Brennan then found that
Sheffield should have sought the attorney general's approval not
only for the referendum but also for the revised governmental
structure adopted as a result of the election.[51] Thus, as one legal
scholar observed, the court remained "willing to sustain a high
degree of federal encroachment upon local legislative processes,
at least when federal action is supported by the 15th amendment."[52]

In keeping with this legal tradition, the high bench also
stretched the definition of suffrage practices affected by section
five. Previously, the court had extended Justice Department supervision to devices that directly molded the electoral process: reapportionment, annexation, the shift to multimember districts, and
relocation of polling places. In a case from Georgia, the Supreme
Court added to the list regulations that indirectly affected the
franchise. One such rule adopted by the Dougherty County Board
of Education in 1972 required its employees to take unpaid leaves
of absence while running for political office. The board approved
this measure a month before a black assistant coordinator of student personnel services, John White, announced his candidacy for
the Georgia House of Representatives. Forced to take a leave
without pay, he lost the election but was then reinstated. Two
years later, White took another leave to campaign, and this time
he won. In 1976, he was reelected. As a result of complying with
the board's rule, the black representative lost over $11,000 in in-
come from the school system. He filed litigation to recover his

back salary, charging that the ordinance was inoperative because the county had not cleared it with the Justice Department. A federal district panel agreed that the regulation should have been submitted, for it "restricts the ability of citizens to run for office."[53]

By a 5-4 split, the Supreme Court affirmed this opinion. Justice Marshall delivered the ruling, brushing aside the county's claim that it had promulgated the measure simply to get "a full day's work for a full day's pay." He found that the board's policy was not a "neutral personnel practice governing all forms of absenteeism," but that it singled out one kind specifically related to the electoral process. Consequently, the disputed measure operated in the same manner as a filing fee, providing an "economic disincentive" for employees contemplating seeking election, and thus, restricted the choices available to voters.[54] Although the county insisted that the policy constituted a routine personnel matter, Marshall, who had spent much of his life challenging ingenious attempts to circumvent racial equality, focused on the law's "potential" for discrimination. Aware that Dougherty County and its chief city of Albany possessed a long history of racial oppression, suspicious of the timing of the measure's adoption, and skeptical of the board's decision to require a mandatory leave based on candidacy rather than on absence during regular working hours, Marshall discerned the discriminatory impact of the rule on electoral participation. He reminded his doubting brethren that section five "must be given broadest possible scope," encompassing the "subtle, as well as obvious," forms of bias.[55]

Speaking for the minority, Justice Powell condemned Marshall's reasoning as "tortuous." He disputed the contention that the personnel regulation of the Dougherty County School Board had anything to do with the electoral system or that the framers of the Voting Rights Act thought such measures applicable. To hold differently, Powell said, "means that any incidental impact on elections is sufficient to trigger the preclearance requirement of section 5 [and] then it is difficult to imagine what sorts of state or local enactments would *not* fall within the scope of that section."[56] Indeed, to the dissenters' chagrin, the majority of the court had significantly broadened the criteria for coverage. The justices upheld the authority of the Justice Department to examine a particular submission for its potential effect on the suffrage and to inquire whether the change was related, however indirectly, to any phase of the electoral process.[57]

While the justices enlarged the procedural scope of section five to cover a variety of franchise practices, they also began looking closely at the substantive features of electoral devices in order to measure their racial impact. By the mid-1970s, the high court addressed the issue of how far state and local governments could go in revising the content of their laws without running afoul of the voting rights law. Consequently, the judiciary struggled to determine what constituted adequate and fair representation for minorities and what obligations state and local governments had for achieving it. The concept of fairness raised a complex legal question for the judges: did the suffrage plans under examination have to afford blacks an opportunity to attain political office in relation to their proportion of the population? Traditionally, the judiciary had considered the issue of representation from the standpoint of equality of individual citizens, i.e., "one person, one vote"; however, following enfranchisement, civil rights advocates petitioned the courts to strike down discriminatory electoral practices that reduced the power of blacks as a cohesive voting bloc. Having suffered disfranchisement on the basis of race, blacks insisted that the bench take their recognizable group identity into account when reversing the effects of past discrimination and fostering their political aspirations.[58]

In pressing their case, black voters found an ally in the Civil Rights Division of the Justice Department. The CRD utilized section five to nullify suffrage submissions that weakened the potential strength of the Negro electorate. In one such instance, on January 28, 1971, the city of Richmond, Virginia, requested approval from the attorney general for its annexation of twenty-three square miles of neighboring land. The city had instituted proceedings to obtain the parcel of land in 1962, and it received permission seven years later. By incorporating over 45,000 whites compared with only 1,557 blacks, this real estate acquisition converted a slight black population majority of 52 percent into a 42 percent minority. At the same time, Richmond retained its nine-member council, which was chosen at-large. Both before and after the annexation, three blacks gained seats on the governing body. Upon review of these facts, the Justice Department declined to consent to the annexation. On May 7, 1971, Washington informed municipal officials that because their action substantially augmented the proportion of whites and diminished the ratio of blacks living in Richmond, it "inevitably tends to dilute the voting strength of black voters."[59] This decision came just as the battle between the Nixon administration and Congress over section five guidelines was drawing to a close, and Attorney General Mitchell heeded the legislative demands for strict enforcement. Mitchell suggested that civic leaders might overcome his objections by establishing single-member districts within the new city boundaries in order to diminish the racial effect of the annexation.

In the meantime, the judiciary also considered the problem. On February 4, 1971, Curtis Holt, a black resident of Richmond, had petitioned the United States district court to stop the annexation on the ground that it violated the Fifteenth Amendment. Finding for the plaintiff, in November the court declared that the territorial merger had an "illegal racial purpose." Rather than voiding the deal, the bench ordered new elections conducted at-large; seven councilmembers would be elected from within the original city limits, which retained a black population majority, and two would come from the mainly white annexed portion. However, the court of appeals soon reversed this decision, holding that Richmond had valid reasons for pursuing the annexation of the adjacent parcel of land. Holt did not give up, and on December 9, he filed another suit to throw out the acquisition because it had not received proper section five clearance. Six months later, the city submitted its plan to the federal district court in Washington, for certification.[60] Before reaching a conclusion, the court resolved a similar controversy from Petersburg, Virginia, where the 52 percent black population had been cut to a minority through an annexation. In canceling this scheme, the judiciary found that the system of at-large elections operating in the city diluted black ballots, and it suggested that Petersburg switch to a ward system of electing councilmembers in order to minimize the detrimental effect upon Afro-Americans. The city complied.[61]

With this lesson in mind, Richmond developed another plan for submission to the attorney general. After a series of negotiations, the Justice Department accepted a proposal for creating a ward system in which blacks held a population advantage in four districts and whites predominated in five. This agreement was sent to the court of appeals in the nation's capital for approval, but the panel rejected it. The judges reasoned that the ward system in effect did not lessen the dilution of black voting strength "to the greatest possible extent," and they expressed preference for a plan drawn up by blacks that gave Negroes a majority in five districts.[62]

At this juncture, the Supreme Court stepped in. When the justices finally heard the oral arguments on April 23, 1975, city council elections had been suspended for five years, pending an outcome of the dispute. On June 24, Justice Byron White, on behalf of a majority of five, announced that the electoral bargain hammered out by Washington and Richmond satisfied section five criteria and should have been sanctioned by the appellate court. He argued that an annexation proposal complied with the letter of the law as long as it provided blacks "representation reasonably equivalent to their political strength in the enlarged community." In so ruling, White denied the claim that any annexation attempt was invalid if it left blacks with potentially fewer seats on a legislative council than they would have commanded before the acquisition took place. "To hold otherwise," White declared, "would be either to forbid all such annexations or to require . . . that the black community be assigned the same proportion of council seats as before, hence perhaps permanently overrepresenting them and underrepresenting other elements in the community, including the non black citizens in the annexed area." The justice did not dispute the lower court's finding that the annexation, as it had taken place in 1969, was "infected by the impermissible purpose of denying the right to vote based on race"; however, he maintained that as long as "verifiable reasons are now demonstrable" in support of the plan, then it was acceptable.[63]

This opinion deeply disturbed a minority on the court as well as civil rights proponents. Joining Justices Marshall and William O. Douglas, William Brennan attacked his opposing brethren's emphasis on discovering the intent of city officials in seeking annexations. To unravel racist from legitimate economic motives in extending municipal boundaries was nearly an impossible task, and he scoffed at "the sort of *post hoc* rationalization which the city now offers." Besides, Brennan asserted, the effect of this annexation diluted black electoral strength as it had previously existed, and thus, contravened the fundamental purpose of section five, "namely, the protection of *present* levels of voting effectiveness for the black population."[64] Outside the courtroom, legal critics argued that the tribunal's ruling virtually encouraged local authorities to manipulate the annexation process to the disadvantage of blacks without fear of reversal. In a clash between a city's nonracial motives for incorporating suburban land and the desire of blacks for maximum political representation, the latter had to yield. "Given the difficulty of ascertaining improper motivations and the multitude of verifiable, legitimate purposes which may plausibly accompany an annexation," a law journal contributor pointed out, "it is now highly unlikely that municipalities will fail to meet the burden of proof on this issue."[65]

The controversial issue of proportional representation treated in *Richmond* also surfaced in litigation involving New Orleans. A city containing a population 55 percent white and 45 percent black, New Orleans was governed by a mayor and seven councilmembers chosen both at-large and by wards. Before 1970, blacks composed a majority of the population in one of five districts, but following reapportionment in that census year, they were granted a slight population edge in two districts. But, in neither locale were blacks a majority of the registered voters. When the Crescent City submitted this plan to the attorney general, he rejected it. Likewise, the Justice Department vetoed a second redistricting measure in which black residents predominated in two areas and in one of them held a registration advantage in the electorate. In each instance, the Civil Rights Division found that municipal officials had drawn new boundary lines in a manner that decreased the "maximum potential of the Negro vote."[66] Turning next to the federal district court in Washington, for section five approval, New Orleans did not fare any better. The judiciary figured that according to their proportion of registered voters, blacks ideally should have been able to select 2.42 members of the city council or 3.15, if computed on the basis of population ratio. However, given the history of racial bloc voting, under the contested reapportionment proposal they could expect to put in office only one Negro councilmember. As a result of these federal government rulings, New Orleans had not conducted a contest for the city council since 1970.[67]

Six years later, the impasse ended in victory for the city. The Supreme Court decided that the second redistricting measure satisfied the requirements of section five. Justice Potter Stewart, who previously had joined his brethren in extending coverage of Washington's preclearance power, swung his support behind an interpretation narrowing the latitude of the national government in blocking electoral revisions. Authoring the court's opinion for five justices, Stewart contended that section five meant that "no voting-procedure changes would be made that would lead to a *retrogression* in the position of racial minorities with respect to their effective exercise of the electoral franchise" [emphasis added].[68] According to this view, any legislative reapportionment or redistricting scheme that actually improved the chance for electing black officials could not at the same time dilute the right to vote. Stewart placed New Orleans' plan into this category. He found it enhanced the possibility for a black victory at the polls, compared with the prior procedure that had excluded nonwhite representation. Thus if blacks could elect only one member of their race, no matter what their current strength, they would be in better shape than they had been in the past.

The opinion struck a blow against those who favored affirmative remedies to heal political disabilities inflicted by generations of racial disfranchisement. Taking into account the existence of racial bloc voting and the presence of electoral features operating to the disadvantage of blacks in New Orleans, Justice Byron White argued in a minority opinion that "to the extent practicable, the new electoral districts [should] afford the Negro minority the opportunity to achieve legislative representation roughly proportional to the Negro population in the community," in this case at least two council members. To reverse the legacy of bias, the justice suggested, state and local officials should deliberately construct districts along racial lines.[69] Moreover, White did not consider Stewart's "retrogression test" an appropriate standard for judgment in section five hearings: he suggested looking at the current effect of redistricting on the black electorate. In this way, he was consistent with his majority opinion in *Richmond,* which decided that blacks had received a fair share of representation according to their population within the newly drawn municipality. White's latest reasoning mirrored that of civil rights advocates who perceived the voting rights law as a weapon to ensure that blacks reached their potential electoral strength.[70]

Meanwhile, the judiciary labored uneasily over the issue of appropriate representation outside the framework of the voting rights statute. Because section five applied only to changes in electoral procedures adopted since 1964, local measures in existence before that date did not have to be submitted for clearance from Washington. In particular, the system of at-large and multimember district elections, generally established around the turn of the century, functioned as roadblocks to black political participation. The adoption of these electoral devices was part of the process that disfranchised blacks and ensured white Democratic hegemony in the South. For example, in Galveston, Texas, the city which originated the commission form of municipal government with at-large elections in 1895, black officeholding quickly ceased, and shortly therafter, the Lone Star State revised its electoral laws to reduce black participation even more sharply.[71] Carried over into the postenfranchisement era of the mid–1960s, these electoral institutions assumed critical importance as methods of diluting black political strength. "It is perfectly possible," one scholar commented, "to have people voting all day long, and the vote to be relatively useless, because of the way the rules of the game are rigged against them."[72] In communities characterized by racial polarization, a phenomenon that did not expire in the South after passage of the 1965 act, recently enfranchised blacks experienced great difficulty in obtaining support for their candidates from the majority white electorate. Those who did manage to wage successful campaigns in at-large elections often had to shape their appeals in a manner that downplayed their role as aggressive advocates for racial advancement. Thus, the electoral structure of numerous southern municipal and state governing agencies operated to hamper effective black political involvement.[73]

During the 1960s, when the federal government had embarked on the "reapportionment revolution," the bench had expressed a preference for plans that emphasized single-member districts. In several early cases, the Supreme Court suggested that multimember districts might "designedly or otherwise . . . minimize or cancel out the voting strength of racial or political elements of the population." Under this system, members of an "insular minority" usually failed to elect representatives who best spoke for them from their own communities.[74] However, the high tribunal stopped short of invalidating the use of multimember districts or of instructing legislators to sketch political boundary lines with maximum black representation as their goal. In a landmark 1971 decision on reapportionment of the Indiana legislature, the court refused to compel the Hoosier State to adopt the single-member form of districting. In upholding the constitutionality of the multimember district system, the justices found that the state had not instituted or perpetuated it deliberately to maintain racial discrimination or to deny blacks access to equal participation in the political process. Repudiating the claim that minorities should be entitled to proportional representation as a matter of fairness, the Court insisted that plaintiffs must show that their lack of legislative representation was attributable to a "built in bias" rather than to voting for the wrong party and losing at the polls. "The mere fact that one interest group or another," Justice White wrote for the majority, "have found themselves [sic] outvoted and without legislative seats of its own provides no basis for invoking constitutional remedies where . . . there is no indication that this segment of the population is being denied access to the political system."[75]

Although the Supreme Court declined to issue a blanket condemnation of multimember districts, its reasoning indicated that the constitutionality of such schemes was most suspect in the

South. Permissible in a northern state such as Indiana, which did not have a long history of racial disfranchisement, multimember districting had much less chance of withstanding a legal assault from blacks in Dixie where this arrangement perpetuated the effects of previous suffrage bias. Indeed, in the early 1970s, the high bench underlined this crucial distinction. The court invalidated a Louisiana reapportionment plan that created four "safe," majority-white state senatorial districts for New Orleans. Recognizing similarities to the Indiana case, *Whitcomb v. Chavis,* the justices nevertheless highlighted an important difference: "In *Whitcomb* it was conceded that the State's preference for multi-member districts was not rooted in racial discrimination. Here, there has been . . . a long 'history' of bias and franchise dilution in the State's traditional drawing of district lines."[76]

The judiciary moved even closer to developing standards that threatened the continued existence of most at-large elections throughout the South. Among other issues raised by a suit concerning the 1970 reapportionment of the Texas House of Representatives, the Supreme Court considered "whether multimember districts provided for Bexar [San Antonio] and Dallas Counties were properly found to have been invidiously discriminatory against cognizable racial or ethnic groups in these counties."[77] Before 1972, only two blacks had ever been elected to the state legislature from Dallas and only five Mexican-Americans from Bexar County. A review of the history of racial disfranchisement in the Lone Star State convinced a three-judge district court panel that the retention of multimember districts was invalid. In 1973, the high tribunal affirmed this opinion. Leading the Court, Justice White reiterated his opinion in *Whitcomb* that "multimember districts are not *per se* unconstitutional" and to prove bias "it is not enough that the racial group allegedly discriminated against has not had legislative seats in proportion to its voting potential." Instead, to sustain their claim, plaintiffs had to demonstrate that they had been denied equal access to the political process and had been prevented from electing lawmakers of their own choice. Having discarded any constitutional right to proportional representation, the justice ruled in this case against an electoral procedure that minimized participation by minorities and checked their opportunities for winning public office. In arriving at this conclusion, White stressed that his colleagues placed great weight on the findings of the lower court, based as they were on a combination of history and "an intensely local appraisal of the design and impact of the . . . multimember district in light of past and present reality, political and otherwise."[78]

The Supreme Court had gone far toward dismantling multimember district and at-large elections without declaring them inherently unconstitutional. Encouraged by the Texas ruling, the lower federal courts implemented this line of reasoning in broad fashion. In vacating an at-large plan for the election of local officials in East Carroll Parish, Louisiana, in 1973, the Fifth Circuit Court of Appeals promulgated guidelines for identifying the "fact of dilution." In *Zimmer v. McKeithen*, the tribunal affirmed that equal entry into the political process, and not population ratios, furnished the proper yardstick for measuring whether minorities were represented fairly. In adjudicating litigation, the court considered the "totality of circumstances" surrounding the electoral system. Besides taking into account the history of racial bias, the panel noted the telltale signs of impermissible voter dilution that "enhanced" the lingering effects of past racial discrimination by thwarting blacks from casting ballots solidly behind their preferred candidates: the consistent failure of minorities to obtain a place on nomination slates; unresponsiveness of elected officials to nonwhite interests; the existence of large electoral districts, requirements for majority runoff and full ticket (antisingle shot) voting. Given these standards, legal commentators were quick to recognize that multimember districts might remain in principle; but in the South, they would have a difficult time meeting the constitutional test. The legacy of racial disfranchisement throughout Dixie, and especially in the states covered by the Voting Rights Act, virtually guaranteed the applicability of the *Zimmer* criteria to this region.[79]

While civil rights plaintiffs praised the judicial guidelines crafted in the Texas and Louisiana suits, more conservative members of the bench and bar deplored their implications. Some law reviewers grumbled that in examining these "aggregate factors" of racial bias, for all practical purposes the courts had decreed a *per se* rule against at-large systems. For any such plan, however worthy, to withstand constitutional challenges, the courts would have to find strong reasons for excepting it from the general doctrine. Embarking on this course, one scholar contended with reference to the years of reapportionment controveries, "the federal courts may be leaving the relative security of the 'political thicket' for an uncharted journey into the 'political jungle.'"[80] Another critic suggested that the judiciary had become a party to "reverse discrimination" by compelling "the affirmative use of racial factors in affording a minority group an impermissible adventage over other voters in a community."[81] In rebuttal, defenders of the judiciary insisted that the rulings did not ensure blacks proportional representation but only improved their opportunity for striving toward this goal. Furthermore, multimember districts, they claimed, *"foreclose the possibility* that blacks will ever be represented in proportion to their population."[82]

By the late 1970s, the Supreme Court began to heed the conservative criticism and retreated from employing the standards on vote dilution in a sweeping manner. The growing public outcry against affirmative action programs in employment and education and the view that compensatory treatment for minorities constituted "reverse discrimination" found expression on the high tribunal. In a series of rulings, the justices held that litigants who alleged racial bias in violation of the equal protection clause of the Fourteenth Amendment had to show that their adversaries *intentionally* adopted discriminatory practices. In contrast, the court's vote dilution decisions had been based upon a result-oriented approach. Rather than merely exploring the purposes of local officials in enacting suffrage regulations, the judiciary had examined their impact on black political participation. This subsequent shift in judicial orientation toward assessing the motives behind a particular action imposed especially severe hardships on suffragists. Considered "race proof," systems such as multimember district and at-large elections usually came into existence after southern blacks had been disfranchised. Moreover, these "neutral" plans were popularly identified as good government reforms and not as undemocratic means for reducing minority participation. Thus, "a strict application of the intent requirement," according to a legal observer, "could raise monumental hurdles for plaintiffs challenging at-large election schemes, and, because of the extraordinary evidentiary problems that would be presented in vote dilution challenges, the burden of proof for plaintiffs . . . could become virtually insurmountable."[83]

While the high tribunal composed stiff standards for determining racial discrimination, the lower courts adapted the new criteria to fit the precedents handed down in vote dilution cases. Nullifying at-large elections in Mobile, Alabama, the federal judiciary resolved the "conscious intent issue" in a novel manner. The district and appellate benches concurred that the Alabama Gulf Coast city had not enacted at-large electoral regulations for racially invalid purposes. Nevertheless, the judges concluded that the system had functioned to submerge black voting strength, and in perpetuating its operation, local officials deliberately practiced racial discrimination. Thus, in judging the legal meaning of intent, the lower courts did not confine their examination to the original purpose in adopting a suffrage plan, but they also inferred from the "totality of circumstances" whether the system was intentionally maintained for the dilution of black ballots.[84] However, it remained for the Supreme Court to determine if this modified test was constitutionally acceptable. (See chapter 9.)

The dilemma facing the judiciary stemmed from the changing goals of the suffrage movement. The struggle that reached its peak with passage of the Voting Rights Act had altered direction from voter registration to electoral representation. In attempting to convert their ballots into political power, blacks had received support from the Democratic party and from the federal courts. Both agencies spurred minority group involvement in political affairs to an extent unmatched since the First Reconstruction. Yet, as Afro-Americans sought greater representation by members of their race, they aroused intense controversy. Pushing to replace the conventional liberal conception of equal opportunity with a desire for representation through compensatory treatment, blacks encountered resistance not only from their traditional civil rights opponents but also from some former allies. Reflecting public wariness over these new demands, both the Democratic party and the judiciary attempted to increase minority participation while explicitly refusing to sanction quotas to guarantee a proportional share of representation to the recently enfranchised. Though southern blacks had not received all they had hoped for, their position within the political arena was more secure.

8.

The Consensus Holds

Ten years later, they came to celebrate. Smaller in number, their ranks depleted by death, disillusionment, and disinterest, a band of civil rights veterans gathered in Selma, Alabama, to commemorate the anniversary of the historic 1965 march that had climaxed the voting rights struggle. The passage of time had not dampened the spirit of John Lewis, who had been bashed in the head by a state trooper a decade earlier. The irrepressible director of the Voter Education Project returned to the former battleground along with Julian Bond, his compatriot in SNCC, who was quietly serving as a Georgia state senator without any hint of the controversy that had accompanied his stormy entry into the legislature in the mid-1960s. The martyred Dr. Martin Luther King was not there to assume leadership of the march once again, but his wife, Coretta, returned to keep his memory alive. The civil rights activists found a different city from the one in which Reverend James Reeb, an original demonstrator, had been murdered on the street and where Dallas County Sheriff Jim Clark had used cattle prods on peaceful protestors. Clark had been turned out of office, and more than 70 percent of Selma's Negro residents had registered to vote, thereby helping to elect a town council that was half black. In contrast to the hostility they experienced in March 1965, those who congregated to remember the days of bloodshed encountered friendly police as they trekked over the Edmund Pettus Bridge. Reverend Frederick Reese, a longtime leader of the local movement and one of five blacks on the city council, underscored the changed racial climate: "We've come a long way. Whites who wouldn't tip their hats have learned to do it. People who wouldn't say 'Mister or Miss' to a black have learned to say it mighty fine. We've got black policemen, black secretaries, and we can use the public restrooms. The word 'nigger' is almost out of existence."[1]

The Selma reunion coincided with efforts to extend once again the temporary provisions of the Voting Rights Act due to lapse in August 1975. A decade after enactment of the landmark statute, suffragists intended to demonstrate that, despite many successes, black electoral participation relied heavily on continued federal surveillance. Andrew Young, a former aide to Dr. King, who was beginning his second term as a congressman from Atlanta, expressed the viewpoint of civil rights leaders that the suffrage law meant more than any other triumph. Although the Montgomery bus boycott and the Civil Rights Act of 1964 had helped demolish Jim Crow, Young insisted, they "didn't do anything to challenge the power relationships in the South" and were "far less consequential than the passage of the '65 act, which began to give blacks access to political power."[2] The task for Young and his legislative allies was to keep the measure alive.

This time they had to convince a new occupant of the White House to join their side, but the situation looked promising. Although the Watergate scandal had thrust Gerald Ford into the Oval Office, his administration displayed the bipartisan agreement that had accompanied expansion of the ballot since World War II. While the presidency had changed hands five times from Truman to Ford, the civil rights bureaucracy in Washington ensured a measure of continuity in suffrage policy. As former Assistant Attorney General Jerris Leonard, who had "grave misgivings" about vital provisions of the voting rights statute, subsequently acknowledged, career staff lawyers tended to "set a style and a mode because they have been part of the development of the previous policy and, therefore, they are wedded to it."[3] Thus, in the Justice Department the Civil Rights Division had built up considerable force behind implementation that carried over from one regime to another.

Shortly after Nixon resigned in 1974, the CRD began to prepare for renewal of the Voting Rights Act. Overseeing the discussion was its newly appointed head, J. Stanley Pottinger, a

Harvard Law School graduate and formerly the chief civil rights official in the Department of Health Education and Welfare, whom Aaron Henry called "the best ray of light the blacks see in this country today" inside the GOP regime.[4] On September 24, Pottinger assured the Congressional Black Caucus that in making a recommendation, his department would "not lose sight of the great symbolic meaning of the Voting Rights Act." Furthermore, the assistant attorney general sought to relieve any anxieties that the minority lawmakers might have had concerning the intention of this Republican administration to tamper with the provisions of the statute as its predecessor had attempted to do in 1970. Referring to Nixon's putative southern strategy, Pottinger promised that "politics will not be a part of the Civil Rights Division's evaluation."[5]

Pottinger's auspicious remarks reflected something of a change in White House thinking. The successor to a disgraced president, Ford saw his tenure as "a time to heal." A congressman from Grand Rapids, Michigan, for over twenty-five years, he had never been closely identified with the black cause. Although Representative Ford had voted for the major civil rights measures enacted on Capitol Hill, he had sponsored alternative versions that would have weakened the statutes. The former GOP minority leader had lined up behind passage of the 1965 Voting Rights Act and its extension in 1970 only after trying unsuccessfully to lift some of the burden from the South. A conservative Republican, Ford preferred that suffrage problems be resolved by federal judges sitting in the South rather than by Justice Department bureaucrats in Washington. In short, his previous record did not inspire confidence among civil rights proponents. However, having reached the nation's highest office without benefit of election, President Ford offered some hope of improvement, pledging to conduct an "open" White House and to appeal to "blacks and other minorities [who] felt—with some justification—that Nixon hadn't cared about their problems at all." Hence, about a month after taking over the reigns of power, Ford invited the Congressional Black Caucus to a meeting, which the group's chairman praised as "absolutely, fantastically good."[6]

Following up this exhibition of good will, the Republican administration decided to support retention of the Voting Rights Act's potent remedies. Appearing on "Meet the Press" on November 17, Attorney General William Saxbe, who, like Ford, owed his position to the Watergate imbroglio, revealed he would recommend to the president that the law be extended with "no major revisions in it."[7] Three weeks later, the attorney general officially asked the president to endorse a simple five-year rewnewal of the law. He urged a continuation of the nationwide ban on literacy tests "because there is evidence that the use of such tests may continue to perpetuate past racial discrimination." Likewise, Saxbe concluded that measures concerning federal examiners and preclearance review were still required "because recent experience under the Voting Rights Act shows a need for such provisions to prevent racial discrimination in connection with elections."[8] Acknowledging that considerable progress in black political participation had occurred in the covered jurisdictions during the previous decade, he noted that old patterns of suffrage bias persisted. As evidence he cited the disproportionately low percentage of black elected officials, the necessity of sending federal observers to monitor elections where race was a divisive factor, the rising number of section five objections, and repeated litigation of voter discrimination suits.[9]

Immediately after the beginning of the new year, President Ford publicly endorsed the Justice Department's recommendation. The chief executive gave his decision special significance by choosing to make the announcement on January 14, King's birthday. In euologizing the slain minister, Ford underscored the revered black leader's role in paving the way for passage of the 1965 act, a measure he celebrated for helping "to open up our political processes to full citizen participation."[10] By the end of the month, the president had transmitted to Capitol Hill legislation extending the key sections of the Voting Rights Act for an additional five years.[11] White House aides realized that a recommendation to the contrary "would be seen as the first step in another Republican effort to torpedo extension of the legislation" and throw the president "into political hot water."[12]

Nevertheless, in making this suggestion, President Ford ran into political flak from another quarter—southern Republi-

cans with whom he had cooperated in the past. David Treen, a
GOP congressman from Louisiana, called the suffrage law "one
of the most abominable pieces of legislation ever adopted by the
U.S. Congress." Yet, he could live with the statute if it were
drastically altered to remove the South from "perpetually different standards." Echoing this sentiment, Clarke Reed, chairman
of the Republican party in Mississippi, favored extension as long
as it applied nationwide. "Other than difficulties that our state
governments have had [in clearing] necessary changes in our
election laws through the Department of Justice," he admitted,
"the law had not been overly difficult to live with." He admonished Ford not to worry about charges of following a "southern
strategy" and claimed that the South was "miles ahead of the rest
of the nation in any aspect of race relations."[13]

In contrast, liberals welcomed the president's initial appeal for renewal. The NAACP's Clarence Mitchell congratulated
Ford for his support and expressed confidence in his "spirit and
continuing wholesome manner."[14] Led by Philip Hart and Hugh
Scott in the Senate, by Peter Rodino and Don Edwards in the
House, and by the Leadership Conference on Civil Rights, suffragists rallied to preserve the act's strength in full force and to
keep it from "becoming a victim of its own success." Despite
tremendous electoral progress since 1965, civil rights supporters
contended that southern blacks trailed whites in voter registration, lacked fair representation in governing councils, and generally held positions without "real power and responsibility." A
decade of federal intervention had not been enough to reverse the
effects of a century of disfranchisement. "The hard-won base of
black political power," Senator Scott wrote, "is still too fragile
to be shorn of the Voting Rights Act and its protection."[15]

In plotting their strategy, the reformers modified slightly
the president's proposal. Instead of a five-year extension as Ford
had recommended, they suggested ten. By enlarging the period
of coverage, the liberals would prolong the act through the 1980
census. In this way, section five would continue in operation while
state and local governments in the South reapportioned their legislative bodies. With preclearance required, the jurisdictions would
be less likely to redraw boundary lines to "wipe out the gains of

the Seventies."[16] The liberal legislators hoped to convert Ford to their viewpoint, and Senator Scott, the Republican minority leader, sought to nudge the chief executive in that direction. Indeed, civil rights advocates minimized their differences with the White House. Clarence Mitchell explained that supporters of the ten-year renewal had not originally recommended this time frame in discussing the legislation with the president. "If it is anybody's fault," Mitchell asserted, "I guess it is that of people like myself who raised the question of extension with the President."[17]

A more serious issue threatened to divide the liberals themselves—the possibility of broadening the scope of the act to include protection for language minorities, particularly Spanish speaking. Mitchell opposed the idea of redrafting the existing sections of the law and believed that to do so would pose a serious risk to renewal by introducing a new source of controversy. To head off a bitter squabble within their ranks, liberals agreed to support a statutory revision that contained a separate title covering non-English speaking groups. Enacted in this manner, it could be adjudicated on its own merits without endangering the constitutionality of the rest of the law.[18]

The language issue notwithstanding, the black franchise loomed as the paramount feature of the renewal battle. Although the record was replete with accomplishments, a great many trouble spots existed in the South where a decade after Selma blacks still struggled for political emancipation. Some improvements had come to southwest Georgia, the site of well-publicized confrontations in Albany and Americus; however, in Terrell County, Afro-Americans continued to experience difficulties in registering to vote. Composing a majority of the total population, blacks in "Terrible Terrell," as early civil rights workers had dubbed it, constituted slightly less than half of the enrolled voters. No black had yet been elected to office in the county seat of Dawson, and the white leaders intended to keep it that way. Mayor J. C. Raines, a defendant in a precedent-setting suffrage discrimination suit brought by the federal government in the late 1950s, helped engineer the effort to hold down black enrollment and to prevent a "take-over." Under his regime, white registration officials purged black voters already on the rolls and thwarted additional black applicants from signing up. In doing so, they devised standards for blacks that whites did not have to satisfy. An attorney from the Civil Rights Division thought that "after 10 years of the Voting Rights Act and several law suits," the situation was "unconscienable" [sic]. She reported that the "most damaging consequence of the city's behavior has been the damper it placed upon political participation by a large portion of Dawson's black population."[19]

Communities throughout Dixie mirrored the contrasting experiences of Selma and Dawson and of Dallas and Terrell counties. Although the surge of registration among southern blacks in the states covered by the 1965 Voting Rights Act had dropped off, the level of enrollment remained steady at about 55 percent of those eligible. Moreover, the decline in the growth rate was somewhat misleading. Since 1970, the number of potential voters had swelled with enfranchisement of eighteen to twenty-year-olds, a group whose lack of enthusiasm for signing up to vote reflected a traditional pattern among the youngest segment of the electorate. Under the circumstances, it was a measure of some progress that the percentage of black registration stayed constant. Indeed, the pace of black enrollment had exceeded that for whites, thus narrowing the registration gap between the races from over 40 percent in the mid-1960s to about 11 percent a decade later.[20] Furthermore, acquisition of the franchise resulted in a marked increase in the number of black elected officials. Across the South in 1975, over 1500 Afro-Americans held offices, including some eighty mayors and three United States representatives. Overall, the seven covered jurisdictions led the way with more than 1,100 blacks in elected posts.[21]

Despite such impressive statistics, southern blacks still found their path toward equal suffrage obstructed by discrimination. The Voter Education Project, which closely monitored the progress of the franchise, reported in the mid-1970s: "It should be abundantly clear that the advocacy of participatory democracy for minorities in the South is a revolutionary concept. The simple process of attempting to register the unregistered, to arouse the apathetic to action, to urge the voiceless to vote is obviously seen by many who hold power as a counter-productive, dangerous challenge to the status quo."[22] In many areas with nearly every white adult on the voter lists, officials manipulated the registration process to hamper Negroes from qualifying. Some enrollment boards proved uncooperative and refused to maintain regular or convenient office hours. Blacks in Sumter County, Alabama, complained that the registration office was closed half the scheduled period, and when it opened, employees conducted business only during normal daytime hours. To make matters worse, they closed for lunch. This problem was compounded for rural blacks who had no way to get to the courthouse when the office did open. In Humphreys County, Mississippi, G. H. Hood, the registrar who had been the target of federal voting rights suits in the early 1960s, still made it tough for blacks to enroll. In 1975, the Justice Department reported his steadfast refusal to provide blacks with an opportunity to register in the outlying areas where they lived and to keep his office functioning in the evening or on Saturday. In Ouachita Parish, Louisiana, another location of perennial suffrage bias, the registrar rebuffed black applicants for failing to identify themselves properly. Hence, he declined to accept forms of documentation such as social security cards, and he required those who were rejected to bring an accepted voter to vouch for them. However, a registrant could not testify on behalf of more than two applicants a year.[23] Managing to hurdle these barriers did not guarantee that blacks would have unimpeded access to the polls. Whites customarily supervised the polling booths and, in many places, rendered aid to black illiterates by marking their ballots improperly. Because few blacks served as authorized poll watchers, this racist ploy often went undetected.[24] In Mississippi's Noxubee County, disillusioned residents "expressed the view that they could not get a black elected even if they all voted . . . or even if a black candidate . . . received a majority of the votes cast."[25]

More than mere nuisances, these biased practices helped foster an atmosphere of fear among blacks that kept them outside of the electoral process. The persistent attempts to discourage minority political participation reinforced traditional attitudes that "politics was white folks' business," particularly in the rural South where blacks depended heavily on whites for their livelihood. The

more black southerners relied upon local whites for their sources
of income—employment, credit, welfare—the less likely they were
to upset traditional patterns of political behavior. Commenting
upon the failure of blacks to vote for more candidates of their
own race, the *Jackson Daily News* declared that "an historic relationship of paternalism of the whites for the blacks still exists
in Mississippi; . . . the blacks look upon the whites for leadership, for guidance, for favors, for loans, for friendship."[26] Robert Clark, who had braved white hostility to become the first black
representative in the Mississippi state legislature since Reconstruction, understood the reluctance of many of his neighbors: "It's
hard for a black man from my age up, when he walks into the
booth, not to get nervous. It's very hard. I mean because it's associated with the past."[27] Although overt violence and other blatant forms of racial control had gradually diminished by the mid-
1970s, their damaging effects lingered in the underlying institutional structures. In 1974, a Justice Department lawyer observed
that only the "degree" of racial bias had changed in Kemper
County, Mississippi, indicating that white officials exhibited a
"more modern attitude of subtle discriminatory action." As a result, blacks were not as much afraid of physical intimidation as
they feared "incurring the wrath of white officialdom, such as the
sheriff" and triggering "economic reprisals," fears "well grounded
in the black experience in the county."[28]

For many, the ravages of discrimination were difficult
to remedy. Generations of fear and vulnerability had left their
victims wary of throwing off old habits. "Our folks," a black
political organizer commented, "have been brainwashed for so long
that it's really hard for them to conceive of themselves having
any power."[29] The act of enfranchisement had not automatically
removed deep-seated structual barriers, psychological and economic, that thwarted expanded political access for Afro-Americans. Within the framework of southern race relations, the man-
ifestations of fear were difficult to distinguish from the usual apathy
associated with political nonparticipation. In fact, the two were
mutually reinforcing. The southern caste system had perpetuated
black subservience on the basis of race and class. Hence, a disproportionate number of Negroes had been denied the economic

and educational resources that stimulated political involvement. Financial dependence combined with segregated and inferior schooling left many black southerners pessimistic about their ability to achieve social change through the electoral process. These perceptions of political futility died hard, especially when whites maintained their domination through racist subterfuges. The old fears were easily aroused each time a registrar frustrated attempts to increase black enrollment and an election official mismarked ballots cast by illiterates at the polls.[30] Filled with painful memories of the past and discouraged by biased practices in the present, many southern blacks did not look to the future with hope. "One of the main problems," a former SNCC field secretary in Greenwood, Mississippi, observed, "is Negroes just haven't seem to reach that point where they want to stick together. There's a lot of people feel if they don't work for Mr. Charlie, they'll perish."[31]

It was essential in these rural regions to wipe out the residue of fear which, as one team of scholars noted, "has a long half life."[32] At the grass roots level, civil rights activists had established ongoing community organizations to mobilize blacks politically; however, before its collapse in the late sixties, the civil rights movement had left many areas virtually untouched. Furthermore, even agencies such as the Voter Education Project which continued to function were severely hamstrung by a shortage of funds and by a federal tax code that limited opportunities for obtaining additional financial resources.[33]

The majority of blacks who overcame these varied obstacles did not necessarily see their political power increase substantially. Indeed, their enthusiasm for voter registration and turning out at the polls had been more than matched by whites. In 1965, Mississippi had discarded its strict educational and character requirements for the franchise; consequently, whites were permitted to register and vote "under the same lenient rules which the federal Voting Rights Act has made applicable to Negroes."[34] Wary of being swept away by the wave of black enfranchisement, white southerners had responded to the challenge and accounted for approximately 60 to 70 percent of the new registrants.[35]

Many of these problems captured the attention of the United States Commission on Civil Rights. For nearly twenty years, the CCR had been a tenacious advocate of vigorous expansion of the suffrage. A gadfly within the federal bureaucracy, this agency consistently pointed out the gaps between the nation's democratic promise and the reality in its treatment of minorities. Not only had the commission investigated racial discrimination on the state and local levels, but it had also criticized Washington for executing federal laws too cautiously against the biased practices it uncovered. In January 1975, ten years after passage of the Voting Rights Act, the CCR wholeheartedly urged its extension for another decade. Noting "the very real gains that have been made," the civil rights panel contended: "Exclusion from the political process left minorities at a decided disadvantage when the opportunity to participate was finally achieved. The years under the Voting Rights Act have been years of catching up, a process well under way but far from complete."[36]

In its report, the commission catalogued the familiar discriminatory obstacles that continued to stand in the way of undiluted black political participation and recommended renewal of section five to combat these subterfuges. As the "cornerstone" of the Justice Department's enforcement policy, the preclearance program really had been utilized only since 1971, the commission maintained. In 1974, it noted, objections to submissions had reached a peak as Civil Rights Division attorneys became increasingly adept at diagnosing subtle as well as obvious efforts to reduce black electoral potency. Furthermore, the commission argued that the preclearance section had a deterrent effect in discouraging localities from enacting measures that could not withstand federal scrutiny. Looking ahead to the 1980 census and to the extensive legislative reapportionment that would follow it, the CCR suggested that Congress extend the Voting Rights Act until 1985 and thus narrow fresh opportunities for discrimination.[37] The commission also asked lawmakers to provide civil penalties against officials who violated section five, to suspend literacy tests for an additional ten years, to remove restrictions on foundation financing of nonpartisan voter education projects, and to protect illiterate voters from manipulation at the ballot box.[38]

In addition to these legislative proposals, the panel advocated some changes in the current enforcement policy. Although generally pleased with the Justice Department's handling of section five, the commissioners noted that local compliance with the submission regulation had been "uneven." It called upon the Civil Rights Division to establish "an effective monitoring system to bring to its attention unsubmitted changes."[39] The CCR found greater fault with the department's resistance to sending federal examiners to boost black registration. An early and frequent critic of Justice's policy of superseding local enrollment officials only as a last resort, the commission pointed out that federal examiners had visited a mere sixty counties during a ten-year span, and since 1972 had functioned in just two jurisdictions in Mississippi for ten days. No examiners had ever gone to North Carolina and Virginia, and overall, those who were dispatched to the remaining areas listed only 15 percent of the more than one million new registrants. The commission did not consider this record good enough, and it advised the department routinely to ship personnel to places "where the minority registration rate is significantly lower than the white rate, registration for minorities is inordinately inconvenient, or purges are burdensome or discriminatory in purpose or effect."[40] Closely related to the matter of registration was the deployment of federal observers. The CCR considered the program inadequate because the Justice Department could not empower these federal watchdogs to correct abuses immediately rather than simply jotting down their observations at the polling booth. The commission also wanted Washington to give extensive publicity to the presence of the observers and to employ a greater number of minority group members for this assignment. Both suggestions were designed to bolster the confidence of local blacks to participate on election day.[41]

Liberal lawmakers incorporated some of these recommendations into their legislative proposals, but the Justice Department rejected them. Although civil rights advocates enthusiastically endorsed the idea of a ten-year extension of the Voting Rights Act, the Ford administration stayed with the shorter time limit. Admitting that there was "some logic" in the commission's reasoning and that it was a "close question," the Justice

Department, nevertheless, favored a renewal for five years. Assistant Attorney General Pottinger argued that his version of the bill would offer "a greater incentive to covered jurisdictions to eliminate the need for special coverage," and the progress of the previous five years made him optimistic that "the job could be completed in the next five years."[42] Furthermore, denying that he did not have sufficient authority to enforce section five, the CRD chief spurned the proposal for initiating civil damage suits against officials who failed to submit electoral changes. He contended that such a measure "would swallow our present resources and detract from the nonpunitive spirit of the act." For similar reasons, Pottinger doubted the merit of providing advance publicity of the deployment of federal observers. Articulating a policy that had characterized enforcement of the voting rights law from its inception, the assistant attorney general asserted: "The Department often negotiates with local officials right up to election day in hopes of finding ways to reconcile differences or dispel fears without sending in observers. We believe this voluntary resolution of problems is important to the concept of federalism."[43] However, Pottinger accepted the CCR's advice in one area—closer review of unsubmitted state electoral codes. After a thorough inspection of measures enacted between 1970 and 1974, the Civil Rights Division had already turned up about three hundred laws that went into effect without the requisite federal clearance. To avoid this situation in the future, Pottinger pledged to conduct regular surveys of state legislative sessions in order to detect unsubmitted changes and to remind local officials of their obligations under section five.[44]

Despite these differences of opinion, the outlook for renewal appeared bright. Both the Ford administration and the suffragists sought to retain the special provisions of the Voting Rights Act for an additional period. Not since 1965 had such a common purpose existed between government and reformers, the executive and legislative branches, and Republicans and Democrats. Faced with this united front, the opposition shouldered the heavy burden of reversing a popular program—indeed, a showcase for the American reform tradition—that yielded rich returns at little financial cost. The 1965 statute had become an accepted feature of the prevailing political system. Thus, foes of renewal, most of them conservatives, in seeking to dismantle the machinery for continued enforcement found themselves in the anomalous position of attempting to upset the status quo.

The consensus on black enfranchisement was evident from the opening legislative deliberations. On February 25, a House Judiciary Subcommittee convened to consider several extension bills, among them a ten-year measure introduced by Peter Rodino and Don Edwards, respectively the chairpersons of the full committee and the subcommittee. The panel also reviewed the administration's five-year version sponsored by Edward Hutchinson of Michigan, the ranking Republican of the group. Their strategies differed sharply. Administration supporters recognized that some form of extension bill was likely to pass, and with the August deadline in mind they wanted to move as quickly as possible. To this end, they hoped to improve the chief executive's bargaining position in case Congress adopted a ten-year renewal. In that event, Ford would veto the measure, and with sufficient time left before the expiration date, he could hold out for a five-year substitute. The liberals reversed this timetable. Although anxious to complete legislative action before the special features of the law lapsed, they believed that by finishing final deliberations close to August 6, they would force the president to sign a ten-year extension or risk termination of the crucial provisions.[45]

The advocates of ten-year renewal dominated the proceedings. Speaking before the Edwards subcommittee, Representative Rodino, whose stature had grown from his judicious handling of the Nixon impeachment hearings, explained that in retaining the act for another decade, "we are more likely to find new officials with new outlooks and attitudes, and you will no longer have those [residual] fears which are now associated with past brutal measures of discrimination and violence."[46] Arthur Flemming, the head of the Civil Rights Commission who had replaced Father Hesburgh and was no less committed to the cause of equal justice, rallied around the Rodino-Edwards bill. Appraising the suffrage situation in the South as his agency had reported it, Flemming noted the substantial gains in voter registration and in officeholding among blacks. However, he warned against becoming complacent before the task was completed: "Blacks are slowly catching up with a moving target, slowly overcoming the effects of their political exclusion, while taking advantage of the hard-won opportunity to participate."[47] Representative Andrew Young offered vivid proof of the need to renew the law. In the early 1970s, the Georgia legislature had sketched the boundary lines of the fifth congressional district to exclude Young's neighborhood. Utilizing section five, the Justice Department had blocked this plan, and when the state redrafted the proposal, Young won election from the district. Had it not been for the preclearance provision, the black congressman told his colleagues on Capitol Hill, "I would not be here today." In light of his experience, he reminded them of the upcoming census in 1980 and the hazard it posed to southern blacks if state lawmakers undertook reapportionment without fear of a federal veto.[48]

Along this line, other black suffragists rushed to the defense of the act. Dr. Oscar Butler, president of the Orangeburg, South Carolina, chapter of the NAACP, called for extended federal surveillance: "If we do not have the big 'daddy' . . . we have no clout, so if you are going to remove that which has given us the opportunity to learn to walk, we are going to be back in the crawling stage."[49] Clarence Mitchell portrayed a more frightening picture of the consequences if the voting rights statute lapsed. Recalling the political abyss into which southern Negroes had fallen during the decades following Reconstruction, the NAACP lobbyist warned that failure to renew the landmark measure would flash a signal to covered jurisdictions to "pass the most horrendous legislation." The resulting "nightmare" would produce catastrophic effects "because the blacks are not going to take it." Elaborating on this gloomy forecast, Eddie Williams, director of the Joint Center for Political Studies, a nonpartisan research group specializing in public policy concerns of Afro-Americans, commented that as long as the Voting Rights Act remained in operation blacks would believe that "change is possible through the political process." He urged the lawmakers to preserve its message: "Cast a ballot, not a brick."[50]

Other witnesses quarrelled over the premise that the law was still needed because it had not yet allowed blacks equal access to the electoral process. A. F. Summer, the attorney general of Mississippi, was under the impression that the act "was for the purpose of creating the atmosphere and creating the position that a black person could go and vote and could participate and enjoy all of the benefits of anybody else in the United States." However, he thought the federal government's obligation ended at clearing away suffrage hurdles and did not include promoting the election of black officials.[51] This view of the statute's intent was disputed by Armand Derfner, a civil rights attorney experienced in the franchise field. Although literacy tests and other impediments to voter registration may have been the main focus of legislation in 1965, he argued that lawmakers had inserted the preclearance authority of section five "to prevent, in advance, stratagems whose nature was unknown but which Congress knew would be forthcoming when literacy tests were abolished."[52] He placed in this category schemes to dilute voting strength and to hinder the opportunity to elect minority group officials.

If the suffragists encountered a friendly response in the committee, the congressmen were only slightly less receptive to the testimony presented by the Ford administration. Because the content of the competing suffrage bills was similar, no serious tension developed between the two camps. The appearance of Pottinger, admired for his enlightened supervision of the CRD, further diminished the chance of a split within the ranks of voting rights supporters. The assistant attorney general vigorously defended the extension of section five, pointing out that many covered jurisdictions had not complied with this measure in the past. He announced that the Justice Department and the FBI were investigating local governments which had not submitted electoral changes, and the administration spokesman promised to take remedial action to correct these violations of the act. Pottinger hailed the preclearance section for its overall effectiveness in challenging discriminatory techniques of diluting the black vote, and he firmly asserted that the "guarantees it provides are more significant to the country than the slight interference to the Federal system which this powerful provision would incur."[53]

Nevertheless, the assistant attorney general did dissent from those suffrage advocates who favored a more vigorous program for using federal examiners. Pottinger informed one of them, Congressman Robert Drinan of Massachusetts, that the Civil Rights Commission was "simply wrong" in suggesting that the Justice Department should send registrars where black enrollment lagged behind that of whites. Statistics alone were not enough, and he insisted that his department responded to reports of any discrepancy in voter registration that resulted from official action. "We will send examiners into such a situation tomorrow," Pottinger claimed, "but we need to know where these places are if they exist."[54] In another point of departure, the CRD representative counseled against a ten-year extension. He argued that Congress had accepted a figure of five years in both 1965 and 1970, and he opposed setting a longer time period, especially when the "goal should be to end the special coverage provisions."[55]

Southern white officials who appeared before the subcommittee agreed with Pottinger's aim but wanted it fulfilled more quickly. The attorney general of Virginia, Andrew P. Miller, contended that his state had not employed a literacy test in a discriminatory manner for over a decade and, thus, should be entitled to bail out from coverage. However, the federal district court in Washington had ruled otherwise. In a 1974 opinion echoing the *Gaston County* verdict, the tribunal held that the state literacy requirement for registration, even though administered fairly, discriminated against black applicants who had matriculated through an officially segregated and inferior school system. On the basis of this decision, none of the designated governmental units could have soon escaped jurisdiction if Congress renewed the law.[56] Representative M. Caldwell Butler, a Virginia Republican who sat on the subcommittee, bemoaned this situation: "Where is there anywhere in the Voting Rights Act anything to inspire the States to do something about this themselves?" he asked dejectedly.[57] To furnish such an incentive, Butler suggested an amendment, fashioned by Attorney General Miller, to relax the court-devised standard for bailout. His proviso declared that so long as a state had not administered its literacy test in a racially biased manner, "previous disparities in the quality of education afforded its citizens" were not sufficient evidence of discrimination.[58]

The Ford administration responded in a mixed fashion to this proposal. At first, Pottinger maintained that the offering was based on a faulty proposition. Contradicting the presumption that a literacy exam was "the sole discriminatory practice which the Voting Rights Act is designed to reach," he contended that it was only an "anchor" or a "targeting device" to identify other forms of suffrage discrimination as well. Consequently, he asserted, any jurisdiction seeking to free itself from coverage ought to prove that it had not "engaged in other practices which the courts have found violate the Voting Rights Act and the Fifteenth Amendment."[59] To meet this objection, Butler drew up another plan that took into account a state's overall performance in fulfilling its obligations under the suffrage law. In order to satisfy the requirements for removal from coverage, during a five-year period a designated jurisdiction had to demonstrate complete compliance with section five, both in furnishing electoral changes to and in having all submissions approved by the Justice Department. This revision impressed the administration, which suggested that with some slight modifications the measure "would be stringent enough . . . to ensure that only those jurisdictions which, in fact, have rooted out the evils which the Act was designed to prohibit, could bail out."[60]

In contrast, Don Edwards and his liberal colleagues took a dim view of this attempt to alter one of the key provisions of the statute. After wrapping up thirteen days of hearings throughout February and March, the members of the subcommittee argued their case before the full Judiciary Committee. On May 3, the proponents of a simple ten-year renewal of the statute barely turned back the Butler amendment. The majority claimed that "while some progress has been made, the covered jurisdictions need to remain under the Act so that retrogression does not occur."[61] They opposed lowering in any way the standards for withdrawal because it had been impossible to erase the effects of voting discrimination in only a decade. Offering the covered areas a convenient escape route was premature while the proportion of black registration and the number of minority elected officials continued to lag considerably behind those of whites. In retaining jurisdiction, Washington could spur new suffrage gains and could prevent attempts to erase some of the achievements already made. Anticipating the wave of legislative reapportionment following the 1980 census and the possibilities of racial gerrymandering it would open, the committee underscored the need for preserving section five and recommended extension of the law until 1985. Furthermore, the group suggested amendments to abolish literacy tests permanently, to afford federal protection to language minorities, and to broaden the opportunity of private citizens to litigate suits under the Voting Rights Act. In order to safeguard the basic provisions of the existing law, the legislators adopted a clause separating the original measure from the proposed amendments in the event that the latter were challenged in the courts.

A minority of the committee dissented. Composed mainly of Republicans and a few white southern Democrats, this faction endorsed the Butler bailout plan. The Virginia congressman admitted the need for retaining the basic provisions of the act. "Many of us," he declared, "have availed ourselves of the opportunity to meet with our constituents representing minorities and found that the complaints set forth in the Report of the Civil Rights Commission do in fact exist in many instances."[62] Butler had redrafted his bill to permit exemption from coverage when a jurisdiction attained a 60 percent voter registration or voter turnout at the most recent presidential election, exhibited an unblemished suffrage record for the previous five years, and successfully introduced "an affirmative action program to revamp voting laws." On behalf of his colleagues, Representative Butler contended that the adoption of these criteria would provide a strong incentive for state and local officials to enhance black political participation. In addition, GOP proponents of the administration bill favored a simple five-year extension, including a suspension of the literacy test during that period. They maintained that passage of biased reapportionment schemes following the 1980 census could be challenged in the federal district court in Washington, which retained jurisdiction for five years after a state bailed out from special coverage. Furthermore, the minority rejected the foreign language proposals, preferring instead to permit the attorney general to file lawsuits to attack discrimination against non-English speaking electorates.[63]

In expressing their opposition, white southern officials had decided against a frontal assault to combat the voting rights law. They realized the immense difficulty in overturning this popular measure, and some had even come to accept it as a political reality. Stone D. Barefield, an influential Mississippi state legislator who had testified before the subcommittee, acknowledged: "After ten years of living under the Voter Rights Act . . . we have learned to live with it. I found out that it did not destroy the State of Mississippi. We still function. We still operate." In a similar vein, Alabama Congressman Walter Flowers, a Judiciary Committee member who had staunchly opposed all civil rights bills, declared, "In all honesty, I must give credit to this [voting rights] legislation for a great deal of . . . success, which we accepted reluctantly." Recognizing the inevitable, the adversaries shifted their customary attack on the extension of the law to revising it to permit southern states a better chance of escaping coverage.[64] Indeed, the generally moderate comments voiced by the dissidents increased the confidence of suffragists. "I guess one of the happiest things for us," a delighted Joseph Rauh explained during the hearings, "is the broad consensus that has grown up behind extending the Voting Rights Act. The President, the Attorney General, the Committee—the minority as well as the majority—all favor extension; we are happy with this consensus in America."[65]

His assessment proved correct. On May 14, a week after the Judiciary panel issued its report the House Rules Committee approved the ten-year extension bill and sent it to the floor. Three weeks later, it moved through the lower chamber without alteration. From the outset, the opponents saw the legislative handwriting on the wall. "I am realistic enough to know," moaned Representative Sonny Montgomery of Mississippi, "that an extension of the Voting Rights Act in some form is going to pass the Congress."[66] Nevertheless, the antagonists still were not willing to surrender meekly. Southern white lawmakers and their conservative Republican allies once again attempted to soften what they considered the harsh features of the law. Congressman Butler offered his bailout proviso, which he dubbed the "impossible bailout amendment," emphasizing to his opponents that the standards for removal would be stringent. Representative Charles Wiggins, a California Republican, introduced a proposal that substituted for the original triggering mechanism one that applied to jurisdictions where minority groups made up at least 5 percent of the population and where less than 50 percent of nonwhite voters had participated in the prior general election. The adoption of these measures would have paved the way for the entrapped southern states to loosen the knot of federal supervision. Acknowledging that they may have sinned in the past, but insisting that the time had arrived for an end to Reconstruction-like treatment of their region, Dixie legislators backed these amendments "which allow formerly errant jurisdictions to be rewarded for having changed their bygone ways."[67]

These appeals went unheeded. Upon hearing white southerners bewail the oppressiveness of the Voting Rights Act, Representative Andrew Young provided a southern black perspective on living under the 1965 law: "It surely feels wonderful."[68] The overwhelming majority of his colleagues empathized with the black congressman. After two days of debate, on June 4 the House rejected by a margin of two to one or better a series of weakening amendments. At the same time, lawmakers easily approved a measure expanding the statute's guarantees to language minorities. On a final tally, 341-70, the congressmen renewed the act for an additional ten years. On the losing side were forty southerners, but more noteworthy were the sixty-six white delegates from Dixie who lined up behind extension. Representative John Buchanan of Alabama expressed the prevailing sentiment of those from his region who joined the victory: "The increased participation of black Americans in the political process through the protections afforded in this act, notwithstanding the fears and dire predictions concerning its effects on States like mine which were voiced in 1965, has hurt our State approximately as much as black participation has hurt Bear Bryant's football team or the University of Alabama's basketball team."[69]

Following this easy triumph, two months before the

special provisions of the Voting Rights Act were due to lapse the suffragists faced a more difficult battle in the Senate. Unlike its counterpart in the House, the upper chamber's Judiciary Committee was presided over by a chairman hostile to civil rights. James Eastland of Mississippi could be counted on to throw up whatever procedural blockades were at his disposal to derail smooth extension of the law. Slowed down in committee, the bill awaited a filibuster once it reached the floor. Unless checked promptly, these dilatory tactics might prevent renewal of the statute before the August 6 deadline.

The reformers did not intend to be caught by surprise, and they followed their own timetable for conducting business. During April and the first day of May, the Judiciary Subcommittee on Constitutional Rights had held hearings on several extension measures paralleling those introduced in the House. Chaired by John V. Tunney of California, who had succeeded the retired Sam Ervin, and dominated by liberals, the panel heard a reprise of the testimony delivered before the Edwards group. Southern white officials complained about the burden imposed in conforming to the preclearance and bailout sections of the law; the Ford administration urged as the safest course a five-year renewal bill excluding special provisions for non-English speaking groups and keeping a temporary ban on literacy exams; and suffragists recited a litany of problems confronting black political participation and called for another decade to implement the act's vital procedures. Listening to the witnesses, most subcommittee members were inclined to agree with the comments of Vernon Jordan, former VEP director who had become head of the National Urban League: "The ten-year period is . . . needed to establish and institutionalize a black voting tradition in the South. A tradition too strong to be tampered with now, just as we are beginning to reap some of the fruits of our labor."[70]

The conclusion of the hearings brought the expected stall, and Tunney maneuvered to beat it. After the House had passed its version of the bill and sent it to the upper chamber in early June, the California senator, along with Republican Minority Leader Hugh Scott, obtained the approval of Mike Mansfield, the majority leader, to hold the measure at the desk. In this way, they kept it from interment in the graveyard of Eastland's Judiciary Committee where similar proposals lay buried. Using this parliamentary device as leverage, Tunney goaded the Judiciary Committee to complete its own work and to forward a report to the floor. On July 17, at a session marking up the voting rights bill, he warned the group to finish its task within four days or the House bill would then be called up. Irked by this threat, Senator Strom Thurmond yelled: "Do it! Do it! And see what happens." When tempers cooled, the committee resumed deliberations, rejected amendments to soften the measure, and adopted S. 1279, a ten-year renewal, 12-4.[71]

Before the Judiciary panel released its final report, the upper chamber decided first to consider the recently passed H.R. 6219. Senate leaders hoped that approval of the House version, even with modifications, would facilitate speedy passage of the law. Desiring to avoid a time-consuming joint conference committee to reconcile differences, they sought to return to the lower body a measure closely resembling the one it had already adopted.[72] On July 21, with less than three weeks to spare, Mansfield offered two cloture motions to avert further delay. The first was aimed at ending discussion on the move to proceed to consider H.R. 6219. The 72-19 vote provided a comfortable margin beyond the sixty votes required to terminate debate. This outcome reaffirmed the consensus on black voting rights. Highlighting this point, eight of fifteen southern Democrats joined the majority to defuse one of Dixie's hallowed legislative weapons. Next, on a 63-13 tally, the senators quickly agreed to consider the House bill. On this occasion, despite a slight erosion in support, five of twelve southern Democrats appeared on the winning side.[73] Two days later on July 23, the Senate supported a second cloture petition, 76-20; in this instance, eight southern Democrats again followed the majority.

Having lost the major procedural struggles, the foes of renewal attempted to write substantive changes into the bill. Southern opponents introduced several proposals to expand enforcement nationwide. Although continuing to prohibit suffrage discrimination, they would require the attorney general to use the cumbersome process of litigation before he could send federal examiners and could exercise preclearance review. Senator Sam Nunn of Georgia advocated this approach to avoid "the rather humiliating experience of having to submit every single change by elected officials in every single city and county ordinance pertaining to elections through some unselected GS-12 bureaucrat over at the Department of Justice."[74]

The voting rights coalition repelled all attempts to overhaul the act's enforcement machinery in this manner, though on July 23, the day of the second cloture vote, the suffragists narrowly defeated an amendment proposed by Richard Stone of Florida. To broaden geographical coverage of the statute, the Sunshine State's senator suggested that the preclearance remedy be applied anywhere in the country the attorney general filed a successful franchise discrimination suit. John Tunney, the floor manager of H.R. 6219, warned against adopting this revision which would "gut" the law by "completely overburden[ing] the Justice Department . . . if they [sic] had to have preclearance for every State or county of the country." By a slim 49-46 vote, thirty-three northern Democrats aligned with two southern Democrats and fourteen northern Republicans in tabling Stone's proposal. On the losing side were a majority of GOP lawmakers—twenty-three out of thirty-seven—several northern Democrats, and nearly all Democrats from the South.[75]

Up to this point in the legislative deliberations, the Ford administration had supported renewal of the act in its current form. The president had taken credit for recommending a simple renewal bill to Congress and considered "the passage of this vital legislation . . . a top priority."[76] Although counseling against incorporating those alterations that strengthened the measure, the GOP regime had indicated that it would not resist including most of them. Assistant Attorney General Pottinger eventually endorsed H.R. 6219, the liberal version that passed the House, as a "basically strong bill" and recommended "that we would not quarrel with a legislative judgment to go with a ten year extension."[77]

Nevertheless, Ford's political strategists had never ceased calculating the administration's stake in meeting its obligation to southern Republicans. In the spring and early summer, presidential counselors and Justice Department officials had quietly assessed the options available to the White House in tailoring the suffrage bill to its moral and political objectives. Southern Republican leaders, they recognized, accepted renewal of the franchise measure as a practical reality but called upon the chief executive to extend it throughout the United States. Clarke Reed, the GOP chairman in Mississippi, admitted that "from the viewpoint of actual federal impact, existence of the Act is not as controversial or undesirable now as it was five or ten years ago, but that . . . singling out the South for disparate treatment . . . is . . . politically 'unfair,' in a general sense of the word."[78] At the same time, the president knew that civil rights groups viewed geographical expansion of the law as a sellout to white southern officials. Richard D. Parsons, a member of Ford's Domestic Council, argued that any move by the chief executive to apply the special provisions of the law nationally "can be interpreted, at best, as an obvious political gesture and, at worst, as an outright attempt to kill extension of the Voting Rights Act."[79] Caught in a dilemma, presidential aides sought to find a delicate way of appeasing both sides in the legislative controversy. In one proposed solution the president accepted the ten-year renewal bill while concurrently instructing the attorney general "to vigorously exercise his authority to root out and eliminate voting discrimination in the North."[80]

In the end, Ford chose a position that exhibited neither finesse nor grace, only clumsiness. On the eve of the debate in the Senate, the president nearly wrecked the chance of renewing the Voting Rights Act before its scheduled expiration. Perhaps with an eye toward the coming year's presidential election, he appeared to be looking southward in search of backing for his nomination with the hope of heading off the opposition of Ronald Reagan, popular with conservatives in Dixie.[81] A former congressional advocate of nationwide expansion of the 1965 statute, Ford suddenly recommended this approach again. Affirming that he favored continuation of suffrage legislation, on July 17 the president publicly announced that he was leaning toward support of extending coverage of the law to all fifty states. The next day, Ford wrote privately to Hugh Scott and Mike Mansfield that either a five or ten-year renewal was suitable because "my first priority is to extend the Voting Rights Act before the August recess"; but he dropped a bombshell by adding, "this is the appropriate time and opportunity to extend the Voting Rights Act nationwide."[82]

The president's eleventh hour invitation drew a mixed reception. When the text of Ford's message to Scott and Mansfield was officially announced immediately following the defeat of the Stone amendment, John Stennis of Mississippi rushed to resurrect it. He introduced a measure authorizing the operation of section five throughout the nation. Linking the chief executive to this plan, Senator James Allen of Alabama, a die-hard foe of the pending renewal proposal, praised him for "the greatest stroke that he has made yet toward fairness and toward the promotion of unity in this country" and pleaded with "this Democratic Congress to meet the President halfway on this issue."[83] This appeal met strong resistance. Senator Edward Kennedy of Massachusetts lambasted Ford for confusing the matter—"He wants to have it all ways"—and his University of Virginia Law School roommate, John Tunney, admonished those lawmakers who followed the president as "voting to kill the Voting Rights Act."[84] Liberal Republicans chimed in agreement. Jacob Javits of New York countered the claim that laws aimed at particular regions were unfair. "My state," he declared, "does not get very much out of the fact that we have some kind of support for cotton, for example, and the same is true for many other States."[85]

The bipartisan alliance won this skirmish, 48-38, a more generous margin than that defeating the Stone amendment. On this occasion, the triumphant coalition picked up five northern Democrats and four Republicans. The Democratic senators who made the switch, including Hubert Humphrey of Minnesota, had long supported civil rights legislation. In revolting briefly against the reform position, they had challenged the notion that civil rights was exclusively a sectional issue. This point demonstrated on the Stone amendment vote, they returned to the fold. The defection of the four GOP senators, though, left only a razor-thin majority of Republicans lined up in favor of enlarging the scope of the act. This nearly even split in GOP ranks reflected the ambiguous role played by the president, who in a manner reminiscent of Nixon's approach to renewal in 1970, did not make himself perfectly clear on this issue. Ostensibly an advocate of a simple renewal of the law, Ford also supported the principle behind the amendments offered by Stone and Stennis. Having staked out all sides of the question, he confused both friends and foes of suffrage extension. On July 23, the morning of the crucial votes, however, he brought this perplexing performance to an end. Alarmed that his last-minute intervention might backfire and might threaten passage of the House bill before adjournment, he abruptly reaffirmed his original stand in support of the measure by telephoning Minority Leader Scott that he really "didn't want to mess up this bill" and by asking him "to put out the fire."[86] Ford's latest about-face came to light after the defeat of the Stone amendment and shortly before the vote on the Stennis proviso, thereby explaining the erosion in support for the latter measure.

Buoyed by these victories, civil rights proponents easily defeated a variety of amendments that would have drastically hampered implementation of the Voting Rights Act. The suffrage juggernaut rolled over plans to defuse the triggering device in the 1965 law, to substitute an updated formula that would have released the original jurisdictions from coverage, and to ease the requirements for bailout. On roll call votes disposing of amendments which in one form or another weakened the bill, the bulk of northern Democrats united against the modifications in each instance. Following the revelation of the latest presidential communication in support of the pending bill, the majority of Republicans only once favored a proposed change.[87] Thus, not only did the lawmakers approve the strong features of the law adopted in 1965 and 1970, but they also agreed to eliminate literacy tests permanently and to establish administrative machinery to assist language minorities.[88]

However, the Republicans did manage to obtain a significant revision of H.R. 6219 that pleased white southerners: renewal of the act for seven years instead of ten. This figure emerged rather casually during a conversation on the Senate floor between Tunney and Robert Byrd, the majority whip from West Virginia who had allied with the South on several attempts to amend the bill. Byrd introduced an amendment for a five-year extension.

Tunney countered with an offer of seven years, although he still favored the full ten-year period. Byrd responded with a suggestion of six years, and John Pastore, a Rhode Island Democrat, raised the ante to eight years. Holding out for the decade approach, Jacob Javits put an end to the bidding by raising a procedural objection that temporarily halted further discussion of the matter.[89]

Given this respite, Tunney conferred with Don Edwards and Peter Rodino in the House to inquire whether the lower chamber would agree to a seven-year renewal without convening a conference committee. Assured that the representatives would accept the Senate revision, Tunney offered only token resistance when the subject again came up on the Senate floor. The California Democrat felt comfortable with the compromise because the preclearance section would continue in operation until August 1982, long enough to review state reapportionment plans adopted after the 1980 census.[90] Modified as a seven-year renewal, the Byrd amendment carried, 52–42. Not unexpectedly, it captured support from twenty-three administration Republicans who previously had favored some weakening amendments and from all sixteen southern Democrats who voted. Nevertheless, the margin of victory was supplied by thirteen northern Democrats, including Majority Leader Mansfield and a few customary defenders of civil rights legislation. Having joined in preventing dilution of the law's powerful enforcement provisions, they acquiesced in a slight shortening of their length of operation.[91]

This was the solitary defeat for the suffragists who deflected all other efforts to carve up H.R. 6219. The voting rights alliance held together and outmaneuvered its adversaries, for Southern opponents could not muster enough votes from conservative Republicans uncertain of firm backing from the White House. After losing showdowns on the Stone and Stennis amendments, Ernest Hollings of South Carolina saw "the writing on the wall." The Palmetto State Democrat acknowledged: "Without the President's support to get some votes on his side of the aisle, we are not going to be able to make it."[92] While not all southern senators were ready to concede defeat, most did not have their heart in waging an all-out fight. By July 24, following three days of deliberations, only a handful could work up as much rage as did James Allen. "General Robert E. Lee just had his citizenship returned to him posthumously," the undaunted Alabama Democrat thundered about a leader of another lost cause. "That is one sign, I guess, that reconstruction is over. Let us end reconstruction of the South somewhere along the line."[93] Unable to alter the regional focus of the law, most southerners resigned themselves to living with it for an additional seven years. Bennett Johnston, a Democrat from Louisiana, spoke for his fellow Dixie senators: "We found that the sky did not fall under the 1965 Voting Rights Act, that things worked pretty well in the South, the deep South of the old Confederacy, which readjusted their patterns of voting, readjusted their attitudes toward all people. It worked."[94] Reflecting this opinion, eleven Democrats and two Republicans from the South, a majority of those representing the region in the Senate, cast their votes in favor of H.R. 6219, which passed 77-12.[95]

Returned to the House for ratification, the slightly modified bill had little trouble winning approval. The legislators agreed to accept the measure containing only one substantial change in the version they had sent to the Senate nearly two months earlier. On July 28, a seven-year renewal of the law sailed through the House, 346-56. The final vote showed that blacks had made significant inroads within the Democratic party in the South following years of affirmative action guidelines and voter registration campaigns. Fifty-two southern Democrats favored H.R. 6219 whereas twenty-six opposed it. Support was particularly solid from congressmen elected since 1972, exhibiting the presence of a new breed of southern Democrat for whom black suffrage was an accepted way of life. In contrast, the Republican party had concentrated its energies on recruiting conservative whites in Dixie. Hence, seventeen of twenty-seven GOP southerners voted against the franchise measure.[96]

On August 6, the day that portions of the Voting Rights Act were due to lapse, Gerald Ford signed the renewal legislation. At a brief ceremony in the White House Rose Garden, congressional leaders and civil rights advocates beamed as the president celebrated the ten-year anniversary of the law by stamping his approval on its continuation. Pursuing the path first opened by Lyndon Johnson, Ford reaffirmed the national commitment to enfranchisement: "The right to vote is the very foundation of our American system. There must be no question whatsoever about the right of each eligible American to participate in our electoral process."[97] Yet President Ford did not exhibit the same moral fervor for racial equality as had his Texas predecessor. Neither did he share the same political aims. LBJ fashioned a voting rights bill primarily designed to appeal to liberals and civil rights lobbyists; in contrast, Ford strove, albeit fleetingly, to shape legislation that pleased conservative whites without greatly disturbing blacks. In choosing this course, he hoped to strengthen his position among southern Republicans for his presidential candidacy in 1976. However feeble his attempt was to revamp the extension bill, its passage did not harm his ambitions. The Voting Rights Act had become a mainstay of the American electoral system, and even its detractors grudgingly accepted that fact. James Buckley, the archconservative senator from New York who had voted for nearly all the southern-inspired amendments to the bills, nevertheless favored its final enactment. He came around because he believed it was important for blacks and other minorities to "understand that those who are labeled 'conservative' are as concerned over the protection of fundamental civil liberties as anyone else in the country."[98] Thus, at mid-decade blacks could take some comfort that the suffrage had made great progress and that the second Reconstruction was still alive.

9.

The Hands
That Picked the Cotton

The presidential election of 1876 sealed the fate of the First Reconstruction and bargained away the civil rights of Afro-Americans for sectional reconciliation instead. One hundred years later, black ballots were instrumental in electing as president a descendant of former Confederates, Jimmy Carter of Georgia. The 1976 election demonstrated the endurance of the Second Reconstruction's policy of enfranchisement and showed that some old racial wounds were healing. However, like the country that stood at its bicentennial crossroads, blacks celebrated their past victories while looking to the future with uncertainty. Samuel DuBois Cook, a political scientist and president of Dillard University, observed, "From the long perspective of history, a new factor in the equation of blacks in the American political system is that today blacks . . . can be creative participants and subjects rather than mere objects and victims of the political process." Yet, as the United States observed its two hundredth birthday, this noted black scholar offered a sober warning against the excesses of self-congratulation. "Black politics in this Bicentennial year," Cook admonished, "is characterized, also, by a deep sense of frustration, anguish, drift, wondering, and a tinge of cynicism and hopelessness."[1] Unless federal commitment to the suffrage and racial equality persisted, the long-promised payoffs from participation in the political system might forever elude Afro-Americans.

The rise of Jimmy Carter to the presidency offered some

encouragement to the aspirations of blacks. Like Lyndon Johnson, Carter came to the Oval Office having undergone something of a transformation on the race issue. In his successful campaign for governor of Georgia in 1970, Carter had assailed his opponent for supporting school busing and racial balancing. Still, while appealing to the same "antiestablishment" white constituency of outgoing governor Lester Maddox, this southwest Georgia peanut farmer did not repeat the crudely Negrophobic remarks of his predecessor. Instead, Carter cast himself in a populist mold and expressed his program mainly in economic rather than in racial terms. This new outlook came through eloquently in his 1971 inaugural address: "I say to you quite frankly that the time for racial discrimination is over. Our people have already made this major and difficult decision. No poor, rural, weak, or black person shall ever have to bear the additional burden of being deprived of the opportunity for an education, a job, or simple justice."[2] Following this stirring declaration, Governor Carter established a biracial commission, increased the number of black governmental appointments, and in a gesture filled with symbolism, gave approval to hang Martin Luther King's portrait in the state capitol building. After two years in office, Carter, musing about the changes that the civil rights movement and the federal government had forced upon the South, said he accepted them with a "sense of relief" and "secret gratitude," and refused "to revert back to a formal attitude of . . . separation of blacks and whites, of lesser degree of citizenship, and so forth."[3]

These sentiments appealed to southern blacks who looked favorably upon Carter's presidential bid in 1976. In contrast, they had reason to reject the Republican incumbent, Gerald Ford, who pursued a different strategy from Carter's by focusing on the South's conservative white electorate. Ford's campaign director, James Baker, conceded the black vote to the Democrats and forecast that the Republican share of it "would be 10 percent, regardless."[4] Virtually ignoring blacks, the GOP received even less than this estimate, as 94 percent of the Negro electorate supported the Carter-Mondale ticket. Overall, blacks turned out at the polls in record numbers—of those registered 64 percent voted—and they led Carter's sweep of every southern state except Virginia.[5] One of Carter's top black advisors, Andrew Young, recalled the election-night drama when the Democrats were losing in the West. "I heard," the Georgia congressman asserted, "that it may depend on how Mississippi went, and I thought 'Lord have mercy.' But when I heard that Mississippi had gone our way, I knew that the hands that picked cotton finally picked the president."[6]

Having lined up solidly behind the triumphant chief executive, blacks looked forward to sharing in the spoils of victory, and they did receive some rewards for their loyalty. The number of blacks nominated and appointed to high governmental posts soared during the Carter administration, the most visible example being the selection of Andrew Young as ambassador to the United Nations. Blacks served in the Cabinet, as solicitor general, and as assistant attorney general in charge of the Civil Rights Division, a position no black had previously occupied. Carter also broke with tradition by choosing blacks to take seats on judicial benches in the Deep South. A president who measured international relations by the yardstick of human rights, Carter stated that his policy "would be undercut and fruitless if we didn't set an example in our country of being very insistent that human rights be protected here."[7] Upon taking command in 1977, the new chief executive affirmed to a gathering of federal bureaucrats: "There will never be any attempt while I am President to weaken the great civil rights acts that have passed in years gone by."[8]

Blacks expected him to do more than hold the line. In legal terms equality existed, but in practice the effects of centuries of racial discrimination lingered. Although the statutes added to the books during the previous decade had eased the economic plight of blacks, recession and inflation not only halted many of the gains that had been made but also opened a wider economic gap between the races. In 1979, black families lived on incomes averaging 57 percent of those earned by whites. This figure had dropped from 60 percent a decade earlier and barely improved on the 1954 figure of 53 percent. In the South, where half the black population resided, times were even harder. In 1975, when the national median income of black families was 62 percent of that for whites, southern black families earned 59 percent of what white families made.[9] As long as white Americans endorsed equality of opportunity without creating the means of achieving the conditions of equality, first-class citizenship for blacks remained just a promise, not a reality. Rejecting full employment and domestic Marshall plans and hostile to affirmative action programs perceived as preferential treatment, the majority of the nation was unwilling to overcome the economic barriers still standing in the path of real equality.

There were limits to what Carter could do to construct an economic foundation for racial equality; after all, more skillful and committed presidents had failed in the past. However, he chose to reserve most of his moral fervor for foreign affairs, and he lacked the power of persuasion to lead Congress and the American people on a crusade toward racial equality at home. Joseph Califano, who served in both the Carter and Johnson administrations, complained: "I never heard Carter speak privately with the burning conviction, much less the passion, of Lyndon Johnson about civil rights or race in America."[10] Certainly, Califano had an axe to grind because Carter had dismissed him as secretary of HEW; but the substance of his criticism was accurate: the Georgian saved his precious presidential resources for programs to which he accorded a higher priority than black equality.[11]

Nevertheless, as had most of his predecessors, President Carter viewed the right to vote as a key element for achieving racial progress. While Congress emasculated full employment and social welfare bills and the Supreme Court weakened affirmative action plans, he exhorted blacks to use the ballot as a means of stemming the conservative tide. During a period of retrenchment in Washington, Carter urged blacks to vote in order to help themselves obtain the benefits governments were increasingly reluctant to deliver. The president admonished black college graduates, many of whom had not yet made an attempt to go to the polls: "Both political candidates and incumbents have got to know that you will both vote and act. How are we going to have leadership to fight for equal opportunity and affirmative action in jobs, schools, and housing if even the act of voting is too great an effort?"[12]

President Carter staffed the Justice Department with policymakers who approached the voting rights issue with the same cautious brand of activism as had their predecessors during the previous decade. Initially, the chief executive's appointment of Griffin Bell as attorney general drew opposition from civil rights groups. Born and raised in Americus, Georgia, near Carter's hometown of Plains, Bell had served as an advisor in the late 1950s to Georgia Governor Ernest Vandiver, who had attempted to slow down school desegregation. Since 1961, Bell had held a seat on the Fifth Circuit federal bench in the Deep South, and his opinions, which he labeled as "about in the middle," had infuriated both liberals and conservatives. Specifically, civil rights advocates complained about Judge Bell's ruling to uphold the Georgia legislature's exclusion of Representative-elect Julian Bond because of his anti-Vietnam War pronouncements, and they questioned his endorsement of G. Harrold Carswell's nomination to the Supreme Court. However, by the time Bell was selected to head the Justice Department, he readily admitted that his views on race, like those of his old friend Jimmy Carter, had become more compatible with the egalitarian principles of the Judeo-Christian ethic.[13]

In choosing Drew Days III as chief of the Civil Rights Division, Bell affirmed his intention of sticking to the established course of safeguarding the suffrage. A graduate of Yale Law School, Days had worked as an attorney for the NAACP Legal Defense Fund and had acquired vast experience in civil rights litigation. Nevertheless, entry into the federal bureaucracy had cooled somewhat the activist tendencies he had displayed in private practice. Before, Days had championed the cause of blacks exclusively; now, as assistant attorney general, he acknowledged that he would have to weigh more considerations in "formulating policy that affects the entire Government." While continuing to press for racial equality, Days would do so in a carefully modulated fashion. "The Justice Department's goal," he asserted, "is to achieve observance of laws and constitutional requirements and not generally to suggest ways to solve social problems that have not been reduced to legal principles."[14]

To facilitate exercise of the black franchise, Carter's Justice Department tried improving existing enforcement of the voting rights statute. The extension of the act in 1975 had added numerous jurisdictions for coverage, including the entire states of Texas and Arizona, under the provisions for non-English speaking minorities. This expansion put a particular strain on the section five responsibilities of the Civil Rights Division. Even before receiving the extra workload, Justice Department attorneys experienced some difficulty in monitoring compliance on the state and local levels. For example, by the mid-1970s, Alabama had failed to ask Washington for approval of over 300 suffrage ordinances. The department attacked this problem during the Ford administration and, after Carter assumed power, reorganized the CRD to allow the Voting Section's paralegal staff to handle a greater share of the preclearance duties. As part of this assignment, paraprofessionals checked on whether the covered jurisdictions supplied the requisite submissions for review. This freed CRD attorneys to prepare additional litigation challenging various attempts to dilute the strength of the black electorate. They also backed up the paraprofessionals by filing suits to enforce the preclearance requirements of section five.[15]

As a result of these efforts, the CRD screened thousands of franchise proposals and disallowed the most flagrantly biased. From 1977 through 1980, the Justice Department received over 20,000 changes for scrutiny and objected to 133 of them.[16] The CRD handled 6,000 more submissions than it had for the previous twelve years. In denying approval to less than 1 percent of the offerings, the division was influenced by the restrictive opinions of the Burger Court. Following the *Richmond* decision in 1975, the attorney general refused to bar annexations merely because they reduced the proportion of the black population in a city. If a municipality showed a valid economic or administrative reason for acquiring a parcel of land and did not hold at-large elections in the expanded territory, then the department usually sanctioned the annexation. Similarly, after the *Beers* opinion in 1976, the CRD did not turn down reapportionment plans so long as blacks had an opportunity to increase their representation over that in the past. Unless redistricting proposals were clearly retrogressive, they obtained the federal government's blessing.[17] Yet, these judicial rulings did not completely handcuff the department overseers. The largest portion of the rejected submissions involved annexations

(30.5 percent) and at-large elections (10.4 percent), whereas the figure for tainted redistricting changes was lower at 7.3 percent.[18]

Although the Justice Department disallowed only a tiny fraction of submissions, its use of section five had a greater impact than the statistics suggest. The government's enforcement of the preclearance requirement had a deterrent effect on the covered jurisdictions. Previous experience had taught local officials what types of proposals would run afoul of Washington, and they were less inclined to adopt biased measures. In 1975, the Commission on Civil Rights reported "the fact that a change must be submitted and renewed by 'outside' officials specifically for its racial purpose or effect inhibits jurisdictions from passing such legislation."[19] In addition, the conciliatory manner in which the CRD managed the review process resulted in fewer objections. Preferring to cooperate with state and local officials, Justice Department personnel supplied information upon request that aided in drafting their electoral plans. Thus, after informal negotiations, a potentially-flawed law might be revised to satisfy Washington and could be spared a refusal letter.[20]

The Justice Department manifested this spirit of cooperative federalism in other areas of voting rights enforcement too. During the Carter years, although eighteen counties in the original states covered under the 1965 act were designated for federal examiners, none were actually sent. When Carter took office, the percentage of voting-age blacks registered in these targeted states varied from 48.2 in North Carolina to 67.4 in Mississippi. In all of these areas, the proportion of black registrants lagged behind that of whites, ranging from a difference of 3.5 percent in South Carolina to 17.3 percent in Alabama.[21] To help close the remaining gaps, the federal government would have to assume a larger share of the registration burden, and, as in the past, it was unwilling to do this.

Instead of sending examiners to stimulate additional registration, the Carter administration dispatched observers to see whether those who had succeeded in enrolling were permitted to cast their ballots fairly. Indeed, the Carter regime designated the eighteen counties for examiners solely as a prerequisite for assigning observers to them. The main problem sparking federal concern was the coercion of illiterate voters. In 1977, a CRD attorney reported a typical situation in Mississippi that prompted federal surveillance: "When illiterate blacks go to the polls to vote [in Tallahatchie County], they are easily manipulated by poll workers. They are generally nervous and intimidated by whites who often stand outside and harass black voters: 'I know you Mary, you know who to vote for.'" These victims suffered a further disadvantage when local officials refused to appoint blacks as poll watchers.[22] The appearance of federal observers, though, generally improved the quality of elections, especially those in which blacks competed against whites in a strained atmosphere. Despite its salutary effects, this program of national vigilance contained some flaws. To guarantee the safety of the observers by holding to a minimum community resentment against their presence, the federal government declined to furnish advance notice of their arrival. This arrangement may have preserved the peace, but it did not give black leaders sufficient time to alert voters. Moreover, most observers were white, and blacks, especially illiterates, did not always feel secure in seeing white bystanders scribbling notes as they entered the polling places. The fact that the federal agents wore identification badges did not comfort those who could not read.[23]

The Justice Department functioned in a manner that spurred black electoral gains without upsetting the traditional contours of the federal system. Whether appointing observers or processing section five submissions, the department sought to operate in a neutral fashion. A high-ranking CRD attorney had expressed this attitude in recommending supervision of a local election in Louisiana: "It is important that federal observers be present for objectivity's sake to discourage and, if necessary, to respond to post-election self-celebrating criticism by leading black political operatives, blind to the black community's possible factionalism, that the election was stolen if black candidates are not elected as anticipated."[24] Furthermore, the Civil Rights Division preferred to coax local officials into compliance, providing them with ample opportunity voluntarily to remove objectionable practices. CRD lawyers who negotiated agreements proved so cooperative that one white Mississippian exclaimed: "It's easier to work with them than with the electric power company."[25] At the same time, the division maintained a network of contacts with blacks and civil rights activists who provided vital information to help evaluate the performance of local officials. Indeed, a southern white mayor complained: "The blacks have a toll-free line to the Justice Department . . . and some blacks make a career out of informing for the Department of Justice."[26] However, as the voting rights arbiter, the CRD sought to execute the suffrage rules impartially without favoring either side. "We're not in this business say to increase the number of black elected officials or to increase the number of black registered voters," a Voting Section attorney revealed. "We're here to vindicate the law and the principles involved."[27]

While the Justice Department walked this fine administrative line, southern blacks were ready to make the most of their enfranchisement. The 1965 suffrage act converted blacks from plaintiffs and street demonstrators into voters. In the mid-1970s, Fannie Lou Hamer refused to pronounce the civil rights movement dead, but the Mississippi freedom fighter remarked: "Every so many years things chang[e] and go into something else. Now, you might never see demonstrations and I'm tired of that. I won't demonstrate no more. But I try to put that same energy, what I wish I had, I try to put that into politics, too."[28] The struggle that consumed Hamer's life had paved the way for the entry of blacks into the political process. Those who had joined in the marches, sit-ins, boycotts, and court suits won more than the right to eat a hamburger or to gain access to assorted activities with whites. In banding together, they had helped emancipate themselves from the psychological chains that had held them in bondage.[29]

In pursuing political power, the newly enfranchised naturally turned for leadership to the men and women who had come out of the ranks of the freedom struggle. They carried with them a sense of mission to extend the humanitarian goals of the civil rights struggle into the political arena. Kenneth Clark, the noted psychologist, analyzed the emerging breed of elected black officials as "the only civil rights leaders who are representative of the aspirations, desires, and the quest for answers posed by their constituencies and elected by their people to speak for them."[30] When SNCC's Julian Bond was first elected to the Georgia House of Representatives, he declared: "This is *our* seat," and his campaign manager remarked: "It was never Julian Bond's seat to Julian. It was always his *district's* seat."[31]

Nevertheless, southern blacks experienced some difficulty in making the transition from civil rights protests to electoral politics. The registration and mobilization of voters lacked the drama of direct action demonstrations that had attracted thousands to participate in the movement. Political success required the construction of a tightly-knit organization that could enroll voters, finance campaigns, turn out the electorate at the polls, and see that the ballots were counted properly. The building of political machines called for the kind of plodding work and attention to detail that was often missing during the heyday of the civil rights struggle. After the demonstrators had come and gone, it remained for the precinct captains, ward heelers, and poll workers to convert the ballot into an effective instrument of protest. John Cashin, who transformed his civil rights activities into the founding of the National Democratic Party of Alabama, explained that some "people were not able to bridge the gap between confrontation politics and electoral politics. The former are emotional and temporary, the latter are tedious but lasting."[32] Charles Evers, who made the transition smoothly, once chided a rally in Mississippi: "C'mon now. . . . This ain't civil rights no more. Y'all got your local candidates. They gotta buy placards, bumper stickers—that stuff ain't free. Prayer and marchin' ain't gonna get elected officials."[33]

Black southerners sought to make the necessary adjustments that would help them compete more favorably for public office because they believed strongly in the electoral process. A victorious black candidate for a chancery clerk position in Mississippi exclaimed that her success gave "the Negro race the feeling that they had made the first step toward overcoming discrimination, poverty and neglect in every area. They feel like they can progress, and this in itself made more people run for public office."[34] In campaigning, blacks helped tear down barriers to equal political participation. Their candidacies had an educational effect on the electorate, providing practical citizenship instruction for those who either were unfamiliar with the political process or never thought that members of their race belonged in elected posts. Fred Gray, a lawyer for the Montgomery bus boycotters who, in 1970, had won a seat in the Alabama Senate representing George Wallace's home district, perceived his election as "a turning point in the history of the state. I think when people see black people in the Legislature, they will realize they're just like everybody else."[35] Even those who failed to triumph at the polls advanced the cause of first-class citizenship. Vernon Jordan, who preceded John Lewis as head of the VEP, observed that "many Negro candidates run primarily to encourage other Negroes in the community to register and vote."[36]

Overall, blacks met the challenge with considerable success. By 1980, in the seven southern states covered under the Voting Rights Act, 1,846 blacks had won elected positions. Blacks throughout the entire South, which contained about half the Afro-American population, constituted nearly 61 percent of all non-white officeholders in the nation. Most of the incumbents held municipal and county posts although around a hundred sat in state legislative bodies. There were over 80 black mayors, including those in some of Dixie's leading cities—Atlanta, New Orleans, Birmingham—and more than 230 held seats on the county governing boards that controlled local affairs.[37]

Despite these impressive achievements, blacks had still not obtained equal representation with whites. In 1980, of the more than 32,350 elected officials in the original covered jurisdictions, approximately 5 percent were black. This figure lagged considerably behind the proportion of black population in the region, which ranged from 18.9 percent in Virginia to 35.2 percent in Mississippi. In these areas, the ratio of black elected officials to the black population was about one in ten thousand, whereas the proportion for whites was sixteen in ten thousand. Compared with their potential, blacks were underrepresented. For example, the Magnolia State led the nation in the number of black elected officials, but only 7.3 percent of the total number of officeholders in the state were black. "Therefore," according to Henry Kirksey, a black political activist who was elected to the state legislature in 1980, "it figures that if we have a fair electoral process here in the State . . . that the black ought to have a much greater and much higher percentage than that."[38]

Although each year black southerners had made steady progress in obtaining greater representation, the pace of those gains had slowed considerably. The annual rate of increase in the number of black elected officials serving in the original covered states from 1970 to 1981 dipped from 27 percent to 8 percent. At the speed blacks were moving, Eddie N. Williams, the director of the Joint Center for Political Studies, complained: "Even when we're running fast we don't seem to be moving much."[39] Furthermore, in many political subdivisions, black southerners had made little or no progress. In 1980, blacks made up at least 50 percent of the population in eighty counties in the original targeted jurisdictions; however, in twenty-one of them, they had yet to send to public office a representative of their own race.[40] Where black candidates did triumph, they tended to serve in minor posts in small towns and cities. Most often, blacks held seats on city councils, but some three-fifths of these positions were in locales with less than 5,000 people. The majority of black mayors officiated in similar places, and they presided over economically impoverished municipalities where the per capita income of the residents was less than $2,000. Still, these mayors had substantial authority to govern their towns compared with those blacks who served in white-dominated legislative bodies.[41]

Most likely, blacks would have come closer to achieving equal representation if the electoral rules had not been utilized to hold them back. In 1975, Arthur Flemming, chairman of the Commission on Civil Rights, put the matter in perspective: "A jurisdiction may seem to conform to the letter of the law by permitting minority registration and voting but rob that participation of its meaning by structuring the system against minority political victories."[42] He had in mind such schemes that diluted the black suffrage as at-large elections and multimember districts. Not only did blacks have a better opportunity to elect representatives from single-member districts, but if they did manage to win at-large, they could not always speak as forceful advocates for fear of alienating white voters. A civil rights lawyer who won an at-large seat on the Birmingham city council reflected the dilemma of having to appeal to a broad and diverse constituency: "Well I campaign in a white community on the basis of trying to have them to know that we're going to represent the citizens of the city for the best interests of the citizens and the city. And the services that the city's required to give, they'all all get a fair shake."[43]

Structural barriers did not stand alone as impediments to electoral success. Within black communities, expanding chances to participate at the polls and to compete for public office produced factionalism. Before gaining the suffrage, black southerners had channeled their organizational energies into religious and civic affairs, and on obtaining the franchise they transferred some of the institutional rivalries that had developed within these spheres into political conflicts. Ambitious black candidates were often looked upon with suspicion. "Blacks don't trust other blacks," the Negro mayor of a majority-black town asserted. "There is jealousy of one who gets power."[44] Consequently, black officeholders felt an enormous amount of pressure to perform even better than did their white counterparts. State Representative Robert Clark of Mississippi explained the problem: "If we elect a black man to office that can't do the job that will be a disgrace us, and the black race will be set back 50 more years."[45] Moreover, long deprived of entry into the political arena, many southern blacks had grown accustomed to having whites represent them, and this deferential attitude did not die suddenly with enfranchisement. In fact, after 1965, shrewd white politicians adjusted their styles to lure black voters. In many cases the fracturing of the black electorate was enough to swing victories to white candidates, even those running in majority-black areas. Such splits hurt the chances of black contestants, especially in localities that conducted elections at-large.

Those blacks who managed to win election were expected to serve as progressive agents of racial reform. Most Afro-Americans were elected from predominantly black districts on the local level, usually from communities with deplorable economic conditions. Consequently, they needed to obtain funds for services from statewide agencies and governing bodies, and everywhere in the South, blacks constituted a small minority of these influential lawmakers. Thus, black politicos, outnumbered in legislative councils, had to find ways of cooperating with the white majority while, at the same time, pressing the demands of their constituents. Kenneth Clark summed up this dilemma: "The Negro political official must assume the additional burdens inherent in defining politics as requiring a tough-minded and realistic appraisal of the power available to him, a determination to obtain and use effectively the power necessary to effect desired and observable changes, and balance this by a stable, deep and broad sense of human values."[46] Little wonder that under these circumstances black functionaries often felt they were walking a dangerous tightrope. "Your position in the black community has to take on a veneer of militancy," observed Leroy Johnson, the first black since Reconstruction to serve in the Georgia State Senate, "but . . . you have to be willing to negotiate, to compromise, in order to be effective."[47] By its very nature this bargaining process opened up black politicians to the charge of shortchanging legitimate grievances to gain support from white power brokers.

Black southerners had placed paramount faith in the suffrage as the means of liberation, and the performances of their elected representatives served to measure whether that confidence was justified. Some enthusiasts held exalted notions that the franchise would smash racist oppression and would shatter the economic caste system accompanying it in one fell swoop. Most blacks set their sights more realistically. For them the ballot would better the quality of their daily lives. They looked forward to improved community services, better treatment by the police, good schools, and benefits that might be brought by officeholders "who believe in justice and fair play."[48]

The election of blacks did raise the standard of living in very basic ways. The rewards they gained included upgraded streets and sanitation services, the extension of park, recreational, and health facilities, and perhaps most dramatically, the decline in abusive law enforcement. The election of black sheriffs and the ouster at the polls of some of the most vicious police chiefs who were replaced by more moderate whites greatly reduced incidents of brutality. Fannie Lou Hamer, who had been severely beaten by several policemen in Winona, Mississippi, in 1963, reflected a decade later about her hometown of Ruleville: "We've got a real change in the police officials. I don't think at this point they could be any better, because brutality is really not [here]. You don't have that! And if something or other comes up, most of the time, whether it's a young black or a young white . . . they can expect something, but the kind of beating and all that kind of stuff—they don't have any of it."[49] If the integration of juries is an accurate barometer of equality before the law, blacks who were arrested were more likely than before to receive fair trials. According to the 1968 Civil Rights Act, juries that reached a verdict had to be selected from updated voter registration rolls. The passage and enforcement of the 1965 suffrage law ensured that an ample number of black names appeared on the jury lists to try the accused.[50]

The election of blacks might also result in expanded job opportunities. Black governmental officials obtained federal grants to enhance public services and, concurrently, employed their constituents on these projects. Furthermore, they recruited blacks to fill municipal and county positions and affirmatively applied federal regulations concerning equal hiring. Many of these elected officials attempted to supplement assistance from Washington by attracting business firms and industry to their areas, thereby increasing the potential for black employment. The victims of long-term neglect, black communities strove to extend the base of their public and private resources. Chances for success were greatest where black officials controlled the reins of government or wielded influence in cities experiencing economic modernization.[51]

The ballot earned more than material dividends. The symbolic yields were profound. For generations the acts of registering and voting in the South were not routine matters for blacks, and when they finally acquired the franchise and affected the outcome of elections, the experience was psychologically liberating. Ed Brown, the brother of "Rap," SNCC's belligerent chairman in the late 1960s, believed the growing political power meant "that all over . . . the South blacks are removing the final shackles from their minds."[52] On a tour of Dixie in 1973, a staff member of the VEP swelled with pride in beholding blacks "casting aside the feelings of inferiority and shame and realizing what a strong and beautiful people we are." She observed a black minister fearlessly challenge white officials in a rural Mississippi county: "I DEMAND that you open the doors to that courthouse. We are here to serve notice upon you that it belongs to us, too, and you will run things no longer."[53] Participating in the political process gave southern blacks an opportunity to exhibit their own sense of worth, to throw off the yoke of submission that had divested them of the most fundamental right of citizenship. Unlike most white Americans, black southerners did not take the ballot for granted, and they looked upon it as an essential tool to shape their destinies free of white domination. A black parish official in Louisiana explained this attitude: "I made up my mind that whenever I got in power, got to be a registered voter, I would run for office. After I registered and voted, there came up an election, and I decided I would run for something. It didn't make any difference what it was. I was doing it to let the white man know that the Negroes in my community wanted their rights."[54]

The admission of blacks to the registration lists and polling places also had a salutary effect on white politicians. In the mid-1970s, Hodding Carter, the Mississippi newspaper editor and Loyalist Democratic Party organizer who served as an aide to President Jimmy Carter, revealed a significant by-product of the civil rights struggle: "By God the white Mississippian is free. That's the hardest thing for me to remember now—how tiny a thing you could do ten years ago and be in desperate difficulty. You know, what few dissenting remarks could destroy you politically or make you fear for your job, or get you run the hell out of the state. That just doesn't happen anymore."[55] In the postenfranchisement South, white candidates actively campaigned for the black vote, which frequently meant the difference between victory and defeat. To this end, the climate of electioneering vastly improved, and race baiting, while still resorted to on occasion, declined markedly. In Tylertown, Mississippi, in the early 1960s, the local registrar had knocked a suffrage worker over the head with a gun for leading a registration drive. A decade later, black residents could vote, and according to one civil rights activist remaining on the scene, "White candidates come around to black homes and give out their cards, and they ask blacks to vote for them, and they make promises to blacks just like they make promises to anybody else."[56] Racial demagoguery also diminished in statewide battles for governor. After surveying gubernatorial contests in the South since 1954, Earl Black concluded: "During the period 1966–73, for the first time in the twentieth century, there were more nonsegregationist than militant segregationist among major candidates."[57] He also noted a departure from tradition because the nonsegregationist contenders ultimately triumphed. In 1974, one of the new breed of governors, George Busbee of Georgia, who had defeated Lester Maddox in the Democratic primary, rejoiced from the capitol in Margaret Mitchell's Atlanta: "The political processes which led to this inauguration proclaim that Georgia has met the challenge of political maturity. The politics of race has gone with the wind."[58]

In state legislative chambers, white lawmakers responded favorably to the augmented presence of black representatives. "I think that the atmosphere has been much better than people would have expected," Georgia state lawmaker Ben Brown declared in 1974. "Many of the white legislators have become educated and more intelligent because we've been there."[59] Similarly, Mississippi Representative Robert Clark observed: "I wouldn't say the Legislature is what it's supposed to be. But it's changed 200 percent."[60]

Even the most bitter foes of civil rights eventually modified their old rabble-rousing ways. As late as 1970 George Wallace, who once had pledged to defend segregation forever in Alabama, campaigned for reelection as governor by attacking the so-called Negro bloc vote. This ploy lost much of its usual charm, and although victorious, Wallace barely emerged triumphant. A year later, the governor was ready to try a new approach, one that courted instead of repelled the state's growing black electorate. In 1971, Wallace announced, "Segregation is dead. It's outlawed, and it won't be again."[61] Seeking another term in 1974, he received the endorsement of some local black elected officials. Johnny Ford, the mayor of Tuskegee who had previously worked for Robert F. Kennedy and John V. Lindsay, threw his endorsement to Wallace for practical reasons to obtain whatever economic benefits his former foes could deliver. "If they're looking for a favorite fellow to give some extra money for his people," Ford declared, "I'll certainly take it. It's business with me—no emotion. What you must do is penetrate the system and, once within the system, learn how it works."[62] Most black Alabamians, though, were not as willing to forgive Wallace for his past sins, and he captured probably not more than 12 percent of the black vote in winning reelection.[63] His opponents acknowledged that the governor had shown some signs of repentance—he made black governmental appointments and planted a well-publicized kiss on the cheek of the black homecoming queen at the University of Alabama—but they insisted "deep down George Wallace is a racist . . .[who] will adjust because . . . he sees that he cannot continue to find a place in history as a racist."[64] Sincere or not, Wallace had to bow to the new ways.

At the national level, too, white southerners calculated the rising impact of the black electorate on their political fortunes. Democratic politicians increasingly came to rely on black votes as the Republican party lured away conservative whites from their customary partisan affiliation. In turn, black ballots influenced the legislative behavior of Democratic congressmen from Dixie. By the mid-1970s, a majority of white southern Democrats in the House of Representatives had swung their support to final pasage of the Voting Rights Act extension. In other measures concerning civil rights, over one-quarter of congressmen from .the South consistently were willing to approve proposals supported by black leaders. The development of a two-party system in the region, with the GOP making substantial inroads on the white electorate, forced many white southern Democrats to pay close attention to the wishes of their black constituents whose backing at the polls was crucial to their reelection. For example,after a 1972 reapportionment plan left the seventh congressional district in Alabama with the highest proportion of black population in the state (38 percent), its representative, Walter Flowers, who had served the area since 1968, boosted his support for civil rights legislation from a rating of zero to 44 percent.[65]

Enlightened white moderates had replaced southern

Negrophobia with civility, but their election did not usher in a complete break from the past. To be sure, progressive New South governors and their legislative allies did not ignore blacks. They recognized the importance of the minority electorate by making black appointments and by issuing proclamations honoring black heroes. Furthermore, blacks benefited from the initiation of "people programs" such as the expansion of public kindergartens, prison reform, and consumer and environmental protection. However, as a rule, white middle-class reformers did little to break down the structure of poverty that left many of both races in economic subservience. Their performance in office did not impress Julian Bond, who remarked: "My colleagues are very clever at ingratiating themselves with a few blacks and think that serves as adequate representation. But most of these people are indifferent to the needs of poor people."[66] Geared toward attracting new industry to the South and to upgrading governmental institutions to accommodate dynamic economic growth, their policies relied on tax and investment incentives and on the guarantee of relatively cheap labor markets. In the process, some of the wealth gained from economic modernization eventually trickled down but scarcely enough to make a diference in the lives of impoverished blacks. Vastly outnumbered in state legislatures, black representatives had to wage defensive battles. When successful, they forged coalitions with liberal white lawmakers to block measures that would have harmed the poor.[67]

Although the ballot served reasonably well as an instrument for removing blatant forms of racial oppression, it had not yet brought economic equality to the mass of southern blacks. "For ten years," Andrew Young remarked in 1973, "we went around yelling 'Freedom Now'—and a lot of people translated that into having a black congressman, meaning we're going to have all of our freedom now, so on Monday morning they come to city hall and say, 'Where is it?' "[68] On the local level, where blacks won the largest share of public offices, there existed the sparsest resources to remedy their hardships. Rural black-belt counties provided Negroes with the greatest opportunity to control decision-making, but these areas ranked among the most poverty-stricken in the nation. Blacks in Lowndes County, Alabama, held all the important electoral posts; yet economic power remained in the hands of whites. One black official commented: "If you're talking about the county putting up money for something, then forget it. You're talking about something far out. There is no money."[69] Hence black elected leaders turned to Washington for grants to improve municipal services, and they frequently obtained them, though often in amounts sufficient only to ameliorate, not eliminate, century-old problems. However, the budgetary retrenchment of the 1970s threatened to dry up these vital sources of revenue.

The continued privation of Afro-Americans in turn limited their ability to improve economic conditions through use of the ballot. This was especially true in the South where black participation in the electoral process was lower than in any other area of the nation. In 1976, 56.4 percent of eligible blacks in the region were registered to vote, but only 46 percent of the voting-age population turned out at the polls. As political scientist Charles Hamilton has noted, Afro-Americans would take greater advantage of the electoral process when they became convinced that their participation in it would yield tangible products such as goods and services. Thus, the situation was cyclical and depressing. Unless black southerners cast their ballots more effectively, they would not receive increased material benefits; however, they would not become more fully involved until they felt their economic position improving.[70]

From its inception, the struggle for enfranchisement had been conceived in political and legal rather than in economic terms. The Voting Rights Act of 1965 equated representative democracy with the removal of artificial racial barriers to the suffrage and with the conduct of free elections. Like their predecessors during the First Reconstruction, modern-day reformers failed to provide southern blacks with the economic means to accompany guarantees of political freedom. Throughout the late 1960s and 1970s, family income in the majority-black counties in the South fell considerably below the median for that of the states in the region. These areas endured a poverty rate double that for other counties in the South, and more than five times as many families residing there lived on public welfare than they did in the rest of

Dixie.[71] These figures provided gloomy evidence for the assessment offered by political scientist Lester Salamon: "The Voting Rights Act reflects . . . America's 'instrumentalist bias,' its preoccupation with the formal, outward trappings of democratic government . . . and its neglect of the substantive underpinnings of real democracy."[72]

However modest the economic gains from the ballot, they were convincing enough for southern blacks to continue working actively through electoral politics. Indeed, black enfranchisement helped strengthen existing institutions. The civil rights movement originally had aimed not at overthrowing the American system of government but at reforming those elements that maintained inequality of treatment between the races. The democratic process, vulnerable to charges of racism, earned new legitimacy from black participation, and the recently enfranchised were expected to fight battles for social change at the ballot boxes in an orderly fashion. The black mayor of Birmingham, Richard Arrington, endorsed this view: "It is good for the community for people to believe that they can come to city hall with their grievances. If they don't, they will seek a solution to problems in other ways."[73] As southern blacks advanced inside the political arena, they demonstrated that a turbulent movement for social change had been swept into the electoral mainstream. "I feel," a southern black mayor proudly remarked, "I've provided a role model for other blacks, especially young blacks, and increased confidence in the black community that they really can do something in the system."[74] Georgia State Senator Julian Bond discerned a difference in attitude when he spoke on northern college campuses and in the South. "Since I've been in Mississippi," he declared on a visit to the state where black electoral participation had improved most dramatically, "nobody's asked me why I am in the system."[75]

In the transition from civil rights to electoral competition, the militant field-workers with a radical vision were generally replaced by individuals who practiced politics as the art of the possible around the bargaining table. Middle-class blacks—professionals, businesspeople, clergymen—possessed the educational skills and the financial resources necessary to wage successful campaigns, and the black electorate looked to them for political guidance. Although providing tangible benefits for their constituents, they were either unable or unwilling to devise policies that reordered legislative priorities on behalf of the black masses. "Many of the region's black elected officials have turned out to be only slightly better than the white officials whose places they took," Bond complained.[76] Working together with white progressives, middle-class black politicians entered the alliance supporting rapid industrial growth in the South. They advocated policies to make government operate more efficiently, to upgrade social and educational services, and to offer financial inducements to attract outside investment. These measures benefited the rising black bourgeoisie, but they did little if anything to ease the distress of rural blacks and impoverished ghetto dwellers in the cities. Indeed, one of the consequences of swift economic development in the modern South has been the dislocation of black tenant farmers and sharecroppers and their migration into the ranks of the urban underclass.[77]

If low-income black southerners were to derive greater profits fom participation in the electoral process, they had to achieve a larger share of representation and choose candidates who favored sweeping changes. Solutions had to be found for the problems of unemployment, substandard housing, inadequate health care, and poor education. To the degree that politics could remedy these ills, blacks and their white allies had to mobilize behind politicians who shared their concerns.[78] By the late 1970s, such prospects appeared to be receding. Registration had leveled off, and as figure 1 shows, the annual rate of increase in the number of black elected officials in the South had slowed to a trickle. The Justice Department kept up its vigilance of potentially harmful suffrage changes, but instances of electoral chicanery occasionally escaped its notice. Southern jurisdictions did not always submit their ordinances for inspection in timely fashion, and sometimes they did not present them at all. In any event, section five preclearance procedures did not apply to laws that were in effect before 1964, while attempts by the judiciary to attack discriminatory devices, such as at-large elections, that had been on the statute books for half a century came to a halt.

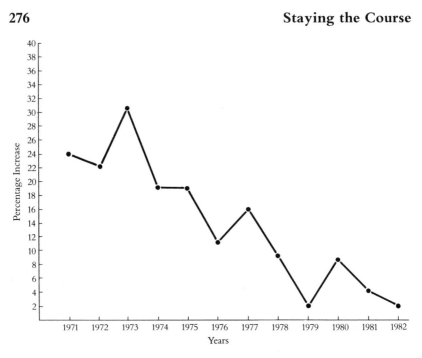

Source: Joint Center for Political Studies, National Roster of Black Elected Officials, vol. 6-12.

Figure 1. Annual Percentage Increase in Black Elected Officials, 1971–1982, in the Seven Southern States Originally Covered under the Voting Rights Act of 1965.

In a 1980 case involving the city of Mobile, the Supreme Court narrowed the opportunity for Negroes to prove that at-large elections violated the constitutional ban against racial discrimination. Not unconstitutional *per se,* this method of election had been declared invalid when it operated on the basis of race to hamper minority group representation. The Albama litigation centered on whether the "practice of electing city commissioners at-large unfairly diluted the voting strength of Negroes in violation of the Fourteenth and Fifteenth Ammendments."[79] Since 1911, Mobile, like many other southern cities during the Progressive Era, had selected a commission form of government whose three members were chosen on a citywide basis. In 1970, blacks constituted about 35 percent of Mobile's population, but no Afro-American had ever won election to the municipal governing body. Consequently, a black plaintiff, Wiley L. Bolden, filed a suit requesting the judiciary to overturn the city's manner of holding elections. In light of recent decisions resolving similar controversies in Texas and Louisiana, the lower federal courts sided with Bolden and ordered the existing type of government disbanded and replaced by a mayor and council elected from single-member districts.[80]

On April 22, 1980, the Supreme Court reversed this judgment although the majority of six split on the reasoning behind the verdict. On behalf of Justices Lewis Powell, William Rehnquist, and Chief Justice Warren Burger, Potter Stewart delivered the plurality opinion. It became the ruling of the bench because Harry Blackmun and John Paul Stevens concurred in the decision. In *City of Mobile v. Bolden,* Stewart rejected the black appellee's contention that the at-large system violated the Fifteenth Amendment. He strictly interpreted the amendment as affording protection against denial of the right to vote. In this instance, the city had not excluded blacks from registering and casting their ballots, and thus, the justice held that no breach of the Fifteenth Amendment had occurred. Speaking to the broader question of what constituted an abridgment of the franchise, Stewart asserted: "The Fifteenth Amendment does not entail the right to have Negro candidates elected."[81]

Dispensing with the Fifteenth Amendment as a means of combating vote dilution, Justice Stewart could not so easily dismiss the Fourteenth Amendment's equal protection safeguard against minimizing or canceling out the voting strength of racial minorities. The lower federal courts had concluded that Mobile's practice of at-large elections, together with racially polarized voting, effectively closed the political process to blacks. They cited the absence of any black elected officials and the unresponsiveness by white officeholders to the interests of minorities in the areas of public employment and municipal services. To buttress their finding of discrimination, the district and appellate court justices noted the long and pervasive history of racism in Alabama. However, these arguments did not persuade Stewart. After considering the evidence offered as proof of racial bias, he labeled it "circumstantial." The Justice refused to accept the proposition that official discrimination could be evaluated on the basis of "disproportionate impact"; instead, he called for a showing that the city fathers "conceived or operated [a] purposeful device to further racial discrimination."[82] In short, the question of intent became the principal standard for constitutional judgment in vote dilution cases. "To prove such a purpose," Stewart wrote, "it is not enough to show that the group allegedly discriminated against has not elected representatives in proportion to its number."[83]

While lending their support to Stewart in reversing the lower court ruling, the two swing justices took issue with significant portions of their brethren's opinion. Blackmun believed that the lower bench had correctly found the necessary "purposeful discrimination" in the at-large scheme. Nevertheless, he argued that the district court had erred in its manner of providing relief. Blackmun disagreed that "in order to remedy the unconstitutional vote dilution . . . it was necessary to convert Mobile's city government to a mayor-council system." According to the justice, the proper judicial response was to examine alternatives "that would have maintained some of the basic elements of the commission system."[84] Whereas Blackmun contended that Mobile's at-large electoral procedure satisfied the criteria for proving infringement of the suffrage, the other concurring jurist, John Paul Stevens, disputed the validity of using that very standard. In his view "the subjective intent of the decisionmakers" was not as important to determine as "the objective effects of the political decision."[85] Indeed, he downplayed the question of intent, arguing that improper motives on the part of some lawmakers were not sufficient to invalidate a legitimate electoral plan such as he considered Mobile's.[86] In spite of these separate points of departure, Blackmun and Stevens agreed with the majority of their colleagues that the Constitution did not sanction proportional representation for minorities.

The dissenters on the bench criticized their brethren for abandoning the guidelines in vote dilution cases that the court had affirmed only recently. Justice Byron R. White, who had authored the majority opinion in *White v. Register,* the Texas case, reminded his adversaries that they had struck down an electoral system similar to that in Mobile. In that decision and subsequent ones, the judiciary inferred the presence of "an invidious discriminatory purpose . . . from the totality of the relevant facts including the fact, if it is true, that the law bears more heavily on one race than another."[87] In probing the constitutionality of electoral plans, the judges had looked for such clues as whether black officials had ever been elected, the responsiveness of white public officials, the history of official racial discrimination, and the existence of racial bloc voting. In this instance, White believed that when taking all the circumstances into account, black candidates could not win a place on the Mobile commission under the at-large system.

Thurgood Marshall, joined by William Brennan, issued an even more vociferous dissent. Stung by Justice Stewart's charge that he was calling for a constitutional standard of proportional representation, the former NAACP chief legal counsel branded this claim "a red herring." Like the majority, he refused to lift from the shoulders of minority groups "the onerous burden" of proving that they had been "effectively fenced out of the political process."[88] However, Marshall did propose an approach making it easier to upset voter dilution schemes. He asserted that the Fifteenth Amendment outlawed all attempts, intentional or otherwise, to lessen the impact of every citizen's vote. Rather than having judges take "an unguided, tortuous look into the minds of officials in the hope of guessing why certain policies were adopted and others rejected," he proposed a "disproportionate-impact test" to "reach only those decisions having a discriminatory effect upon the minority's vote."[89] In closing his arguments, Marshall blasted the plurality opinion for making "this Court an accessory to the perpetuation of racial discrimination." He warned that if the high tribunal ignored the legitimate aspirations of Afro-Americans, "it cannot expect the victims of discrimination to respect political channels of seeking redress."[90]

The bitterness of Marshall's remarks underscored the severe blow that the ruling dealt to the suffragists. The case was remanded to the district court for a rehearing in light of the Supreme Court's ruling. Lawyers for black Mobileans embarked on a search to find specific proof that white officials had adopted at-large elections for consciously racial reasons. To discover evidence of such discriminatory "smoking guns" would be a difficult assignment, and a sympathetic attorney predicted "only those challenges will win . . . where elected officials are caught making overtly racial defenses of voting procedures."[91] In a similar vein, one of the leading historians of southern disfranchisement decried *Mobile* as "an announcement that a credulous court is ready to defer to any state and local authorities who can offer plausible reasons besides race for their actions."[92]

Yet the suffrage outlook was not all gloomy. The same day on which the Supreme Court proclaimed the *Mobile* ruling, it handed down a decision strengthening the preclearance provision of the Voting Rights Act. Rome, Georgia, disputed the authority of the federal government to object to voting changes that had a biased effect unless they also had a discriminatory purpose to infringe upon the right to vote. In contrast to *Mobile,* in which the high court upheld this line of reasoning, the jurists reached a different verdict. Significantly, Justice Marshall wrote the opinion distinguishing the two lawsuits. Unlike the *Mobile* decision, the outcome in *Rome* hinged on the interpretation of the Fifteenth Amendment and the Voting Rights Act. Marshall conceded that the language of the amendment may have been directed at prohibiting only purposeful discrimination, but he argued that Congress retained the power to enforce the article so as to ban practices producing a racially biased effect as well. According to the justice, the framers of the amendment had conferred upon lawmakers broad discretion to take whatever measures they deemed appropriate to protect black suffrage, and they had done so in passing the voting rights statute. Thus, to implement the Fifteenth Amendment, legislators "rationally have concluded that, because electoral changes by jurisdictions with a demonstrable history of intentional racial discrimination in voting create the risk of purposeful discrimination, it was proper to prohibit changes that have a discriminatory effect."[93]

This opinion divided the bench. Justices Burger, Blackmun, and Stevens, all of whom had supported the judgment in *Mobile,* shifted to Marshall's side. Apparently, they agreed with the majority spokesman that the enforcement power of the Fifteenth Amendment permitted Congress to invalidate state action, which although free of intentional racial bias, "perpetuates the effects of past discrimination."[94] In contrast, three justices—Powell, Rehnquist, and Stewart—had trouble separating the reasoning between the two cases. In dissent, William Rehnquist wondered how one city could maintain its electoral system without offending the Constitution while another could not use the same type of suffrage plan because the Fifteenth Amendment gave Congress the authority to prevent the practice. "It would be a topsy-turvy judicial system," Rehnquist scoffed, "which held that electoral changes which have been affirmatively proven to be permissible under the Constitution nonetheless violate the Constitution."[95]

These disparate decisions in 1980 left the suffragists in an ambiguous position. Vote dilution techniques instituted before 1964 would be difficult to overthrow by private litigants, but the federal government could employ section five to halt such practices initiated after that date. Washington might remain vigilant as long as the Voting Rights Act was in effect; however, the preclearance section of the statute was scheduled to lapse in 1982. Without renewal, southern blacks would find themselves at the mercy of white officials ready to undercut the strength of the minority electorate. Nevertheless, the *Mobile* and *Rome* rulings posed both a challenge and an opportunity.[96] Whereas one narrowed the means of combating franchise bias, the other indicated a way to advance the assault. Justice Marshall's opinion for the Court suggested that by virtue of the Fifteenth Amendment, Congress could pass legislation attacking vote dilution schemes, regardless of the original intent behind their adoption, if they perpetuated the effects of racial discrimination. Thus, entering the decade of the eighties, the suffragists had an added incentive to extend the voting rights law once more and to expand it as a vehicle for launching a fresh offensive against the dilution of black ballots.

10.

Preserving the Second Reconstruction

The suffragists had their work cut out for them. Extended in 1975 for seven years, the Voting Rights Act came up for renewal at a time when the forces of reform in Washington were in retreat. In 1980, Republicans had captured the White House and had installed a dedicated advocate of federal retrenchment. Swept in with Ronald Reagan's victory, conservative Republicans replaced key liberals from the Senate and ended Democratic control of that body. With a majority in the upper chamber, the GOP elevated Strom Thurmond to the chairmanship of the Judiciary Committee, placing him in a strategic position to threaten the outcome of suffrage proposals. As the Reagan administration and its congressional allies prepared their assault against fifty years of liberal reform measures, the voting rights proponents manned the barricades to protect one of the Great Society's most successful achievements. The battle to renew the 1965 statute offered the most severe test yet to the durability of the Second Reconstruction.

Although the 1980 elections saw the political mood of the nation swing to the right, the supporters of suffrage extension still retained considerable strength. Defending an existing program, they again placed the onus on their adversaries to explain why the statute's vital provisions should be allowed to lapse. As the two prior renewals had demonstrated, the Voting Rights Act commanded widespread support. First Nixon and then Ford had attempted to weaken the law, only to abandon their efforts in the face of strong, bipartisan congressional opposition. Even in the South, lawmakers had lowered their voices against renewal of the legislation as the size of the black electorate mounted in their constituencies. Less controversial than busing or fair housing measures, the franchise law had been enforced unobtrusively from Washington and at minimal cost. The Justice Department's devotion to conciliation, a policy of restraint carrying through four successive presidential regimes, had become a political asset in resisting appeals to shift the balance of power back to the states. This approach, which suffragists had criticized for limiting the effectiveness of the franchise law, now served to enhance its extension.

To thwart the expected drive against extension of the Voting Rights Act, the suffragists launched the offensive. They introduced renewal bills in Congress well in advance of August 1982, the date the covered jurisdictions could extricate themselves from the law's special provisions pertaining to race. When the Ninety-Seventh Congress convened in January 1981, House and Senate liberals on both sides of the aisle quickly moved to prolong the act for another ten years. Not only did civil rights proponents fix their sights on renewal, but they also aimed to repair the damage caused by the *Mobile* decision. Their plan incorporated into the suffrage statute language authorizing the judiciary to find vote dilution unconstitutional based on discriminatory impact as well as intent. The reformers chose to push their proposal first in the lower chamber where the crucial Committee on the Judiciary remained in sympathetic hands. A subcommittee chaired by Don Edwards conducted hearings, and the liberal representative from California provided his customary favorable forum.

From May 6 to July 13 more than 150 witnesses testified before the panel as Edwards took his hearings on the road to Montgomery and Austin. Most of them were civil rights advocates who sought to prevent the Voting Rights Act from falling victim to its own successes. Conceding the accomplishments in voter registration and in the election of black officials, supporters warned that failure to renew the legislation would bring progress in minority political participation to a virtual standstill and, more frightening, might lead to a reversal of earlier achievements. They pointed to ongoing attempts by southern officials to devise and implement schemes for reapportionment, annexation, and at-large elections that sapped black strength at the polls. Notwithstanding well-publicized victories of black mayoral candidates in Atlanta, Birmingham, New Orleans, and Richmond, the proportion of elected black representatives remained low in the South as a whole. Sheriff John Hulett of Lowndes County, Alabama, predicted that if the temporary provisions of the voting rights law were permitted to expire, "there will be other things to replace it, such as bills to purge voters from the rolls." Should this occur, he feared, "we'll end up with many of our positions going back to white people."[1] To forestall this possibility, suffragists urged continuation of section five giving the federal government power to block discriminatory suffrage practices from going into effect in the future.

The weight of the evidence presented to the subcommittee eventually swayed even the most conservative members of the group in favor of extending the preclearance procedure. Initially condemning section five as an unwarranted intrusion upon the authority of state and local governments to manage their own electoral affairs, Representative Henry Hyde, an Illinois Republican, finally admitted that federal surveillence was still necessary to curtail suffrage abuses. "During the course of the hearings," Hyde acknowledged, "it has become progressively clear to me that certain areas of the country have not aggressively sought to improve their electoral systems in a way which would permit minorities to become active participants. For these jurisdictions, perhaps administrative preclearance is the proper recourse, as much as it pains me to say so."[2] Nevertheless, Hyde suggested that the law be modified to free from the "penalty box" those locales that had complied with its letter and spirit. Consequently, the congressman favored a bailout proposal that political subdivisions could satisfy by meeting three conditions: 1) not employing a biased test or device for the previous ten years, 2) routinely submitting their laws for preclearance without the Justice Department offering any "substantial" objections, and 3) undertaking "constructive efforts" to stimulate minority electoral involvement.[3]

The liberals decided they could accept some relaxation in the bailout criteria in exchange for retaining section five and adding a provision that permitted a result-oriented approach in suffrage dilution cases. In early August, Representative Edwards hammered out a revised bailout measure, and although Hyde thought its terms too stringent, he went along with a nearly unanimous Judiciary Committee in reporting the bill to the floor, where he still hoped to win concessions that improved the chances of covered areas for release. "A workable bail out is necessary to gain Southern support," Hyde reasoned. "It's necessary to reward those who have honored the . . . law and isolate those who have not."[4]

The backers of renewal diligently mobilized sentiment in favor of the law. The Leadership Conference on Civil Rights, composed of over 150 organizations, conducted weekly strategy sessions in Washington, and along with such groups as the NAACP, the Joint Center for Political Studies, and the Lawyers Committee for Civil Rights Under Law, supplied expert witnesses and cranked out press releases in behalf of a strong bill. In September, before the floor debate had begun, the United States Commission on Civil Rights issued a detailed report attesting to the need for continuing the Voting Rights Act and recommending changes similar to those approved by the Judiciary Committee. The CCR also called upon the Justice Department to assume "an affirmative responsibility . . . to enforce more vigorously compliance with the preclearance provision of section 5." The commission suggested a requirement that all covered jurisdictions submit an annual report listing their election law changes.[5] Cheered by these efforts, the lobbyist for the AFL-CIO exulted: "The strength of feeling about maintenance of the Voting Rights Act is phenomenal."[6]

In contrast to this well-orchestrated campaign the opposition fizzled. Congressman Hyde lamented: "There was no organized constituency for the kinds of amendments we offered. They don't touch a great number of people. There was no pressure to vote for the amendments."[7] On October 5, by a lopsided vote of 389-24, the House passed H.R. 3112. Indeed, the traditional resistance to voting rights legislation had greatly diminished. Among those lining up in support of H.R. 3112 were seventy-one southerners, nearly double the number of representatives who had voted for passage of the original statute in 1965. The black electorate in Dixie had grown too large for lawmakers to ignore. Taking note of this situation, a legislative aide from the South admitted: "You have to cater to these interests, just like you cater to other interests."[8]

Although the final measure contained a bailout procedure granting covered jurisdictions increased opportunity for their removal from inclusion under the law, overall the House version strengthened the existing law. It established section five as a permanent feature of the act, beginning in 1985, and thus avoided the periodic battles for extension of this controversial provision. Furthermore, the bill permitted a suffrage litigant to prove discrimination by demonstrating that an election ordinance operated "in a manner which results" in voting bias. In this way, the measure offset the harm caused by the *Mobile* ruling with its onerous requirement of finding the intent behind a disputed electoral practice.[9]

Throughout this opening skirmish, the Reagan administration had watched from the sidelines. A foe of school busing and a proponent of allowing tax-exempt status for colleges practicing racial segregation, the president nevertheless sought to tread lightly on the suffrage issue. In mid-June, Reagan instructed Attorney General William French Smith to explore whether the Voting Rights Act was "the most appropriate means of guaranteeing" the ballot. At the same time, the chief executive affirmed his commitment to "full constitutional and political equality for black Americans"; however, he also expressed concern about provisions of the law "which impose burdens unequally upon different parts of the nation."[10] To resolve the conflict, Reagan asked the attorney general to report back by October 1 with recommendations for a course of action. Not until early November, a month after the House had approved a renewal bill, did the White House publicly reveal its position. Calling the right to vote "the crown jewel of American liberties," Reagan proposed a ten-year extension of the act that allowed covered jurisdictions a greater chance of bailing out than the House bill permitted them; moreover, in contrast to H.R. 3112, his suggestion sanctioned exclusive use of the intent standard enunciated in *Mobile*. Though the president did not choose to extend the law in its current form, neither did he seek to apply the obligations of the preclearance section nationally, as his GOP predecessors had attempted. Thus, while showing sympathy to the South, the conservative Republican regime nonetheless failed to remedy the specific complaint of southerners such as Senator Thad Cochran, a Mississippi Republican who had replaced Eastland: "Local officials have to go to Washington, get on their knees, kiss the ring and tug their forelock to all these third-rate bureaucrats."[11]

Compared to the House version, the administration recommendation constituted a presidential retreat; however, the Reagan plan did represent something of a compromise. Reportedly, Attorney General Smith had argued for taking an even harder line against the liberal House measure, but the president declined to do so. Political realities reinforced his decision. A special congressional election that had taken place in Mississippi in July warned GOP leaders about the risks involved in tampering with suffrage enforcement. The victorious Democratic candidate had approved extension of the Voting Rights Act, unlike his Republican opponent, and black voters had responded by flocking to the polls in large enough numbers to guarantee his triumph. In evaluating the loss of this seat, previously held by a Republican, one White House aide had concluded: "We dare not weaken the act substantially."[12] This view also reflected the opinion of Clarke Reed, GOP national committeeman from Mississippi, who commented: "A lot of us think the Voting Rights Act wasn't all that bad. We've lived with it 16 years, and a lot of good came out of it."[13] Thus, figuring the political balance sheet, the administration was reluctant to wage an all-out struggle against a strongly emplaced civil rights law.

Nevertheless, the president intended to press for modifications in the House bill, and he looked to the Republican-controlled Senate to back him. Though sixty-one senators, forty Democrats and twenty-one Republicans, had signed up as cosponsors of a proposal similar to H.R. 3112, GOP conservatives occupied positions of influence for shaping the final version of the measure. Administration allies could not count on sufficient support to wage a successful filibuster, but they still had an opportunity to slash at the bill in the Judiciary Committee where Strom Thurmond reigned as chairman and Orrin Hatch of Utah headed the subcommittee scheduled to conduct hearings. The South Carolina senator displayed no enthusiasm for any franchise legislation, and Hatch welcomed revisions sketched along the lines advocated by the chief executive. Given this situation, the suffragists had taken precautions to ensure that the committee did not stall and, consequently, hinder full Senate deliberation before the August 6 renewal deadline. A parliamentary maneuver kept H.R. 3112 from assignment to the Judiciary Committee, leaving it on the Senate calendar and available for consideration in case the Thurmond panel delayed in reporting a recommendation to the floor.[14]

In no rush to convene hearings following passage of the House bill in October 1981, the Hatch subcommittee finally got underway in January 1982. The main point of contention no longer concerned section five but focused on the result-oriented standard for proving impermissible vote dilution that the lower chamber had written into section two of the statute.[15] The Reagan administration and its allies shrewdly framed the issue as one of affirmative action and reverse discrimination; hence, they shifted attention away from the right to vote, which had widespread appeal, toward the question of proportional representation, which generated much controversy. The president had signaled this approach at a news conference held the month before the Judiciary subcommittee initiated its investigation. Substitution of an "effect rule" for one of intent, Reagan claimed on December 17, "could lead to the type of thing in which effect could be judged if there was some disproportion in the number of public officials who were elected at any government level, and so forth." According to him, the ultimate danger "would come down to where all of society had to have an actual quota system."[16]

This theme was taken up by Attorney General Smith and William Bradford Reynolds, the newly appointed head of the Civil Rights Division. They asserted that the House revision of section two had established "a quota system for electoral politics," and Smith decried "the abhorrent notion that blacks can only be represented by blacks and whites can only be represented by whites."[17] Similarly Reynolds, who had served in the solicitor general's office during the Nixon administration but had scant experience in the field of civil rights, held views that were detrimental to the cause of equality for Afro-Americans. Affirming a commitment to the "color blind ideal of equal opportunity for all," the assistant attorney general deplored "race conscious remedies which require preferential treatment for minorities."[18] His argument minimized the significance of past racial bias in perpetuating current inequalities between whites and blacks and equated affirmative action with "reverse discrimination" against whites.

The subject of racial quotas was a particularly explosive one, and the suffragists attempted to defuse it. Denying any aim to rig the political process to benefit blacks and disadvantage whites, they insisted on preventing local and state governments from "strangl[ing] a cohesive minority's bid for influence."[19] Reformers pointed out that even before the *Mobile* opinion the courts had found franchise violations only upon concluding that blacks had been systematically denied political access for racial reasons. In no decision had the judiciary fashioned its ruling around proportional representation nor did the judges impose a quota to foster that goal. Instead, they had reached their decisions after reviewing a combination of factors contributing to vote dilution. Defenders of the House version of renewal emphasized that modification of section two had been necessary only to restore the standard of judgment in suffrage suits so recently upset by *Mobile*. These proponents endorsed the language contained in H.R. 3112, proclaiming that the failure of a minority group to elect officials "in numbers equal to the group's proportion of the population shall not, in and of itself, constitute a violation of"the act.[20] This disclaimer did not assuage the Reagan administration.

As the debate over quotas continued, the judiciary rendered a final verdict in the Mobile lawsuit that each side in Washington used to justify its position. Following its 1980 ruling, the Supreme Court had remanded the case to the federal district bench for a rehearing on the question of whether the city had introduced at-large elections with the intent to discriminate. Two years later on April 15, Judge Virgil Pittman decided in favor of the black litigants. Civil rights supporters hailed the outcome but underscored "the wastefulness and unfairness" of the intent test. Both expensive and time-consuming, the ultimate victory in the case occupied over a year of the judge's attention and required thousands of hours of labor by a battery of attorneys, expert witnesses, and paralegals who eventually found long-buried evidence of purposeful discrimination. Despite this triumph, civil rights advocates reminded Congress not to forget the heavy burden required to satisfy the Supreme Court's intent standard. In contrast, the Justice Department drew the opposite conclusion. Pointing to the favorable lower court judgment, its officials rebutted the argument that the intent principle handicapped minority suffrage rights and should be abandoned.[21]

With both camps digging in, the need for some type of compromise became apparent. In the Senate Judiciary Committee, seven Republicans were expected to line up against nine Democrats on a bill containing an effect standard. Only Robert Dole of Kansas, a Republican, and Howell Heflin, an Alabama Democrat, appeared undecided, leaving neither side with a clear majority. The fate of the measure rested in their hands, and Dole emerged as the pivotal figure. Gerald Ford's former running mate had customarily supported passage of civil rights laws while maintaining strong ties with GOP conservatives. Disagreeing with some of Reagan's advisors who were willing to write off the black vote for the Republican party, Dole asserted: "I don't think we throw in the towel and say well, only eight percent vote for us and don't worry about it." He suggested making "the extra effort to erase the lingering image of our party as the cadre of the elite, the wealthy, the insensitive. . . . Our job now is to demonstrate concern to blacks and others who doubt our sincerity."[22]

The Kansas senator staked out a moderate position on the House bill. He recommended extension of section five for twenty-five years, instead of permanently, and endorsed the need for a result-oriented standard written into section two. Concerning the latter, Dole inserted language that explicitly restored the criteria of proof applicable before *Mobile*. Accordingly, in vote dilution suits the courts would scrutinize the "totality of circum-

stances" resulting in the denial of equal political access for minorities, a doctrine originally affirmed in 1973. The Dole compromise broke the stalemate, and on May 4, the Judiciary
Committee voted to adopt it as S. 1992.[23] Although not fully satisfied, conservatives did have something to cheer about. They came
away with an alteration in the length of coverage of section five,
an unequivocal statement against proportional representation, and
a limited bailout procedure. In recognition of these changes,
President Reagan praised the measure as "constructive." By
comparison, the liberals had done even better. They managed to
extend preclearance for another twenty-five years—by far the
longest expansion period to date—and returned the standard of
proof in vote dilution cases to an emphasis on the effect of racial
bias. Civil rights attorney Joseph Rauh had nothing but tribute
for Dole. "He was superb. He got us the perfect bill. We couldn't
have done it without him. It was no compromise bill at all. We
got everything we wanted."[24]

Only the diehards lambasted S. 1992 when it came up
for discussion on the Senate floor on June 9. Their efforts proved
as futile as they were short-lived. Jesse Helms mounted a feeble
filibuster against the bill. Vowing to continue his opposition "until
the cows come home," Helms stopped considerably short of that
mark because he did not want his delaying tactic to endanger
consideration of proposals closer to his heart—antiabortion and
balanced budget amendments. Besides, GOP moderates did not
want the Democrats to reap exclusive credit for passage of the
measure, and they deplored the stalling attempt undertaken by
the North Carolina Republican.[25]

Nor did most southern senators sympathize with Helms.
The Voting Rights Act had swelled their constituencies with black
electors who could be ignored only at substantial political peril.
Never before had John Stennis, the octogenarian Mississippi
Democrat, supported a civil rights proposal, but, facing a tough
reelection battle, he prepared to join the ranks of the majority on
this occasion. Russell Long voiced the sentiments of many of his
Dixie colleagues: "There have been violations of voting in Southern states in years gone by. To some extent we have to pay for
that." The South had joined the national consensus favoring en-

franchisement. Also gathered in support of suffrage renewal were influential segments of corporate America. During May, eleven major business firms had run an advertisement in the *New York Times, Washington Post,* and *Los Angeles Times* backing the strong House version of the bill.[26]

Up against a broad-based coalition, the opposition easily collapsed. On June 15, after a week of debate the Senate invoked cloture by an overwhelming vote of 86–8, thereby opening the way for speedy action on the proposal. Within three days, after having rejected a series of weakening amendments, lawmakers voted 85–8 to approve S. 1992. Only a handful of conservative Republicans, three of them from the South, held out to the bitter end; significantly, Strom Thurmond was not counted among them as he cast his first vote in favor of a civil rights law since becoming a senator. Nor did they have the backing of their ideological confederate in the Oval Office, since Ronald Reagan proclaimed the final outcome a "statesmanlike decision."[27]

The president received the renewal measure for his signature shortly after the House agreed to accept the Senate version, and on June 29, he became the fourth chief executive to place his name on the Voting Rights Act.[28] In words reminiscent of those of his predecessors, Reagan hailed the legislation as evidence of "our unbending commitment to voting rights."[29] However, the brief four-minute ceremony before 350 guests in the East Room of the White House contrasted sharply with the fanfare that had accompanied the signing of the law by Lyndon Johnson in 1965. On that occasion, Johnson fulfilled the goals of civil rights proponents with whom he had closely identified. Seventeen years later, the civil rights advocates in attendance did not generally view the chief executive as an ally, but in this instance they joined with him in common cause to keep alive the suffrage program of the Second Reconstruction. By 1982, the Voting Rights Act had transcended partisan, regional, and ideological boundaries, and President Reagan lacked any real incentive to wage an all-out struggle against its renewal. Furthermore, in lending support for the franchise measure, the Reagan administration highlighted the conservative dimension of suffrage reform.

The renewal and strengthening of the Voting Rights Act in 1982 marked the latest triumph in the long struggle to extend the ballot to southern blacks. For over a half-century civil rights advocates had litigated, legislated, and demonstrated against barriers erected to evade the Fifteenth Amendment. Although the judiciary had overturned various subterfuges and Congress had enacted two pieces of legislation increasing the power of the federal government to challenge discriminatory suffrage practices, by 1965 less than 40 percent of the black adults in the South had been enrolled on the voter lists and only about one hundred elected officials in the region were nonwhite. However, seventeen years after the Voting Rights Act went into effect, approximately 60 percent of black southerners had qualified to vote and more than 2,500 held public office. Not since the period following the Civil War had blacks participated so extensively in the political process.

In flocking to the polls, Afro-Americans evoked contrasting images of the First Reconstruction Era. The Voting Rights Act elicited in some white southerners painful memories. Opposing revival of the law in 1970, Representative George W. Andrews of Alabama complained that the southern states "have been singled out for special harassment and humiliation. In the name of decency, civility, and indeed democracy," he pleaded, "the act should die. The Civil War ended about a century ago. It is time that Reconstruction ended too."[30] Blacks held a more favorable impression of Reconstruction. "In ten years," Chuck Stone, a journalist and political commentator, predicted in 1968, "the black South is going to be the leading force among black people and, as was true during Black Reconstruction, spawn a race of brilliant and articulate black men whose capacity for innovative social legislation may well help to save America from the self destruction of its own white racism."[31]

But the history of Reconstruction also held bitter lessons for blacks. White commitment to racial equality, never wide or deep, had been brief, and a caste system which kept southern blacks segregated socially, impoverished economically, and impotent politically was the era's ultimate legacy. If by the mid-1960s the shroud of oppression was beginning to lift, few blacks could forget the hopes raised and then dashed a century before. In the early 1970s, Vernon Jordan found the similarities to the previous epoch disturbing. "There is persuasive evidence that the Second Reconstruction . . . is coming to an end," he discerned, and enumerated the worrisome signs: "Once again, the North seems weary of the struggle. Once again, the righteous cause of black people seems relegated to national neglect. Once again, a period of national reconstruction and reform seems doomed to be unfinished and uncompleted."[32] Victims of an earlier change in political climate, blacks were naturally fearful of the erosion of the gains they had only so recently achieved.

So far, however, the political gains of the Second Reconstruction have outlasted those of the first. Maintenance of the suffrage during the Second Reconstruction reflected the continuing consensus on enfranchisement. Unlike the era following the Civil War when extension of the vote to blacks was considered an extreme measure, the period since the end of World War II has witnessed an acceptance of the ballot as a moderate instrument for social change. When the tactics of the civil rights movement shifted from litigation to direct action confrontation, the ballot commanded even wider appeal. Registering to vote and going to the polls proved less of a threat to national peace and to the established order than did massive street demonstrations and boycotts. Furthermore, compared to such goals as the desegregation of schools, public facilities, and housing and the removal of racial bias in employment, extending the franchise posed fewer direct challenges to prevailing social and economic patterns.[33]

Nor did southern whites feel as threatened by a black electorate as they had during the First Reconstruction. In the modern civil rights era, black enfranchisement was not accompanied by any white disqualification or federal military intervention as was the case during Radical Republican rule. Moreover, demographic changes reduced the potential for black control. The huge migration of blacks northward since World War I diminished the possibility that whites could be substantially outnumbered at the polls. In fact, while the gap between the percentage of registrants of each race has narrowed, since the mid-1960s the actual number of new white voters has exceeded that of blacks.

In the southern states blacks fell far short of constituting a majority of the electorate, and in many of the counties where blacks predominated in absolute numbers, they did not command a majority of the crucial voting-age population. Thus, when the voting rights bill swept through the national legislative halls in 1965, it encountered less opposition from southern politicos than any of the other four civil rights plans enacted from 1957 to 1968. Thereafter, each attempt to extend the measure attracted increased southern support.

Throughout the period, enthusiasm for this strong suffrage remedy remained high among blacks and whites. Although serious disagreements over tactics and goals cracked the civil rights movement after 1965, moderates and radicals alike viewed the ballot as an important weapon for black emancipation. Bayard Rustin applauded the channeling of energies from "a protest movement into a political movement."[34] Rustin's "Black Power" critics, who belittled the strategy of working within an interracial liberal coalition, themselves emphasized the use of the franchise to establish political domination in local black communities. SNCC's Julian Bond explained: "In the South, where Negroes are voting for the first time, the opportunities are fantastic—control school boards, city halls. Up North, the Democratic machine has got everything all sewed up, but there is no machine in Jackson, Mississippi."[35]

At the national level, most politicians also agreed on the importance of protecting black enfranchisement. Their appreciation of the value of the suffrage heightened as black radicalism grew during the latter half of the 1960s. Liberal and conservative lawmakers differed over what form the Voting Rights Act should take, but they did not seriously quarrel with the assumption that participation in the political process had a soothing effect on black militancy. Indeed, expansion of the suffrage helped cool black hostility and directed protest into traditional political activities. Having fought hard and sacrificed much to obtain the right to vote, southern blacks did not regard it lightly as a weapon for liberation. In pursuing electoral politics as an avenue of obtaining freedom, they gradually moved away from reliance on disruptive techniques that were their only means for social change when they were excluded from the voting booth. Consequently, the shift away from civil rights confrontation to political participation narrowed the acceptable choices for achieving racial advancement. The exercise of the franchise, a suffragist explained, "provides evidence that the political process is adaptable to the needs and aspirations of all citizens."[36]

As a device for increasing black registration, the Voting Rights Act enjoyed great success. As table 1 shows, when the statute went into effect in 1965, only 31 percent of the eligible blacks in the seven covered southern states were enrolled to vote. By 1982, the percentage had soared to nearly 60 (57.7). The most spectacular changes came in Mississippi, the state subject to the most federal supervision and to the extensive organizing efforts of civil rights groups. The Magnolia State came in first among the seven states with 75.8 percent of voting-age blacks registered, up from 6.7 in 1965, and with 8.3 percent of elective offices held by blacks.[37] However, the effects of the suffrage statute on voter participation were more modest. While blacks continued to trail behind whites throughout the region in turning out at the polls, in a few cases they were beginning to participate at a higher rate than did whites.[38] It remains to be seen whether the climb in black registration and voting accompanying the 1984 presidential challenge of Jesse Jackson is the start of a new long-term growth pattern.

In enforcing the voting rights law, the Johnson administration charted the path that successive presidential regimes followed. Cherishing a belief in federal-state comity, Justice Department lawyers consistently attempted to secure compliance with a minimum of national intrusion in the local electoral process. This strategy did produce impressive gains. No longer permitted to administer literacy tests after 1965, local enrollment officers accounted for most of the names of new black registrants appearing on the polling lists. Although federal examiners never operated in more than a fraction of the covered counties, sixty out of 533, they were a reminder to southern registrars that their failure to cooperate brought the risk of outside intervention.[39]

Despite the accomplishments, the federal government might have gone even further to expand the size of the black

Table 1. Estimated Percentage of Adult Black and White Voter Registrants in Seven Southern States: 1964–1982.

	1964[a]		1966[a]		1976[b]		1982[c]	
	Black	White	Black	White	Black	White	Black	White
Alabama	22.8	68.4	51.2	88.1	58.1	75.4	57.7	79.4
Georgia	44.1	65.8	47.2	76.7	56.3	73.2	51.9	66.8
Louisiana	31.7	79.7	47.1	83.1	63.9	78.8	68.5	71.9
Mississippi	6.7	70.2	32.9	62.7	67.4	77.7	75.8	90.6
North Carolina	46.8	92.5	51.0	82.4	48.2	63.1	43.6	65.5
South Carolina	38.8	78.5	51.4	80.2	60.6	64.1	53.3	55.0
Virginia	29.1	50.1	46.9	61.8	60.7	67.0	53.6	58.3
Total	31.4	72.1	46.8	76.4	59.3	71.3	57.7	69.6

[a] Pat Watters and Reese Cleghorn, *Climbing Jacob's Ladder* (New York: Harcourt, Brace & World), pp. 376–77.
[b] United States Commission on Civil Rights, *The Voting Rights Act: Unfulfilled Goals* (Washington, D.C.: GPO, 1981), p. 19.
[c] Joint Center for Political Studies, *Focus* (June, 1983), 11:8, for figures on blacks, and U.S Department of Commerce, Bureau of Census, *Statistical Abstract of the United States, 1982–83* (Washington, D.C.: GPO, 1982), p. 488, for figures on whites.

electorate and to challenge the remaining obstacles to equal representation. When the Justice Department took affirmative steps to compel southern officials to rectify the effects of past bias, its attorneys did so more to encourage and measure voluntary consent than to foster maximum black involvement. By sending examiners to areas where blacks continued to encounter suffrage barriers, the Justice Department could have boosted political participation more significantly than it did. Had the percentage of registrants been higher, black voters would have had a greater opportunity to elect candidates of their own race, especially in counties with a black population majority. In 1980, there were as yet no black elected officials in about one-quarter of the majority-black population counties in the seven states originally covered under the Voting Rights Act.[40] In a racially neutral society, such figures would have had little meaning; however, given the long history of southern disfranchisement, if the proportion of black officeholders falls considerably below the percentage of blacks in the population, it is not unreasonable to assume the persistence of racial discrimination.

However, the Johnson administration and its successors could be held only partly responsible for lingering suffrage problems. The rate of voter enrollment had dropped after the most highly motivated blacks placed their names on the rolls in the first months after the Voting Rights Act went into effect. Many of those who remained disfranchised suffered from the same socioeconomic handicaps that curtailed political participation by the poor and ill educated throughout the nation. In addition, fear and intimidation continued to hamper prospective black registrants in the South. Breaking down the habit of nonvoting, nurtured throughout the years by white supremacy, required not only increased federal intervention but also the resumption of grass roots civil rights activities like those conducted in the early 1960s. Yet the concerted efforts necessary to remove the vestiges of racial subordination never materialized in the wake of the disintegration of several of the most militant civil rights groups. SNCC and CORE, ruptured from within by ideological disputes, virtually abandoned the South, and SCLC, unable to recover from the assassination of the charismatic Martin Luther King, barely survived. The withering of these private organizations and the inability of the financially troubled NAACP and VEP to take up the slack left civil rights advocates almost wholly dependent on the federal government for vigorous implementation of the Voting Rights Act.

The first major challenge to black enfranchisement and the Second Reconstruction came with the transfer of presidential regimes in 1969, for Richard Nixon owed his nomination and election to elements hostile to a robust execution of civil rights laws. His southern strategy, which undercut traditional Democratic electoral support in the South and reduced the third party appeal of George Wallace, allied him with perennial foes of racial equality. Yet if civil rights troops did not have an ally in the Oval Office, they still possessed enough clout in Congress to defy the administration's wishes, as shown by their victories in renewing the Voting Rights Act in 1970 and in strengthening the guidelines for its enforcement in 1971.

In addition to bowing to the congressional will on the black franchise, the Nixon administration took its cue from the judiciary and from the established bureaucracy. Reluctantly at first, the president's men followed the lead of the Supreme Court, which had liberally construed the language of section five of the Voting Rights Act to apply to a second generation of suffrage barriers— those designed with the purpose or having the effect of diluting the influence of the black electorate. Hence, the statute was conceived less as a means of handling registration problems and more as a tool for extending to blacks an opportunity to make their ballots count to the fullest extent. With the first phase of enfranchisement considered at an end, a cadre of career attorneys in the Civil Rights Division turned section five into a potent instrument for combating artful forms of discrimination. The CRD contained a devoted and resourceful band of lawyers who developed into experts in the field and were able to spot subtle practices crafted to diminish the impact of black ballots. Although the Nixon administration received scant praise from suffragists, its voting rights attorneys generally adhered to the approach established by Johnson's lawyers.

Some of the continuity resulted from a holdover of CRD

personnel, but a good deal of it reflected a common belief in the suitable role of law enforcement within the federal system. From 1965 to 1982, the Justice Department under the direction of both Democratic and Republican chief executives fixed a cautious brand of affirmative action on black suffrage advancement. Federal officials adhered to this policy out of deference to the smooth functioning of the federal system and because it generally encouraged conformity with the law. Southern election officials grumbled about the special burdens section five placed upon them, but they usually tendered the required submissions secure in the knowledge that Washington rejected only a tiny fraction of their offerings.

This process avoided much of the friction that existed between national and state governments during the years following the Civil War, but it demanded ongoing vigilance on the part of civil rights groups. Three times they managed to convince Congress and the president to renew the Voting Rights Act, and they exerted enough pressure to ensure that the Department of Justice did not stray far from its obligations under the statute. Civil rights litigants filed lawsuits to identify sophisticated forms of racially biased voting practices, thereby enabling the CRD to attack most of the schemes invented to dilute black electoral strength. Local civil rights groups in the South also proved adept at monitoring and reporting to Washington changes in election requirements that might otherwise have gone undetected.

In 1975 and most recently in 1982, Republican presidents again followed the congressional lead in sanctioning federal enforcement of black enfranchisement. The votes of newly registered blacks figured little into the partisan calculations of the GOP's southern strategists in the White House, for most blacks cast their ballots for Democratic candidates. Nevertheless, Republican administrations caved in easily on the issues of perpetuating and enforcing the Voting Rights Act. Actually, congressional Republicans from the North never wrote off the black electorate. They sided with northern Democrats to thwart conservative presidents from successfully implementing their southern strategy on the suffrage. President Gerald Ford, who on two occasions as Republican minority leader in the House had unsuccessfully labored to weaken the act, signed into law a seven-year extension of the landmark statute. Furthermore, an initially unsympathetic Ronald Reagan agreed to renew the crucial provisions of the law into the beginning of the twenty-first century. Whatever policy changes his administration wrought concerning race relations in general, "on voting rights cases," one aide remarked, "we're not going to be all that different."[41] Once again, a president learned the difficulty of altering the direction in which the career bureaucracy headed, especially when Congress supported the prevailing policy. After seventeen years, the statute had become a bipartisan fixture, in contrast to the identification of black franchise with a single political party during the First Reconstruction.

This trend became evident by the early 1980s when the majority of southern lawmakers threw their support behind bills to resuscitate the Voting Rights Act. Their approval reflected the editorial comment of the *Birmingham News:* "Black votes . . . are . . . a significant factor—and a force which exerts pressure on elected officials regardless of race to represent blacks fairly."[42] Recent experience had shown white southerners that the federal government could extend black suffrage without disrupting their lives or forcing substantial federal intrusion into Dixie. They also had little reason to be dissatisfied with the growing number of blacks elected to office. Still very much in the minority and usually holding office in predominantly black areas, these public officials performed their duties without threatening white political or economic domination.

The political process has benefited greatly from black ballots. Race baiting has virtually ceased, white candidates campaign regularly for black votes, and the lines of communication between the races have improved. Moreover, the psychological accomplishment cannot be quantified. Lawrence Guyot, a black political organizer in Mississippi, accurately reflected that "the number of victories isn't as important as the fact that they symbolize a bit of black authority, a gradual return to respect for those accustomed to having their lives manipulated by white hands."[43]

By comparison, the franchise has been a marginal instrument for black economic advancement. Services such as garbage collection, street maintenance, sewage and sanitation, and police and fire protection have shown the most notable improvement. Too often, however, blacks failed to capture control of posts in all but the poorest areas. In most places, obtaining the franchise has resulted only in slight economic gains. Although the Second Reconstruction has legitimized the black suffrage, like the first it has failed to remove the serious economic impediments hampering racial equality. Many southern blacks today face as bleak an economic future as their ancestors of a century ago. Increased mechanization and agribusiness practices have hastened the migration of impoverished black farm laborers to the cities where the double-digit rate of unemployment among Afro-Americans has reached depression-era levels. Although the amount of formal education attained by Afro-Americans has risen since 1965, the improvements in schooling still have not allowed blacks to catch up with whites in acquring the skills or training to compete satisfactorily for well-paying jobs in high technology industries. Indeed, the economic disparities between the races remain wide. From 1979 to 1981, the median income of black families continued to decline from 57 to 56 percent of that earned by whites. This downward spiral, begun in the mid-1970s, has been further aggravated by Reaganomics, as Republican administration cutbacks in social service programs have affected blacks most adversely.[44]

On balance, the Second Reconstruction has been most successful in preserving black ballots. Southern black political power has not reached the level of strength achieved during Radical Republican rule, but it is based on a more solid foundation of acceptance. The principle of correcting the consequences of past discrimination has unleashed a storm of controversy; however, the type of affirmative action applied to black enfranchisement has generated much less bitter conflict. Nevertheless, this general agreement has been approaching its limits as the emphasis on enforcement of the Voting Rights Act shifts from the right to register to the opportunity to be elected. Serious questions remain as to how far Washington should or legally can go in restructuring the electoral process so that blacks may maximize their potential power in winning election to public office. Yet, the lesson suggested by the First Reconstruction is that a premature withdrawal of federal supervision poses a serious danger to the achievement of racial equality. Neither the fears of white southerners nor the hopes of the suffragists have been realized. Vigilance thus remains necessary, and the political system still needs to be made more responsive to the aspirations of the recently enfranchised.

Notes

Preface

1. Thomas Cavanaugh, "Black Gains," p. 8.

2. *New York Times,* October 16, 1892, p. A30.

3. Quoting Alvin Holmes, a black Alabama state representative, *New York Times,* November 3, 1982, p. A22.

4. *New York Times,* October 14, 1982, p. B12. On the legal battles over suffrage and redistricting, see Hester, "Mississippi and the Voting Rights Act."

5. *New York Times,* November 3, 1983, p. A22, November 4, 1982, p. 24. Whites split their tickets along racial lines. In majority-white counties, voters cast 60 percent of their ballots for United States Senator John Stennis but only 40.3 percent for Clark. Cavanaugh, "Black Gains," p. 3.

6. From 1982 to 1984, black voter registration jumped 31.4 percent in Texas, 29.7 percent in South Carolina, 14.6 percent in Virginia, 14.4 percent in Louisiana, 11 percent in Alabama, and 9.7 percent in Georgia. This surge in black enrollment can be attributed not only to the voter registration drives stimulated by Jesse Jackson's presidential candidacy but also to strong sentiments against the Reagan administration. See Robert A. Jordan, *Boston Globe,* May 6, 1984, p. A25.

7. For the provocative suggestion that "racial identity expressed through the electoral process is one way to relate the citizen to the system," see Hamilton, "Response," p. 191.

1. Ballots, Not Bullets

1. *Washington Post,* January 18, 1969, p. 1. On Johnson's relations with the press, see Culbert, "Johnson and the Media," in Divine, ed., *Exploring the Johnson Years.*

2. *Public Papers of the Presidents: Lyndon B. Johnson, 1965,* p. 841; Johnson, *The Vantage Point,* p. 161.

3. *Public Papers of the Presidents, LBJ, 1968,* p. 1354; *New York Times,* January 18, 1969, p. 12.

4. *Crisis* (January 1969), 76:8.

5. Quoted in Carson, *In Struggle,* p. 221.

6. Quoted in *ibid.,* p. 255.

7. *Ibid.,* p. 256.

8. O'Neill, *Coming Apart,* p.389.

9. Harry McPherson to Nicholas Katzenbach, September 20, 1966, Box 21(2), McPherson Files, Lyndon B. Johnson Library (LBJL).

10. Nicholas Katzenbach to Harry McPherson, September 17, 1966, Box 21(2), McPherson Files, LBJL.

11. Marvin Watson to the President, September 6, 1967, Box 15, EX FG 1, LBJL. For the increasing level of stridency among some Johnson aides, see Larry Temple to the President, February 14, 1968, Box 7, EX HU 2, LBJL.

12. *New York Times,* January 7, 1966, p. 2; Forman, *Sammy Younge, Jr.,* p. 223.

13. Roy Wilkins column, January 15–16, 1966, EX HU/2, Box 4, LBJL; Jack Valenti to Frank A. Clark, January 21, 1966, wrote that the president "has a measureless respect and regard for Mr. Wilkins." See Clifford Alexander, Memo for the President, January 7, 1966, Box 3, EX HU 2; Whitney Young column, May 10, 1966, Box 4, EX HU 2. Later, Young changed his mind and concluded that the administration's Vietnam policy interfered with the extension of domestic reform. Whitney Young, Oral History Memoir, LBJL.

14. Simeon Booker to Louis Martin, August 13, 1965; Louis Martin to Marvin Watson, August 16, 1965, ND 19/LO 312; Bill Moyers to the President, August 30, 1965, Box 3, EX HU 2; Joseph Califano to the President, July 25, 1966, Diary Backup, July 26, 1966; Perry Barber to Jack Valenti, August 31, 1965, "Louis Martin" Name File, White House Confidential Files; "Remarks by the President to Democratic Elected Negro Officials," June 2, 1967, Will Sparks Files, LBJL.

15. Louis Martin to Joseph Califano, December 7, 1966, HU 2, White House Confidential Files, LBJL.

16. Goldman, *The Tragedy of Lyndon Johnson,* pp. 312, 370.

17. Clifford Alexander, Memo for the President, January 7, 1966, EX HU 2, Box 3, LBJL.

18. Lewis, *King,* p. 360.

19. Harry McPherson, Oral History Memoir, Tape 7, p. 12, LBJL; Garrow, *The FBI and Martin Luther King, Jr.;* Harry McPherson to the President, April 4, 1967, Box 14, Harry McPherson Files, LBJL; Clifford Alexander to the President, April 18, 1967, Diary Backup, LBJL.

20. George Christian, Memo for the President, April 8, 1967, Box 4, EX HU 2, LBJL; Rowan, "Martin Luther King's Tragic Decision," *Reader's Digest,* September 1967, reprinted as "The Consequences of Decision," in Lincoln, ed., *Martin Luther King, Jr.*

21. *New Pittsburgh Courier,* May 27, 1967; *New York Times,* April 11, 1967, p. 1; for a concurring view, see also Evers, *Evers,* pp. 127–29.

22. Halberstam, "Martin Luther King," pp. 40, 47.

23. Hubert Humphrey to Joseph Califano, January 28, 1966, Box 4, EX HU 2, LBJL.

24. Miroff, "Presidential Leverage Over Social Movements."

25. Harry McPherson to the President, July 26, 1967, Box 5, EX HU 2, LBJL.

26. Matthew Nimetz, Oral History Memoir, LBJL.

27. Harry McPherson to the President, September 12, 1966, Box 21(2), McPherson Files; McPherson, Oral History Memoir, tape 7, p. 12, LBJL.

28. Nicholas Katzenbach to Harry McPherson, September 17, 1966, Box 21(2), McPherson Files; see also, Clifford Alexander to Harry McPherson, October 3, 1966, Box 22, McPherson Files, and Harry McPherson to the President, July 26, 1967, Box 5, EX HU 2, LBJL.

29. *Public Papers of the Presidents, LBJ, 1966,* p. 1137.

30. Louis Martin to Jim Jones, October 3, 1966, "Democratic Elected Negro Officials" folder, Will Sparks Files, LBJL.

31. U.S. Senate, Committee on the Judiciary, Subcommittee on Constitutional Rights, *Hearings* (Civil Rights Act of 1967), 90th Cong., 1st sess., p. 291.

32. Jordan, "New Forces of Urban Political Power," p. 51.

33. Booker, "Black Politics at the Crossroads," p. 42.

34. Rustin, "The Southern Negro Vote," p. 49.

35. Dunbar, "Public Policymaking," p. 6.

36. King, "Martin Luther King Defines 'Black Power,' " p. 101; King, *Where Do We Go From Here?* p. 15.

37. Carmichael and Hamilton, *Black Power,* p. 104.

38. Ladner, "What Black Power Means," p. 145.

39. "Address by Nicholas deB. Katzenbach to the Southern Regional Council," February 28, 1966, Press Release, "Civil Rights," Will Sparks Files, LBJL.

40. Louis Martin to John Criswell, August 29, 1967, EX PL; Louis Martin to Jim Jones, October 3, 1966, "Democratic Elected Negro Officials" folder, Will Sparks Files, LBJL.

41. Ben Wattenberg to the President, February 29, 1968, FG 11-8-1, "Douglas Cater" Name File, White House Confidential Files, LBJL.

2. A Cautious Advance

1. Lawson, *Black Ballots;* Garrow, *Protest at Selma;* Bass, *Unlikely Heroes;* Read and McGough, *Let Them Be Judged.*

2. Public Law 89-110, 79 STAT. 437. Virginia and thirty-four counties in North Carolina were also covered. Texas had a poll tax but no literacy test. Florida had neither.

3. John Doar to Stephen Pollak, July 14, 1965, Administrative History, Department of Justice, Volume VII, Part X; Alan G. Marer to Stephen Pollak, June 11, 1965, Stephen Pollak to John Doar, July 14, 1965, Administrative History, Department of Justice, Volume VII, Part X, LBJL; Garrow, *Protest at Selma,* p. 185.

4. John Macy to the President, November 3, 1965, Box 55, EX HU 2-7, LBJL. The administration had filed a lawsuit challenging the poll tax and defended the constitutionality of the 1965 act in litigation brought by South Carolina. In both cases, the Department of Justice emerged victorious. *Harper v. Virginia State Board of Elections,* 383 U.S. 663 (1966) and *South Carolina v. Katzenbach* 383 U.S. 301 (1966).

5. Orfield, *The Reconstruction of Southern Education,* pp. 308–9.

6. Navasky, *Kennedy Justice,* pp. 163, 167, 241; Oberdorfer, "Daily Dilemmas," pp. 28, 82.

7. Navasky, *Kennedy Justice,* pp. 219–20.

8. John Doar, Memo to the Attorney General, August 1965, Civil Rights Division (CRD) office files, Department of Justice (DOJ).

9. Doar, "Civil Rights and Self-Government," p. 105; Marshall, *Federalism and Civil Rights.*

10. John Doar, testimony before the Special Equal Rights Committee (SERC), October 5, 1965, Box 91, Democratic National Committee (DNC) Files, LBJL.

11. Wolk, *Presidency and Black Civil Rights,* pp. 75–76; Nicholas Katzenbach, testimony before the U.S. Senate, Committee on the Judiciary, Subcommittee on Constitutional Rights, *Hearings* (Civil Rights), 89th Cong., 2d sess., 1966, p. 114.

12. Garrow, *Protest at Selma,* pp. 11, 19, 189; Lawson, *Black Ballots,* p. 334. For views sympathetic to the Justice Department's position, see Brauer, *John F. Kennedy,* chapter

4, and Wofford, *Of Kennedy and Kings,* pp. 225–27. As David Garrow correctly pointed out, registration figures based on race are estimates and not precise counts.

13. Lawson, *Black Ballots,* pp. 279 ff.

14. "Complaint of Robert Moses *et. al.* Against Robert F. Kennedy and J. Edgar Hoover," filed in the U.S. District Court for Washington, D.C., and reprinted in U.S. Congress, House of Representatives, Committee on the Judiciary, *Hearings on Civil Rights,* 1963, 88th Cong., 1st sess., pp. 1280–83.

15. Quoted in Wirt, *Politics of Southern Equality,* p. 82.

16. John Lewis to Lyndon B. Johnson, February 3, 1966, Box 40, GEN HU 2/ST 24, LBJL. This subject is treated more extensively in Lawson, *Black Ballots,* pp. 274–83.

17. Oberdorfer, "Daily Dilemmas," p. 82.

18. Richard Russell to Carey Williams, February 17, 1966, IFIA Dictation, Richard Russell Papers, University of Georgia; Watters and Cleghorn, *Climbing Jacob's Ladder,* p. 262. While preparing to enforce the act in anticipation of its passage, CRD lawyers did not view the magnitude of the suffrage problem in Georgia as being as great as it was in Mississippi, Alabama, and Louisiana. Alan Marer to Stephen Pollak, June 11, 1965, Administrative History, Department of Justice, Volume VII, Part X, LBJL.

19. Quoted in *Delta Democrat-Times,* April 22, 1966, cited in U.S. House of Representatives, Committee on the Judiciary, Subcommittee No. 5, *Hearings* (Civil Rights), 89th Cong., 2d sess., 1966, p. 1488.

20. Quoted in Marvin Watson to the President, April 5, 1967, Box 55, EX HU 2–7, LBJL.

21. Nicholas Katzenbach to William L. Taylor, December 4, 1965, Box 3, Lee White Files, LBJL.

22. John Doar to Bradford J. Dye, January 26, 1966, CRD Office Files, DOJ.

23. Nicholas Katzenbach to state and local registration officials, January 8, 1966, Administrative History, Department of Justice, Vol. VII, Part X, LBJL.

24. For examples, see Justice Department reports, "Clarendon County, South Carolina," September 21, 1965, and "Autauga, Alabama," October 29, 1965, CRD Office Files, DOJ. Lyndon B. Johnson to Nicholas Katzenbach, February 2, 1966, Box 184, EX FG 135, LBJL.

25. John Doar to St. John Barrett, May 21, 1967, CRD Office Files, DOJ.

26. Wolk, *Presidency and Black Civil Rights,* p. 77; Doar, "Civil Rights and Self-Government," p. 112; Stephen Eilperin and Alan Marer to Stephen Pollak, July 14, 1965, Administrative History, Department of Justice,, Vol. VII, Part X, LBJL.

27. John Macy to the President, November 1, 1965, Box 55, EX HU 2–7, LBJL.

28. Nicholas Katzenbach, Memo for the President, November 2, 1965, Box 55, EX HU 2–7, LBJL.

29. Alan G. Marer to Stephen Pollak, June 11, 1965, Administrative History, Department of Justice, Vol. VII, Part X, LBJL.

30. St. John Barrett to Stephen Pollak, June 15, 1965, *ibid.*

31. Alan Marer to John Doar, August 2, 1965, *ibid.* According to the Civil Service Commission, it "sought Negroes for this, but could not persuade any others to accept."

32. *Public Papers of the Presidents, Lyndon B. Johnson, 1965,* p. 843.

33. *Ibid.,* p. 636.

34. Harry McPherson, Oral History Memoir, Tape 16, p. 9, LBJL.

35. Hubert H. Humphrey to the President, August 5, 1965, Box 2, Richard

Goodwin Files; Ben Heineman, Oral History Memoir, LBJL. On planning for the conference and the controversy generated by the issue of the Negro family, see Rainwater and Yancey, *Moynihan Report*, p. 146; McPherson, *A Political Education*, pp. 339–42.

36. Rainwater and Yancey, *Moynihan Report*, pp. 195–96.

37. Sterling Tucker and Wiley Branton, Agenda Paper #3, "Voting and Citizenship Participation," November 16, 17, 18, 1965, Box 71, White House Conference on Civil Rights (WHCCR) Papers, LBJL.

38. Panel #3, "Transcript," pp. 140–41, WHCCR Papers.

39. *Ibid.*, p. 142.

40. *Ibid.*, pp. 157–58.

41. *Ibid.*, p. 159. For a slightly different view of private responsibility, see pp. 143–44 (Arnold Aronson and Henry L. Moon).

42. Thurgood Marshall to the President, January 14, 1966, Box 3, EX HU 2, LBJL.

43. U.S. Commission on Civil Rights, *Political Participation*, p. 186. However, the administration might have conducted citizenship training as part of the Great Society's adult education projects administered by HEW, the Department of Labor, and the Office of Economic Opportunity.

44. Panel #3, "Transcript," pp. 195–96, 213–14, 216, WHCCR Papers.

45. *Ibid.*, p. 216.

46. *Ibid.*, p. 262.

47. *Ibid.*, p. 228. For linkages in strategy between foreign and domestic affairs, see Walt Rostow to the President, July 28, 1967, Box 6, EX HU 2, LBJL.

48. Carl Holman, Berl Bernhard, Harold Fleming to Lee White, December 1965, Box 16, WHCCR Papers.

49. Sterling Tucker and Wiley Branton to Carl Holman, December 15, 1965, Box 15, WHCCR Papers.

50. Herbers, *Lost Priority*, pp. 158–59; Wiley Branton, personal interview with the author, October 21, 1970. Nothing came of Branton's plans, and he quit this post several months later.

51. Council Meeting, Minutes, March 5, 1966, Box 4, WHCCR Papers; Garrow, *Protest At Selma*, p. 185; Lyndon Johnson to Nicholas Katzenbach, February 2, 1966, Box 184, EX FG 135, LBJL.

52. "Battlefront," *Crisis* (January 1966); 73:41–42; Arnold Aronson to Nicholas Katzenbach, December 2, 1965, Box 96, Leadership Conference on Civil Rights (LCCR) Papers, Library of Congress.

53. "A Letter From Mrs. Devine," January 7, 1966, Key List Mailing 12A f.15, Eugene Cox MSS., Mississippi State University.

54. United States Commission on Civil Rights, *The Voting Rights Act . . . the first months*, pp. 3–4.

55. Nicholas Katzenbach to William L. Taylor, December 4, 1965, Box 3, Lee White Files, LBJL.

56. William Taylor, Memo, December 15, 1965, Box 67, Theodore M. Hesburgh MSS., Notre Dame University.

57. Forman, *Sammy Younge*, pp. 121, 183–84, 185, 207–8, 223.

58. Clifford Alexander to the President, January 7, 1966, Box 184, EX FG 135. Johnson's remarks, scrawled at the bottom of the memo, were unusual for him. See also Jack Rosenthal to Bill Moyers, January 7, 1966, Box 184, EX FG 135; Gwendolyn M. Patton to Lyndon B. Johnson, January 11, 1966, Box 29, GEN HU 2/St 1, LBJL.

59. Forman, *Sammy Younge,* p. 25.

60. John Doar to Earl Morgan, December 31, 1965; Landsberg-Thomas, "Jefferson County, Alabama," December 20, 1965; Wiley A. Branton to Nicholas Katzenbach, January 5, 1966, CRD Office Files, DOJ; U.S. Commission on Civil Rights, *Political Participation,* p. 226, for figures on Birmingham (Jefferson County).

61. Earl C. Morgan to John Doar, January 7, 1966; George Rayborn, "Conversations With Jefferson County District Attorney Earl C. Morgan and Jefferson County Negro Leaders," January 22, 1966, CRD Office Files, DOJ. Neither the local white officials nor conservative black leaders wanted it to appear that examiners were sent in direct response to SCLC demonstrations. John Doar to James G. O'Hara, March 7, 1966, Box 50, James G. O'Hara MSS, Michigan Historical Collection, University of Michigan.

62. Nicholas Katzenbach to state and local registration officials, January 8, 1966, April 23, 1966, Administrative History, Department of Justice, Vol. VII, Part XA; *New York Times,* January 3, 1966, p. 25; Arnold Aronson to Nicholas Katzenbach, December 2, 1965, Box 96, LCCR MSS.

63. Jim Martin to Dear Colleague, January 25, 1966, B 34-28, Gerald Ford Congressional Files, Gerald R. Ford Library.

64. "Address by Attorney General Nicholas deB. Katzenbach to the Southern Regional Council," February 28, 1966, Will Sparks Files, LBJL.

65. Southern Regional Council, "The Effects of Federal Examiners and Organized Registration Campaigns on Negro Voter Registration," July 1966. For confirmation of the SRC's findings, see Joubert and Crouch, "Mississippi Blacks"; Terchek, "Political Participation." Garrow, *Protest At Selma,* pp. 185–90.

66. Nicholas Katzenbach, Memo for the President, April 26, 1966, Box PL 31, EX PL/ST 1, LBJL; Walton, *Black Political Parties,* p. 145.

67. Garrow, *Protest at Selma,* pp. 187–88; Walton, *Black Political Parties,* p. 143.

68. *New York Times,* August 5, 1966, p. 11; "Number of Persons Listed by Federal Examiners Under the Voting Rights Act, 1965–74," in U.S. Senate, Committee on the Judiciary, Subcommittee on Constitutional Rights, *Hearings,* "Extension of the Voting Rights Act of 1965," 94th Cong., 1st sess., 1975, p. 633.

69. "Black Power at the Dixie Polls," *Time* (June 15, 1970), 95:17.

70. Garrow, *Protest at Selma,* p. 191; Morris, *The Politics of Black America,* p. 163.

71. Roy Wilkins, "State of the NAACP," *Crisis* (February 1966), 73:80; "Battlefront," *Crisis* (August-September 1966), 73:387.

72. Gaile Noble to Father Henry Parker, January 9, 1969, Delta Ministry MSS, Mississippi State University; Noble, "The Delta Ministry," p. 148. For the Delta Ministry's voter registration activities, see Delta Ministry, "Report," February 17–18, June 1967, folder 19, 1972 add., Eugene Cox MSS; Delta Ministry Commission, Minutes of Executive Committee, November 15, 1968, Delta Ministry MSS.

73. Nicholas Katzenbach, Memo for the President, November 2, 1965, Box 55, EX HU 2-7, LBJL.

74. "Summary" B-457, NAACP Papers; Roy Wilkins to John M. Brooks, April 4, 1966; Vernon Jordan to Roy Wilkins, April 9, 1966; John A. Morsell to John M. Brooks, April 24, 1966, B-408, NAACP Papers; John A. Morsell to Gilbert Jonas, "Interim Report on 1967–68 NAACP Voter Registration Activity," B-411, NAACP Reports.

75. *New York Times,* January 18, 1966, p. 18; Executive Director of the Southern Regional Council, "Annual Report, 1966," Southern Regional Council Office Files; Executive Committee Meeting, Minutes, December 1–3, 1967, SRC Office Files; Voter Education Project, *Annual Report, 1967.*

76. King, *Where Do We Go from Here?* p. 34.

77. Vernon Jordan, Interview, January 26, 1968, Civil Rights Documentation Project, Howard University.

78. U.S. Senate, Committee on the Judiciary, Subcommittee on Constitutional Rights, *Hearings on the Extension of the Voting Rights Act of 1965,* 94th Cong., 1st sess., 1975, pp. 631–33, 657; Watters and Cleghorn, *Climbing Jacob's Ladder,* pp. 376–77; U.S Department of Commerce, *Statistical Abstract of the United States, 1970,* p. 369.

79. Marvin Wall, "New South Notes," p. 82; *VEP News,* January 1969, p. 30.

80. The figures were calculated from U.S. Department of Commerce, *Statistical Abstract of the United States, 1970,* p. 369. The gaps between white and black enrollment were as follows: Alabama, 33.3 percent; Georgia, 28.1 percent; Louisiana, 26.3 percent; Mississippi, 23.3 percent; North Carolina, 24.7 percent; South Carolina, 16.9 percent; and Virginia, 18.9 percent.

81. Wolk, *Presidency and Black Civil Rights,* p. 76.

82. Pollak, "Effective Anti-Discrimination Legislation," p. 36; R. Pressman to D. Robert Owen, June 2, 1966; Bob Murphy to James P. Turner, July 3, 1967; "Interview with Angie [sic] Moore, October 17, 1970, by James M. Fallon and Dorothy E. Mead," CRD Office Files.

83. Wolk, *Presidency and Black Civil Rights,* p. 78.

84. *Public Papers . . . LBJ, 1966,* pp. 615, 859. See also Elizabeth W. Reeves to Edward Sylvester, June 28, 1966, pp. 6–7, Box 14, WHCCR Papers.

3. The Land of the Tree and the Home of the Grave

1. Carl Holman, Berl Bernhard, Harold Fleming to Lee White, December 3, 1965, Box 4, WHCCR Papers.

2. Morris Abram to the President, November 24, 1965, Box 22, EX HU 2/MC, LBJL.

3. John Lewis, Marion Berry, Jr., Betty Garman to A. Philip Randolph, Morris Abram, William Coleman, December 14, 1965, Box 66, WHCCR Papers; Panel #3, "Transcript," p. 160, WHCCR Papers.

4. Harry McPherson to Bill Moyers, December 10, 1965, Box 22, EX HU 2/MC, WHCCR Papers. For a contrasting view, see Hayes Redmon to Bill Moyers, December 1, 1965, Box 22, EX HU 2/MC, WHCCR Papers.

5. Harry McPherson, Oral History Memoir, Tape 6, p. 16; Rainwater and Yancey, *Moynihan Report,* p. 258.

6. Joseph Califano to the President, February 3, 1966, Box 22, EX HU 2/MC; Clifford Alexander, Memo for the Record, December 9, 1965, Box 22, EX HU 2/MC, WHCCR Papers.

7. Berl I. Bernhard and Ronald B. Natalie to the Council, March 19, 1966, Box 9, WHCCR Papers.

8. Press Release, "SNCC Statement on White House Conference," May 23, 1966, III, B-452, NAACP MSS; Carson, *In Struggle,* pp. 204–5.

9. Harry McPherson to the president, May 18, 1966, Box 52, McPherson Files; see also Robert Kintner to the President, May 25, 1966, Confidential File, Box 4, FB 100/MC, LBJL.

10. White House Conference on Civil Rights, *To Fulfill These Rights,* 1966, p. 3, EX HU 2/MC, WHCCR Papers; Rainwater and Yancey, *Moynihan Report,* pp. 276, 278.

11. Committee No. VII, "Transcript of Proceedings, Morning Session," p. 14, June 1, 1966, Box 32; Council Meeting, Minutes, April 1, 2, 1966, Box 6, WHCCR Papers. See also, Committee No. V, "Transcript," p. 67, June 2, 1966, linking voting rights enforcement with administration of justice. For a dissenting view warning against using the FBI as a national police force, see Committee No. VII, "Transcript . . . ," pp. 39–42, for the statement of Archibald J. Carey, Jr.

12. "Administration of Justice Resolutions," n.d., Box 52; "Summary of Conference Discussions on Administration of Justice," June 23, 1966, Box 7, WHCCR Papers.

13. The recommendations also included financial compensation for victims of civil rights crimes. *To Fulfill These Rights*, pp. 81–90. At the same time, a CORE-sponsored resolution against the Vietnam War was voted down.

14. Joseph Califano to the President, June 5, 1966, Box 22, EX HU 2/MC, WHCCR Papers.

15. Cliff Carter to the President, June 3, 1966, Marvin Watson Files, LBJL.

16. John Herbers, *New York Times*, June 4, 1966, p. 12; Richard Miles to Marvin Wall, June 22, 1966, VEP Office Files, Atlanta, Georgia; Kopkind, "No Fire This Time," p. 15. See also Muse, *The American Negro Revolution*, p. 256; Rainwater and Yancey, *Moynihan Report*, p. 291.

17. *Public Papers of the Presidents, LBJ, 1966*, p. 574; McPherson, *Political Education*, p. 348.

18. Harry McPherson to the President, June 10, 1966, Confidential File HU 2, LBJL.

19. *Public Papers . . . LBJ, 1966*, p. 895; Harry McPherson to the President, August 12, 1966, Box 52, McPherson Files, LBJL; McPherson, *Political Education*, p. 351.

20. *New York Times*, June 4, 1966, p. 12.

21. Committee Number V, Administration of Justice, "Transcript of Proceedings," June 2, 1966, pp. 66–71, WHCCR Papers; *New York Times*, June 12, 1966, IV, p. 1.

22. Charles Cobb, quoted in *The Christian Science Monitor*, September 17, 1966, clipping, "Civil Rights 1965–1966," Fred Panzer Files, LBJL.

23. *New York Times*, May 23, 1966, p. 27; June 5, 1966, p. 78.

24. "Is Meredith Right?" p. 765; *New York Times*, June 5, 1966, p. 78.

25. *Memphis Press Scimitar*, June 7, 1966, clipping, Box 1A folder 46, Eugene Cox MSS; "The Meredith Ambush," p. 731.

26. Rovere, "Letter from Washington," p. 143.

27. *New York Times*, June 8, 1966, p. 1.

28. *New York Times*, June 7, 1966, p. 28.

29. *Memphis Commercial Appeal*, June 8, 1966, clipping, Box IA folder 46, Eugene Cox MSS.

30. Sellers with Terrell, *The River of No Return*, p. 162; Carson, *In Struggle*, p. 207; Muse, *American Negro Revolution*, pp. 236–37.

31. King, *Where Do We Go From Here?*, p. 30; *New York Times*, June 7, 1966, p. 28.

32. Roy Wilkins to Delegates to the 57th Annual NAACP Convention, July 5, 1966, B-374, NAACP MSS.

33. Roy Wilkins to NAACP Branch Offices, "On Meredith March, Memphis to Jackson," June 10, 1966, B 374, NAACP MSS: *New York Times*, June 12, 1966, p. 82. The NAACP believed that the manifesto did not properly emphasize support for the

congressional civil rights proposals, and although the organization called for the appointment of federal examiners, it did not agree the problem "will be solved simply by sending in registrars into 600 counties."

34. Muse, *American Negro Revolution*, p. 238. Evers remarked: "I don't want this to turn into another Selma where everyone goes home with the cameramen and leaves us holding the bag." Despite initial reports to the contrary, Evers did not sign the manifesto. *New York Times*, June 11, 1966, p. 1.

35. *New York Times*, June 8, 1966, p. 26.

36. "The Meredith Ambush," p. 731.

37. United States Senate, Committee on the Judiciary, *Hearings Before the Subcommittee on Constitutional Rights*, 89th Cong. 2d sess., 1966, pp. 111–12; *New York Times*, June 7, 1966, p. 29.

38. *New York Times*, June 7, 1966, p. 29.

39. Handwritten notes, n.d., Box 22, Civil Rights folder 5, Harry McPherson Files, LBJL; John Doar to Byron G. Rogers, August 11, 1966, Box 40, GEN HU 2 ST 24, LBJL.

40. *New York Times*, June 7, 1966, p. 29; June 8, 1966, p. 1. The law provided a maximum penalty of five years in prison and a $5,000 fine "to intimidate, threaten or coerce any person for urging or aiding any person to vote or attempt to vote."

41. Fred L. Shuttlesworth to Lyndon B. Johnson, June 7, 1966, Box 22, McPherson Files; John W. Macy to the President, June 13, 1966, Box 86, EX PL2, LBJL.

42. *New York Times*, June 12, 1966, p. 1.

43. *Memphis Commercial Appeal*, June 10, 1966, clipping, Box 1A folder 46, Eugene Cox MSS.

44. *New York Times*, June 12, 1966, p. 1.

45. Neil A. Maxwell, *Wall Street Journal*, June 22, 1966, clipping, "Civil Rights 1965–1966," Fred Panzer Files, LBJL; Arthur C. Thomas to Dear Friend, n.d., Box 2 folder 6, Eugene Cox MSS.

46. Maxwell, *Wall Street Journal*, June 22, 1966, clipping, Panzer Files.

47. *New York Times*, June 15, 1966, p. 1; June 16, 1966, p. 35.

48. Jaffe, "Grenada, Mississippi," pp. 18–19.

49. *Ibid.*, p. 19; Good, "Meredith March," p. 7.

50. Sellers, *River of No Return*, pp. 166–67.

51. King, *Where Do We Go From Here?* p. 29; *New York Times*, June 17, 1966, p. 1.

52. King, *Where Do We Go From Here?*, pp. 30–31.

53. Good, "Black Power," p. 114.

54. *New York Times*, June 18, 1966, p. 28.

55. Ruby Magee Interview, Mississippi Oral History Program, University of Southern Mississippi.

56. *New York Times*, June 17, 1966, p. 1.

57. Jacob Rosenthal to Bill Moyers, June 17, 1966, Box 184, EX FB 135, LBJL.

58. The Delta Ministry *Newsletter* (January 1966) 3, Box 2 folder 6, Eugene Cox MSS; Hilton, *The Delta Ministry*, p. 82; *New York Times*, January 11, 1966, p. 10. In March, the FBI arrested thirteen Klansmen for killing Dahmer, and on June 23, 1966, a biracial grand jury returned an indictment against the Kluxers for violating the Voting Rights Act. *New York Times*, March 29, April 13, June 24, 1966.

59. *New York Times*, June 22, 1966, p. 1.

60. Lyndon B. Johnson to Martin Luther King, Jr., June 23, 1966, Box 59 EX

HU 4; Floyd McKissick to Lyndon B. Johnson, June 20, 1966, Box 40, GEN HU ST24, LBJL.

61. Nicholas Katzenbach to the President, July 6, 1966, Monthly Report to the Cabinet, Box 28, Confidential File EX FG 120, LBJL; "Possible questions at a press conference," June 1966, Civil Rights folder 5, McPherson Files; *Christian Science Monitor,* June 15, 1966, clipping, Fred Panzer Files, LBJL.

62. Good, "Black Power," p. 116.

63. *New York Times,* June 24, 1966, pp. 1, 20; June 25, 1966, p. 1.

64. Roy Wilkins to Lyndon B. Johnson, June 24, 1966, Box 40, GEN HU 2/ST 24, LBJL.

65. *New York Times,* June 24, 1966, p. 20; "Possible questions at press conference," McPherson Files, LBJL.

66. Meredith, "Big Changes Are Coming."

67. *New York Times,* June 27, 1966, p. 29.

68. *Lexington [Mississippi] Advertiser,* June 30, 1966, clipping, Box 1A folder 46, Eugene Cox MSS.

69. Roy Wilkins to Delegates to the 57th Annual NAACP Convention, July 5, 1966, B-374, NAACP MSS; "Mississippi and the NAACP," p. 317. *New York Times,* June 27, 1966, p. 1.

70. *Jackson Clarion Ledger,* June 28, 1966, clipping, Box 1A folder 46, Eugene Cox MSS.

71. John Doar, Memo to the Attorney General, August 4, 1966, CRD Office Files, DOJ. The county was designated on July 20, 1966, but protests continued over desegregation of schools and public facilities. Over the next two years, 1,500 citizens were listed on the voter rolls. Racial violence flared in the late summer and early fall. White mobs viciously attacked black youths seeking to desegregate public schools. Jaffe, "Grenada," pp. 15–27.

72. *New York Times,* June 26, 1966, p. 1.

73. *New York Times,* August 22, 1966, p. 36; King, *Where Do We Go From Here?,* pp. 34–35.

74. *Public Papers . . . LBJ, 1966,* p. 710.

75. Good, "Meredith March," p. 13.

76. Harry McPherson, Oral History Memoir, Tape 6, p. 22, LBJL.

77. Harry McPherson to George Christian, August 1, 1967, Box 6, EX HU 2, LBJL; Miroff, "Presidential Leverage."

78. "Up the Political Ladder," *Newsweek* (November 20, 1967), 70:66.

79. U.S. Commission on Civil Rights, Minutes of 68th Meeting, September 8, 1965, Box 78, Theodore M. Hesburgh MSS, Notre Dame University Law School, reporting the observations of commission staff director, William L. Taylor, who attended the meeting of the task force.

80. Nicholas Katzenbach to Joseph Califano, December 13, 1965, Box 65, LE HU 2, LBJL.

81. *Ibid;* George Reedy to the President, October 2, 1965, Box 56, CF HU 2; Joseph Califano to the President, October 25, 1965, CF HU 2, LBJL.

82. *Public Papers . . . LBJ, 1966,* p. 6.

83. Clarence Mitchell to Roy Wilkins, January 25, 1966, B 386, NAACP MSS.

84. Section 241 provided for penalties of ten years in prison and a $5,000 fine; section 242 imposed a one-year prison term and a $1,000 fine. Department of Justice, CRD Staff, "Interference With Rights Proposal No. 1," n.d., Joseph Califano Files, LBJL.

85. The federal government also had the authority to punish intimidation against those who exercised or counseled others to exercise the franchise under Section 11b of the Voting Rights Act. Violation of this provision resulted in a $5,000 fine and imprisonment for not more than five years. John Doar to Director, Federal Bureau of Investigation, August 9, 1965, Administrative History of the Department of Justice, Volume VII, Part X, LBJL.

86. Department of Justice, CRD Staff, "Interference With Rights Proposal No. 1"; Alan G. Marer to David L. Norman, February 11, 1966, Administrative History of the Department of Justice, Volume VII, Part X, LBJL; see testimony of Nicholas Katzenbach, U.S. House of Representatives, Committee on the Judiciary, Subcommittee No. 5, *Civil Rights,* 89th Cong., 2d sess., 1966, p. 1182, and U.S. Senate, Committee on the Judiciary, *Civil Rights,* 89th Cong., 2d sess., 1966, p. 110.

87. *United States v. Guest,* 383 U.S. 782 (1966). Potter Stewart, who wrote the majority opinion, thought it unnecessary to consider the issue of the constitutionality of the enforcement legislation under the Fourteenth Amendment. Justice John Marshall Harlan dissented. For a view unsympathetic to the majority, see Alfred Avins, "The Ku Klux Klan Act of 1871: Some Reflected Light on State Action and the Fourteenth Amendment," reprinted in Senate Judiciary Committee, *Civil Rights,* 1966, pp. 772–805. In the retrials, the defendants were found guilty, and their sentences varied from three to ten years in prison. Berry, *Black Resistance,* p. 201.

88. Henry Wilson to the President, March 11, 1966, Box 11, Henry Wilson Files, LBJL; Nicholas Katzenbach to the President, March 17, 1966, Diary Backup, LBJL.

89. Ramsey Clark to Lawrence F. O'Brien, April 7, 1966, Box 19, Reports on Legislation, LBJL. The internal debate within the administration dealt with the question of whether the president should seek legislation on housing or issue an executive order. Nicholas Katzenbach, Memo for the President, March 17, 1966, Box 2, EX HU 2, MC, LBJL.

90. April 28, 1966, Diary Backup, LBJL. Among those in attendance were Martin Luther King, Roy Wilkins, Clarence Mitchell, A. Philip Randolph, Floyd McKissick, Joseph Rauh, and Dorothy Height.

91. *Public Papers . . . LBJ, 1966,* p. 462.

92. *Ibid.,* p. 463. He also requested an additional appropriation for 100 FBI agents to help deal with civil rights infractions.

93. *Ibid.,* pp. 466, 469.

94. Sam Ervin to C. A. McKnight, August 12, 1966, Box 36, Sam Ervin MSS, Southern Historical Collection, University of North Carolina.

95. Senate Judiciary Committee, *Civil Rights,* 1966, p. 65.

96. *Ibid.,* p. 103.

97. *Ibid.,* p. 150.

98. *Congressional Record,* 89th Cong. 2d sess., p. 17487; Tucker, *Memphis Since Crump,* pp. 149–51.

99. *New York Times,* June 28, 1966, p. 1. See testimony of Dr. Benjamin Payton, Senate Judiciary Committee, *Civil Rights,* 1966, p. 1491.

100. Everett Dirksen to Harry W. Knatz, June 28, 1966, Box 5, Working Papers, folder 329, Everett Dirksen MSS.

101. Howard Smith to G. Glenn Whitlock, June 1, 1966, Box 100, Howard Smith MSS; *Congressional Record,* 89th Cong., 2d sess., pp. 16838–39.

102. Clifford Alexander to Harry McPherson, June 8, 1966, Box 22, McPherson Files, LBJL.

103. Clifford Alexander to Harry McPherson, June 8, 1966, Box 52, McPherson Files, LBJL.

104. Edward Hutchinson to Cecil J. Dixon, June 10, 1966, Box 31, Edward Hutchinson MSS, Michigan Historical Collection, University of Michigan.

105. U.S. Senate, Committee on the Judiciary, *Hearings (Civil Rights)*, 1966, pp. 558–59.

106. Senate Judiciary Committee, *Civil Rights*, 1966, p. 117.

107. *Congressional Record*, 89th Cong., 2d sess., p. 16833.

108. *Ibid.*, p. 17112.

109. *Ibid.*, p. 17120. For similar expressions, see pp. 17114, 17118, 17180, 17219, 17226, 17496, and 17516.

110. Horace Kornegay to James W. Morrison, July 21, 1966, Box 39, Horace Kornegay MSS, Southern Historical Collection, University of North Carolina.

111. *Congressional Record*, 89th Cong., 2d sess., p. 17227.

112. *Ibid.*, p. 17505. See also pp. 16834, 17115, 17229, and 17490.

113. Lader, *Power on the Left*, p. 208; Downes, "A Critical Reexamination," p. 352.

114. "A 'Black Power' Speech That Has Congress Aroused," *U.S. News & World Report* (August 22, 1966), 61:6.

115. *Congressional Record*, 89th Cong., 2d sess., p. 18456.

116. *Ibid.*, p. 18469. Ryan noted the difference between Title V, which was made necessary because of the refusal of state and local authorities to investigate and prosecute offenders in certain states, and the antiriot provision, which was not based on any evidence that law enforcement was unwilling to handle riots on the state and local levels. See also pp. 18464 and 18474.

117. *Ibid.*, pp. 18457, 18462, 18467, 18475, 18477. The Republicans voted unanimously, 138-0, for the antiriot amendment, while the Democrats split 251-24.

118. Nicholas Katzenbach, Memo for the President, July 28, 1966, Box 4, EX HU 2; Katzenbach to the President, July 6, 1966, Monthly Report to the Cabinet, Box 28, CF EX FG 120; Clifford Alexander to Joe Califano, July 20, 1966, Box 65, EX LE HU 2; Clarence Mitchell to Lyndon B. Johnson, August 12, 1966, Clarence Mitchell Name File, LBJL.

119. Edward Hutchinson to Harriet K. Brooks, August 11, 1966, Box 31, Hutchinson MSS.

120. Arnold Aronson, Memo, No. 90, August 16, 1966, Box 26, LCCR MSS; *Congressional Record*, 89th Cong., 2nd sess., p. 18484.

121. Everett M. Dirksen to John H. Bishop, July 29, 1966, Box 5, Working Papers, folder 334; Everett M. Dirksen to Walter E. Wiles, August 2, 1966, Box 5, Working Papers, folder 336, Dirksen MSS.

122. Reports on Legislation, September 2, 1966, Box 26, LBJL; Nicholas Katzenbach Memo to the President, September 9, 1966, Box 65, EX LE HU 2, LBJL; Philip Hart to Bill Welsh, August 19, 1966, Box 453, Michigan Historical Collection, University of Michigan.

123. Richard Russell to A. Willis Robertson, August 25, 1966, 1F 1A, Dictation, Richard Russell MSS.

124. Richard Russell to Donovan E. Smith, September 6, 1966, Box 9, Russell MSS.

125. Sundquist, *Politics and Policy*, p. 282, points out that twelve Republicans

and Frank Lausche, an Ohio Democrat, who had supported cloture in 1964 and 1965, opposed it in 1966. The cloture votes on September 14 and 19 were 54-42 and 52-41.

126. Richard Russell to Henry L. Wells, May 17, 1966, IF-1 Dictation, Russell MSS; *Congressional Record,* 89th Cong., 2d sess., p. 22384; Tom Wicker, *New York Times,* September 14, 1966, p. 46; "Negro Strategy," *Commonweal* (September 1966), 84:626–27.

127. *Congressional Record,* 89th Cong., 2d sess., p. 23034.

128. *Pittsburgh Courier,* editorials, October 1, October 29, 1966.

129. John Herbers, *New York Times,* September 13, 1966, p. 22; Sherrill, *The Accidental President,* p. 195; Harvey, *Black Civil Rights,* p. 40.

130. *Public Papers . . . LBJ, 1966,* p. 1047.

131. Sundquist, *Politics and Policy,* p. 286. Senator Thruston Morton, a Kentucky Republican, explained the political problems for those voting on the omnibus bill: "This is an election year, and in my opinion, not the appropriate time to consider legislation on such a highly emotional issue. I think it would be better to implement those laws which are already on the books." Thruston Morton to Lillian Jackson, September 14, 1966, Box 8, Legislative Files, Thruston Morton Collection, University of Kentucky. For the administration's differing perspective on the outcome of the 1966 congressional election, see Nicholas Katzenbach, Oral History Memoir, LBJL.

132. Ramsey Clark, Report of the Civil Rights Task Force, November 1966, 1966 Task Force on Civil Rights (1), Joseph Califano Files, LBJL; Memo, December 8, (1966), Box 12, 1966 Task Force on Civil Rights, LBJL.

133. In this version there were several changes from the bill passed by the House in 1966. The prosecution was required to prove that racial assaults were for the purpose of interfering with the stipulated civil rights activity because the assailants did not want Negroes to participate in that activity. In the House-passed bill, the federal government merely had to prove that interference occurred while the victim was engaging or seeking to engage in designated conduct. The Justice Department had questioned the constitutionality of this provision because a direct connection between racial motivation and the exercise of federal rights was missing. The 1967 version also contained a measure creating a civil action for damages for victims of civil rights crimes. This was not as sweeping as the previous proposal for indemnification. The new bill also removed the word "lawfully" inserted in the Grider amendment and repealed the criminal provisions of the Voting Rights Act which overlapped Title V. This last action was opposed by the Civil Rights Commission, which charged that it would remove the Voting Rights Act's criminal sanctions against economic intimidation. The Justice Department wanted one statute to avoid "election" of an appropriate remedy and suggested that economic coercion interfering with the rights in Title V would be subject to civil litigation. "Criminal Legislation Dealing with Interference with Exercise of Federal Rights," n.d., Administrative History of the Department of Justice, Volume VII, Part X; John Doar, Memo for the Acting Attorney General, January 26, 1967, Administrative History of the Department of Justice, Volume VII, Part X; Stephen J. Pollak, Memo, December 5, 1966, Box 12, Task Force on Civil Rights, 1966; Stephen J. Pollak to the President, February 15, 1967, Box 12, Task Force on Civil Rights, 1966; Stephen J. Pollak to Ramsey Clark, January 20, 1967, Administrative History of the Department of Justice, Volume VII, Part X; William J. Taylor to James Frey, February 13, 1967, Administrative History of the Department of Justice, Volume VII, Part X, LBJL; Seess, "Federal Power."

134. Harvey, *Black Civil Rights,* p. 42; Memo for the Record, February 15, 1967, Box 55, Diary Backup, February 13, 1967, LBJL.

135. Arnold Aronson, Memo No. 3-67, February 1967, Box 26, LCCR MSS.

136. *New Pittsburgh Courier,* March 4, 1967; Ramsey Clark, Reports on Pending Legislation, February 24, 1967, Box 29, LBJL.

137. Ramsey Clark, Reports on Pending Legislation, March 17, 1967, Box 30, LBJL; *New York Times,* March 19, 1967, p. 1.

138. Quoted in *Congressional Record,* 90th Cong., 1st sess., p. 22686.

139. Minutes of the 152nd Meeting of the Republican Leadership, November 2, 1967, Legislative Minutes and Statements, August–November 1967, Dirksen MSS; Edward Hutchinson to Jessie Martan, April 19, 1967, Box 37, Hutchinson MSS; Edward Hutchinson to Phil Adkins, November 13, 1967, Box 37, Hutchinson MSS; James G. O'Hara to Mr. and Mrs. Carl Prytula, August 9, 1967, Box 70, James G. O'Hara MSS, Michigan Historical Collection, University of Michigan; Sherwin Markman to Barefoot Sanders, August 14, 1967, Box 6, EX HU 2, LBJL.

140. *Congressional Record,* 90th Cong., 1st sess., pp. 22752, 22757, 22772, 22765, 22771, 22773; *New York Times,* June 23, 1967, p. 1, June 28, 1967, p. 23; Ramsey Clark, Reports on Pending Legislation, June 23, June 30, 1967, Box 34, July 6, 1967, Box 35, LBJL. The House had already approved the antiriot measure when, on July 25, Brown delivered a speech in Cambridge, Maryland, which helped trigger an ensuing riot. Among other things he declared: "Burn this town down if this town don't turn around." Lader, *Power on the Left,* p. 225.

141. *New Pittsburgh Courier,* July 16, 1967; *New York Times,* June 25, 1967, pp. 1, 48, June 26, 1967, p. 14, July 5, 1967, p. 1, August 16, 1967, p. 40, October 22, 1967, IV, p. 10.

142. *Congressional Quarterly Almanac* (1967), 23:786; *Congressional Quarterly Weekly Report,* August 11, 1967, p. 1518.

143. U.S. Senate, Committee on the Judiciary, *Hearings on the Civil Rights Act of 1967,* 90th Cong., 1st sess., pp. 287–88.

144. *Ibid.,* p. 220.

145. Larry Temple to the President, January 22, 1968, Box 7, EX HU 2, LBJL.

146. *New York Times,* October 11, 1967, p. 35, October 26, 1967, p. 1; George B. Autry to Ralph Hemphill, October 6, 1967, Box 224, Ervin MSS.

147. Sam Ervin to T. J. Sellers, June 4, 1968, Box 3, Ervin MSS.

148. Philip Hart to Clarence Mitchell, December 19, 1967, Box 306, Hart MSS; Lyndon B. Johnson to Roy Wilkins, November 20, 1967, Box 7, EX HU 2, LBJL.

149. *Crisis* (February 1968), 75:44.

150. Diggs Datrooth, "National Hotline," *New Pittsburgh Courier,* January 30, 1968.

151. Philip Hart to Terry Segal, January 15, 1968, Box 456, Hart MSS; *New York Times,* January 19, 1968, p. 19.

152. *Public Papers . . . LBJ, 1968,* p. 62; Barefoot Sanders to the President, January 13, 1968, Box 7, EX HU 2, LBJL.

153. "1968 Constructive Republican Programs—State of the Union Message by Republicans," n.d., folder 87, Republican National Convention Files, Dirksen MSS. The Johnson administration pondered the pros and cons of endorsing an antiriot bill. The Justice Department recommended against sending one to Congress but "rather holding it back as leverage to enact other parts of your program which may be in trouble." Johnson, however, wanted to include a riot bill as part of his crime program. Joseph Califano to the President, January 29, 1968, Box 79, EX LE JL, LBJL.

154. Bart Hertzbach to Senator Scott, January 30, 1968, S-2-10, Hugh Scott MSS, University of Virginia.

155. *Congressional Record,* 90th Cong., 2nd sess., p. 333.

156. *Ibid.,* p. 320, and pp. 332, 535, 918, 2084, 2269. Mike Manatos to the President, January 22, 1968, Box 66, EX LE HU 2; Larry Temple to the President, January 22, 1968, Box 7, EX HU 2, LBJL; Richard Russell to Michael L. Glover, January 23, 1968, IF 3, Russell MSS; Berry, *Black Resistance,* p. 214.

157. *Congressional Record,* 90th Cong., 2d sess., p. 1027.

158. *Ibid.,* p. 670.

159. Richard Russell to R. L. Sherrill, February 13, 1968, Box 6, Civil Rights, Russell MSS.

160. *New York Times,* February 7, 1968, p. 23.

161. *Congressional Record,* 90th Cong., 2d sess. p. 2267; Everett Dirksen to Dear ———, robo, February 1, 1968, Box 34, folder 2161, Chicago Office Files, Dirksen MSS. Ervin insisted: "Many Senators who voted against my bill confided to me privately that it was a better bill, but that they could not vote for it because it was not aimed solely at Negroes and civil rights workers and thus would appear to 'dilute' the protection given to them." Sam Ervin to H. E. Myers, April 2, 1968, Box 3, Ervin MSS.

162. The votes taken on February 20 and 26 were 57-37 and 56-37.

163. Ramsey Clark to the President, February 20, 1968, Box 7, EX HU 2; Larry Temple to the President, February 23, 1968, Box 7, EX HU 2; Barefoot Sanders to the President, Februaary 23, 1968, EX HU 2-2, LBJL; *Congressional Record,* 90th Cong., 2d sess., pp. 3806, 4049; *Public Papers . . . LBJ, 1968,* p. 242.

164. Ramsey Clark to the President, February 17, 1968, Box 66, EX LE HU 2, LBJL.

165. Roy Wilkins and Clarence Mitchell to Lyndon B. Johnson, February 24, 1968, Clarence Mitchell Name File, LBJL; Louis Martin to Joseph Califano, March 1, 1968, Box 7, EX HU 2, LBJL. Senators I. Jack Miller, Albert Gore, Edward Bartlett, Howard Cannon, and Frank Carlson switched their votes in favor and Frank Church, Joseph Tydings, and Gale McGee voted in support, whereas they had been absent previously.

166. Herbers, *Lost Priority,* p. 111.

167. *Congressional Record,* 90th Cong. 2d sess., pp. 4574, 5990; Everett Dirksen to Dear ———, robo, March 13, 1968, Box 34, folder 2161, Chicago Office Files, Dirksen MSS; Tom Wicker, *New York Times,* February 27, 1968, p. 42; John Herbers, *New York Times,* February 28, 1968, p. 35; Orfield, *Congressional Power,* p. 70. Thruston Morton praised Dirksen for "a good job in easing the Administration proposal." Thurston Morton to Willie Philips, April 10, 1968, Box 8, Legislative Series, Morton MSS.

168. *Congressional Record,* 90th Cong. 2d sess., pp. 5201–21, 5532–51. Proposals also adopted subjected rioters to the same penalties for those convicted of harming civil rights workers, exempted National Guardsmen and law enforcement officers quelling riots from prosecution under the worker protection clause, and made it a federal crime to teach or demonstrate the use of firearms or explosive devices for participation in a riot.

169. *Ibid.,* p. 5998.

170. *Public Papers . . . LBJ, 1968,* p. 374.

171. Barefoot Sanders to the President, February 29, 1968, Box 66, LE HU 2; Meeting Notes of the President's Leadership Breakfast (March 5, 1968), Box 94, Diary Backup, March 14, 1968, LBJL.

172. Barefoot Sanders to the President, March 13, 1968, Box 66, EX LE HU 2,

LBJL; Gerald R. Ford to Dwight W. Johnson, April 19, 1968, B-85-42, Congressional files, Gerald R. Ford Library. Ford wrote: "While I do think that some votes were changed because of this development, I am sure that most of the members of the House would have voted the same way had there been no murder in Memphis."

173. Barefoot Sanders, Oral History Memoir, LBJL. See *Congressional Record,* 90th Cong., 2d sess., pp. 9571, 9583, 9598, and 9604.

174. Lyndon Baines Johnson to John McCormack, April 5, 1968, Box 66, EX LE HU 2, LBJL.

175. George Romney to All Members of the Michigan Delegation, April 8, 1968, Box 139, Hart MSS. Romney had taken this position before King's death. See George Romney telegram to Robert Griffin, February 20, 1968, Box 0688, Robert Griffin MSS, Central Michigan University.

176. Edward Hutchinson to A. Scott Petersen, April 23, 1968, Box 38, Hutchinson MSS. For similar views, see Maston O'Neal to Jeff Goolsby, April 19, 1968, Box 8, Maston O'Neal MSS, Richard Russell Library; Sam Ervin to J.G. Freeman, April 18, 1968, Box 3, Ervin MSS; Charles Griffin to Warren Schenck, April 12, 1968, Box 31, Charles Griffin MSS, Mississippi State University; Harry McPherson, Oral History Memoir, Tape 8, p. 4, LBJL; Button, *Black Violence,* pp. 78–79; John Finney, *New York Times,* April 14, 1968, IV, p. 2.

177. *Congressional Record,* 90th Cong., 2d sess., p. 9598.

178. *Ibid.,* p. 9576.

179. Emanuel Celler to Joyce Rosenthal, April 15, 1968, Box 476, Celler MSS.

180. Barefoot Sanders to the President, April 8, 1968, Box 66, EX HU 2; Barefoot Sanders to the President, March 26, 1968, Box 7, EX HU 2; Barefoot Sanders to Jim Jones, March 21, 1968, Box 7, EX HU 2, LBJL. For a contrary view, see Orfield, *Congressional Power,* p. 70.

181. Philip Hart to George R. Laure, April 15, 1968, Box 139, Hart MSS. In agreement was the other Michigan senator, Robert Griffin, a Republican. Robert Griffin, Press Release, April 10, 1968, Box 1028, Robert Griffin MSS.

182. The votes were 229–195 on moving the previous question and 250–171 to adopt the resolution. On the first vote, 77 Republicans joined 152 Democrats against 106 Republicans and 89 Democrats. On the second vote, 100 Republicans and 150 Democrats beat 84 Republicans and 88 Democrats. For those like Edward Hutchinson, who preferred the conference route but finally voted for approval, the key factor was the inclusion in the measure of an antiriot clause. Edward Hutchinson to Warren Gast, August 11, 1968, Box 37, Hutchinson MSS.

183. *Public Papers . . . LBJ, 1968,* pp. 509–10. The law banned discrimination in the sale or rental of about 80 percent of all housing. Homes built with federal assistance were covered immediately. Beginning on January 1, 1969, the prohibition would extend to all multiple-unit dwellings except for owner-occupied homes with no more than four units. As of January 1, 1970, privately owned single-family dwellings sold or rented by real estate agents would be covered. Only private owners selling houses on their own were exempt.

4. Black Power, Ballot Power

1. Sellers with Terrell, *River of No Return,* p. 167; Carson, *In Struggle, passim.*

2. Quoting James Jolliff, Jr., in Bond, *Black Candidates,* p. 15.

3. Whittemore, *Together,* p. 128.

4. King, *Where Do We Go From Here?* p. 15; Watters, "South Carolina," p. 20.

5. Kopkind, "The Lair of the Black Panther," p. 12.

6. Rustin, "Black Power," pp. 35, 36, 40; Rustin, "The Southern Negro Vote," p. 49; "Negro Voting Power," pp. 36–37; Graham, "The Storm Over Black Power," p. 559.

7. King, *Where Do We Go From Here?,* pp. 48–49; Millspaugh, "Black Power," p. 502; Whittemore, *Together,* pp. 160–61.

8. Glick, "Black Power Enclave," p. 11.

9. Minutes of the COFO Convention, March 7, 1965, Part 2, Box 5, Aaron Henry Papers, The Archives of Labor History and Urban Affairs, Wayne State University; Joseph Rauh, Oral History Memoir, LBJL; McMillen, "Black Enfranchisement"; Walton, *Black Political Parties,* pp. 114–15.

10. Aaron Henry Oral History Memoir, LBJL; *Memphis Commercial Appeal,* January 15, 1967, clipping, Box 3B folder 20, Eugene Cox MSS.

11. *Delta Democrat Times,* August 20, 1965, clipping, Box 1A folder 27, Eugene Cox MSS.

12. McLemore, "Mississippi Freedom Democratic Party," p. 491; Noble, "Delta Ministry," p. 162.

13. "NAACP Freedom Democratic Party in Bitter Feud in Canton," August 16 (1966), n.p., clipping, Box 1 folder 27, Eugene Cox MSS; Walton, *Black Political Parties,* p. 116.

14. Fannie Lou Hamer, COFO Minutes, March 17, 1965, Part 2, Box 5, Aaron Henry Papers; Rudwick and Meier, "Integration vs. Separatism."

15. *Memphis Press-Scimitar,* June 29, 1966, clipping, Box 1A folder 46, Eugene Cox MSS.

16. *New York Times,* June 11, 1966, p. 1.

17. Roy Wilkins to Delegates to the 57th Annual NAACP Convention, July 5, 1966, B374, NAACP MSS; Berry, "Mississippi Post Mortem," p. 8; Berry, *Amazing Grace,* p. 33. One of the principal noncivil rights issues dividing the NAACP from the FDP was the Vietnam War. The NAACP lined up behind the Johnson administration's southeast Asian policies, while the Freedom Democrats, in mid-1965, urged blacks not to "honor the draft" and to do what "we can . . . to stop the war in Vietnam." *Memphis Commercial Appeal,* August 1, 1965, Box 1A folder 27, Eugene Cox MSS.

18. Simpson, "Loyalist," pp. 52–53.

19. Kenneth Fairly, "Two Major Groups Split By Bickering," clipping, n.d., n.p., Box 3B folder 19, Eugene Cox MSS.

20. Paul Pittman, February 1966, clipping, n.p., Young Democratic Club File, Mississippi State University; Meier, "Dilemmas," p. 9. For a different view of the relationship between the Johnson administration and the MDC, see Radosh, "From Protest to Black Power," p. 291.

21. Simpson, "Loyalist," p. 55; Terry Alford, "Integrationists Split," August 14, 1965, typewritten manuscript, vertical file, Mississippi State University Library; *Harvard Crimson,* October 7, 1965, clipping, Ed King MSS, Tougaloo College; penned note on back of flyer, "Young Democrats Convention," Ed King MSS.

22. William Silver to Aaron Henry, November 1, 1965, Box I 3, Aaron Henry MSS.

23. Hodding Carter, Oral History Interview, Billy Simpson Loyalist Democratic Collection, Mississippi State University Library.

24. *Harvard Crimson,* October 7, 1965, clipping, Ed King MSS. Ed King was one of a handful of white members of the MFDP. A member of the party's challenge delegation to the Democratic convention in 1964, he stuck with the FDP after its split from the NAACP-white liberal faction.

25. Simpson, "Loyalist," p. 58; Noble, "Delta Ministry," pp. 96–97. The two factions also battled over control of the Office of Economic Opportunity's Headstart program, with the radicals forming the Child Development Group of Mississippi to administer the funds, while the moderates endorsed the Mississippi Action Program.

26. Lee Dilworth to Reverend C. Whitley, October 7, 1965, Ed King MSS; Fortenberry and Abney, "Mississippi," p. 493; Simpson, "Loyalist," p. 60; Walton, *Black Political Parties,* p. 118.

27. Mississippians United To Elect Negro Candidates to Dear Friend, n.d., Delta Ministry Files, Mississippi State University.

28. Freedom Information Service, "Mississippi Newsletter," July 14, 1967, Mississippi State University; Walton, *Black Political Parties,* p. 125.

29. FDP, Minutes of the State Executive Committee meeting, March 20, 1967, Ed King MSS. National Committee For Free Elections in Sunflower, "Analysis and Statement on Behalf of the Negro Citizens of Sunflower County," press release, April 26, 1967, Ed King MSS. Robert Analavage, "The Sunflower Election, Negroes Not Represented," *Southern Patriot,* May 1967, pp. 1, 8. In Moorhead, white registrants barely outnumbered black registrants 418–412, while in Sunflower, blacks surpassed whites, 185–154. McLemore, "Mississippi Freedom Democratic Party," p. 363.

30. McLemore, "Mississippi Freedom Democratic Party," p. 366.

31. John Doar to G. W. Manning, Jr., April 25, 1967, CRD office files, DOJ.

32. John Doar to Joseph Harris, July 27, 1967, James P. Turner to John Doar, September 13, 1967, CRD Office Files, DOJ. Civil rights leaders contended that local registrars conducted business in stores where Negroes had credit accounts and were afraid to go to register. The federal government declined to send examiners. Joseph Harris to John Doar, July 11, 1967, Charles Quaintance to J. Harold Flannery, September 22, 1967, CRD Office Files, DOJ. Only 40 percent of the black voting-age population of the county had registered.

33. McLemore, 'Mississippi Freedom Democratic Party," p. 363.

34. *New York Times,* May 3, 1967, p. 32, May 4, 1967, p. 31; Salamon, "Protest, Politics, and Modernization," p. 487.

35. McLemore, "Mississippi Freedom Democratic Party," p. 375.

36. D. Robert Owen to Ramsey Clark, May 5, 1967, CRD Office Files, DOJ.

37. Hinds County FDP, *Newsletter,* February 26, 1968, Ed King MSS; McLemore, "Mississippi Freedom Democratic Party," p. 396.

38. *New York Times,* February 25, 1968, p. 54, February 28, 1968, p. 1, February 29, 1968, p. 24; McLemore, "Mississippi Freedom Democratic Party," pp. 401–2.

39. *New Pittsburgh Courier,* March 9, 1968.

40. Robert Canzoneri, "Evers," p. 73; *New York Times,* March 28, 1968, p. 17, April 4, 1968, p. 22.

41. Bond, *Black Candidates,* p. 12.

42. McLemore, "Mississippi Freedom Democratic Party," p. 421; Simpson, "Loyalist," pp. 65, 67; MFDP, Minutes, September 17, 1967, Ed King MSS.

43. Bond, *Black Candidates,* p. 13.

44. Carmichael and Hamilton, *Black Power,* p. 101.

45. Carson, *In Struggle,* p. 165.

46. *New York Times,* October 31, 1966, p. 1. Enrolled blacks numbered 2,681 and whites, 2,519.

47. Kopkind, "Lair of the Black Panther," p. 14; Corry, "Visit to Lowndes County," p. 30; United States Commission On Civil Rights, *Hearings, April 27–May 2, 1968, Montgomery Alabama,* p. 603.

48. *New York Times,* April 20, 1966, p. 27; Walton, *Black Political Parties,* p. 140.

49. Meier, "Dilemmas of Negro Protest Strategy," pp. 2–3.

50. W. C. Patton, "Political Activism," February and March 1966, B-410, NAACP MSS.

51. Campbell, "The Lowndes County (Alabama) Freedom Organization," p. 52; Meier, "The Dilemmas of Negro Protest Strategy," p. 5; Kopkind, "The Lair of the Black Panther," p. 13.

52. *New York Times,* May 5, 1966, pp. 1, 30, May 8, 1966, IV, p. 10; Roberts, "Wilcox County" p. 26.

53. Lucius Amerson, Interview, October 24, 1967, Civil Rights Documentation Project, Howard University.

54. U. S. Commission on Civil Rights, *Hearings, Montgomery, Alabama, 1968,* p. 611; Holloway, *Politics of the Southern Negro,* pp. 104–4, 107; *New York Times,* April 21, 1966, p. 30, June 2, 1966, p. 23; Fred Gray, personal interview with the author, March 24, 1970.

55. Campbell, "Lowndes County Freedom Organization," p. 39.

56. "Alabama's New Era," *Newsweek* (May 16, 1966), p. 29.

57. Kopkind, "Lair of the Black Panther," p. 11.

58. Campbell, "Lowndes County Freedom Organization," p. 57.

59. *Ibid.,* p. 77; *New York Times,* November 10, 1966, p. 30. Of 2,681 black registrants about 500 or 600 did not vote.

60. Charles Quaintance, "Investigative File Report on November 8, 1966, Election," n.d., CRD Office Files, DOJ; John Hunter interview by Charles Nesson, March 5, 1966, CRD Office Files, DOJ; United States Commission on Civil Rights, *Hearings, Montgomery Alabama, 1968,* p. 597; Fager, *White Reflections,* p. 88; Lillian McGill, Interview, May 29, 1968, Civil Rights Documentation Project, Howard University.

61. Carmichael and Hamilton, *Black Power,* p. 115.

62. Thomas Gilmore, Interview, August 3, 1968, Civil Rights Documentation Project, Howard University.

63. Campbell, "Lowndes County Freedom Organization," pp. 82–90; Walton, *Black Political Parties,* pp. 148, 150, 154–56; Kopkind, "Lowndes County," p. 10; Frye, *Black Parties.*

64. Campbell and Feagin, "Black Politics," pp. 141–42; Jones, "Black Office-holders," p. 53.

65. "New South Notes," p. 86.

66. Hobart Taylor, Oral History Memoir, LBJL.

67. Louis Martin to John M. Bailey, November 17, 1964, Box 86, EX PL 2, LBJL.

68. Hubert Humphrey to John M. Bailey, February 11, 1965, Box 86, EX PL 2, LBJL.

69. Marvin Watson to Hubert Humphrey, February 12, 1965, Box 86, EX PL 2, LBJL; Piven and Cloward, *Poor People's Movements,* pp. 232, 252.

70. David Lawrence to the President, March 10, 1965, Box 3, EX HU 2; "Resolution Adopted at Democratic National Committee Meeting," January 19, 1965, Box

91, Democratic National Committee Files; Marvin Watson to the President, September 15, 1965, EX PL, LBJL. The members of the SERC were Helen Gunseth of Ohio, Edgar A. Brown of South Carolina, Mildred Jeffrey of Michigan, Eugene Wyman of California, Stephen McNichols of Colorado, Mrs. Eugene M. Locke of Texas, Mrs. May E. Fantasia of Massachusetts, and Reverend E. Franklin Jackson of Washington D. C. An advisory panel of political scientists included Evan Kirkpatrick, Richard Scammon, Austin Ranney, Donald Matthews, Jack Peltason, and Ronald Hertzberg.

71. SERC, "Proceedings," Box 101, pp. 47–48, Democratic National Committee Files, LBJL. See also the testimony of Clarence Mitchell, pp. 139–40.

72. SERC, "Report," April 20, 1966, Box 88, Democratic National Committee Files; Berl Bernhard to Orzell Billingsley, Jr., March 1, 1966, Box 88, Democratic National Committee Files.

73. Aaron Henry to Lyndon B. Johnson, June 10, 1966, Aaron Henry Name File; Berl Bernhard to Marvin Watson, December 5, 1966, Democratic National Committee/Equal Rights Committee Folder, Marvin Watson Files, LBJL; Louis Martin to Aaron Henry, June 21, 1966, I 2, Aaron Henry MSS, Wayne State University.

74. Marvin Watson to the President, November 7, 1967, Richard Hughes Name File; James Rowe to Marvin Watson, December 16, 22, 1966, Democratic National Committee/Equal Rights Folder, Watson Files; William Connell to Marvin Watson, January 23, 1967, David Lawrence Name File; John Criswell to Marvin Watson, March 8, 1967, Democratic National Committee/Equal Rights Folder, Watson Files, LBJL. Another candidate under serious consideration for the post was Senator Walter Mondale of Minnesota.

75. Richard Hughes to Dear Chairman, July 26, 1967, Ed King MSS. Tougaloo College; "Remarks by Louis Martin, Deputy Chairman of the Democratic National Committee, at Young Democratic Clubs of Mississippi, Jackson, Mississippi, September 29, 1967," press release, Marvin Watson Files, LBJL.

76. Joseph Rauh to David Lawrence, June 22, 1966, Joseph Rauh Office Files, Washington D.C.; Joseph Rauh, Interview, August 28, 1967, Civil Rights Documentation Project, Howard University.

77. "Recommendations of the Special Equal Rights Committee to the Democratic National Committee," February 1, 1967, Democratic National Committee/Equal Rights Folder, Marvin Watson Files, LBJL.

78. *New York Times,* Feburary 14, 1967, clipping, Box 15, Democratic National Committee Files, LBJL. On the leak, see John Criswell to Marvin Watson, February 13, 1967, Democratic National Committee/Equal Rights Folder, Watson Files; Marvin Watson to the President, February 14, 1967, Watson Files, LBJL. The administration considered Rauh a troublemaker whose antiwar views were damaging to party unity. Indeed, Rauh welcomed integrated delegations in Mississippi and Alabama as favorable to the adoption of a peace plank at the Democratic National Convention. Joseph Rauh, "A Proposal to Maximize Political Support for an End to the War in Vietnam," July 31, 1967, Box 115, EX PL 5, LBJL. The administration appointed a second associate counsel to SERC "to offset Rauh's militant attitude toward the quota system." Marvin Watson to the President, July 7, 1967, EX PL 1, LBJL.

79. *New York Times,* March 8, 1967, *New York Post,* February 23, 1967, *Chicago Sun Times,* February 24, 1967, *Providence Journal,* February 17, 1967, *Des Moines Tribune,* July 15, 1967, *Washington Star,* February 19, 1967, clippings, Box 15, Democratic National Committee Files, LBJL. On George Wallace, see John Roche to the President June

6, 1967, Confidential File, PL/Wallace, Box 76; Fred Panzer to the President, September 13, 1967, Box 77, Confidential File PL 2; Hubert Humphrey to the President, April 17, 1967, EX PL ST 10, LBJL.

80. *The Democrat,* July–August 1967, Joseph Rauh Office Files; "Statement by Governor Richard Hughes," April 19, 1967, Democratic National Committee/ Equal Rights Folder, Marvin Watson Files, LBJL. The liberals did not consider the plan a mandatory quota system because it gave the regular state party organizations the opportunity to defend the poor black turnout in local affairs.

81. McLemore, "Mississippi Freedom Democratic Party," p. 453; Hanes Walton, *Black Political Parties,* pp. 128–30; Simpson, " 'Loyalist' Democrats," pp. 70–72; Ed King, "Possible Coalition Delegation at Various Levels of 'Compromise,' " n.d., Ed King MSS. The FDP originally demanded half the seats but wound up with ten of forty-four or five votes of twenty-four alloted. McLemore, p. 441.

82. Simpson, "Loyalist," p. 84; McLemore, "Mississippi Freedom Democratic Party," pp. 466–79. The presence of Doug Wynn as cocounsel to the loyalists was important. Wynn, a friend of President Johnson and a member of the regular delegation in 1964, had supported the chief executive and had worked for party reform. Douglas Wynn to Hubert Humphrey, December 7, 1965, Box 77, Confidential File PL ST 24; Memo, October 7, 1966, Box 77, EX PL ST 24; Marvin Watson to the President, December 5, 1967, Marvin Watson Files, LBJL.

83. Simpson, "Loyalist," pp. 87–88; *Delta Democrat Times,* August 13, 1968, clipping, Delta Ministry Files, Mississippi State University; McLemore, "Mississippi Freedom Democratic Party," p. 477.

84. Neary, *Julian Bond,* pp. 181–212; Morris, "The Georgia Challenge," p. 60–61; Bass and DeVries, *Transformation of Southern Politics,* p. 260; James L. Felder, "Annual Report of the South Carolina VEP," July 1, 1967 through July 1, 1968, VEP Files; W. H. Samuel, Director, Louisiana VEP, "Democratic National Convention," n.d., VEP Files; Howard, "Louisiana," pp. 577–78. Challenges were rejected in North Carolina and Texas. Booker, "Black Politics," p. 36.

85. Walton, *Black Political Parties,* pp. 150–52; Morgan, *One Man One Voice,* pp. 93–99; Frye, *Black Parties,* p. 155; Arthur Shores, Interview, July 17, 1974, Southern Oral History Project (Bass and DeVries), University of North Carolina, p. 25; Strong, "Alabama," p. 460; Peirce, *Deep South,* p. 300; "The 1968 Alabama Situation," February 5, 1968, EX PL ST 1; James Rowe to Marvin Watson, January 1, 1968, EX PL 1; Memo to Mr. President, February 7, 1968, Watson Files; John Cashin to John M. Bailey, July 22, 1968, EX PL 1, LBJL. AID provided the opportunity to vote for the national ticket in its column on the ballot, thereby protecting "loyal Democratic Senators and Congressmen who would not have to run against the very strong Wallace sentiment in Alabama, but who are and will be supporters of the President in Washington." James Rowe to Marvin Watson, January 19, 1968 (Alabama), Watson Files, LBJL. On one Johnson aide sympathetic to the NDPA (Louis Martin), see Mike Manatos to the President, February 5, 1968, Louis Martin Name File, LBJL.

86. Crotty, *Decision for the Democrats,* p. 16; McGovern, *Grassroots,* pp. 133–34; "Special Equal Rights, Democratic National Committee," August 24, 1968, Rauh Office Files; U.S. Commission on Civil Rights, *Political Participation,* pp. 133–51.

87. Booker, "Black Politics," p. 32; *New Pittsburgh Courier,* September 7, 1968; Rustin, *Down the Line,* p. 246.

88. Berry, *Amazing Grace,* pp. 37–38; *Memphis Press Scimitar,* December 16, 1968,

clipping, folder 7, 1971 add., *Jackson Clarion Ledger,* August 21, 1968, January 8, 1969, clippings, folder 7, 1971 add., folder 6, 1972 add., Eugene Cox MSS; Kenneth Dean, "Observations on the Loyalists."

89. Bass and DeVries, *Transformation of Southern Politics,* pp. 76–77; Arthur Shores, Interview, p. 8; U.C. Clemon, Interview, August 17, 1974, Southern Oral History Project (Bass and DeVries), University of North Carolina, p. 17; Richard Arrington, Interview, June 18, 1974, Southern Oral History Proejct (Bass and DeVries), University of North Carolina, p. 20; Frye, *Black Parties,* pp. 153–56.

90. W. H. Samuel to Vernon Jordan, August 12, 1968, VEP Office Files; Ethel Payne, *New Pittsburgh Courier,* August 17, 1968; *New York Times,* April 13, 1966; Peirce, *The Deep South,* p. 57; Bartley and Graham, *Southern Politics,* p. 193; Jordan, "New Game in Dixie," p. 398; Dent, *The Prodigal South,* p. 178; Roy Wilkins to Roy C. Bliss, August 31, 1968, B 367, NAACP MSS; for the views of liberal Republicans in making an effort to appeal to Negro voters, see "A Ripon Society Press Release," December 30, 1965, D65, Congressional files, Gerald R. Ford Library.

91. U.S. Commission on Civil Rights, *Political Participation,* p. 144; Simpson, "Loyalist," p. 107; Strong, "Alabama," p. 460. In Mississippi and Alabama, the focus of the convention challenges, Wallace captured 63% and 65% of the popular vote, Humphrey 23% and 13.6% (AID), Nixon 14% and 16.2%, and NDPA 5.2%.

92. Harry McPherson, Oral History Memoir, Tape 6, p. 18, LBJL.

5. Bring Us Together

1. Evans and Novak, *Nixon in the White House,* pp. 33–34.

2. Robert Finch quoted in *ibid.,* p. 59.

3. Dent, *Prodigal South,* pp. 75, 96, 111, 159; Murphy and Gulliver, *The Southern Strategy,* p. 249.

4. A. Philip Randolph, "An Open Letter to Black Voters," n.d. [1968], Box 68, Chicago Office Files, Everett Dirksen MSS.

5. Diggs Datrooth, "National Hotline," *New Pittsburgh Courier,* September 7, 1968. See also, Whittemore, *Together,* p. 50, for the statement of Julian Bond and *Newsweek* (December 30, 1968), 72:21, for the comments of Hosea Williams.

6. U.S. Senate, Committee on the Judiciary, Subcommittee on Constitutional Rights, *Hearings* (Bills to Amend the Voting Rights Act of 1965), 91st Cong., 1st and 2d sess., 1969 and 1970, p. 444; Murphy and Gulliver, *Southern Strategy,* p. 2; Panetta and Gall, *Bring Us Together,* pp. 5–6.

7. Panetta, *Bring Us Together,* p. 106.

8. Richard Russell to Olin L. Spence, January 31, 1969, Box 5, Richard Russell MSS. Some twenty of Thurmond's friends and allies held posts in the Nixon administration. Peirce, *Deep South,* p. 377.

9. Quoted in *New York Times,* January 27, 1969, p. 18; Panetta, *Bring Us Together,* p. 92; Harris, *Justice,* pp. 151–52; Phillips, *The Emerging Republican Majority.*

10. Marvin Caplan to Allan Wolk, August 11, 1969, Box 117, Leadership Conference on Civil Rights MSS.

11. *Public Papers of the Presidents, Richard M. Nixon, 1969* (Washington, D.C.: GPO 1970), p. 750; Dent, *Prodigal South,* pp. 125–38.

12. *Alexander v. Holmes County Board of Education,* 396 U.S. 19 (1969); Read and McGough, *Let Them Be Judged,* pp. 486–87.

13. *New York Times,* April 23, 1969, p. 32; Evans and Novak, *Nixon in the White House,* pp. 211–22.

14. Louis Martin, *New Pittsburgh Courier,* June 25, 1969, p. 7; "Nixon, the NAACP and Civil Rights," *Crisis* (June–July 1969); 76:234–36; *New York Times,* June 14, 1969, p. 32, November 19, 1969, p. 37.

15. Ed Sexton to Harry Dent, November 24, 1969, "Civil Rights—Minorities," Republican National Committee Files, Rogers C. B. Morton MSS, University of Kentucky; Roy Wilkins, Memo for Files, May 1, 1969, B-445, NAACP MSS.

16. Edwin T. Sexton Jr., "Election Analysis: 1968 and the Black American Voter," January 1969, "Civil Rights—Minorities," Republican National Committee Files, Rogers Morton MSS. For the view that Republicans should do more to recruit blacks, see Clarence L. Towne, Jr., to Rogers C. B. Morton and Jim Allison, May 15, 1969, Republican National Committee Files, Rogers C. B. Morton MSS.

17. *New York Times,* August 8, 1969, p. 32; U.S. Senate, Committee on Finance, *Hearings on Tax Reform Act of 1969,* 91st Cong., 1st sess., 1969, Part 6, pp. 5371, 5911.

18. Voter Education Project, "Annual Report 1969"; "Report of the Voter Education Project, Inc., Executive Committee Meeting, Capahosic, Virginia, July 24–26, 1970," VEP Office Files.

19. Voter Education Project, "Annual Report 1969," and "Annual Report, 1970."

20. Hinson, "Voter Education Project"; *Atlanta Constitution,* May 23, 1975, clipping, VEP Files.

21. Owen Brooks, "A Delta Ministry Proposal for the Foundation of the 1969 Municipal Elections," November 25, 1968, Delta Ministry Files, Tougaloo College.

22. Kimball, *The Disconnected,* p. 272.

23. Clarence Hall, Jr., to Marvin Wall, July 21, 1966, Issaquena Mississippi Voters League, VEP Office Files.

24. Quoted in Charles Sherrod, "Southwest Georgia Voter Education Project, 1969–70;" Willard M. Cooper, "Narrative Report of Wilkinson County," July 27, 1967; Charles Sherrod to Voter Education Project, December 21, 1966, to January 18, 1967; "Narrative Report, Yazoo County," July 28, 1969, to August 1, 1969; Glen Allan Improvement Association, "Report on Voter Registration Activities," November 24–30, 1968, VEP Office Files.

25. Kimball, *The Disconnected,* p. 3; Washington Research Project, *Shameful Blight,* pp. 5 ff.; Ruby Magee, Interview, Mississippi Oral History Project, University of Southern Mississippi, p. 45; James David Campbell, "Electoral Participation and the Quest for Equality," pp. 58–61.

26. Lawrence Tardy to Richard Bourne, June 10, 1970, CRD Office Files; Herbert Clay to John Lewis, August 25, 1971, VEP Office Files. For earlier complaints against Hood, see U.S. Commission on Civil Rights, *Hearings in Jackson Mississippi* (Washington, D.C.: GPO, 1965), pp. 52–93.

27. U.S. Commission on Civil Rights, Staff Report, May 13, 1969, "Municipal Elections in Mississippi, June 13, 1969," in Senate Judiciary Committee, *Hearings on Amendments to the Voting Rights Act of 1965,* 1970, pp. 36–45.

28. U.S. Commission on Civil Rights, *Political Participation* (Washington, D.C.: GPO, 1968) chapters 2 and 3; statement of Birch Bayh, *Congressional Record,* 91st Cong., 2d sess., pp. 6357–58; McCarty and Stevenson, "The Voting Rights Act of 1965," pp. 386, 401.

29. *Hadnot v. Amos,* 294 U.S. 360 (1969); Morgan, *One Man, One Voice,* pp.

101, 110; Jenkins, "Majority Rule," pp. 64–66; Ross, "Black Power Alabama," pp. 14–15; Emmons, "Black Politics"; Peirce, *Deep South,* p. 275; Murphy and Gulliver, *Southern Strategy,* p. 211.

30. Even if the covered areas extricated themselves, the U.S. District Court in Washington, D.C., retained jurisdiction for an additional five years.

31. *Public Papers LBJ, 1968–1969,* p. 1266; Ramsey Clark to Speaker John McCormack, January 15, 1969, Box 437, Emanuel Celler MSS; Stephen J. Pollak, Memorandum for the Attorney General, December 13, 1968, Appellate Section, Department of Justice Office Files. Pollak pointed out that the prime goal for renewal was to keep literacy tests suspended and to maintain authority to dispatch federal observers. He admitted that federal registrars were used sparingly and local enrollment officers were performing their duties satisfactorily. On January 23, 1969, Celler introduced the administration bill.

32. "Memorandum on Meeting with Attorney General John N. Mitchell, February 18, 1969," LCCR MSS.

33. Daniel P. Moynihan to Theodore M. Hesburgh, April 16, 1969, Box 74, Hesburgh MSS; Clarence Mitchell to Daniel P. Moynihan, April 16, 1969, B-376, NAACP MSS. Moynihan, *Maximum Feasible Misunderstanding.*

34. Jerris Leonard, Memorandum for the Attorney General, February 27, 1969, Appellate Section, Department of Justice Office Files.

35. *Ibid.*

36. Howard "Bo" Calloway to John Mitchell, February 24, 1969, B 134-29, Ford Congressional Papers, Gerald R. Ford Presidential Library.

37. Jerris Leonard, Memorandum for the Attorney General, May 6, 1969, Appellate Section, Department of Justice Office Files. At the same time, the assistant attorney general rejected a plan to allow covered jurisdictions to free themselves if they had raised the level of registration or voter participation to over 50 percent in the 1968 presidential election. This would have worked against blacks.

38. *Gaston County v. United States,* 395 U.S. 296 (1969). For an appraisal of the decision, see Fiss, *"Gaston County v. U. S."*

39. Box 476, Celler MSS.

40. Jerris Leonard, Memorandum for John Ehrlichman, June 9 [1969], Appellate Section, Department of Justice Office Files; testimony of John Mitchell, U.S. House of Representatives, Committee on the Judiciary, Subcommittee No. 5, *Hearings on Voting Rights Extension,* 91st Cong., 1st Sess., 1969, pp. 222, 279.

41. *Allen et. al. v. State Board of Elections et. al.,* 393 U.S. 544 (1969) 565; Pollak, "Effective Anti-Discrimination Legislation"; Gary Greenberg to Jerris Leonard, March 4, 1969, Appellate Section, DOJ. *Allen* also affirmed the right of private citizens to sue under section five to prevent changes from taking effect without federal clearance.

42. *Allen v. Board of Elections,* 393 U.S. 585 (1969).

43. *Ibid.,* p. 595.

44. Jerris Leonard Memorandum for John Ehrlichman, June 9 [1969], Appellate Section, DOJ. Leonard had "grave misgivings" about the constitutionality and practicality of section five of the act, the preclearance provision. He believed it presented an "administrative nightmare" for the Justice Department and imposed an "onerous and unreasonable burden" on the jurisdictions covered in the South. Jerris Leonard, Interview with author, July 31, 1979.

45. Sid Bailey to Senator Scott, June 10, 1969, S-2-67, Hugh Scott MSS.

46. *Ibid.;* Roy Reed, *New York Times,* June 11, 1969, p. 18.

47. House Judiciary Committee, Subcommittee No. 5, *Hearings on Voting Rights Extension,* 1969, p. 3.

48. Statement of Joseph Rauh, *ibid.,* p. 179; see also Vernon Jordan, *ibid.,* p. 193.

49. House Judiciary Committee, Subcommittee No. 5, *Hearings on Voting Rights Extension,* 1969, p. 195.

50. *Ibid.,* p. 193. Jordan suggested removing the discretionary power of the attorney general to appoint registrars and requiring the automatic appointment of examiners when nonwhite registration fell below two-thirds of the eligible number. Jordan, "The Black Vote in Danger," p. 6.

51. House Judiciary Committee, Subcommittee No. 5, *Hearings on Voting Rights Extension,* 1969, p. 129.

52. *New York Times,* June 19, 1969, p. 19.

53. House Judiciary Committee, Subcommittee No. 5, *Hearings on Voting Rights Extension,* 1969, p. 219.

54. *Ibid.,* p. 279.

55. *Ibid.,* pp. 225–27, 220, 222, 286–87.

56. *Ibid.,* p. 233.

57. *Ibid.,* p. 269.

58. *Ibid.,* p. 239.

59. *Ibid.,* p. 246; Harris, *Justice,* p. 202; *New York Times,* June 29, 1969, p. 30; Louis Martin, *New Pittsburgh Courier,* July 26, 1969, p. 7.

60. House Judiciary Committee, *Hearings on Voting Rights Extension,* p. 222.

61. Mitchell charged that in 1968 the two congressional districts in the nation with the lowest turnout were located in the black ghettos of New York City's Bedford-Stuyvesant and Harlem where literacy tests were imposed. He argued that this illustrated "a prima facie relationship between Northern literacy tests and ghetto Negro nonvoting," *ibid.* pp. 296–97. However, Mitchell's figures did not reveal the entire picture. In 1968, a generally higher proportion of northern blacks registered and voted than did southern blacks, although the gap was closing. In 1966, 69 percent of the black voting-age population in the North was registered to vote compared with 53 percent in the South. In 1968, the figures were 72 and 62 percent, respectively. Of those registered to vote in 1968, 90 percent in the North and 84 percent in the South reported that they cast ballots. Viewed another way, in 1968, in the North 65 percent of the black voting-age population reported voting compared with 52 percent in the South. Morris, *Politics of Black America,* pp. 150–51.

62. *Jackson Clarion Ledger,* July 9, 1969, clipping, folder 9, 1972 add., Eugene Cox MSS.

63. Senate Judiciary Committee, Subcommittee on Constitutional Rights, *Hearings on Amendments to the Voting Rights Act of 1965,* 1969, p. 7.

64. U.S. House of Representatives, Committee on the Rules, *Hearings to Extend the Voting Rights Act of 1965,* 91st Cong., 1st sess., 1969, p. 50.

65. U.S. House of Representatives, Committee on the Judiciary, *Report to Accompany H. R. 4249,* 91st Cong., 1st sess., 1969, pp. 8–9; Warren Weaver, Jr., *New York Times,* July 18, 1969, p. 10.

66. U.S. House of Representatives, Committee on the Judiciary, *Report to Accompany H. R. 4249,* p. 13. Poff did not challenge the constitutionality of the 1965 act, but Walter Flowers of Alabama did. See p. 22.

67. Sam Ervin to Harrison Williams, July 30, 1969, Box 3, Ervin MSS; Senate

Judiciary Committee, *Hearings on Amendments to the Voting Rights Act of 1965,* 1969, p. 5.

68. Senate Judiciary Committee, *Hearings on Amendments to the Voting Rights Act of 1965,* 1969, p. 128.

69. *Ibid.,* p. 120.

70. *Ibid.,* pp. 164, 189, 201–2 ff.

71. Emanuel Celler to John McCormack, September 26, 1969, Box 437, Celler MSS; *New York Times,* October 29, 1969, p. 23.

72. House Rules Committee, *Hearings to Extend the Voting Rights Act of 1965,* 1969, p. 18.

73. *Ibid.,* pp. 13, 20, 22, 39; Orfield, *Congressional Power,* p. 98.

74. Bryce Harlow, "Congressional Report," September 4, 1969, Box 30, Republican National Committee Files, Rogers C. B. Morton MSS.

75. John W. Finney, *New York Times,* December 11, 1969, p. 35; *Detroit Free Press,* July 3, 1969, clipping, Box 0509, Robert Griffin MSS, University of Central Michigan; *St. Louis Post Dispatch,* June 19, 1969, clipping, D 118, Ford Congressional Files, Gerald R. Ford Presidential Library.

76. *Congressional Record,* 91st Cong., 1st sess., pp. 38129, 38132.

77. *Ibid.,* p. 38138.

78. *Ibid.,* p. 38488.

79. *Ibid.,* p. 38135.

80. *Ibid.,* p. 38501.

81. *Ibid.,* p. 38490.

82. *Ibid.,* p. 38535.

83. *Ibid.,* p. 38512; see also the statement of Joe Waggoner, p. 38531, and in contrast, Bob Eckhardt of Texas, p. 38497.

84. Harris, *Justice,* p. 207.

85. Quoted in House Rules Committee, *Hearings to Extend the Voting Rights Act of 1965,* 1969, p. 20. In addition to Delaney, the supporters included one from Colorado, three from Kentucky, three from Missouri, one from Nevada, one from Oklahoma, and two from Oregon.

86. Orfield, *Congressional Power,* p. 98. Edward Hutchinson, a Michigan Republican, opposed the administration bill on constitutional grounds, specifically the residency provision. However, on the final vote, he joined the majority in favor of the entire measure. Ags [Mrs. A. G. Schultz] to EH [Edward Hutchinson], December 10, 1969, "Judiciary Voting Rights," Box 76, Edward Hutchinson MSS. Nine southerners voted for the administration substitute to replace the Judiciary Committee version and then cast a "nay" tally on the final balloting on the bill.

87. E. W. Kenworthy, *New York Times,* December 14, 1969, IV, p. 2.

88. William F. Timmons to Mark Gelfand, August 26, 1981, courtesy of Mark I. Gelfand.

89. *New York Times,* December 12, 1969, pp. 1, 54.

90. Marvin Caplan to Harry and Ruth Kingman, January 19, 1970, Box 117, LCCR MSS.

91. David Johnson to Sid Bailey, December 10, 1969, S-26-7, Hugh Scott MSS; *New York Times,* December 13, 1969, p. 72, December 17,1969, p. 63, and December 19, 1969, p. 71.

92. Bart Hertzbach to Senator Scott, February 9, 1970, S-26-7, Hugh Scott MSS; John Finney, *New York Times,* February 16, 1970, p. 18; Fred Graham, *New York Times,* February 18, 1970, p. 23.

93. Gene Cowen to Senator Scott, June 25, 1969, S-26-7, Hugh Scott MSS.

94. For a revealing attempt by the administration to persuade Griffin to change his mind and to lead the White House congressional forces, thereby increasing his chances of displacing Scott as minority leader, see Memo, n.d., Box 0509, Robert Griffin MSS. Also, Detroit *News,* December 16, 1969, clipping, Box 045, Griffin MSS.

95. "Outline for Review of 'Compromise' Amendment to Voting Rights Act of 1965," February 18, 1969 [1970], Box 313, and Burton V. Wides to Archibald Cox, February 16, 1970, Box 168, Philip Hart MSS; Bart Hertzbach to Senator Scott, February 18, 1970, S-26-7, Hugh Scott MSS.

96. Theodore Hesburgh to Michael J. Mansfield, March 8, 1970, Box 74, Hesburgh MSS.

97. Department of Justice Routing Slip, Jerris Leonard To Ben Mintz, February 20, 1970, Appellate Section, Department of Justice Office Files. In his scrawled note, Leonard wrote "Sen. passed bill," but the date on the memo, "2-20," suggests that he meant the House.

98. Senate Judiciary Committee, *Hearings on Amendments to the Voting Rights Act of 1965,* 1970, pp. 257, 346.

99. *Ibid.,* p. 440.

100. *Ibid.,* p. 262–63.

101. *Ibid.,* p. 449.

102. *Ibid.,* p. 523.

103. *Ibid.,* p. 398.

104. *Ibid.,* p. 530.

105. *Congressional Record,* 91st Cong. 2d sess., pp. 6151, 5678, 5687, 6353.

106. *Ibid.,* p. 6168.

107. *Ibid.,* p. 6150. This theme had also been sounded by moderate blacks. Senate Judiciary Committee, *Hearings on Amendments to the Voting Rights Act of 1965,* 1969, p. 130.

108. *Congressional Record,* 91st Cong., 2d sess., p. 6167. Hruska did not prove any more adept in defending Carswell than in passing his tabling motion. During the debate on the Florida judge, Hruska declared that even if Carswell "were mediocre, there are a lot of mediocre judges and people and lawyers. They are entitled to a little representation, aren't they, and a little chance. We can't have all Brandeises and Frankfurters and Cardozos and stuff like that there." Quoted in Orfield, *Congressional Power,* p. 113.

109. *Congressional Record,* 91st Cong., 2d sess., pp. 6519, 6172, 6344-45, 6506, 6518; Senate Judiciary Committee, *Hearings on Amendments to the Voting Rights Act of 1965,* 1970, p. 434; U.S. Commission on Civil Rights, "Voting Rights Act Trigger: Use of 1968 General Elections," Box 0509, Robert Griffin MSS.

110. *Congressional Record,* 91st Cong., 2nd sess., p. 6172; Burt Wides to Senator Hart, March 9, 1970, Box 313, Hart MSS; Theodore Hesburgh to Hugh Scott, March 8, 1970, S-26-7, Scott MSS.

111. Supporters of Ervin's efforts never mustered more than thirty-two votes. One of the defeated amendments would have permitted a bailout from coverage through litigation before federal district courts other than the one in Washington, D.C..

112. Burt Wides to Senator Hart, March 9, 1970, Box 313, Hart MSS.

113. John Sherman Cooper to Samuel Starks, November 17, 1971, Box 117, John Sherman Cooper MSS, University of Kentucky; *Congressional Record,* 91st Cong., 2d sess., pp. 6654, 6656, 6659.

114. On the Cooper Amendment, twenty-four Republicans and twenty-six

Democrats were in favor, and eleven Republicans and twenty-six Democrats were opposed. In contrast to the tabling resolution which one northern Democrat approved, the Cooper plan attracted sixteen Democrats from the North. Eighteen Republicans had supported Hruska's motion compared with the twenty-four who backed Cooper's. One of the latter was Robert Griffin, a supporter of the Scott-Hart version. The Michigan senator had considered a proposal like Cooper's the previous December. It would have geared the triggering mechanism to the 1968 presidential election. Dave [?] to Senator Griffin, December 16, 1969, Box 0509, Griffin MSS; Saul Friedman, *Detroit Free Press,* March 2, 1970, clipping, Robert A. Hoving, *Grand Rapids Press,* March 7, 1970, clipping, Box 0451, Griffin MSS.

115. Emanuel Celler to Edward Kennedy, February 25, 1970, Box 437, Celler MSS; *New York Times,* March 12, 1970, p. 22, March 13, 1970, p. 14.

116. Gelfand, "The 18-Year-Old Vote." The northern Democrats were unanimously in support, no doubt believing that the bulk of young people would likely vote for their party's candidates. The Republicans divided twenty-six to eight, and the southern Democrats divided six in favor and nine opposed; *New York Times,* February 23, 1970, p. 8.

117. In addition to Spong, the other southerners voting for the bill were J. William Fulbright (D. Ark.), Marlow Cook (R. Ky.), John Sherman Cooper (R. Ky.), Albert Gore (D. Tenn.), and Howard Baker (R. Tenn.). Also, Ralph Yarborough, a Texas Democrat, had announced that he was for the measure, but he did not record his vote.

118. Quoted in Orfield, *Congressional Power,* p. 102. Hollings had also supported the Mansfield amendment lowering the voting age to eighteen. Orfield quotes Herman Talmadge of Georgia in hesitating to participate in a filibuster: "Look fellows, I was the principal speaker at the NAACP Conference in my state last year," pp. 99–100. See also Arnold Aronson, Memo No. 9–70, May 26, 1970, Box 27, LCCR MSS.

119. *Congressional Record,* 91st Cong., 2d sess., p. 10715.

120. *Public Papers . . . RMN, 1970,* pp. 401, 404.

121. William E. Timmons to Mark Gelfand, August 26, 1981; Evans and Novak, *Nixon in the White House,* pp. 129–30.

122. *New York Times,* May 11, 1970, p. 45; Bart Hertzbach to Senator Scott, June 1, 1970, S-26-7, Hugh Scott MSS.

123. Edward Hutchinson to C. A. Allen, June 19, 1970, Box 64, Edward Hutchinson MSS.

124. John B. Anderson et. al. to Dear Fellow Republican, April 13, 1970, Box 81, James G. O'Hara MSS, University of Michigan. The Republican Policy Committee split, 10-7, against the bill including the teenage voting provision. *New York Times,* June 3, 1970, p. 33.

125. *New York Times,* June 5, 1970, p. 71; Orfield, *Congressional Power,* p. 103. The second vote in the Rules Committee was 9–6.

126. See the remarks of Richard Poff, who expressed these sentiments, but could not bring himself to vote "aye." *Congressional Record,* 91st Cong., 2d sess., p. 20166. Of the congressmen from states covered under the 1965 law, only seven—one from Virginia, one from Alabama, two from Louisiana, and three from North Carolina—voted for adoption of the Senate measure.

127. Press Release, June 19, 1970, Box 99, Marlow Cook MSS, University of Louisville.

128. *Congressional Record,* 91st Cong., 2d sess., p. 20164.

129. Evans and Novak, *Nixon in the White House,* pp. 129–30, report that the

president pledged to Hugh Scott that if Congress passed the Senate version of the voting rights bill, he would most reluctantly sign it. For a harsh view of Nixon's performance in civil rights, see Schell, *The Time of Illusion*, pp. 39–44.

130. In *Oregon v. Mitchell*, 400 U.S. 112 (1970), the Supreme Court upheld the nationwide literacy test ban and residency requirements. It also affirmed congressional authority to lower the voting age for national but not for state and local elections. Subsequently, a constitutional amendment was ratified that lowered the voting age in state and local contests. Foster, "Constitutional Bases."

131. *Public Papers . . . RMN, 1970*, p. 512. In contrast to the celebration five years earlier, Nixon quietly signed the bill in the presence of a single aide. *New York Times,* June 23, 1970, p. 31.

132. *New Pittsburgh Courier,* July 11, 1970, p. 10. For the view that Nixon should get no credit for passage of the act's extension, see *Baltimore Afro-American*, July 11, 1970, p. 4.

133. Senator John Stennis, T.V. Transcript, March 1, 1970, John Stennis MSS, Mississippi State University.

134. John W. Finney, *New York Times,* March 15, 1970, IV, p. 2; Orfield, *Congressional Power,* p. 103; Harris, *Justice,* p. 202; Press Release, February 12, 1970, Box 99, Marlowe Cook MSS, for the view of a moderate Republican from Kentucky who denounced the southern strategy.

6. The Battle Over Guidelines

1. *Congressional Record,* 91st Cong., 2d sess., pp. 7102–3.

2. Gerald Jones, head of the Voting Rights Section, quoted in Ball, Krane, and Lauth, *Compromised Compliance,* p. 58.

3. *United States v. Crooks,* 253 F. Supp. 915 (M.D. Ala. 1966); U.S. Department of Justice, Attorney General, *Annual Report for the Fiscal Year Ended June 30, 1966,* p. 190; U.S. Commission on Civil Rights, *Political Participation,* pp. 41–42; Pollak, "Effective Anti-Discrimination Legislation," p. 19.

4. Morgan, *One Man, One Voice,* pp. 99–101; Walton, *Black Political Parties,* p. 154; *Hadnott v. Amos,* 394 U.S. 358 (1969); Jerris Leonard to MacDonald Gallion, August 1, 1969, Box 437, Emanuel Celler MSS. The plaintiffs also wanted the recalcitrant probate judge, James Dennis Herndon, to be cited for contempt.

5. *Allen v. State Board of Elections,* 393 U.S. 556 (1969). The Court also stressed that the federal district bench could adjudicate lawsuits concerning the types of practices covered under section five, but it could not make a substantive determination on whether the electoral change had a discriminatory purpose or effect. Only the attorney general or the federal district court in the nation's capital had that authority.

6. *Ibid.,* pp. 571–72; Roman, "Section 5," p. 119.

7. *Hadnott v. Amos,* 394 U.S. 366 (1969).

8. U. S. Senate, Committee on the Judiciary, *Hearings,* "Extension of the Voting Rights Act of 1965," 94th Cong., 1st sess., 1975, p. 123.

9. For a different opinion of the court's interpretation of the Voting Rights Act, see Thernstrom, "The Odd Evolution." In contrast, see the testimony of Armand Derfner, U.S. Congress, House of Representatives, Committee on the Judiciary, *Hearings,* "Extension of the Voting Rights Act of 1965," 94th Cong., 1st sess., 1975, p. 629.

10. Engstrom, "Racial Vote Dilution," p. 150; Binion, "Implementation of Section 5," pp. 155, 157 n. 21; Derfner, "Racial Discrimination," pp. 580–81.

11. Gary J. Greenberg to Jerris Leonard, March 4, 1969, Appellate Section, DOJ.

12. *New York Times,* September 25, 1969, p. 23; Thernstrom, "Odd Evolution," p. 58; Ball et. al., *Compromised Compliance,* pp. 68–69; Harris, *Justice,* p. 220; Derfner, "Racial Discrimination," pp. 580–81; Jerris Leonard, Interview with author, July 31, 1979. One of the leaders of the CRD revolt was Gary Greenberg, who had advised Leonard to enforce *Allen* vigorously. See note 11 above.

13. Ball et. al., *Compromised Compliance,* pp. 72, 78; Senate Judiciary Committee, *Hearings on the Voting Rights Act,* 1975, p. 597.

14. *Delta Democrat Times,* March 26, 1970, and see also September 23, 24, 1970, clippings, Delta Ministry Papers, Mississippi State University; Washington Research Project, *Shameful Blight,* pp. 139, 142; see testimony of Howard Glickstein, U.S. House of Representatives, Committee on the Judiciary, The Civil Rights Oversight Subcommittee, *Hearings on the Enforcement and Administration of the Voting Rights Act of 1965, As Amended,* 92d Cong., 1st sess., 1971, p. 88.

15. Washington Research Project, *Shameful Blight,* pp. 139–40.

16. Howard Glickstein to John Mitchell, November 3, 1970, Box 74, Theodore Hesburgh MSS.

17. Jerris Leonard to Howard Glickstein, November 12, 1970, Box 74, Hesburgh MSS.

18. Howard Glickstein to Jerris Leonard, February 12, 1971, Box 75, Hesburgh, MSS.

19. *Wesberry v. Sanders,* 376 U.S. 1 (1964); Parker, "County Redistricting."

20. In *Connor v. Johnson,* 402 U.S. 691 (1972), the high tribunal ruled that court-ordered reapportionment plans did not have to be cleared in Washington.

21. Jerris Leonard to Julius L. Latterhos, Jr., October 16, 1970, Notebook, Voting Rights Act Hearings, CRD Files, DOJ.

22. House Judiciary Committee, Civil Rights Oversight Subcommittee, *Hearings,* pp. 81, 82.

23. Washington Research Project, *Shameful Blight,* p. 25.

24. House Judiciary Committee, Civil Rights Oversight Subcommittee, *Hearings,* pp. 88–89, 203; Martin Waldron, *New York Times,* March 24, 1971, p. 37; Washington Research Project, *Shameful Blight,* pp. 30–31; Mervyn M. Dymally to members of the National Conference of Black Elected Officials, April 2, 1971, Box 185, Philip Hart MSS.

25. House Judiciary Committee, Civil Rights Oversight Subcommittee, *Hearings,* p. 18; Washington Research Project, *Shameful Blight,* p. 45. The reregistration experience of South Carolina in 1967 appeared to confirm Norman's analysis. See Kimball, *The Disconnected,* p. 272 and Watters, "South Carolina." In South Carolina black voter registration campaigns swelled Negro enrollment which in several areas exceeded that of whites. Leonard left the CRD to become head of the department's Law Enforcement Assistance Administration. Later, he went into private practice in Washington, D.C., and has represented the state of Mississippi in suffrage suits.

26. This category of federally registered voters could not be removed from the books except through procedures stipulated by the attorney general and the Civil Service Commission.

27. The statistics were fragmentary and varied among counties. See David Norman to Don Edwards, June 25, 1971, Notebook, Voting Rights Hearings, CRD Office

Files; Gerald W. Jones to David L. Norman, May 10, 1971, and David Norman to Marvin Oates, June 8, 1971, CRD Files, DOJ.

28. House Judiciary Committee, Civil Rights Oversight Subcommittee, *Hearings,* p. 3.

29. Washington Research Project, *Shameful Blight,* p. 144.

30. Jacob Javits, Philip Hart, and Hugh Scott to Jerris Leonard, March 3, 1971, S3 54, Hugh Scott MSS.

31. Howard Glickstein to Philip Hart, March 11, 1971, Box 75, Hesburgh MSS: U.S. Commission on Civil Rights, "Minutes, 123rd meeting," April 4, 1971, Box 78, Hesburgh MSS; Howard Glickstein to John N. Mitchell, April 14, 1971, Box 75, Hesburgh MSS; House Judiciary Committee Civil Rights Oversight Subcommittee, *Hearings,* p. 87.

32. Pollak, "Effective Anti-Discrimination Legislation," p. 21, cited the efforts of Armand Derfner and the Lawyers' Committee for Civil Rights Under Law; Robert Packwood to Jerris Leonard, March 16, 1971, Box 0509, Robert Griffin MSS, for a copy of a letter from a Republican senator from Oregon.

33. Burt Wides to Bill Hildebrand April 7, 1971, S3 54, Scott MSS; Burt Wides to Ira M. Heyman, April 16, 1971, Box 185, Hart MSS; Philip Hart to David Norman, May 7, 1971, Box 185, Hart MSS.

34. Bob to Senator [Griffin], March 23 and March 28, 1971, Box 0509 Robert Griffin MSS. At the same time, Attorney General Mitchell felt considerable pressure from southern lawmakers. See Memo "Wally", n.d., Voting Rights folder, Box 344, Sam Ervin MSS. Mitchell wanted assurance that Ervin would support him "when he gets heat."

35. *Charles Evers et. al. v. State Board of Election Commissioners,* 327 F. Supp. 640, 642 (S.D. Miss, 1971); House Judiciary Committee, Civil Rights Oversight Subcommittee, *Hearings,* 446–49; U.S. Commission on Civil Rights, "Minutes of the 124th meeting," May 9 and 10, 1971, Box 78, Hesburgh MSS. The state did not resubmit the law for clearance.

36. *Perkins v. Matthews,* 400 U.S. 388, 397 (1971). The issue of shifting from ward to at-large elections had a peculiar twist. *Allen* had decided the matter, but in this case the law had not actually changed. A 1962 Mississippi statute required that aldermanic elections be held at-large; however, in 1961 and 1965, Canton used wards. In 1969, the city claimed it had no choice but to obey the 1962 law. The court held otherwise, pointing out that section five applied to procedures "in force or effect on November 1, 1964," the period during which Canton conducted elections by ward. Later, when the city submitted these changes, the Justice Department cleared them. See Washington Research Project, *Shameful Blight,* p. 164; Roman, "Section 5," p. 122.

37. David Norman agreed that Canton failed to make proper submissions, but he opposed having the court order new elections for its failure to do so. David Norman to Jim Turner, June 2, 1970, CRD Files, DOJ. The CRD chief explained: "I think if Congress had intended that harsh a remedy it would have said so expressly . . . [that] elections could be set aside when no one but the Attorney General's feelings have been hurt."

38. BW [Burt Wides] to PAH [Philip A. Hart], Memo, n.d. [1971], Box 185, Hart MSS.

39. Burt Wides to Bill Hildebrand, April 7, 1971, S3 54, Scott MSS.

40. Burt Wides to Philip Hart, Memo, n.d. [1971], and "Standard for decision concerning submissions," n.d. [1971], Box 185, Hart MSS; Arnold Aronson, Memo No. 9-71, June 8, 1971, Box 27, LCCR MSS. The Department of Justice also agreed to establish a registry to ensure that civil rights organizations were notified each time a proposed

electoral law was submitted, and they would be given an opportunity to comment. Warren Weaver, *New York Times,* May 31, 1971, p. 6; David A. Brody to Philip Hart, May 25, 1971, Box 185, Hart MSS.

41. House Judiciary Committee, Civil Rights Oversight Subcommittee, *Hearings,* p. 238; Burt Wides to Philip Hart, n.d. [1971], Box 185, Hart MSS.

42. House Judiciary Committee, Civil Rights Oversight Subcommittee, *Hearings,* p. 10.

43. *Ibid.,* p. 69.

44. *Ibid.,* p. 63.

45. *Ibid.,* p. 62.

46. *Ibid.,* pp. 206, 239.

47. *Ibid.,* p. 10.

48. *Ibid.,* p. 44.

49. *Ibid.,* pp. 67, 68. See also Jerris Leonard to Howard Q. Davis, April 10, 1969, Gerald W. Jones to Jerris Leonard, September 12, 1970, and Gerald Jones, Memo to Files, September 15, 1970, CRD Files, DOJ. The Civil Rights Commission had offered a suggestion to send examiners when black registration fell below a fixed percentage. Washington Research Project, *Shameful Blight,* p. 13.

50. House Judiciary Committee, Civil Rights Oversight Subcommittee, *Hearings,* p. 4.

51. *Ibid.,* p. 19.

52. *Ibid.,* pp. 31, 43, 48, 50, 106. When his adversaries recommended using the criminal sanctions of the Voting Rights Act against jurisdictions which did not obtain prior approval for electoral changes, Norman correctly noted that the government could invoke these penalties only when a person had been denied a ballot as a result of the uncleared procedure. Thus, the crime was deprivation of the right to vote; failure to submit was not a crime.

53. *Ibid.,* p. 13; Burt Wides to Philip Hart, n.d. [1971], Box 185, Hart MSS. Norman denied that the administration "was trying to get around section 5 for the purpose of getting rid of it." See p. 7 of the hearings.

54. House Judiciary Committee, Civil Rights Oversight Subcommittee, *Hearings,* p. 102.

55. *Ibid.,* p. 242.

56. *Ibid.,* p. 231.

57. *Ibid.,* p. 225. He did admit that in absolute terms, since 1969, the Department of Justice had stepped up implementation of section five. But as the law had developed, more was expected from Washington. Acknowledging that the department had done "many good things," Derfner complained, "they in many ways failed to do things we thought would be useful and effective under the Voting Rights Act," p. 264.

58. *Ibid.,* pp. 77–78.

59. Committee on the Judiciary, Civil Rights Oversight Subcommittee, *Report: Enforcement of the Voting Rights Act of 1965 in Mississippi,* 92d Cong., 2nd sess., 1972.

60. *Ibid.,* pp. 14–15.

61. Charles Evers to Philip A. Hart, July 21, 1971, Box 185, Hart MSS. The committee report was not issued publicly until 1972 ,and it was adopted unanimously.

62. Aaron Henry, Oral Memoir, Tape 2, p. 22, LBJL.

63. Charles Evers to John Lewis, April 17, 1971, and Charles Evers to Dear Friend, October 6, 1971, VEP Office Files.

64. Charles Evers, "Interview," p. 186.

65. "Two Years in Fayette: A Background Memorandum on the Achievements of the Evers Administration," n.d. [received June 28, 1971] and "Closer to the Promised Land . . ." pamphlet, VEP Office Files; Haines, "Evers Administration."

66. House Judiciary Committee, Civil Rights Oversight Subcommittee, *Hearings*, pp. 14–17.

67. Berry, *Amazing Grace*, p. 39.

68. Janet C. Shortt, "The Mississippi Tour," June 22, 24, 28–30, 1971, VEP Office Files.

69. Neil Maxwell, "Black Ballots," *Wall Street Journal*, June 22, 1971, clipping, VEP Office Files.

70. Lewis and Allen, "Black Voter Registration," pp. 119–20.

71. *VEP News* (April–June 1971), vol. 5.

72. Lewis and Allen, "Black Voter Registration," pp. 117–18.

73. *New York Times*, July 6, 1971, p. 17.

74. Lewis and Allen, "Black Voter Registration," p. 116.

75. Quoted in Berry, *Amazing Grace*, p. 120; see also pp. 40–41.

76. *Ibid.*, p. 123.

77. *Ibid.*, p. 185; Bass and De Vries, *Transformation of Southern Politics*, p. 209; Peirce, *Deep South*, p. 188. Both Waller and Charles Sullivan promised to promote fair employment practices and to bring blacks into state government. Mississippi Negroes split their votes between the two, apparently giving Waller a slight edge.

78. Black, *Southern Governors*, p. 65. Berry, *Amazing Grace*, pp. 17, 154–55.

79. Berry, *Amazing Grace*, p. 87; *Delta Ministry Reports*, July 1971, folder 19, 1972 add., Eugene Cox MSS; Jake Ayers, Sr., to John Lewis, May 10, 1971, VEP Office Files; National Committee to Elect Charles Evers Governor of Mississippi, "Press Release," June 2, 1971, VEP Office Files.

80. John Lewis to John N. Mitchell, June 28, 1971, VEP Office Files.

81. *New York Times*, June 10, 1971, p. 21; see testimony of Aaron Henry, House Judiciary Committee, Civil Rights Oversight Subcommittee, *Hearings*, p. 215.

82. "Dateline Washington," taped transcript, July 1, 1971, John Stennis MSS.

83. James Eastland to John Mitchell, July 23, 1969, Robert T. Moore to Jerris Leonard, n.d., Jerris Leonard to Irby Turner, Jr., August 29, 1969, and Gerald Jones to David Norman, June 21, 1971, CRD Office Files, DOJ.

84. Jerris Leonard to Jack Edwards, n.d., reprinted in House Judiciary Committee, *Hearings on the Voting Rights Act, 1975*, p. 338.

85. Archie Allen, "Federal Registrars in Mississippi—1971, Madison and Tallahatchie Counties," September 2, 1971, VEP Office Files; Gerald Jones to David Norman, August 11, 1971, and Peter Mear to Gerald Jones, August 6, 1971, CRD Office Files; *Delta Ministry Reports*, September 1971, folder 19, 1972 add., Eugene Cox MSS; Washington Research Project, *Shameful Blight*, p. 29.

86. Aaron Henry testimony, House Judiciary Committee, Civil Rights Oversight Subcommittee, *Hearings*, p. 223; Lewis and Allen, "Black Voter Registration," p. 123.

87. Bass and De Vries, *Transformation of Southern Politics*, p. 208; Fortenberry and Abney, "Mississippi," p. 522.

88. *Delta Ministry Reports*, November 1971, folder 19, 1972 add., Eugene Cox MSS, Berry *Amazing Grace*, pp. 304, 324.

89. Berry, *Amazing Grace*, pp. 302, 330; Washington Research Project, *Shameful Blight*, p. 87.

90. Delta Ministry, "Election Analysis, 1971," VEP Office Files; Jason Berry, an Evers campaign aide offered another perspective. "The election may have been the fairest in Mississippi's history," he wrote, "but it was still crooked." *Amazing Grace*, p. 330.

91. Berry, *Amazing Grace*, pp. 263, 331; Simpson, "Loyalist," p. 118. Tom Ethridge column, Jackson *Clarion Ledger*, December 15, 1971, clipping, folder 16, 1972 add., Eugene Cox MSS. For the view that Evers' campaign served as an "adrenalin builder" for other black candidates, see Aaron Henry, Interview, Southern Oral History Collection (Bass and De Vries), University of North Carolina.

92. Berry, *Amazing Grace*, pp. 268, 333–34; Delta Ministry, "Election Analysis, 1971"; Peirce, *Deep South*, p. 186. In some instances, white trickery rather than black apathy explained why blacks voted for Evers but not for other candidates of their own race. Professor John Dittmer, who was teaching history at Tougaloo College at the time, has informed the author that in Madison County precincts, white poll managers would cast the illiterates' vote for Evers and then pull the remaining levers for white candidates. A typical conversation went this way: "I want to vote for Evers for governor." "Fine. Now you want to vote for Billy Nobles for Sheriff, don't you?"—and so on down the line. John Dittmer, letter to author, March 1, 1983. For recent evidence of ongoing election-day chicanery by polling officials in Mississippi, see McLemore, "Response," pp. 41–42.

93. Quoting Bill Rose in the *Lexington Advertiser*, reprinted in the *Delta Democrat Times*, December 9, 1971, clipping, folder 16, 1972 add., Eugene Cox MSS.

94. Delta Ministry, "Election Analysis," p. 15; Berry, *Amazing Grace*, p. 331; Peirce, *Deep South*, p. 189. Some civil rights workers blamed the loss on the paternalistic attitude of whites who did not allow blacks to exert leadership. Charles M. Saunders to James E. Cheek, November 22, 1971, VEP Office Files.

95. Julius Harris to John Lewis, February 22, 1971, VEP Files; Prince, "Black Voting Strength"; Simpson, "Loyalist" p. 118; William B. Stuart, *Commercial Appeal*, February 12, 1971, clipping, folder 16, 1972 add., Eugene Cox MSS; Neil Maxwell, *Wall Street Journal*, November 2, 1971. clipping, VEP Office Files; U.S. Commission on Civil Rights, *The Voting Rights Act: Ten Years After*, p. 210; Salamon, "Mississippi Post-Mortem"; Ed King, Interview with author, February 11, 1979.

96. VEP, "Press Release: What Happened in the South, 1971: Advances in Black Political Participation," and Larry Rand to John Lewis, "Report of Activities of the Mississippi Center for Elected Officials From July 1, 1971, through December 31, 1971," VEP Office Files.

97. Peirce, *Deep South*, p. 163; Berry, *Amazing Grace*, p. 132.

98. Quoted in Tom Ethridge column, Jackson *Clarion Ledger*, December 15, 1971, clipping, 1972 add., Eugene Cox MSS.

99. Peirce, *Deep South*, p. 205.

100. Leuchtenburg, "White House and Black America," p. 142. Data compiled from U.S. General Accounting Office, Report of the Comptroller General of the United States, *Voting Rights Act—Enforcement Needs Strengthening*, p. 57, and Senate Judiciary Committee, *Hearings on the Voting Rights Act*, 1975, p. 597. The proportion of voting-age blacks registered to vote in the seven covered states held constant at 57 percent when Nixon resigned. This percentage was drawn from the larger pool of eligible voters created by the enfranchisement of eighteen to twenty-year olds. This statistic is striking because newly emancipated youths generally registered at lower rates than did their elders, which meant that a greater number of citizens over the age of twenty-one had to enroll just to keep the figure at the same overall level.

101. Wells, "Voting Rights," p. 11. On the disappointment with the Nixon ad-

ministration, see Wilson, "Voices From Mississippi," p. 63. On bureaucratic continuity, see Orfield, *Congressional Power*, p. 83, and Button, *Black Violence*, p. 101.

7. Beyond the Ballot: The Suffrage and Political Representation

1. Testimony of Howard Glickstein, U.S. House of Representatives, Committee on the Judiciary, *Hearings on Extension of the Voting Rights Act*, 94th Cong., 1st sess., 1975, p. 344.
2. Parmet, *The Democrats*, p. 294, gives the figure at 5.5 percent. The Joint Center for Political Studies estimated 6.7 percent. See note 11 below.
3. "Proposed Guidelines Commission on Party Structure and Delegate Selection," September 23, 1969, Box 220, James G. O'Hara MSS.
4. Crotty, *Decision for the Democrats*, pp. 26–27, 31. See also Byron E. Shafer, *Quiet Revolution*, for a nicely detailed account.
5. "Proposed Guidelines," September 23, 1969.
6. *Ibid.*
7. Commission on Party Structure and Delegate Selection, "Official Guidelines for Delegate Selection," November 19–20, 1969, II, Box 5, Aaron Henry MSS.
8. McGovern, *Grassroots*, pp. 145–47; Crotty, *Decision for the Democrats*, p. 64. For a critical account of the work of the commission by one of its members, see Ranney, *Curing the Mischiefs*, pp. 111–15, 188–91, 195–96. Ranney had originally supported some form of preferential representation for blacks based on a history of past bias. However, he wound up opposing proportional representation after women and the young were included under it. See also White, *Making of the President 1972*, pp. 28–34.
9. McGovern, *Grassroots*, pp. 143–48.
10. *Ibid.*, pp. 148, 149; Crotty, *Decision for the Democrats*, pp. 75, 124; Parmet, *Democrats*, p. 295.
11. Quoted in Crotty, *Decision for Democrats*, p. 136; Joint Center for Political Studies, *Guide To Black Politics 1976, Part 1*,—pp. 30–31 for the figures. For slightly varying data see Crotty, *Decision for Democrats*, pp. 76, 143; Lewis and Allen, "Black Voter Registration," pp. 129–30; Conyers and Wallace, *Black Elected Officials*, p. 148.
12. Fannie Lou Hamer, Oral Interview, University of Southern Mississippi; *Delta Ministry Reports*, March 1972, folder 11, 1972 add., Eugene Cox MSS. Henry blocked Hamer's selection for national committeewoman. He contended that the "spirit" of the McGovern rules required a white woman be chosen because another black, Charles Evers, had been appointed as national committeeman. Pat Derrian, a close associate of Hodding Carter III got the position.
13. Donald M. Fraser to Aaron Henry, September 25, 1969, II, Box 1, Aaron Henry MSS; Fred R. Harris to Aaron Henry, January 7, 1970, II, Box 2, Henry MSS.
14. Simpson, "Loyalist" p. 110.
15. Charles H. Griffin to David Ethridge, December 17, 1970, Box 31, Charles Griffin MSS.
16. Charles Griffin to John Bell Williams, February 3, 1969, Box 31, Griffin MSS. The congressman rejected the idea of switching his affiliation to the Republican party.
17. Peirce, *Deep South*, p. 194.
18. Arnold Aronson, Memo 1-71, January 15, 1971, Box 27, LCCR MSS. See also the attached affidavit of Aaron Henry.
19. The vote was 111-55. Simpson " 'Loyalist' Democrats," p. 113.

20. Charles Griffin to John Bell Williams, February 3, 1969, Box 31, Griffin MSS.

21. Simpson, "Loyalist," p. 117. Such statements did win over the leaders of the Mississippi AFL-CIO, who abandoned the loyalist cause. Bass and DeVries, *The Transformation of Southern Politics*, p. 207.

22. Aaron Henry to J. Wesley Watkins III, December 20, 1971, Jan Lewis Loyalist Democrat Papers.

23. Simpson, "Loyalist," pp. 125, 126, 129, 130; Berry, *Amazing Grace*, pp. 346–47.

24. Hodding Carter, Oral Interview, Billy Simpson Loyalist Democrat Collection, Mississippi State University.

25. Statement of Charles H. Griffin, n.d., Box 69, Griffin MSS. The regulars had already pressed this claim in federal court, trying to enjoin the loyalists from representing themselves as the official state Democratic party at the convention. The appeal was rejected. Simpson, " 'Loyalist' Democrats," pp. 136, 137, 143.

26. Simpson, " 'Loyalist' Democrats," pp. 151–52; Bass and DeVries, *Transformation of Southern Politics*, p. 208.

27. Donald M. Fraser, "Press Release," April 28, 1972, Box 220, James G. O'Hara MSS.

28. Crotty, *Decision for Democrats*, p. 109; Bass and DeVries, *Transformation of Southern Politics*, p. 172; Murphy and Gulliver, *Southern Strategy*, p. 170; Edsall and Williams, "North Carolina," pp. 392–93.

29. William F. Walsh, Hearing Officer, to Patricia Roberta Harris, June 10, 1972, Robert S. Vance to Ken Bode, June 15, 1972, Jan Lewis Loyalist Democrat Papers; Robert S. Vance to Aaron Henry, July 25, 1969, I, Box 3, Aaron Henry MSS; Strong, "Alabama," p. 471; Walton, *Black Political Parties*, p. 155; Frye, *Black Parties*, pp. 155–56. The NDPA challenge aroused little enthusiasm compared to 1968, as evidenced by the failure of the loyalist delegation from Mississippi to endorse it. Simpson, "Loyalist," p. 167.

30. Peirce, *Deep South*, p. 64.

31. Crotty, *Decision for Democrats*, chapters 5 and 6.

32. Coalition for a Democratic Majority Task Force on Democratic Party Rules and Structure, "Toward Fairness and Unity for '76," draft, Box 220, James G. O'Hara MSS; Crotty, *Decision for Democrats*, pp. 226 ff. For a contrary point of view on quotas and reaffirmation of party reform, see Americans for Democratic Action, "Let Us Continue . . . ," August 1973.

33. Crotty, *Decision for Democrats*, p. 223.

34. *Ibid.*, pp. 236, 246. The AFL-CIO sought to eliminate the clause related to representation based on presence in the Democratic electorate, but it failed. Parmet, *Democrats*, p. 313; Costello, "Minority Voting Rights," p. 156. For criticism of the Mikulski Commission, see Walters, "Democratic Panel," p. 7.

35. Legal Advisory Council to Compliance Review Commission, May 28, 1975, Box 222, and Aaron Henry to Robert Wagner, June 16, 1975, Box 222, James G. O'Hara MSS.

36. Joint Center for Political Studies, *Guide to Black Politics, 1976*, pp. 30–31. In Mississippi, the percentage fell from 56.0 to 33.3.

37. *Delta Ministry Reports*, April 1976, Delta Ministry MSS, Mississippi State University; *Tupelo Daily Journal*, October 29, 1973, *Delta Democrat Times*, March 20, 1974, *Meridian Star*, June 10, 1974, *Hattiesburg American*, June 13, 1974, clippings, Mitchell Memorial Library, Mississippi State University; New York Times, December 30, 1975, p. 15; Bass and DeVries, *Transformation of Southern Politics*, p. 208.

38. Bass and DeVries, *Transformation of Southern Politics,* p. 217. However, after testing the political waters further, Eastland decided not to run.

39. Thernstrom, "Odd Evolution," p. 60; Zimmerman, "Federal Voting Rights Act," p. 382; Dauer, "Multi Member Districts," p. 633; Bonapfel, "Minority Challenges," p. 692; Birenbaum "Effect of Elections At-Large," p. 387; Bass and DeVries, *Transformation of Southern Politics,* p. 14. Supporters of multimember districts and at-large elections argued that minority voters would actually have more influence in the selection of a large number of officials throughout the entire city or county.

40. Berry and Dye, "Discriminatory Effects" p. 85; Note, *"Chavis v. Whitcomb,"* p. 523.

41. Birenbaum, "Effect of Elections At-Large," p. 370; Horwitz, "Jurisprudence of *Brown,"* p. 184. In contrast, see Thernstrom, "Odd Evolution," 59–60.

42. *Georgia v. United States,* 411 U.S. 527, 530 (1973). The other requirements were numbered posts and majority runoff. Also, the state had departed extensively from its previous policy of respecting county lines in drawing districts.

43. *Ibid.,* p. 530.

44. *Ibid.,* pp. 531, 533, 534. Joining Stewart were William O. Douglas, William Brennan, Thurgood Marshall, and Harry Blackmun. Chief Justice Burger concurred.

45. *Ibid.,* pp. 538, 540. William Rehnquist and Lewis Powell concurred with Justice Byron White, who wrote the minority opinion. It agreed that section five covered reapportionment plans but argued that the attorney general "should not be able to object by simply saying he cannot make up his mind or that the evidence is in equipoise." See p. 545. Halpin and Engstrom, "Racial Gerrymandering," p. 40. Before the Supreme Court ruling, Georgia had submitted a revised plan for congressional and state senate redistricting. The attorney general approved it, paving the way for the election of Representative Andrew Young from the Fifth Congressional District, in which blacks comprised 43.8 percent of the population. The Supreme Court permitted elections for the state house of representatives to be held under the 1972 plan. U.S. Commission on Civil Rights, *The Voting Rights Act: Ten Years After,* pp. 230–33; Eisenstat and Barutio, *Andrew Young,* pp. 9–11.

46. *Morris v. Gressette,* 432 U.S. 493, 498 (1977). The Court of Appeals in the District of Columbia approved on appeal.

47. *Ibid.,* pp. 500, 501, 502, 504, 506. The decision was ultimately rendered on June 20, 1977.

48. *Ibid.,* pp. 516, 509, 510, 513; Yoste, "Section 5," pp. 850–51. At the same time, in a per curiam opinion, the Supreme Court strengthened the attorney general's authority to review reapportionment changes. It overturned a lower federal court ruling approving a redistricting plan that had not been cleared by the Justice Department. *United States v. Board of Supervisors of Warren County,* 429 U.S. 642 (1977).

49. *United States v. Board of Commissioners of Sheffield, Alabama,* 435 U.S. 113, 114, 116 (1978).

50. *Ibid.,* pp. 118, 124, 131.

51. *Ibid.,* pp. 136, 137. Despite having reservations about the constitutionality of section five, Justices Blackmun and Powell concurred because they considered the issue settled by precedent. *Ibid.* at 138, 139. The minority interpreted the statutory history differently than did the majority. Justices Stevens, Burger, and Rehnquist believed that in passing the act, Congress had been concerned mainly with literacy tests and other devices to hinder black voter registration. Thus, the lawmakers had intended section five to apply only to governmental entities engaged in the registration process and not to political bodies, like Sheffield, that adopted electoral changes. *Ibid.* at 144, 145, 147, 149.

52. Ramundo, "Voting Rights," p. 185. In *Rome v. United States,* 446 U.S. 156 (1980), the court ruling followed this precedent. The high tribunal concluded in light of *Sheffield,* that if a city or any political unit came under the Voting Rights Act because it was part of a covered state, it could not bail out separately from coverage unless the entire state sought to do so. The court also declared that the sixty-day period for the attorney general to furnish a response should be calculated from the time when the jurisdiction provided supplemental material requested by the Justice Department.

53. *Dougherty County Board of Education v. White,* 439 U.S. 34 (1979).

54. *Ibid.,* p. 50.

55. *Ibid.,* pp. 41, 43, 47. Marshall also argued that the county board of education was a political entity subject to section 5, as interpreted in *Sheffield.*

56. *Ibid.,* pp. 51, 54. Justice Stevens was the swing vote. He concurred on the basis of precedent but disagreed with Marshall's portrayal of congressional intent.

57. MacCoon, "Enforcement of the Preclearance Requirement," p. 112; Goulder, "Reconstructed Right," p. 70. For recognition of the limits of what constituted a voting change, e.g., zoning ordinances, see Hunter, "Administrators' Dilemmas."

58. For contrasting viewpoints, see Horwitz, "Jurisprudence," pp. 184–85; Binion, "Implementation of Section 5," pp. 169–70; Thernstrom, "Odd Evolution," pp. 60, 64.

59. *City of Richmond v. United States,* 422 U.S. 362, 363 (1975). Richmond had not submitted the change until 1971 when the *Perkins* ruling decreed that annexations were covered under section five.

60. *Ibid.,* pp. 364–65; "Securing a Valid Annexation," pp. 568–69.

61. The Supreme Court affirmed, *City of Petersburg v. United States,* 410 U.S. 962 (1973). Stronach, "Anatomy of a Black Victory," p. 147. Derfner and Taylor, "Court Cases," p. 3. Petersburg agreed to make the alterations, and on June 12, 1973, a black mayor and a black majority were elected to the city council.

62. *City of Richmond v. United States,* 422 U.S. 366 (1975).

63. *Ibid.,* pp. 370, 371, 372–73; Thernstrom, "Odd Evolution," p. 66; Powers, "Annexations," pp. 207, 213–14, points out that under the ward plan, whites were guaranteed maximum representation if blacks became a majority of the new city. The Civil Rights Division agreed that legitimate purposes existed for the annexation and approved the plan for single-member districts in the enlarged municipality. *Annual Report of the Attorney General of the United States for the Fiscal Year Ended June 10, 1976,* p. 107. Justice Lewis Powell, a prominent Richmond attorney at the time of the annexation, did not participate in the decision.

64. *City of Richmond v. United States,* 422 U.S. 383, 388 (1975). Brennan had no difficulty finding discriminatory purpose in the record as well. He also cited the rejection of an alternative plan that could have given blacks greater opportunity to elect a majority.

65. Powers, "Annexations," p. 215; Ozog, "Judicial Review," pp. 319, 320; Wernz, " 'Discriminatory Purpose,' " pp. 339, 340; Yoste, "Section 5," p. 823. The immediate impact of the Richmond plan did not work against black representation. In March 1977, the city held council elections, and blacks won five of nine seats. Henry Marsh was chosen as the first black mayor. Harris, "Richmond."

66. *Beer v. United States,* 425 U.S. 133, 134, 135 (1976). The districts were constructed in a north to south pattern, while predominantly black neighborhoods were located along an east–west axis.

67. *Ibid.,* p. 136.

68. *Ibid.,* p. 141; Binion, "Implementation of Section 5," p. 170.

69. *Beer v. United States,* 422 U.S. 143, 144 (1976).

70. Marshall and Brennan joined White in dissent; Stevens took no part. Marshall insisted that as long as "vestiges of discrimination" remained, submissions from covered jurisdictions should be approved only with "compelling justification" (*ibid.,* pp. 151, 161). Engstrom, "Racial Vote Dilution," p. 162, points out that under the "retrogression rule" it would be nearly impossible for any reapportionment plan to contravene section five because in most southern localities before 1965, the proportion of black voters was exceedingly low. Almost any redistricting plan based on current voter registration would mean an increase of black representation. Wernz, " 'Discriminatory Purpose,' " pp. 343, 347, 350; Thernstrom, "Odd Evolution," p. 65.

71. Rice, *Progressive Cities,* p. 5. Tampa, Florida, offers another example of the link between white racism and the institution of at-large elections. During the first decade of the twentieth century, Tampa had a council form of government whose members were elected partly at-large and partly by districts. In 1910, the White Municipal Party was formed, and a year later blacks were excluded from participation in its primary contests. The White Municipal Party campaigned for the creation of a commission system of government with at-large elections, and in 1920, Tampans voted to adopt it. I am grateful to Randolyn Kay Gardner for conducting the research on this point. These examples do not preclude the fact that motives other than race were involved in the adoption of at-large election procedures. The desire for "good government" played a major role, especially in areas where the bulk of southern blacks had already lost the right to vote. Nevertheless, even in these places, at-large plans served as a second line of defense in case restrictive franchise requirements were subsequently outlawed by the courts or became the target of congressional action under the Fifteenth Amendment.

72. Quoting Professor Clifton McCloskey in Derfner, "Multi Member Districts," p. 128; Sloan, " 'Good Government' ", p. 174; Jordan, "The Challenge and the Promise," p. 50; Kousser, "Undermining of the First Reconstruction," pp. 20–21.

73. Derfner, "Multi Member Districts," p. 120; Berry and Dye, "Discriminatory Effects," pp. 86–88, 93, 121; Hull, "Challenges to At-Large Election Plans," p. 77; Davidson and Korbel, "At-Large Elections"; Howell Raines, "Legislative Districts as an Obstacle to Equality," *St. Petersburg Times,* part 1, January 2, 1977, p. 1B and part 2, January 3, 1977, p. 1B. Also see Dauer, "Multi Member Districts in Dade County," p. 5; MacManus, "City Council Election Procedures"; Engstrom and McDonald, "Election of Blacks." One indication of continued racial polarization was the increase in white voter registration as a response to black enfranchisement during the 1960s. For example, whites on the registration rolls in Mississippi rose between 1960 and 1970 from 41 percent to 70 percent. Parmet, *Democrats,* p. 240.

74. *Burns v. Richardson,* 384 U.S. 73 (1966); *Fortson v. Dorsey,* 379 U.S. 433 (1965); Note, *"Chavis v. Whitcomb,"* p. 533.

75. *Whitcomb v. Chavis,* 403 U.S. 124 (1971); Washington, "Fair and Effective Representation," p. 394; Berry and Dye, "Discriminatory Effects of At-Large Elections," pp. 110–12, 122. Justices Douglas, Brennan, and Marshall dissented.

76. *Taylor v. McKeithen,* 407 U.S. 194 (1972). See also *East Carroll Parish v. Marshall,* 424 U.S. 636 (1976), and contrast with *Wise v. Lipscomb,* 437 U.S. 535 (1978). The protracted litigation (1965–79) involving reapportionment of the Mississippi legislature also underlined the sectional distinctions noted by the Supreme Court in considering the legitimacy of multimember districts. Parker, "County Redistricting in Mississippi," p. 400; *Connor v. Johnson,* 402 U.S. 690 (1971); *Connor v. Waller,* 421 U.S. 656 (1975); *Connor v. Finch,* 431 U.S. 407 (1977); Bass, *Unlikely Heroes,* p. 294.

77. *White v. Register,* 412 U.S. 756 (1973).

78. *Ibid.,* p. 769. Part of that historical assessment included the way the white primary was run, the use of the majority runoff requirement, numbered posts, racist campaign tactics, and disregard for slating blacks for posts in the Democratic primary. Cotrell, "Effect(s) of At-Large Elections," reprinted in U. S. Congress, House of Representatives, Committee on the Judiciary, *Hearings on Extension of the Voting Rights Act,* 94th Cong., 1st sess., 1975, p. 434; Bonapfel, "Minority Challenges," p. 371. Under the single-member district system, three blacks were elected to the eighteen-member delegation from Dallas, and four Mexican-Americans and one black were elected to the Bexar County delegation. The ruling also increased the number of minority candidates competing for office and prompted a move to single-member districts in the state legislature and to a lesser extent in the city councils.

79. *Zimmer v. McKeithen,* 485 F.2d 1297 (5th Cir. 1973); Note, "Equal Protection of the Laws," pp. 1853–54, 1856–57; Bonapfel, "Minority Challenges," p. 379; Bell, "Constitutional Law," p. 184; Carr, "Vote Dilution," p. 408; Hull, "Challenges to At-Large Election," p. 69; Birenbaum, "Discriminatory Effect of Election At-Large," pp. 382–83; Derfner, "Multi Member Districts," pp. 124, 127; Peters, "At-Large Elections," p. 175.

80. Bonapfel, "Minority Challenges," p. 383; Note, "Equal Protection," p. 1859.

81. Peters, "At-Large Elections," p. 175.

82. Berry and Dye, "The Discriminatory Effects of At-Large Elections," p. 111.

83. Carr, "Vote Dilution," pp. 401, 415, 416, 417; Birenbaum, "Discriminatory Effect of Election At-Large," pp. 380; Note, "Racial Vote Dilution," pp. 694, 716, 718–19; *Washington v. Davis,* 426 U.S. 229 (1976); *Village of Arlington Heights v. Metropolitan Housing Authority,* 429 U.S. 250 (1977). On the seven voting rights cases from the South discussed in the text of this chapter, the Supreme Court broke into three blocs. Justices Thurgood Marshall, William Brennan, and William O. Douglas supported the position of the suffragists in every ruling in which they participated; Byron White, John Paul Stevens, and Harry Blackmun endorsed the voting rights side in 57 to 71 percent of the rulings; Potter Stewart, William Rehnquist, Lewis Powell, and Warren Burger favored civil rights advocates less than 43 percent of the time. Clearly, the Nixon presidency had a negative influence on the court in franchise suits. Nixon had appointed four justices to the bench, and three of them—Burger, Powell, and Rehnquist—were squarely in the ranks of the antivoting rights contingent. On these cases, the fourth Nixon appointee, Blackmun, proved to be the exception.

84. Carr, "Vote Dilution," pp. 409, 411; Note, "Racial Vote Dilution," p. 715; Birenbaum, "Discriminatory Effect of Election At-Large," 379; Irwin, "At-Large Voting," pp. 450–51. *Nevitt v. Sides,* 571 F.2d 209 (5th Cir. 1978); *Bolden v. City of Mobile,* 571 F.2d 268 (5th Cir. 1978).

8. The Consensus Holds

1. Jim Squires, *Chicago Tribune,* March 9, 1975, *Birmingham News,* March 9, 1975, *Atlanta Constitution,* March 7, 1975, clippings, VEP Office Files. The Selma council contained eleven members, including the mayor who was white, thus placing blacks in the minority. A similar memorial gathering had been held in 1972. Although it took place peacefully, the mayor had tried to block it. This time the same official, Joe Smitherman, did not interfere and proclaimed the convocation as the "last hurrah of the civil rights

marches. This should be the end of it." *Atlanta Journal,* April 12, 13, 15, 18, 1972, *Birmingham News,* April 13, 14, 15, 16, 1972, *Birmingham Post-Herald,* April 13, 14, 15, 1972, *Atlanta Constitution,* April 13, 15, 16, 1972, *Selma Times-Journal,* April 14, 1972, *Alabama Journal,* April 15, 16, 1972, clippings, VEP Office Files.

2. Andrew Young, Oral Interview, Southern Oral History Project, (Bass and DeVries), University of North Carolina, p. 5.

3. Jerris Leonard, Interview with author, July 31, 1979.

4. Henry's comment can be found in House Judiciary Committee, *Hearings,* "Extension of Voting Rights Act," 94th Cong., 1st Sess., 1975, p. 671.

5. J. Stanley Pottinger, "Justice and the Voting Rights Act," speech to Congressional Black Caucus, September 27, 1974, Appellate Section Files, DOJ.

6. Ford, *A Time To Heal,* pp. 139–40; Stan Scott to the President, August 21, 1974, PR 7-1, White House Central Files, Gerald R. Ford Library (GRFL).

7. "Excerpt from Attorney General [William] Saxbe's interview on "Meet the Press,'" November 17, 1974, Appellate Section Files. DOJ. Saxbe, a former Ohio senator, was appointed in the wake of Nixon's "Saturday Night Massacre" firing of Attorney General Eliot Richardson and his deputy, William Ruckelshaus.

8. William B. Saxbe, Memorandum for the President, December 6, 1974, Appellate Section Files, DOJ.

9. *Ibid.*

10. *Public Papers of the Presidents, Gerald R. Ford, 1975,* p. 35. See also his remarks to the National Newspaper Publishers Association, January 23, 1975, p. 89. Ford counted himself as a supporter of the 1965 act and its extension in 1970, a view that was technically correct but was misleading in light of his prior attempts to substitute weaker versions before Congress voted for final passage.

11. Letter to the Speaker of the House and the President of the Senate, January 27, 1975, *Public Papers . . . GRF, 1975,* p. 113.

12. Jerry H. Jones to Ken Cole, January 13, 1975, HU 2-4, WHCF, GRFL.

13. David C. Treen to Gerald R. Ford, February 6, 1975, HU 2-4, WHCF, GRFL; Clarke Reed to Gerald R. Ford, April 9, 1975, GEN HU 2-4, WHCF, GRFL.

14. Clarence Mitchell to Gerald R. Ford, January 15, 1975, HU 2-4, WHCF, GRFL.

15. "Remarks of Senator Hugh Scott—Conference on the Voting Rights Act," n.d., drafted by Burt Wides, Burt Wides to Senator Philip Hart, Box 244, CR 6, Philip A. Hart MSS. Scott did not deliver the speech because he was unable to attend the conference held at the Martin Luther King, Jr., Center for Social Change in Atlanta. See also comments of Frank R. Parker to the 26th Annual Board Meeting of the Leadership Conference on Civil Rights, Minutes, January 27, 1975, LCCR MSS.

16. Burt Wides to Philip A. Hart, n.d. [1975], Box 244, CR 6, Hart MSS.

17. Senate Judiciary Committee, *Hearings,* "Extension of the Voting Rights Act of 1965," 94th Cong. 1st sess., 1975, p. 63.

18. Burt Wides to Philip Hart, n.d. [1975], Box 244, CR 6, Hart MSS; House Judiciary Committee, *Hearings,* "Extension of the Voting Rights Act,", 1975, p. 920; Sam Gibbons to Edward Hutchinson, May 2, 1975, Box 158, Edward Hutchinson MSS. The Tampa congressman, representing a large Spanish-speaking district to which the act would have applied, opposed the measure. A previous supporter of the Voting Rights Act and its 1970 extension, he pledged to vote against it if language provisions were included. He later changed his mind.

19. "Action Memorandum," draft, Katharine I. Butler to J. Stanley Pottinger,

n.d., and Barry Weinberg to J. Stanley Pottinger, August 4, 1976, CRD Office Files; Katz, "The Other Side of the New South," p. 17.

20. U.S. Commission on Civil Rights, *The Voting Rights Act: Ten Years After,* p. 42; "Progress in Minority Registration and Voting," Briefing Notebook, 1975 extension, CRD Files; "Estimated Voter Registration in the South, 1976," Research Department, VEP. At the same time, the gap in percentage between white and black registrants in the North grew from 7.0 in 1968 to 11.2 in 1972. See testimony of Kenneth N. Klee, U.S. Congress, House of Representatives, Committee on the Judiciary, Subcommittee on Civil and Constitutional Rights, *Hearings,* "Extension of the Voting Rights Act," 1975, 94th Cong., 1st sess., p. 851.

21. "Black Elected Officials in the South, January, 1975," Voter Education Project, Joint Center for Political Studies, *National Roster of Black Elected Officials,* August 1976, pp. xxvii–xxviii. The three representatives came from Atlanta (Andrew Young), Houston (Barbara Jordan), and Memphis (Harold Ford). Among the southern cities with black mayors were Atlanta, Charlottesville and Roanoke, Virginia, Tallahassee, Florida, Gastonia, North Carolina, and Prichard, Alabama.

22. Voter Education Project, "Barriers to Minority Political Progress in the South," c. 1975–1976.

23. U.S. Commission on Civil Rights, *The Voting Rights Act: Ten Years After,* p. 81; John Hoard to William Holman, September 7, 1976, and "VEP Local Program Proposal, Forest, Mississippi, May 30, 1978," VEP Files; Carl W. Gabel to James Turner, August 14, 1975, and David L. Norman to Hugh Cutrer, Jr., December 15, 1971, CRD Files.

24. Sidney R. Bixler to Gerald Jones, October 29, 1975, Alexander M. Peters to Gerald Jones, October 22, 1974, Carl Gabel and S. Michael Scadron to Gerald Jones, May 15, 1974, Dorothy Mead to Gerald Jones, August 23, 1972, Sidney R. Bixler to J. Stanley Pottinger, July 22, 1975, CRD Files.

25. U.S. Commission on Civil Rights, *The Voting Rights Act: Ten Years After,* p. 154.

26. Quoted in Salamon, "Mississippi Post-Mortem," p. 47; Salamon and Evera, "Fear, Apathy, and Discrimination," p. 1295.

27. Robert Clark, Interview (Bass and DeVries), Southern Oral History Project, University of North Carolina. For similar thoughts, see Whittemore, *Together,* p. 291.

28. Charles W. Aycock to Gerald Jones, October 30, 1974, CRD Files.

29. Quoted in Whittemore, *Together,* p. 277

30. For examples of complaints concerning manipulation of black illiterates, see John P. Mac Coon to Gerald Jones, October 28, 1975, Alexander M. Peters to Gerald Jones, October 24, 1974, John J. Roman to Walter Gorman, October 26, 1971, Ronald L. Oleson to Gerald Jones, October 23, 1975, Naomi White and S. Michael Scadron to Gerald Jones, October 23, 1975, CRD Files; testimony of Aaron Henry, House Subcommittee on Civil and Constitutional Rights, *Hearings,* 1975, p. 661; Berry, *Amazing Grace,* pp. 296, 298, 299, 352; Charles Saunders to James E. Creek, November 22, 1971, Howard Law School Project, VEP Files. In Mississippi, the federal court ordered any person chosen by an illiterate to be allowed to assist. *James v. Humphreys County Board of Election* as noted in John P. Mac Coon to Gerald Jones, August 7, 1975, CRD Files.

31. Silas McGhee, Oral Interview, July 12, 1969, Civil Rights Documentation Project, Howard University; testimony of Albert Turner and John Hulett, U.S. Commission on Civil Rights, *Hearings in Montgomery, Alabama, April 27–May 2, 1968,* pp. 370, 602; testimony of Frank Parker, U.S. Senate, Committee on the Judiciary, *Hearings,* "Extension of the Voting Rights Act of 1965," 94th Cong., 1st sess., 1975, p. 217; Salamon

and Van Evera, "Fear, Apathy, and Discrimination," p. 1304; Kernell, "Comment," p. 1311; Boykin, "Black Political Participation," p. 64; Morris, *The Politics of Black America,* pp. 153–65; Carmen L. Jones to Gerald W. Jones, May 3, 1977, CRD Files; Jake Ayers, Sr., to Sherrill Marcus, August 1, 1973, "Hollandale Municipal Election Analysis," VEP Files.

32. Salamon and Van Evera, "Fear, Apathy, and Discrimination," 1300–1; Kernell, "Comment," p. 1314; Daniel, "Negro Political Behavior," p. 277.

33. In 1971, the VEP funded 92 projects, in 1972, 129 projects, in 1973, 19 projects, in 1974, 16 projects, and in 1975, 25 projects. In 1975, John Lewis reported that the VEP operated with the lowest level of funding since its inception. VEP, *Annual Report, 1975,* p. 4; Atlanta *Constitution,* May 23, 1975, clipping, VEP Files. In addition to sponsoring voter registration, the VEP allocated grants for citizenship education, for technical assistance to black elected officials, for youth involvement in the political process, and for educational workshops.

34. "Vote Your Intelligence," clipping, n.p., n.d. (c. August 1965), attached to *Memphis Commercial-Appeal,* August 18, 1965, clipping, Box 3B, folder 19, Eugene Cox MSS.

35. Bartley and Graham, *Southern Politics,* pp. 109–10; Garrow, *Protest at Selma,* pp. 190, 302, n.33. Black and Black, "The Changing Setting of Minority Politics," p. 38; Peirce, *Deep South,* pp. 187, 298, 317; Bullock, "Election of Blacks," p. 730; Feagin and Hahn, "Second Reconstruction," p. 46; Hammond, "Race and Electoral Mobilization," p. 24; Levesque, "White Response," p. 247; Jones, "Black Officeholders," p. 53; Bass and De Vries, *The Transformation of Southern Politics,* pp. 178, 273.

36. U.S. Commission on Civil Rights, *Voting Rights Act: Ten Years After,* pp. 1, 329.

37. *Ibid.,* pp. 30, 326, 345.

38. *Ibid.,* pp. 346, 352, 354. The CCR also called upon Congress to enhance economic independence of all citizens by passing a plan for a negative income tax (p. 351). Frankie M. Freeman advocated a permanent abolition of literacy tests instead of suspending them for an additional ten years. Stephen Horn disagreed and favored a ban on literacy exams for five years. Robert Rankin supported extension of the act for ten years, but he believed that past accomplishments should have received greater emphasis and that recognition should have been given to the importance of voluntary compliance by southern whites (pp. 357, 360, 363).

39. *Ibid.,* p. 337.

40. *Ibid.,* pp. 33, 348.

41. *Ibid.,* pp. 37, 348.

42. House Judiciary Committee, *Hearings,* "Voting Rights Act," 1975, p. 175; "Summary and Evaluation of the 1975 Voting Rights Act Report of the U.S. Commission on Civil Rights," Briefing Notebook, CRD Files.

43. "Summary and Evaluation," Briefing Notebook, CRD Files; Senate Judiciary Committee, *Hearings,* "Voting Rights Act," 1975, p. 559.

44. "Summary and Evaluation," Briefing Notebook, CRD Files.

45. Ken Klee to Minority Members of the Subcommittee on Civil and Constitutional Rights, February 19, 1975, Box 158, Edward Hutchinson MSS.

46. House Judiciary Committee, *Hearings,* "Voting Rights Act," 1975, p. 12.

47. *Ibid.,* p. 36. Nixon had removed Father Hesburgh as chairman and had appointed Flemming, who had served in the Eisenhower administration as secretary of the Department of Health, Education and Welfare.

48. *Ibid.,* pp. 62–63.

49. *Ibid.*, p. 589.

50. *Ibid.*, pp. 119, 920.

51. *Ibid.*, p. 680. See also the testimony of David Satterfield, p. 729.

52. *Ibid.*, 640–41. Derfner participated in the *Allen* Case. A member of the Lawyers' Committee on Civil Rights Under Law, he placed in this category schemes to dilute voting strength and to hinder the opportunity to elect minority group officials.

53. *Ibid.*, p. 381; *New York Times*, March 9, 1975, p. 59.

54. House Judiciary Committee, *Hearings*, "Voting Voting Rights Act," 1975, p. 297.

55. *Ibid.*, p. 174.

56. *Ibid.*, pp. 745–46; *Virginia v. United States*, 420 U.S. 901 (1975).

57. House Judiciary Committee, *Hearings*, "Voting Rights Act," 1975, p. 304.

58. *Ibid.*, pp. 750, 791.

59. *Ibid.*, p. 791; J. Stanley Pottinger to Don Edwards, May 6, 1975, Box 158, Edward Hutchinson MSS.

60. Pottinger to Edwards, May 6, 1975, Box 158, Hutchinson MSS.

61. The vote on the Butler amendment was a tie, 17–17. U.S. House of Representatives, *Report Number 94-196* (Voting Rights Extension), 94th Cong., 1st sess., pp. 7, 8, 10, 11, 13–15, 29, 33–34; 37; *New York Times*, May 2, 1975. The proposal would have extended the automatic trigger to cover language minorities, thereby affording protection through administrative rather than through judicial means.

62. House of Representatives, *Report Number 94-196*, p. 76.

63. *Ibid.*, pp. 77, 81, 82, 83. These minority plans received support from slightly varying lineups. Another substitute offered by Charles Wiggins, Caldwell Butler, William Moorehead, Henry Hyde, Walter Flowers, and James R. Mann prevented covered jurisdictions from bailing out until February 5, 1977, and then placed all states on an equal basis. A new trigger would take effect covering jurisdictions in which less than 50 percent of the voting-age population of racial or language minorities had cast ballots in the previous presidential election. Every two years thereafter coverage would cease unless the criterion was met in the next presidential election (*ibid.*, p. 97). Only John Ashbrook opposed any extension of the Voting Rights Act (*ibid.*, p. 121). The minority position on language minorities generally reflected presidential thinking. Pottinger told civil rights advocates that the president would have increased doubts about the bill as more provisions were added. However, he added, "he did not see any serious Administration problems with the legislation." "Summary of Discussion with Attorney General Edward Levi," April 23, 1975, LCCR MSS.

64. House Judiciary Committee, *Hearings*, "Voting Rights Act," 1975, p. 698. Barefield had sponsored the 1968 open primary law directed at cutting down the chances of a minority candidate being elected. The bill was dubbed the "Charles Evers bill," after the civil rights leader who ran for Congress in 1968. See chapter four above and Lawyers' Committee for Civil Rights Under Law, *Voting in Mississippi: A Right Still Denied* (Washington, D.C.: 1981), p. 75. In contrast to Barefield's comments, see those of A. F. Summer, House Judiciary Committee, *Hearings*, "Voting Rights Act," 1975, p. 681. Other remarks are on pp. 585 and 649–50. On the shift in the behavior of Representative Flowers, see Stern, "Southern Congressional Civil Rights Voting," p. 16.

65. House Judiciary Committee, *Hearings*, "Voting Rights Act," 1975, p. 904.

66. *Congressional Record*, 94th Cong., 1st sess., p. 16758.

67. *Ibid.*, pp. 16263, 16288, 16758, 16905.

68. *Ibid.*, p. 16774.

69. *Ibid.,* pp. 16904, 16772.

70. Senate Judiciary Committee, *Hearings,* "Voting Rights Act," 1975, p. 846.

71. John V. Tunney to Mike Mansfield, May 31, 1975, Box 55, Hugh Scott MSS; *New York Times,* July 18, 1975, p. 34; U.S. Senate, Committee on the Judiciary, *Report 94-295,* "Voting Rights Act Extension," 94th Cong., 1st sess.; Jordan and Hearon, *Barbara Jordan,* p. 211.

72. *New York Times,* July 25, 1975, p. 28.

73. Democratic southerners voting yes on the first cloture motion were Lawton Chiles and Richard Stone of Florida, Wendell Ford and Walter D. Huddleston of Kentucky, Bennett Johnston and Russell Long of Louisiana, Ernest Hollings of South Carolina, and Lloyd Bentsen of Texas. Southern Republicans in favor were Howard Baker and William Brock of Tennessee and John Tower of Texas. Robert Morgan, a North Carolina Democrat, voted present. On the motion to consider, Long, Ford, and Huddleston went unrecorded. Morgan announced that he would support the final bill but not cloture because he resented the procedure of deliberating on the House bill rather than the version reported out of the Senate Judiciary Committee. *Congressional Record,* 94th Cong., 1st sess., p. 23760.

74. *Ibid.,* p. 24120; *Senate Report 94-295,* "Voting Rights Act Extension," minority view, p. 73.

75. The northern Democrats included several prominent liberals: Abe Ribicoff of Connecticut, Hubert Humphrey of Minnesota, Gaylord Nelson of Wisconsin and Lee Metcalf of Montana. Ribicoff summed up their position: "The time has come when we cannot be dividing this country on a sectional basis. All I am asking is that when we pass a law in the U.S. Senate, the same principles, the same rules, the same regulations should apply to the entire Nation." He had taken a similar position on busing. *Congressional Record,* 94th Cong., 1st sess., p. 2424.

76. Richard D. Parsons to Willa K. Goodson, May 22, 1975, Box 18, Domestic Council, Richard Parsons Files, GRFL.

77. J. Stanley Pottinger Memorandum for the Attorney General, June 13, 1975, Appellate Section, Department of Justice; J. Stanley Pottinger to James M. Cannon, May 19, 1975, Box 39, Domestic Council, Richard Parsons Files, GRFL; Edward H. Levi to the President, July 1, 1975, Box 19, Domestic Council, Richard Parsons Files, GRFL. Pottinger expressed doubts about the constitutionality of a permanent prohibition on literacy tests and suggested, "It would make more sense to tie the extension of special coverage with a nationwide ban on literacy tests, so both were extended for the same time period."

78. J. Stanley Pottinger to James M. Cannon, May 19, 1975, Box 39, Domestic Council, Richard Parsons Files, GRFL, reports on the conversation with Reed.

79. Richard Parsons to James Cannon, June 24, 1975, Box 39, and Parsons to Cannon, June 11, 1976, Box 39, Domestic Council, James M. Cannon Files, GRFL.

80. Richard Parsons to James Cannon, June 11, 1975, Box 39, Domestic Council, James M. Cannon Files, GRFL. The claim for a need to enforce the law in the North had apparently been substantiated by Reverend Jesse Jackson, who reportedly told the president: "There are more blacks denied the right to vote in Chicago than live in the entire State of Mississippi." Ken Cole to the President, December 13, 1974, Box 18, Domestic Council, Richard Parsons Files, GRFL.

81. Rowland Evans and Robert Novak, "The Incompetency Factor," *Washington Post,* July 31, 1975, clipping, Box 19, Domestic Council, Richard Parsons Files, GRFL.

82. Gerald R. Ford to Hugh Scott, July 18, 1975, *Public Papers . . . GRF, 1975,*

p. 1016. For his statement of the previous day, see *Public Papers,* p. 410. See also Gerald Ford to Hugh Scott, July 18, 1975, Box 54, Hugh Scott MSS, and Ford to Mike Mansfield, July 21, 1975, *Congressional Record,* 94th Cong., 1st sess., p. 24220.

83. *Congressional Record,* 94th Cong., 1st sess., p. 24221.

84. *Ibid.,* pp. 24225, 24230.

85. *Ibid.,* p. 24228.

86. See Dick Parsons to Dick Dunham, July 22, 1975, Box 19, Domestic Council, Parsons Files, GRFL, for the claim that Clarence Mitchell and Vernon Jordan had been notified of the letter "and neither has any problem with it." However, Joseph Rauh was furious with the president and felt that the suffragists had been double-crossed. Joseph Rauh, Interview with author, July 16, 1979. The details of the conversation between Ford and Scott are sketchy. See *Congressional Record,* 94th Cong., 1st sess., p. 24731; *Congressional Quarterly Weekly,* July 26, 1975, p. 1596; *Washington Post,* July 24, 1975, p. A4. Sam Nunn to Gerald R. Ford, July 25, 1975, HU 2–4, WHCF, GRFL. Nunn was dismayed over the "rumors and allegations" that the president had weakened his commitment to the amendments "in subsequent conversations with the leaders of the Senate."

87. GOP support for amendments ranged from twelve votes to twenty-three. On thirteen ballots, a majority of Republicans supported alterations on four occasions, opposed on eight instances, and divided evenly one time. The majority of northern Democrats opposed revisions on all thirteen votes. The most active support against amendments came from Republicans in the Northeast, and the most vigorous support for the amendments came from Republicans in the Midwest and Rocky Mountain regions.

88. Two provisions applied: A jurisdiction was eligible for federal examiners and observers and was subject to preclearance review if it used English-only registration and election materials on November 1, 1972, and less than 50 percent of the voting-age citizens were registered on November 1, 1972, or voted in the presidential election of 1972, and more than 5 percent of the citizens of voting age belonged to a sizable language minority group. Second, if more than 5 percent of citizens were part of a single language minority and the illiteracy rate of such groups was higher than the national average, then registration and election materials had to be furnished in the language of the minority group as well as in English.

89. Once an amendment had been placed on the floor for consideration, unanimous consent was necessary to revise it.

90. *Congressional Record,* 94th Cong., 1st sess., pp. 24241–43. Representative Robert Drinan first mentioned the figure of seven years during hearings before the House Judiciary Committee, 94th Cong., 1st sess., 1975, p. 296.

91. Since the Stone amendment defeat, the majority had picked up the votes of six Democrats: Mike Gravel (Alaska), Gary Hart (Colorado), Mansfield, Quentin Burdick (North Dakota), George McGovern (South Dakota), and Frank E. Moss (Utah).

92. *Congressional Record,* 94th Cong., 1st sess., p. 24731.

93. *Ibid.,* p. 24731.

94. *Ibid.,* p. 24229.

95. *Ibid.,* pp. 24224 and 24948 for the comments of two of the bill's southern Democratic supporters, Hollings and Nunn. Baker and Brock of Tennessee were the only two southern Republicans in favor of the final measure. The other four—Jesse Helms of North Carolina, Strom Thurmond of South Carolina, William L. Scott of Virginia, and John Tower of Texas—came from covered states.

96. Bass and DeVries, *Transformation of Southern Politics,* pp. 38, 377–78. The authors note the differences in voting patterns between southerners who represented cov-

ered jurisdictions and those who did not. On the Democratic side, 80.5 percent of congressmen from exempt districts approved the bill compared with 51.5 percent from designated areas. The figure for Republicans was more striking: 64.3 percent from uncovered districts were in support in contrast to only 7.7 percent from nonexempt units. In the Senate, the configuration was similar: 75 percent of southern Democrats from exempt states approved compared with 54.5 percent from covered states. For the GOP, 100 percent of the senators in favor came from the exempt states. In this tabulation, the senators from Florida and Texas were counted as representing covered jurisdictions because the act's language minority trigger brought their states or part of them under coverage. Black, "Racial Composition of Congressional Dictricts," p. 435.

97. *Washington Post,* August 7, 1975, p. A1.

98. *Congressional Record,* 94th Cong., 1st session., p. 24145.

9. The Hands That Picked the Cotton

1. Cook, "Democracy and Tyranny," pp. 392–93, 394.

2. Peirce, *Deep South,* p. 328; Murphy and Gulliver, *The Southern Strategy,* p. 196.

3. Jimmy Carter, Oral History Interview (Bass and DeVries), Southern Oral History Collection, University of North Carolina, p. 20. For books on Carter, see Fink, *Prelude to the Presidency;* Glad, *Jimmy Carter;* St. John, *Jimmy Carter's Betrayal;* Straud, *How Jimmy Won;* Witcover, *Marathon;* Wooten, *Dasher.*

4. Dent, *Prodigal South,* p. 16.

5. In 1972, the black turnout had been 58 percent. Cromwell, "Black impact on the 1976 elections," pp. 4–5.

6. Young made these remarks at the funeral of Mrs. Fannie Lou Hamer. *Jackson Clarion Ledger,* March 21, 1977, clipping, folder 3, 1978 add., Eugene Cox MSS. In Mississippi, Carter carried nineteen of the state's twenty-one predominantly black counties, *Jackson Clarion Ledger,* November 4, 1976, clipping, folder 31, 1978 add., Cox MSS.

7. *Public Papers of the Presidents, Jimmy Carter, 1978,* p. 695, *1979,* p. 759.

8. Califano, *Governing America,* p. 243.

9. Sitkoff, *Struggle for Equality,* pp. 234–35. The median figure hit a high of 62 percent in 1975.

10. Califano, *Governing America,* p. 230.

11. Leuchtenburg, "White House and Black America," p. 145. Carter did much better in securing a Panama Canal Treaty and the deregulation of gasoline.

12. *Public Papers . . . JC, 1979,* p. 910; see also, *1977,* pp. 481–82.

13. Read and McGough, *Let Them Be Judged,* pp. 172–74; Navasky, "The Greening of Griffin Bell," pp. 41 ff.; Washington *Post,* January 12, 1977, p. A1; Bell with Ostrow, *Taking Care of the Law,* pp. 54, 59, for the attorney general's criticism of the workings of the federal bureaucracy, including the Voting Rights Section of the Civil Rights Division.

14. *New York Times,* February 17, 1977, p. 23; see testimony of Drew Days, U.S. House of Representatives, Committee on the Judiciary, Subcommittee on Civil and Constitutional Rights, *Hearings on GAO Report on the Voting Rights Act,* 95th Cong., 2nd sess., 1978, p. 41.

15. *Annual Report of the United States Attorney General, 1977,* pp. 159–60, *1978,* p. 142, *1979,* pp. 116–17. Assistant Attorney General Drew Days reported that the num-

ber of department lawsuits in vote dilution cases rose from eleven in 1977 to twenty-two in 1979. For criticism of the CRD in not keeping track of unsubmitted changes, see General Accounting Office, *Voting Rights Act—Enforcement Needs Strengthening* (1978), pp. 27–29. For evidence of widespread failure to submit electoral changes in North Carolina, see Suitts, "Blacks in the Political Arithmetic After *Mobile,"* p. 72. For a rebuttal, see Hunter, "The Administrators' Dilemmas," p. 3. Hunter, the CRD attorney in charge of the preclearance program, responded that the GAO report "is more concerned with the number of unsubmitted changes than with the existence of discriminatory unsubmitted changes."

16. U.S. Commission on Civil Rights, *The Voting Rights Act: Unfulfilled Goals,* p. 66.

17. Engstrom, "Racial Vote Dilution," p. 152. J. Stanley Pottinger wrote Ford aide, Philip W. Buchen: "Frankly, our view of the law has been moderate, so we usually win in court challenges, but this is not always so—(*Beer v. U.S.,* involving New Orleans)." Pottinger to Buchen, April 6, 1976, HU 2-4, White House Central Files, GRFL. For the view that *Beer* had an important, but not controlling, influence on preclearance reviews, see Motomura, "Preclearance Under Section Five."

18. Parker, "County Redistricting in Mississippi," pp. 414, 418, contends that when the Justice Department did review reapportionment schemes, it was more sensitive to black voting rights than were the district courts. The department's authority to review reapportionment plans under section five had been restricted by the Supreme Court in *Connor v. Johnson,* 402 U.S. 690 (1971).

19. U.S. Commission on Civil Rights, *The Voting Rights Act: Ten Years After,* p. 30.

20. Ball, Krane, and Lauth, *Compromised Compliance,* pp. 88–90.

21. U.S. Commission on Civil Rights, *The Voting Rights Act: Unfulfilled Goals,* p. 19.

22. Carmen L. Jones to Gerald Jones, May 3, 1977, CRD Office Files. A Mississippi Supreme Court ruling, *O'Neal v. Simpson,* 350 So. 2d 998 (1977), decreed that illiterates desiring assistance must identify themselves to the poll manager, who then determined if they were in fact illiterate. If so, the voter could select anyone of his choice for assistance. Gerald Jones to Drew Days III, March 30, 1978, CRD Office Files. On criteria for sending federal observers, see testimony of J. Stanley Pottinger, U.S. Senate, Committee on the Judiciary, *Hearings,* "Extension of the Voting Rights Act of 1965," 94th Cong., 1st sess., 1975, p. 538.

23. Contrast Jeremy I. Schwartz to Gerald Jones, December 22, 1978 and R. W. Rodriguez et. al. to Gerald Jones, November 21, 1978, CRD Office Files, for favorable views of the examiner program with Government Accounting Office, *Voting Rights Act,* pp. 24–25.

24. Gerald W. Jones to J. Stanley Pottinger, March 18, 1974, CRD Office Files.

25. Ball, Krane, and Lauth, *Compromised Compliance,* p. 120.

26. *Ibid.,* p. 124.

27. *Ibid.,* pp. 142–43.

28. Fannie Lou Hamer, Oral History Interview, University of Southern Mississippi, p. 42; see also the remarks of Maynard Jackson, mayor of Atlanta, in Peirce, *Deep South,* p. 354.

29. Salamon, "Protest, Politics, and Modernization," p. 434; Hamilton, "Blacks and the Crisis in Political Participation," p. 191.

30. Clark, "The Present Dilemma," p. 76; Peirce, *Deep South,* p. 24; Bond, *Black Candidates,* p. 47; Salamon, "Leadership and Modernization," p. 641; Neary, *Julian Bond,*

p. 78; John Lewis, Oral Interview (Bass and DeVries), Southern Oral History Project, University of North Carolina, p. 31; "Black Mayors: Playing Politics," *Newsweek* (December 3, 1973), 82:38.

31. Neary, *Julian Bond*, p. 80.

32. Whittemore, *Together*, p. 268.

33. Berry, *Amazing Grace*, p. 11.

34. Mrs. Geneva Collins in Bond, *Black Candidates*, p. 88; see also pp. 17, 29, 32.

35. Murphy and Gulliver, *Southern Strategy*, p. 208.

36. *VEP News*, (November 1967), 1:2; Abney, "Factors Related to Negro Voter Turnout," p. 1061, found that turnout was related positively to the presence of black candidates.

37. Joint Center for Political Studies, *The National Roster of Black Elected Officials* (Washington, D.C.: Joint Center for Political Studies, 1978), *passim;* U.S. Commission on Civil Rights, *Voting Rights Act: Unfulfilled Goals*, p. 12.

38. Freedom Summer Revisited, "Politics and the Civil Rights Movement," November 2, 1979, Millsaps College, transcript, courtesy of John Dittmer; Jackson *Clarion Ledger*, July 7, 1975, clipping, folder 31, 78 add., Cox MSS; U.S. Commission on Civil Rights, *Voting Rights Act: Unfulfilled Goals*, p. 15; Eddie Williams testimony, U.S. Congress, House of Representatives, Committee on the Judiciary, *Hearings*, "Extension of the Voting Rights Act," 94th Cong., 1st sess., 1975, p. 117; Goldstein, "Black Registration in State Legislatures," pp. 3, 6; Henry Kirksey, Interview with author, Jackson, Mississippi, February 18, 1979. However, the Mississippi percentage was the highest in the nation.

39. Quoted in Cook, "Democracy and Tyranny in America," pp. 290–91.

40. U.S. Commission on Civil Rights, *Voting Rights Act: Unfulfilled Goals*, p. 17.

41. Campbell and Feagin, "Black Politics in the South, pp. 141, 142, 146; Colburn, *Southern Black Mayors*, pp. 2, 13; Bullock, "Election of Blacks," pp. 733–34; Melvin Smith (a Mississippi constable), Interview, Civil Rights Documentation Project, Howard University; Jones, "Black Officeholders," pp. 55, 58; "Baker County Community Profile," May 22, 1976, VEP Office Files; Harry J. Bowie to Vivian Jones Malone, September 1, 1977, VEP Office Files.

42. House Judiciary Committee, *Hearings*, "Extension of Voting Rights Act," 1975, p. 41.

43. Arthur Shores, Interview (Bass and DeVries), Southern Oral History Project, University of North Carolina, p. 5; Button, "Impact of Black Elected Municipal Officials," p. 17, concludes: "The black official has the difficulty of not being too white nor too black, otherwise he would offend one group or the other and not get anything done." Button also makes the point that even when black officials were outnumbered by whites on governing bodies, their presence ensured access to information that would have been denied them previously. "No matter what happened," he quotes the lone black member of a city council in Florida as saying, "the others on the council knew I was listening to everything that went on" (p. 12). According to Margaret K. Latimer, at-large elections also had a depressing effect on black political participation, reinforcing underrepresentation of blacks on governmental bodies. See Latimer, "Black Political Representation."

44. Button, "Impact," p. 14; Kimball, *The Disconnected*, p. 268; *Delta Ministry Reports*, December 1975, folder 11, 78 add., Cox MSS.

45. Robert Clark, Interview (Bass and DeVries), Southern Oral History Collection, University of North Carolina; Berry, *Amazing Grace*, p. 335.

46. Clark, "Negro Elected Official," p. 159.

47. Peirce, *Deep South*, p. 328; Bullock, "Election of Blacks," p. 737; Jordan, "New Forces," pp. 49–50.

48. Clarence Hall, Jr., to Marvin Wall, June 16, 1967, VEP Office Files.

49. Fannie Lou Hamer, Oral History Interview p. 33. See Watters and Cleghorn, *Climbing Jacob's Ladder*, pp. 362–95 for an account of the beating. John Cashin agreed with Mrs. Hamer's assessement, *New York Times*, September 19, 1973, p. 33.

50. Bass, *Unlikely Heroes*, pp. 284–85; Eichel, "What Happens When Blacks Gain Strength." p. 3.

51. Button and Scher, "Impact of the Civil Rights Movement"; Scher and Button, "Voting Rights Act," p. 46; Campbell, "Electoral Participation," pp. 271, 445. On the relationships between business leaders and civil rights, see Jacoway and Colburn, eds., *Southern Businessmen and Desegregation*.

52. *New York Times*, September 19, 1973, p. 33.

53. Janet Shortt, "The Mississippi Tour," June 22, 24, 28–30, 1971, VEP Office Files.

54. Quoting Eddie Davis, a police juror, in Bond, *Black Candidates*, p. 8; Morris, *The Politics of Black America*, p. 165; Conyers and Wallace, *Black Elected Officials*, pp. 6, 138; Conyers, "Politics and the Black Revolution," p. 165. Fannie Lou Hamer to Dear Friends, May 11, 1976, folder 31, 78 add., Cox MSS.

55. Bass and DeVries, *The Transformation of Southern Politics*, p. 407.

56. Ruby Magee, Oral History Interview, University of Southern Mississippi, p. 68.

57. Black, *Southern Governors*, p. 152.

58. Bass and DeVries, *Transformation of Southern Politics*, p. 148. For other governors, see Peirce, *Deep South*, pp. 61, 209; *New York Times*, October 17, 1971, p. 46; Bass and DeVries, pp. 168, 176, 212.

59. Ben Brown, Interview (Bass and DeVries), Southern Oral History Collection, University of North Carolina, p. 13.

60. *Lexington-Advertiser*, April 3, 1975, clipping, folder 31, 78 add., Cox MSS.

61. Peirce, *Deep South*, p. 256; Black *Southern Governors*, p. 57; Murphy and Gulliver, *Southern Strategy*, p. 201.

62. Peirce, *Deep South*, pp. 281–82; Fulwood, "Blacks for Wallace," p. 13. Wallace announced plans to build a $25 million oil refinery in Tuskegee, and a black-owned company received the contract for its construction.

63. Bass and DeVries, *Transformation of Southern Politics*, p. 69; Jackson, "How Much Black Support for Wallace?" p. 3. In contrast, the *New York Times* (May 9, 1974, p. 50) estimated that Wallace would pick up 25 percent of the black vote.

64. Quoting Joe Reed, president of the Alabama Democratic Conference, the largest black political organization in the state, in Bass and DeVries, *Transformation of Southern Politics*, p. 70.

65. Stern, "Southern Congressional Civil Rights Voting," pp. 16, 10, 19. This support did not show up to the same extent in the Senate: See Stern and Baker, "Civil Rights Voting in the United States Senate," pp. 12, 13; Bass and DeVries, *Transformation of Southern Politics*, pp. 370, 378–79; Black, "Racial Composition," p. 679; "JCPS voting study," *Focus* (April 1978), 6:3. The correlation between the size of the black population of a congressional district and responsiveness of whites representatives to black concerns

was not linear. One study of congressional voting behavior during the 1970s finds that southern congressmen tend to vote less conservatively where blacks are most numerous but also where they constitute 16 to 25 percent of the population. See Bullock, "Congressional Voting."

66. Quoted in Kotz, "The Other Side of the New South," p. 18; Bass and DeVries, *Transformation of Southern Politics,* p. 12; Black, *Southern Governors,* pp. 304, 342.

67. Occasionally, they successfully opposed increased sales taxes and right to work laws. Bass and DeVries, *Transformation of Southern Politics,* p. 335; Bobby Hill, Interview (Bass and DeVries), Southern Oral History Collection, University of North Carolina, p. 14.

68. Bass and DeVries, *Transformation of Southern Politics,* p. 45; Morris, *Black Politics,* p. 178.

69. Corry, "A Visit to Lowndes County," p. 35; Kopkind, "Lowndes County, Alabama," pp. 8, 12.

70. Preston, Henderson, and Puryear, eds., *New Black Politics,* p. xix; Morris, *The Politics of Black America,* p. 178; Williams, "Black Voter Participation," pp. 4–5. On the positive side, the Census Bureau reported that while black turnout in the South still trailed behind the national average for whites in 1980, the gap had narrowed. White turnout declined from 70.7 percent in 1964 to 60.9 percent in 1980, and black turnout in the South rose from 44 percent to 48 percent." *St. Petersburg Times,* March 8, 1984, p. 14A.

71. Bullock, "Election of Blacks," p. 735.

72. Salamon, "Protest, Politics, and Modernization," p. 627–28.

73. Campbell, "Electoral Participation," p. 291. Arrington was a councilman at the time of the statement.

74. Button, "Impact," p. 11.

75. Austin Scott, "Sketches, We Shall Overcome, Charleston, Mississippi," June 30, 1971, VEP Office Files; Bass and DeVries, *Transformation of Southern Politics,* p. 400.

76. Bond, "Better Voters, Better Politicians," p. 69; Jones, "Black Officeholders," pp. 64, 70; Salamon, "Leadership and Modernization," pp. 625–28, 633, 640; Marable, "The Post Movement Reaction," p. 24; Kilson, "From Civil Rights to Party Politics," p. 198.

77. Salamon, "Protest, Politics, and Modernization," pp. 696, 711, 714, 716. The movement of blacks from the farm to the cities had been accelerating as a result of mechanization and falling crop prices since the Great Depression and New Deal. See McAdam, *Political Process.*

78. Dent, "New Orleans Versus Atlanta."

79. *City of Mobile v. Bolden,* 446 U.S. 55 (1980).

80. *Bolden v. City of Mobile,* 423 F. Supp. 384 (S.D. Ala. 1976), affirmed in 571 F. 2d 238 (5th Cir. 1978).

81. *Mobile v. Bolden,* 446 U.S. 65 (1980).

82. *Ibid.,* p. 70.

83. *Ibid.,* p. 66.

84. *Ibid.,* pp. 80, 82.

85. *Ibid.,* p. 90.

86. *Ibid.,* p. 92. Stevens also disagreed with the Stewart plurality opinion that the Fifteenth Amendment could be used only to eradicate practices directly affecting access to the ballot rather than devices that inhibited the political strength of minority groups, 85–86.

87. *Ibid.*, pp. 102–3.

88. *Ibid.*, p. 122.

89. *Ibid.*, pp. 134, 137. If a "discriminatory purpose" test had to be applied, Marshall favored the common law "foreseeability presumption." Plaintiffs had to prove that maintenance of multimember districts or at-large elections would have the foreseeable effect of perpetuating the submerged electoral influence of minorities. In that instance, the discriminatory impact would have to be corrected by implementation of a single-member district plan.

90. *Ibid.*, p. 141.

91. McDonald, "Voting Rights on the Chopping Block," p. 94.

92. Kousser, "Undermining of the First Reconstruction," p. 34. The majority of law review articles on the case attacked the *Mobile* ruling for its inconsistency with recent precedents, its confusion in setting standards for future vote dilution cases, and its deleterious effect on black political participation. See Bebout, *"City of Mobile v. Bolden";* Fuller, "Multimember Electoral Systems"; Gorman, *"City of Mobile v. Bolden";* Note, "At-Large Electoral Schemes and Vote Dilution"; Snyder, "Voting Rights"; Wolfson, *"City of Mobile v. Bolden";* Wasserman, "The Voting Rights Act." Also see, Watts, *"City of Mobile v. Bolden."* For a favorable contrasting assessment, consult *Wall Street Journal,* April 25, 1980, p. 18.

93. *City of Rome Georgia v. United States,* 446 U.S. 156, 177 (1980).

94. *Ibid.*, 176.

95. *Ibid.*, 214–15. For a scathing commentary on the majority opinion, see McClellan, "Fiddling with the Constitution." For agreement with Rehnquist see also Leedes, "State Action Limitations." For an analysis critical of both the *Mobile* plurality and the *Rome* majority, see Butler, "Constitutitional and Statutory Challenges."

96. Armand Derfner, "Implications of the *City of Mobile* Case."

10. Preserving the Second Reconstruction

1. Reginald Stuart, *New York Times,* April 14, 1981, p. 1.

2. Robert Pear, *New York Times,* July 2, 1981, p. D1.

3. *Ibid.*

4. Reginald Stuart, "Once Again," p. 105. The vote was 23–1. Hyde wanted a bill that would allow bailout cases to be heard by a three-judge federal panel in the circuit where the jurisdiction was located, but the liberals insisted that the litigation be heard in Washington, D.C. Although the bill permitted counties to escape coverage independently of states, Hyde wanted the states to be able to remove themselves even if some of their counties had a flawed record. Cohodas, "Judiciary Panel," p. 1343.

5. U. S. Commission on Civil Rights, *The Voting Rights Act: Unfulfilled Goals,* (1981), p. 93.

6. Cohodas, "Opposition Fading," p. 1111.

7. Cohodas, "House Passes Bill," p. 1965.

8. Steven V. Roberts, *New York Times,* October 7, 1981, p. B10. In 1970, thirty-four southerners supported renewal, and in 1975, fifty-six joined the majority. Wyche Fowler of Atlanta and twelve of his southern colleagues wrote the president urging him to endorse extension of the act as reported by the House Judiciary Committee. Wyche Fowler to the President, August 3, 1981, letter courtesy of Representative Sam Gibbons. Most southerners, however, lined up behind the final version once they had voted for the weakening amendments offered by Hyde and others.

9. Cohodas, "House Passes Bill," p. 1965. The House rejected amendments: permitting a jurisdiction to bail out if it had signed a consent decree in a voting suit within the previous ten years; allowing jurisdictions to file for removal in federal courts outside of Washington, D.C.; and letting a state bail out if two-thirds of its counties were eligible to do so. The House bill, H.R. 3112, stipulated that beginning in 1984, qualified counties could escape before a covered state did but required proof that during the previous ten years local officials had not employed a discriminatory test or device; that a federal court had not issued a final judgment finding a violation of the voting rights statute; that no consent decrees had been issued concerning suffrage infractions; that the attorney general had not dispatched federal examiners; that covered areas had submitted all changes for preclearance with the Justice Department and had removed all ordinances to which an objection had been lodged; and that local officials had made "constructive efforts" to involve minority groups in the electoral process and to eliminate coercion or intimidation of eligible voters.

10. *New York Times,* June 16, 1981, p. B11. Max L. Friedersdorf, an assistant to the president, wrote Congressman Sam Gibbons of Florida: "As you know, this Administration intends to maintain our Nation's commitment to full equality for all Americans, regardless of race, color, or national origin. Before making a final determination on the extension or revision of the Voting Rights Act, we want to be assured that we have received and evaluated the opinions of concerned parties." Friedersdorf to Gibbons, August 24, 1981, leetter courtesy of Sam Gibbons.

11. Quoted in Isaacson, "Pondering the Voting Rights Act." For a recommendation by a federal judge in Mississippi to extend section 5 nationwide, see Keady and Cochran, "Section 5."

12. Adam Clymer, *New York Times,* July 9, 1981, p. A21. For options under consideration see the *Times,* June 4, 1981, p. B15, November 1, 1981, p. 1, November 7, 1981, p. 1.

13. *St. Petersburg Times,* June 13, 1981, p. 10A.

14. "Senators Try To Protect Voting Rights Options," *Congressional Quarterly Weekly,* October 17, 1981, p. 2028; Robert Pear, *New York Times,* December 17, 1981, p. A22. Howard Baker, Senate majority leader, floated a short-lived trial balloon in suggesting a ten-year extension of the act in its present form, thereby hoping to avoid extended public hearings. Civil rights groups rejected it for not including a "result" test. Robert Pear, *New York Times,* December 3, 1981, p. A18, December 4, 1981, p. A22.

15. Section two of the original statute stipulated: "No voting qualification or prerequisite to voting, or standard, practice or procedure shall be imposed or applied by any State or political subdivision to deny or abridge the right of any citizen of the United States to vote on account of race or color." The House had struck out, "to deny or abridge" and inserted "in a manner which *results* in a denial and abridgement of" [emphasis added].

16. *New York Times,* December 18, 1981, p. B6.

17. William French Smith, "The Voting Rights Act," *New York Times,* March 27, 1982, p. 23. See also, *New York Times,* March 2, 1982, p. A11. In support of Smith, see Konigsberg, "Amending Section 2," and Berns, "Voting Rights and Wrongs."

18. Speech to the Delaware Bar Association, February 22, 1982, reprinted in U.S. House of Representatives, Committee on the Judiciary, *Hearings on Department of Justice Authorization for Fiscal Year 1983,* 97th Cong., 2d sess., 1982, p. 92.

19. "Voting Rights Are Not Quotas," *New York Times,* March 19, 1982, p. A30.

20. Frank R. Parker, "Saving Voting Rights," *New York Times,* February 5, 1982, p. A31, and see issue of February 18, 1982, p. A22 for replies.

21. Cohodas, "Senate Panel Split," p. 921. The brief against the city cited the

statement of state senator Frederick Bromberg in 1909: "We have always, as you know, falsely pretended that our main purpose was to exclude the ignorant vote when, in fact, we were trying to exclude not the ignorant vote, but the Negro vote. . . . By adopting remedial measures now we shall cause no discontent, because of the present apathy of our colored citizens. This is fully recognized by all statesmen." *New York Times,* April 27, 1982, p. A22. Under the auspices of the NAACP, the civil rights attorneys arguing the case, James Blacksher and Larry Menefee, convened a meeting of political scientists, sociologists, lawyers, and historians at the Biltmore Hotel in Atlanta in November 1981. Among those present, J. Morgan Kousser and Peyton McCrary, served as expert witnesses. See McCrary, "Subtle Gerrymander." For an appraisal of the courts' peripatetic attempts to set judicial standards in vote dilution suits and a recommendation for a redefinition of those criteria by the attorneys representing the Mobile black litigants, see Blacksher and Menefee, "From *Reynolds v. Sims.*" See also, Parker, "Impact of *City of Mobile v. Bolden.*"

    22. Cohodas, "Senator Robert Dole," p. 1042.

    23. *Ibid,* p. 1041. The vote to adopt S. 1992 was 14–4. Senators Thurmond, John P. East of North Carolina, Hatch, and Jerimiah P. Denton of Alabama, all Republicans, dissented. The vote to send the measure to the floor was 17–1, with only East opposing it.

    24. *New York Times,* May 4, 1982, p. 1; Mary McGrory, Boston *Sunday Globe,* May 9, 1982, p. A27; see also Steven V. Roberts, *New York Times,* April 28, 1982, p. A25, and Robert Pear, *New York Times,* May 1, 1982, p. 12.

    25. Steven V. Roberts, *New York Times,* June 10, 1982, p. A27.

    26. *Ibid;* Derfner, "Senate Hearings"; Williams, "Perspective," p. 2; *New York Times,* May 31, 1982, p. A9, June 13, 1982, p. 2. Stennis won reelection with black support.

    27. *New York Times,* June 18, 1982, p. D17, June 19, 1982, pp. 1, 11. Voting against passage were Helms, East, Denton, Hayakawa of California, Humphrey of New Hampshire, McClure and Symms of Idaho, and Harry F. Byrd, an Independent from Virginia.

    28. A few days after Reagan signed the bill, the Supreme Court retreated from its own *Mobile* ruling. In *Rogers v. Lodge,* the justices ruled that "circumstantial evidence" could be used to determine whether an electoral system was created for the purpose of racial discrimination. Thus, the court backed away from a strict "intent" test promulgated two years earlier. The case concerned Burke County, Georgia, where blacks constituted about half the population but had never elected a member of their race to serve on the five-person county commission, which was chosen at-large. *New York Times,* July 2, 1982, p. A18. See Cardwell, "Voter Dilution."

    29. *New York Times,* June 30, 1982, p. A16.

    30. *Congressional Record,* 91st Cong., 1st sess., p. 38525.

    31. Stone, *Black Political Power,* p. 242.

    32. Jordan, "End of the Second Reconstruction?" p. 553.

    33. Gillette, *Retreat from Reconstruction,* chapters 1 and 2; Wiebe, "White Attitudes," pp. 157–58.

    34. Rustin, "From Protest to Politics," p. 25.

    35. Quoted in Neary, *Julian Bond,* p. 25.

    36. Testimony of Eddie N. Williams, House of Representatives, Committee on the Judiciary, *Hearings,* "Extension of the Voting Rights Act," 94th Cong., 1st sess., 1975, p. 119.

37. "Black Voter Registration, 1982," p. 8; Joint Center For Political Studies, *National Roster of Black Elected Officials* (1981), 11:16.

38. Tampa *Tribune-Times,* November 27, 1983, p. 5A. In the 1982 congressional elections, a higher percentage of blacks in Louisiana and South Carolina went to the polls than did whites. The black turnout rate also exceeded that of whites in California, Indiana, Kentucky, Missouri, and Tennessee.

39. Scher and Button, "Voting Rights Act," pp. 41, 43.

40. U.S. Commission on Civil Rights, *The Voting Rights Act: Unfulfilled Goals,* p. 17. The data for counties in the seven covered states with 20 percent or more black population show no black officeholders in 46.9 percent of them.

41. Quoting Thomas P. De Cair, chief information officer of the Justice Department, *New York Times,* September 17, 1981, p. B4. Indeed, the Justice Department disapproved of statewide redistricting plans in Georgia, South Carolina, North Carolina, Virginia, and Texas. It also objected to a congressional plan for Mississippi ("An Update on Voting Changes in the South," *Southern Changes,* April 1982, p. 5). Nevertheless, civil rights advocates found reason to complain about the direction in which Justice was heading. In 1982, Frank Parker of the Lawyers' Committee for Civil Rights Under Law charged that departmental "enforcement has been increasingly marked by political interference and significant retreats from strict enforcement of the Act. Rather than taking steps to block political meddling, high Justice Department officials seem to invite it by complying with Congressional requests not to file and amend pleadings and to withdraw Voting Rights Act objections." Parker and Phillips, "Justice Department Voting Rights Act Enforcement."

42. *Birmingham News,* February 22, 1973, clipping, Voter Education Project Office Files.

43. Quoted in Garland, "A Taste of Triumph," p. 27. On the positive relationship between developing black consciousness and increased political participation, see Carlson, "Political Context."

44. U.S. Department of Commerce, Bureau of the Census, *Statistical Abstract of the United States, 1982–83,* p. 432; *New York Times,* June 2, 1981, p. B11, July 5, 1981, p. 1; Sitkoff, *Struggle for Black Equality,* pp. 232–33.

Bibliography

Manuscript Collections

Califano, Joseph A. Files. Lyndon B. Johnson Presidential Library, Austin, Texas.

Cannon, James M. Files. Gerald R. Ford Presidential Library, Ann Arbor, Michigan.

Celler, Emanuel. Papers. Library of Congress, Washington, D.C.

Civil Rights Division. Files. Offices of the Department of Justice, Washington, D.C.

Cook, Marlow. Papers. University of Louisville, Louisville, Kentucky.

Cooper, John Sherman. Papers. University of Kentucky, Lexington, Kentucky.

Cox, Eugene. Papers. Mississippi State University, Starkville, Mississippi.

Delta Ministry. Papers. Mississippi State University, Starkville, Mississippi.

Delta Ministry. Papers. Tougaloo College, Tougaloo, Mississippi.

Democratic National Committee. Papers. Lyndon B. Johnson Presidential Library, Austin, Texas.

Department of Justice. Administrative History. Lyndon B. Johnson Presidential Library, Austin, Texas.

Dirksen, Everett M. Papers. Everett M. Dirksen Congressional Leadership Research Center, Pekin, Illinois.

Ervin, Sam. Papers. Southern Historical Collection, University of North Carolina, Chapel Hill, North Carolina.

Ford, Gerald R. Papers. Gerald R. Ford Presidential Library, Ann Arbor, Michigan.

Goodwin, Richard. Files. Lyndon B. Johnson Presidential Library, Austin, Texas.

Griffin, Charles. Papers. Mississippi State University, Starkville, Mississippi.

Griffin, Robert P. Papers. Central Michigan University, Mt. Pleasant, Michigan.

Hart, Philip A. Papers. Michigan Historical Collection, University of Michigan, Ann Arbor, Michigan.

Henry, Aaron. Papers. Archives of Labor History and Urban Affairs, Wayne State University, Detroit, Michigan.

Hesburgh, Theodore M. Papers. Notre Dame University Law School, South Bend, Indiana.

Hutchinson, Edward. Papers. Michigan Historical Collection, University of Michigan, Ann Arbor, Michigan.

Johnson, Lyndon B. Papers. Lyndon B. Johnson Presidential Library, Austin, Texas.

King, Ed. Papers. Tougaloo College, Tougaloo, Mississippi.

Kornegay, Horace. Papers. Southern Historical Collection, University of North Carolina, Chapel Hill, North Carolina.

Leadership Conference on Civil Rights. Papers. Library of Congress, Washington, D.C.

Lewis, Jan. Loyalist Democrat Papers. Mississippi State University, Starkville, Mississippi.

McCulloch, William. Papers. Northern Ohio University Law School, Ada, Ohio.

McPherson, Harry. Files. Lyndon B. Johnson Presidential Library, Austin, Texas.

Morton, Rogers C. B. Papers. University of Kentucky, Lexington, Kentucky.

Morton, Thruston. Papers. University of Kentucky, Lexington, Kentucky.

National Association for the Advancement of Colored People. Papers. Library of Congress, Washington, D.C.

O'Neal, Maston. Papers. Richard Russell Library, University of Georgia, Athens, Georgia.

Panzer, Fred. Files. Lyndon B. Johnson Presidential Library, Austin, Texas.

Parsons, Richard. Files. Gerald R. Ford Presidential Library, Ann Arbor, Michigan.

Rauh, Joseph. Files. Offices of Joseph Rauh, Washington, D.C.

Russell, Richard. Papers. Richard Russell Library, University of Georgia, Athens, Georgia.

Scott, Hugh. Papers. University of Virginia, Charlottesville, Virginia.

Smith, Howard W. Papers. University of Virginia, Charlottesville, Virginia.

Southern Regional Council. Files. Offices of the Southern Regional Council, Atlanta, Georgia.

Sparks, Will. Files. Lyndon B. Johnson Presidential Library, Austin, Texas.

Stennis, John. Papers. Mississippi State University, Starkville, Mississippi.

Taylor, Hobart. Papers. Michigan Historical Collection, University of Michigan, Ann Arbor, Michigan.

Voter Education Project. Files. Offices of the Voter Education Project, Atlanta, Georgia.

Watson, Marvin. Files. Lyndon B. Johnson Presidential Library, Austin, Texas.

White, Lee. Files. Lyndon B. Johnson Presidential Library, Austin, Texas.

White House Conference on Civil Rights. Records. Lyndon B. Johnson Presidential Library, Austin, Texas.

Wilson, Henry. Files. Lyndon B. Johnson Presidential Library, Austin, Texas.

Young Democratic Club. Papers. Mississippi State University, Starkville, Mississippi.

Public Documents

All of the following, unless otherwise noted, were published at various dates by the Government Printing Office in Washington, D.C.

Public Papers of the Presidents of the United States.
  Jimmy Carter, 1977–1981.
  Gerald R. Ford, 1974–1976.
  Lyndon B. Johnson, 1965–1969.
  Richard M. Nixon, 1969–1974.
  Ronald Reagan, 1981–1982.
U.S. Commission on Civil Rights. *Hearings in Montgomery, Alabama.* 1968.
—— *Law Enforcement: A Report on Equal Protection in the South.* 1965.
—— *Political Participation,* 1968.
—— *The Voting Rights Act: Ten Years After.* 1975.
—— *The Voting Rights Act . . . the first months.* 1965.
—— *The Voting Rights Act: Unfulfilled Goals.* 1981.
U.S. Department of Commerce. *Statistical Abstract of the United States, 1982–1983.* 1982.
U.S. Department of Justice, Attorney General. *Annual Report for the Fiscal Year Ended June 30, 1966.* 1966.
—— *Annual Report for the Fiscal Year Ended June 30, 1967.* 1967.
—— *Annual Report for the Fiscal Year Ended June 30, 1968.* 1968.
—— *Annual Report for the Fiscal Year Ended June 30, 1969.* 1969.
—— *Annual Report for the Fiscal Year Ended June 30, 1970.* 1970.
—— *Annual Report for the Fiscal Year Ended June 30, 1971.* 1971.
—— *Annual Report for the Fiscal Year Ended June 30, 1972.* 1972.
—— *Annual Report for the Fiscal Year Ended June 30, 1973.* 1973.
—— *Annual Report for the Fiscal Year Ended June 30, 1974.* 1974.
—— *Annual Report for the Fiscal Year Ended June 30, 1975.* 1975.
—— *Annual Report for the Fiscal Year Ended June 30, 1976.* 1976.
—— *Annual Report for the Fiscal Year Ended June 30, 1977.* 1977.
—— *Annual Report for the Fiscal Year Ended June 30, 1978.* 1978.
—— *Annual Report for the Fiscal Year Ended June 30, 1979.* 1979.
—— *Annual Report for the Fiscal Year Ended June 30, 1980.* 1980.
—— *Annual Report for the Fiscal Year Ended June 30, 1981.* 1981.
U.S. General Accounting Office, Comptroller General. *Voting Rights Act—Enforcement Needs Strengthening,* 1978.
U.S. House of Representatives. Committee on the Judiciary. Subcommittee No. 5. *Hearings on Civil Rights.* 89th Cong., 2d sess., 1966.
—— Committee on the Judiciary. Subcommittee No. 5. *Hearings on Voting Rights Act Extension.* 91st Cong., 1st sess., 1969.
—— Committee on the Judiciary. The Civil Rights Oversight Subcommittee. *Hearings on the Enforcement and Administration of the Voting Rights Act of 1965, As Amended.* 92d Cong., 1st sess., 1971.
—— Committee on the Judiciary. Subcommittee on Civil and Constitutional Rights. *Hearings on Extension of the Voting Rights Act.* 94th Cong., 1st sess., 1975.
—— Committee on the Judiciary. Subcommittee on Civil and Constitutional

Rights. *Hearings on the GAO Report on the Voting Rights Act.* 95th Cong., 2d sess., 1978.

—— Committee on the Judiciary. *Hearings, Department of Justice Authorization for Fiscal Year 1983.* 97th Cong., 2d sess., 1982.

—— Committee on the Judiciary. *Report 397.* 91st Cong., 1st sess., 1969.

—— Committee on the Judiciary. Civil Rights Oversight Subcommittee. *Report: Enforcement of the Voting Rights Act of 1965 in Mississippi.* 92d Cong., 2d sess., 1972.

—— Committee on the Judiciary. *Report 94-196.* 94th Cong., 1st sess., 1975.

—— Committee on Rules. *Hearings to Extend the Voting Rights Act of 1965 with Respect to the Discriminatory Use of Tests and Devices.* 91st Cong., 1st sess., 1969.

U.S. Senate. Committee on Finance. *Hearings on Tax Reform Act of 1969.* 91st Cong., 1st sess., Part 6, 1969.

—— Committee on the Judiciary. Subcommittee on Constitutional Rights. *Hearings on Civil Rights.* 89th Cong., 2d sess., 1966.

—— Committee on the Judiciary. Subcommittee on Constitutional Rights. *Hearings on Civil Rights Act of 1967.* 90th Cong., 1st sess., 1967.

—— Committee on the Judiciary. Subcommittee on Constitutional Rights. *Hearings on Bills to Amend the Voting Rights Act of 1965.* 91st Cong., 1st and 2d sess., 1969, 1970.

—— Committee on the Judiciary. Subcommittee on Constitutional Rights. *Hearings on Extension of the Voting Rights Act of 1965.* 94th Cong., 1st sess., 1975.

—— Committee on the Judiciary. *Report 94-295.* 94th Cong., 1st sess., 1975.

Court Cases

Allen v. State Board of Elections, 393 U.S. 544 (1969).

Beer v. United States, 425 U.S. 130 (1976).

Bolden v. City of Mobile, 423 F. Supp. 384 (S.D. Ala. 1976), affirmed in 571 F.2d 238 (5th Cir. 1978).

Burns v. Richardson, 384 U.S. 73 (1966).

City of Mobile v. Bolden, 446 U.S. 55 (1980).

City of Petersburg v. United States, 410 U.S. 962 (1973).

City of Richmond v. United States, 422 U.S. 358 (1975).

City of Rome v. United States, 446 U.S. 156 (1980).

Connor v. Finch, 431 U.S. 407 (1977).

Connor v. Johnson, 402 U.S. 690 (1971).

Connor v. Waller, 421 U.S. 656 (1975).

Dougherty County Board of Education v. White, 439 U.S. 32 (1979).

East Carroll Parish School Board v. Marshall, 424 U.S. 636 (1976).

Evers v. State Board of Election Commissioners, 327 F. Supp. 640 (S.D. Miss. 1971).

Fortson v. Dorsey, 379 U.S. 433 (1965).
Gaston County v. United States, 411 U.S. 525 (1973).
Georgia v. United States, 411 U.S. 527 (1973).
Hadnott v. Amos, 394 U.S. 358 (1969).
Morris v. Gressette, 432 U.S. 491 (1977).
Nevitt v. Sides, 571 F. 2d 209 (5th Cir. 1978).
Oregon v. Mitchell, 400 U.S. 112 (1970).
Perkins v. Matthews, 400 U.S. 388 (1971).
South Carolina v. Katzenbach, 383 U.S. 301 (1966).
Taylor v. McKeithen, 407 U.S. 194 (1972).
United States v. Board of Commissioners of Sheffield, Alabama, 435 U.S. 110 (1978).
United States v. Board of Supervisors of Warren County, 429 U.S. 642 (1977).
United States v. Guest, 383 U.S. 745 (1966).
United States v. Price, 383 U.S. 787 (1966).
Village of Arlington Heights v. Metropolitan Housing Authority, 429 U.S. 250 (1977).
Virginia v. United States, 420 U.S. 901 (1975).
Washington v. Davis, 426 U.S. 229 (1976).
Wesberry v. Sanders, 376 U.S. 1 (1966).
Whitcomb v. Chavis, 403 U.S. 124 (1971).
White v. Register, 412 U.S. 755 (1973).
Wise v. Lipscomb, 437 U.S. 535 (1978).
Zimmer v. McKeithen, 485 F.2d 1297 (5th Cir. 1973).

Books, Articles, and Other Secondary Materials

Abney, F. Glenn. "Factors Related to Negro Turnout in Mississippi." *Journal of Politics* (November 1974), 37:1057–63.
"Alabama: A Black Day in Eutaw." *Newsweek* (August 11, 1969), 74:24–25.
Ball, Howard, Dale Krane, and Thomas P. Lauth. *Compromised Compliance: Implementation of the 1965 Voting Rights Act*. Westport, Connecticut: Greenwood Press, 1982.
—— "Judicial Impact on the Enforcement of Voting Rights Policy by Attorneys in the Department of Justice." Paper, Southern Political Science Association, 1977.
Bartley, Numan V. and Hugh D. Graham. *Southern Politics and the Second Reconstruction*. Baltimore: Johns Hopkins University Press, 1975.
Bass, Jack. *Unlikely Heroes*. New York: Simon & Schuster, 1981.
Bass, Jack and Walter DeVries. *The Transformation of Southern Politics: Social Change and Political Consequence Since 1945*. New York: Basic Books, 1976.
Bebout, Cawood K. "*City of Mobile v. Bolden:* The Uncertain Future of Racial Vote Dilution." *Saint Louis University Law Journal* (1981), 25:657–88.
Bell, Griffin with Gilbert Ostrow. *Taking Care of the Law*. New York: Morrow, 1982.

Bell, Robert L. "Constitutional Law—Change to At-Large Election System Which Has the Inevitable Effect of Denying or Abridging the Right of Blacks to Vote Violates the Fifteenth Amendment of the United States Constitution—*Paige v. Gray,*" *Howard Law Journal* (Spring 1976), 19:177–89.

Berns, Walter. "Voting Rights and Wrongs." *Commentary* (March 1982), 73:31–36.

Berry, Barbara L. and Thomas R. Dye. "The Discriminatory Effects of At-Large Elections." *Florida State University Law Review* (1979), 7:85–122.

Berry, Jason. *Amazing Grace: With Charles Evers in Mississippi.* New York: Saturday Review Press, 1973.

—— "Mississippi Post Mortem: Evers' Race For Governor." *New South* (Summer 1973), 28:2–17.

Berry, Mary F. *Black Resistance, White Law.* New York: Appleton-Century-Crofts, 1971.

Bickel, Alexander M. "The Belated Civil Rights Legislation of 1968." *New Republic* (March 30, 1968), 158:11–12.

—— "Civil Rights' Dim Prospects." *New Republic* (September 17, 1966), 155:17–18.

Binion, Gayle. "The Implementation of Section 5 of the 1965 Voting Rights Act." *Western Political Quarterly* (June 1979), 32:154–73.

Birenbaum, Jonathan. "Discriminatory Effect of Elections At-Large: The 'Totality of Effect Circumstances Doctrine.' " *Albany Law Review* (1977), 4:363–87.

Black, Earl. *Southern Governors and Civil Rights: Racial Segregation as a Campaign Issue in the Second Reconstruction.* Cambridge: Harvard University Press, 1976.

Black, Earl and Merle Black. "The Changing Setting of Minority Politics in the American Deep South." *Politics 73,* pp. 35–50.

Black, Merle. "Racial Composition of Congressional Districts and Support for Federal Voting Rights in the American South." *Social Science Quarterly* (December 1978), 59:435–50.

—— "Regional and Partisan Bases of Congressional Support for the Changing Agenda of Civil Rights Legislation." *Journal of Politics* (1979), 41:665–79.

"Black Power at the Dixie Polls." *Time* (June 15, 1970), 95:17.

Blacksher, James U. and Larry T. Menefee. "From *Reynolds v. Sims* to *City of Mobile v. Bolden:* Have the White Suburbs Commandeered the Fifteenth Amendment?" *Hastings Law Journal* (September 1982), 34:1–64.

"Black Voter Registration, 1982." *Focus* (June 1983), 11:8.

Bonapfel, Paul W. "Minority Challenges to At-Large Elections: The Dilution Problem." *Georgia Law Review* (1976), 10:353–90.

Bond, Julian. "Better Voters, Better Politicians." *Southern Exposure* (Spring 1979), 7:70–78.

—— *Black Candidates: Southern Campaign Experiences.* Atlanta: Voter Education Project, 1978.

Booker, Simeon. "Black Politics at the Crossroads." *Ebony* (October 1968), 23:31–42.

Boykin, Milton Lee. "Black Political Participation in Greene County, Alabama: An Information-Efficacious Hypothesis." *Politics 73*, pp. 51–64.

Brauer, Carl. *John F. Kennedy and the Second Reconstruction*. New York: Columbia University Press, 1977.

Bullock, Charles S., III. "Congressional Voting and the Mobilization of a Black Electorate in the South." *Journal of Politics* (1981), 43:662–82.

—— "The Election of Blacks in the South: Preconditions and Consequences." *American Journal of Political Science* (November 1975), 19:727–39.

Bullock, Charles, S., III, and Charles M. Lamb, eds. *Implementation of Civil Rights Policy*. Monterey, California: Brooks/Cole, 1984.

Butler, Katharine I. "Constitutional and Statutory Challenges to Election Structures: Dilution and the Value of the Right to Vote." *Louisiana Law Review* (Spring 1982), 42:851–947.

Button, James W. *Black Violence: Political Impact of the 1960s Riots*. Princeton: Princeton University Press, 1978.

—— "Impact of Black Elected Municipal Officials: A Descriptive Analysis." Paper, Southern Political Science Association, 1978.

Button, James W. and Richard K. Scher. "Impact of the Civil Rights Movement: Elite Perceptions of Black Municipal Service Changes." Paper in possession of the author, 1978.

Califano, Joseph A., Jr. *Governing America: An Insider's Report from the White House and the Cabinet*. New York: Simon & Schuster, 1981.

Campbell, David. "The Lowndes County Freedom Organization: An Appraisal." *New South* (Winter 1972), 37:37–42.

—— "The Lowndes County (Alabama) Freedom Organization: The First Black Panther Party, 1965–1968." Masters thesis, Florida State University, 1970.

Campbell, David and Joe R. Feagin. "Black Politics in the South: A Descriptive Analysis." *Journal of Politics* (February 1975), 37:129–62.

Campbell, James David. "Electoral Participation and the Quest For Equality: Black Politics in Alabama Since the Voting Rights Act of 1965." Doctoral dissertation, University of Texas, 1976.

Canzoneri, Robert. "Charles Evers: Mississippi's Registration Man." *Harper's* (July 1968), 237:67–74.

Cardwell, David. "Voter Dilution and the Standard of Proof." *Urban Lawyer* (Fall 1982), 14:863–67.

Carlson, James M. "Political Context and Black Participation in the South." In Robert P. Steed, Laurence W. Moreland, and Tod A. Baker, eds., *Party Politics in the South*, pp. 180-96. New York: Praeger, 1980.

Carmichael, Stokely and Charles V. Hamilton. *Black Power: The Politics of Black Liberation in America*. New York: Vintage Books, 1967.

Carpeneti, Walter L. "Legislative Apportionment: Multi Member Districts and Fair Representation." *University of Pennsylvania Law Review* (April 1972), 120:666–700.

Carr, Davis D. "Vote Dilution Challenges After *Washington v. Davis.*" *Alabama Law Review* (Winter 1979), 30:396–418.

Carson, Claiborne. *In Struggle: SNCC and the Black Awakening of the 1960s.* Cambridge: Harvard University Press, 1981.

Cavanaugh, Thomas. "Black Gains Offset Losses in '82 Elections." *Focus* (November-December 1982), 10:3–4, 8.

Chafe, William H. *Civilities and Civil Rights: Greensboro, North Carolina, and the Black Struggle for Freedom.* New York: Oxford University Press, 1980.

Chatfield, Jack. "Port Gibson Mississippi: A People of the Future." *New South* (Summer 1969), 24:45–55.

Chubbick, James, Edwin Rennick, and Joe E. Walker. "The Emergence of Coalition Politics in New Orleans." *New South* (Winter 1971), 26:16–25.

Clark, Kenneth B. "The Negro Elected Official in the Changing American Scene." In Lenneal J. Henderson, ed., *Black Political Life in the United States,* pp. 150–60. San Francisco: Chandler, 1972.

—— "The Present Dilemma." *New South* (Fall 1969), 24:74–80.

Cohodas, Nadine. "House Passes Bill To Extend Voting Rights Act." *Congressional Quarterly Weekly* (October 10, 1981), pp. 1965–66.

—— "Judiciary Panel Approves Voting Rights Bill." *Congressional Quarterly Weekly* (July 25, 1981), p. 1343.

—— "Opposition Fading to Voting Act Renewal." *Congressional Quarterly Weekly* (June 20, 1981), p. 1111.

—— "Senate Panel Split Over Voting Rights Bill." *Congressional Quarterly Weekly* (April 24, 1982), p. 921.

—— "Senator Robert Dole: The Man in the Middle." *Congressional Quarterly Weekly* (May 8, 1982), pp. 1042–43.

Colburn, Kenneth S. *Southern Black Mayors: Local Problems and Federal Responses.* Washington, D.C.: Joint Center for Political Studies, 1974.

Comment. "Voting Rights: A Case Study of Madison Parish, Louisiana." *University of Chicago Law Review* (Summer 1971), 38:726–87.

Conyers, James E. and Walter L. Wallace. *Black Elected Officials.* New York: Russell Sage Foundation, 1976.

Conyers, John, Jr. "Politics and the Black Revolution." *Ebony* (April 1969), 24:164–66.

Cook, Samuel DuBois. "Democracy and Tyranny in America: The Radical Paradox of the Bicentennial and Blacks in the American Political System." *Journal of Politics* (August 1976), 38:276–94.

—— "The Tragic Myth of Black Power." *New South* (Summer 1966), 21:58–64.

Corry, John. "A Visit to Lowndes County, Alabama." *New South* (Winter 1972), 27:28–36.

Costello, Mary. "Minority Voting Rights." *Editorial Research Reports* (February 28, 1975), 1:143–59.

Cotrell, Charles L. "The Effect(s) of At-Large Elections on the Political Access and Voting Strength of Mexican Americans and Blacks in Texas." Reprinted in U. S. House of Representatives, Committee on the Judiciary, Subcommittee on Civil and Constitutional Rights, *Hearings on Extension of the Voting Rights Act,* 94th Cong., 1st sess., 1975, pp. 408–79.

Cromwell, Oliver W. "Black Impact on the 1976 Elections." *Focus* (November 1976), 4:4–5.

Crotty, William J. *Decision for the Democrats: Reforming the Party Structure.* Baltimore: Johns Hopkins University Press, 1979.

Culbert, David. "Johnson and the Media." In Robert A. Divine, ed., *Exploring the Johnson Years,* pp. 214–48. Austin: University of Texas Press, 1981.

Cumming, Joseph B. "Greene County, Alabama: The Hope of the Future." *Southern Voices* (March–April 1974), 1:22–30.

Current, Gloster B. "Death in Mississippi." *Crisis* (February 1966), 73:103–9.

Daniel, Johnnie. "Negro Political Behavior and Community Political and Socioeconomic Structural Factors." *Social Forces* (March 1969), 47:274–80.

Dauer, Manning J. "Multi Member Districts in Dade County: Study of a Problem of a Delegation." *Journal of Politics* (1966), 28:617–38.

—— Multi Member Districts vs. Single Member Districts in the Florida Legislature: An Analysis." University of Florida, Civic Information Series, No. 60, 1977.

Davidson, Chandler and George Korbel. "At-Large Elections and Minority-Group Representation: A Re-Examination of Historical and Contemporary Evidence." *Journal of Politics* (November 1981), 43:982–1005.

Dean, John. *The Making of a Black Mayor: A Study of Campaign Organization, Strategies, and Techniques in Prichard, Alabama.* Washington, D.C.: Joint Center for Political Studies, 1973.

Dean, Kenneth. "Observations on the Loyalists." *New South* (Summer 1968), 23:55–56.

DeMuth, Jerry. "Powerless Politics: Blacks and Voting Rights." *America* (September 27, 1975), 133:170.

Dent, Harry S. *The Prodigal South Returns to Power.* New York: Wiley, 1978.

Dent, Tom. "New Orleans Versus Atlanta." *Southern Exposure* (Spring 1979), 7:64–68.

Derfner, Armand. "The Implications of the *City of Mobile* Case for Extension of the Voting Rights Act." In *The Right To Vote: A Rockefeller Foundation Conference, April 22–23, 1981,* pp. 194–216. New York: The Rockefeller Foundation, 1981.

—— "Multi-Member Districts and Black Voters." *Black Law Journal* (1972), 2:120–28.

—— "Racial Discrimination and the Right to Vote." *Vanderbilt Law Review* (April 1973), 26:523–84.

—— "Senate Hearings on Voting Rights Act," *Focus* (January 1982), 10:6–7.

Derfner, Armand and Joe Taylor. "Court Cases Knock Down At-Large Voting Barrier." *Focus* (July 1973), 1:3.

Detwiler, Bruce. "A Time To Be Black." *New Republic* (September 17, 1966), 155:19–22.

Divine, Robert A., ed. *Exploring the Johnson Years*. Austin: University of Texas Press, 1981.

Doar, John. "Civil Rights and Self-Government." In Dona Baron, ed., *The National Purpose Reconsidered*, pp. 97–118. New York: Columbia University Press, 1978.

Downes, Bryan T. "A Critical Reexamination of the Social and Political Characteristics of Riot Cities." *Social Science Quarterly* (September 1970), 51:349–60.

Dunbar, Leslie. "Public Policymaking and the Art of Peacemaking." *New South* (Winter 1966), 21:2–10.

Edsall, Preston W. and J. Oliver Williams. "North Carolina: Bipartisan Paradox." In William C. Havard, ed., *The Changing Politics in the South*, pp. 366–423. Baton Rouge: Louisiana State University Press, 1972.

Eggler, Bruce W. "Blacks in Politics: A Long Way to Go in Mississippi." *New Republic* (June 28, 1969), 160:19–21.

Eichel, Henry. "What Happens When Blacks Gain Strength." *Focus* (September 1975), 3:3.

Eisenstat, Stuart E. and William H. Barutio. *Andrew Young: The Path to History*. Atlanta: Voter Education Project, 1973.

Emmons, David. "Black Politics in the South—Holmes County, Mississippi: Robert Clark and the Politics of Intimacy." Paper prepared for the Voter Education Project, 1968.

Engstrom, Richard L. "Racial Vote Dilution: Supreme Court Interpretations of Section 5 of the Voting Rights Act." *Southern University Law Review* (Spring 1978), 4:139–64.

Engstrom, Richard L. and Michael D. McDonald. "The Election of Blacks to City Councils: Clarifying the Impact of Electoral Arrangements on the Seats/Population Relationship." *American Political Science Review* (June 1981), 75:344–54.

Evans, Rowland, Jr., and Robert D. Novak. *Nixon in the White House: The Frustration of Power*. New York: Vintage Books, 1972.

Evers, Charles. *Evers*. New York: World, 1971.

—— "Interview." *Playboy* (October 1971), 18:77–90, 168–91.

Fager, Charles E. *White Reflections on Black Power*. Grand Rapids, Michigan: Erdmans, 1967.

Feagin, Joe R. and Harlan Hahn. "The Second Reconstruction: Black Political Strength in the South." *Social Science Quarterly* (June 1970), 51:42–56.

Fink, Gary M. *Prelude to the Presidency: The Political Character and Legislative Leadership Style of Governor Jimmy Carter*. Westport, Connecticut: Greenwood Press, 1980.

Fiss, Owen M. "*Gaston County v. United States:* Fruition of the Freezing Principle." *Supreme Court Review* (1969), pp. 379–445.

Ford, Gerald R. *A Time to Heal*. New York: Harper & Row and The Readers' Digest Association, 1979.

Forman, James. *The Making of Black Revolutionaries*. New York: Macmillan, 1972.

—— *Sammy Younge, Jr*. New York: Grove, 1968.

Fortenberry, Charles N. and F. Glenn Abney. "Mississippi Unreconstructed and Unredeemed." In William C. Havard, ed., *The Changing Politics of the South*, pp. 472–524. Baton Rouge: Louisiana State University Press, 1972.

Foster, Frank. "Constitutional Bases for Upholding the Voting Rights Act Amendments of 1970." *De Paul Law Review* (Summer 1971), 28:1002–28.

Frederickson, George M. *White Supremacy: A Comparative Study in American and South African History*. New York: Oxford University Press, 1981.

Freedom Summer Revisited. "Politics and the Civil Rights Movement." Transcript, November 2, 1979, Millsaps College.

Frye, Hardy T. *Black Parties and Political Power: A Case Study*. Boston: G.K. Hall, 1980.

Fuertsch, David Francis. "Lyndon B. Johnson and Civil Rights: The Rhetorical Development of a Political Realist." Doctoral dissertation, University of Texas, 1974.

Fuller, Jamie L. "Multimember Electoral Systems and the Discriminatory Purpose Standard: *City of Mobile v. Bolden*." *Texas Tech Law Review* (1981), 12:743–63.

Fulwood, Charles. "Blacks for Wallace." *Ramparts* (November 1974), 13:13–14.

Garland, Phil A. "A Taste of Triumph for Black Mississippi." *Ebony* (February 1968), 23:25–32.

Garrow, David J. *The FBI and Martin Luther King, Jr*. New York: Norton, 1981.

—— *Protest At Selma: Martin Luther King, Jr., and the Voting Rights Act of 1965*. New Haven: Yale University Press, 1978.

Gelfand, Mark I., "The 18-Year-Old Vote and the Decline of the Youth Movement." Paper, American Historical Association, 1981.

Gettleman, Marvin E. and David Mermelstein, eds. *The Great Society Reader: The Failure of American Liberalism*. New York: Random House, 1967.

Gillette, William. *Retreat from Reconstruction 1869–1879*. Baton Rouge: Louisiana State University Press, 1979.

Glad, Betty. *Jimmy Carter: In Search of the Great White House*. New York: Norton, 1980.

Glick, David S. "Black Power Enclave," *New Republic* (January 16, 1971), 164:11–12.

Goldman, Eric. *The Tragedy of Lyndon Johnson*. New York: Dell, 1969.

Goldstein, Michael. "Black Representation in State Legislatures." *Focus* (February 1979), 7:3, 6.

Good, Paul. "Beyond the Voting Rights Act." *Reporter* (October 7, 1965), 33:25–29.

—— "The Meredith March." *New South* (Summer 1966), 21:2–16.

—— "A White Looks at Black Power." *Nation* (August 8, 1966), 203:112–17.

Gorman, Terry. "*City of Mobile v. Bolden*: Voter Dilution and New Intent Requirements Under the Fifteenth and Fourteenth Amendments." *Houston Law Review* (March 1981), 18:611–27.

Goulder, Gerald P. "The Reconstructed Right to Vote: Neutral Principle and Minority Representation." *Capital University Law Review* (1979), 9:31–96.

Graham, Hugh Davis. "The Storm Over Black Power." *Virginia Quarterly Review* (Autumn 1967), 43:545–65.

Guillory, Ferrel. "Emerging Black Politics." *America* (September 9, 1972), 127:147–49.

Haines, Aubrey. "The Evers Administration: Two Years of Progress in Fayette." *Christian Century* (July 28, 1971), 88:908–11.

Halberstam, David. "The Second Coming of Martin Luther King." *Harper's* (August 1967), 235:39–51.

Halpin, Stanley A. and Richard L. Engstrom. "Racial Gerrymandering and Southern State Legislative Redistricting: Attorney General Determinations Under the Voting Rights Act." *Journal of Public Law* (1973), 22:37–66.

Hamilton, Charles V. "Blacks and the Crisis in Political Participation." *Public Interest* (Winter 1974), 34:188–210.

—— "Response." In *The Right to Vote: A Rockefeller Foundation Conference, April 22–23, 1981,* pp. 189–93. New York: The Rockefeller Foundation, 1981.

Hammond, John L. "Race and Electoral Mobilization: White Southerners, 1952–1968." *Public Opinion Quarterly* (Spring 1977), 41:13–27.

Harris, Richard. *Justice: The Crisis of Law, Order, and Freedom in America.* New York: Dutton, 1970.

Harris, Ron. "Richmond: Former Confederate Capital Finally Falls to Blacks." *Ebony* (June 1980), 35:44–52.

Harvey, James C. *Black Civil Rights During the Johnson Administration.* Jackson: University and College Press of Mississippi, 1973.

Hassan, Kirke M. "*MacGuire v. Amos:* Application of Section 5 of the Voting Rights Act to Political Parties." *Harvard Civil Rights-Civil Liberties Review* (January 1973), 8:199–210.

Havard, William C., ed. *The Changing Politics of the South.* Baton Rouge: Louisiana State University Press, 1972.

Henderson, Lenneal J., Jr., ed. *Black Political Life in the United States.* San Francisco: Chandler, 1972.

Herbers, John. *The Lost Priority: Whatever Happened to the Civil Rights Movement in the United States?* New York: Funk & Wagnalls, 1970.

Hester, Kathryn Healy. "Mississippi and the Voting Rights Act: 1965–1982." *Mississippi Law Journal* (December 1982), 52:803–76.

Hilton, Bruce. *The Delta Ministry.* London: Macmillan, 1969.

Hinson, William J., Jr. "The Voter Education Project and Minority Political Participation in the South." Paper prepared for the Voter Education Project.

Holloway, Harry. *The Politics of the Southern Negro: From Exclusion to Big City Organization.* New York: Random House, 1969.

Horwitz, Morton J. "The Jurisprudence of *Brown* and the Dilemmas of Liberalism." In Michael V. Namorato, ed., *Have We Overcome? Race Relations Since Brown*, pp. 173–87. Jackson: University Press of Mississippi, 1979.

Howard, Perry H. "Louisiana: Resistance and Change." In William C. Havard, ed., *Changing Politics in the South*, pp. 525–87. Baton Rouge: Louisiana State University Press, 1972.

Hull, John David, IV. "Challenges to At-Large Election Plans: Modern Local Governments on Trial." *University of Cincinnati Law Review* (1978), 47:64–77.

Hunter, David H. "The Administrators' Dilemmas in the Enforcement of Section 5 of the Voting Rights Act of 1965." Paper, National Conference of the American Society for Public Administration, 1978.

Irwin, Ann S. "At-Large Voting Dilution Claims: The Fifth Circuit Requires Racially Motivated Discrimination." *Cumberland Law Review* (Fall 1978), 9:443–55.

Isaacson, Walter. "Pondering the Voting Rights Act." *Time* (May 11, 1981), p. 24.

"Is Meredith Right?" *Nation* (June 27, 1966), 202:765.

Jackson, Emory O. "How Much Black Support for Wallace?" *Focus* (June 1974), 2:3.

Jacoway, Elizabeth and David Colburn, eds. *Southern Businessmen and Desegregation*. Baton Rouge: Louisiana State University Press, 1982.

Jaffe, Andrew. "Grenada, Mississippi: Perspective on the Backlash." *New South* (Fall 1966), 21:15–27.

Jenkins, Ray. "Majority Rule in the Black Belt: Greene County, Alabama." *New South* (Fall 1969), 24:60–67.

Johnson, Lyndon B. *The Vantage Point: Perspectives of the Presidency, 1963–1969*. New York: Holt, Rinehart & Winston, 1971.

Joint Center for Political Studies. *Guide to Black Politics 1976, Parts I (Democratic National Convention) and II (Republican National Convention)*. Washington, D.C.: Joint Center for Political Studies, 1976.

—— *National Roster of Black Elected Officials*. 12 volumes. Washington, D.C.: Joint Center for Political Studies, 1970–1982.

Jones, Mack H. "Black Officeholders in Local Governments of the South: An Overview." *Politics 71*, pp. 49–72.

—— "The 1965 Voting Rights Act and Political Symbolism: A Research Note." Paper, Southern Political Science Association, 1979.

Jordan, Barbara and Shelby Hearon. *Barbara Jordan: A Self Portrait*. Garden City, New York: Doubleday, 1979.

Jordan, Vernon E., Jr. "The Black Vote in Danger." *Civil Rights Digest* (Spring 1969), 2:1–7.

—— "The Challenge and the Promise." *New South* (Summer 1966), 21:81–84.

—— "End of the Second Reconstruction?" *Vital Speeches* (July 1, 1972), 38:552–55.

—— "New Forces of Urban Political Power." *New South* (Spring 1968), 23:46–51.

—— "New Game in Dixie." *Nation* (October 21, 1968), 207:397–99.

—— "The Second Reconstruction Period." *Vital Speeches* (September 15, 1972), 38:725–28.

Joubert, Paul E. and Ben M. Crouch. "Mississippi Blacks and the Voting Rights Act of 1965." *Journal of Negro Education* (Spring 1977), 46:157–67.

"Judge Branch of Greene County." *Ebony* (August 1971), 26:82–85.

Keady, William C. and George C. Cochran. "Section 5 of the Voting Rights Act: A Time for Revision." *Kentucky Law Journal* (1980–81), 69:741–97.

Kernell, Sam. "Comment: A Re-evaluation of Black Voting in Mississippi." *American Political Science Review* (December 1973), 67:1307–18.

Kilson, Martin. "From Civil Rights to Party Politics: The Black Political Transition." *Current History* (November 1974), 67:193–99.

Kimball, Penn. *The Disconnected.* New York: Columbia University Press, 1972.

King, Martin Luther, Jr. "Martin Luther King Defines 'Black Power.' " *New York Times Magazine* (June 11, 1967), pp. 26–27.

—— *Where Do We Go From Here: Community or Chaos?* New York: Harper & Row, 1967.

Konigsberg, Charles S. "Amending Section 2 of the Voting Rights Act of 1965." *Case Western Reserve Law Review* (1982), 32:500–58.

Kopkind, Andrew. "The Lair of the Black Panther." *New Republic* (August 13, 1966), 155:10–13.

—— "Lowndes County, Alabama: The Great Fear Is Gone." *Ramparts* (April 1975), 13:8–12, 53–55.

—— "No Fire This Time." *New Republic* (June 18, 1966), 154:15–16.

Kotz, Nick. "The Other Side of the New South," Parts I and II. *New Republic* (March 25, 1978), 178:16–19; (April 1, 1978), 178:18–23.

Kousser, Morgan J. "The Undermining of the First Reconstruction: Lessons for the Second." *Humanities Working Paper 64* (June 1981), California Institute of Technology.

Lader, Lawrence. *Power on the Left: American Radical Movements Since 1946.* New York: Norton, 1979.

Ladner, Joyce. "What Black Power Means to Negroes in Mississippi." In August Meier ed., *The Transformation of Activism,* pp. 131–54. Chicago: Aldine, 1970.

Latimer, Margaret K. "Black Political Representation in Southern Cities: Election Systems and Other Causal Variables." *Urban Affairs Quarterly* (September 1979), 15:65–86.

Lawson, Steven F. *Black Ballots: Voting Rights in the South, 1944–1969.* New York: Columbia University Press, 1976.

Lawyers' Committee For Civil Rights Under Law. *Voting in Mississippi: A Right Still Denied.* Washington, D.C.: Lawyers' Committee for Civil Rights Under Law, 1981.

Leedes, Gary C. "State Action Limitations on Courts and Congressional Power." *North Carolina Law Review* (April 1982), 60:747–97.

Leuchtenburg, William E. "The White House and Black America: From Eisenhower to Carter." In Michael V. Namorato, ed., *Have We Overcome? Race Relations Since Brown,* pp. 121–45. Jackson: University Press of Mississippi, 1979.

Levesque, Russell J. "White Response to Nonwhite Voter Registration in the Southern States." *Pacific Sociological Review* (April 1972), 15:245–55.

Lewis, David L. *King: A Critical Biography.* New York: Praeger, 1970.

Lewis, John and Archie Allen. "Black Voter Registration in the South." *Notre Dame Lawyer* (October 1972), 48:105–32.

McAdam, Doug. *Political Process and the Development of Black Insurgency 1930–1970.* Chicago: University of Chicago Press, 1982.

McCarty, L. Thorne and Russell B. Stevenson. "The Voting Rights Act of 1965: An Evaluation." *Harvard Civil Rights-Civil Liberties Review* (Spring 1968), 3:357–411.

McClellan, James. "Fiddling with the Constitution While *Rome* Burns: The Case Against the Voting Rights Act of 1965." *Louisiana Law Review* (Fall 1981), 42:5–77.

MacCoon, John P. "The Enforcement of the Preclearance Requirement of Section 5 of the Voting Rights Act of 1965." *Catholic University Law Review* (Fall 1979), 29:107–27.

McCrary, Peyton. "The Subtle Gerrymander: Discriminatory Purposes of At-Large Elections in the South, 1865–1982." Paper, Organization of American Historians, 1983.

McDonald, Laughlin. *Voting Rights in the South: Ten Years of Litigation Challenging Continuing Discrimination Against Minorities.* New York and Atlanta: American Civil Liberties Union, 1983.

—— "Voting Rights on the Chopping Block." *Southern Exposure* (Spring 1981), 9:89–94.

McGovern, George S. *Grassroots: The Autobiography of George McGovern.* New York: Random House, 1977.

McLemore, Leslie Burl. "The Mississippi Freedom Democratic Party: A Case Study of Grass-Roots Politics." Doctoral dissertation, University of Massachusetts, 1971.

—— "Response." In *The Right To Vote: A Rockefeller Foundation Conference, April 22–23, 1981,* pp. 33–44. New York: The Rockefeller Foundation, 1981.

MacManus, Susan. "City Council Election Procedures and Minority Representation: Are They Related?" *Social Science Quarterly* (June 1978), 59:153–61.

McMillen, Neil R. "Black Enfranchisement in Mississippi: Federal Enforcement and Black Protest in the 1960s." *Journal of Southern History* (August 1977), 21:1–18.

McPherson, Harry. *A Political Education.* Boston: Little, Brown, 1972.

Marable, Manning. "The Post Movement Reaction." *Southern Exposure* (Spring 1979), 7:60–64.

—— "Tuskegee Alabama: The Politics of Illusion in the New South." *Black Scholar* (May 1977), 8:13–24.

Marshall, Burke. *Federalism and Civil Rights.* New York: Columbia University Press, 1964.

Meier, August. "The Dilemmas of Negro Protest Strategy." *New South* (Spring 1966), 21:1–18.

Meier, August and Elliott Rudwick. *Along the Color Line.* Urbana: University of Illinois Press, 1976.

—— *CORE: A Study of the Civil Rights Movement, 1942–1968.* New York: Oxford University Press, 1973.

"The Meredith Ambush." *Nation* (June 20, 1966), 202:731–32.

Meredith, James H. "Big Changes Are Coming." *Saturday Evening Post* (August 13, 1966), 239:23–27.

Millspaugh, Frank. "Black Power." *Commonweal* (August 5, 1966), 84:500–3.

Miroff, Bruce. "Presidential Leverage over Social Movements: The Johson White House and Civil Rights." *Journal of Politics* (February 1981), 43:2–23.

"Mississippi and the NAACP." *Crisis* (June-July 1966), 73:315–18.

Mitchell, Clarence. "Spotlight on Political Conventions." *Crisis* (October 1968), 75:277–82, 294.

Morgan, Charles. "How Many Minutes Until Midnight?" *New South* (Summer 1968), 23:52–55.

—— *One Man, One Voice.* New York: Holt, Rinehart & Winston, 1979.

Morris, John B. "The Georgia Challenge: An Interpretation." *New South* (Summer 1968), 23:59–61.

Morris, Milton D. *The Politics of Black America.* New York: Harper & Row, 1975.

Motomura, Hiroshi. "Preclearance Under Section Five of the Voting Rights Act." *North Carolina Law Review* (January 1983), 61:189–246.

Moynihan, Daniel Patrick. *Maximum Feasible Misunderstanding.* New York: Free Press, 1969.

Murphy, Reg and Hal Gulliver. *The Southern Strategy.* New York: Scribner's, 1971.

Murray, Richard and Arnold Vedlitz. "The Life Cycle of Black Political Organizations: A Study of Voter Groups in Five Southern Cities." Paper, Symposium on Southern Politics, The Citadel, 1978.

—— "Race, Socioeconomic Status, and Voting Participation in Large Southern Cities." *Journal of Politics* (November 1977), 39:1064–72.

—— "Racial Voting Patterns in the South: An Analysis of Major Elections from 1960 to 1977 in Five Cities." *Annals of the American Academy of Political and Social Science* (September 1978), 439:29–39.

Muse, Benjamin. *The American Negro Revolution From Nonviolence to Black Power 1963–1967.* Bloomington: University of Indiana Press, 1968.

Navasky, Victor. "The Greening of Griffin Bell." *New York Times Magazine,* February 27, 1977, pp. 41 ff.

—— *Kennedy Justice.* New York: Atheneum, 1971.

Neary, John. *Julian Bond: Black Rebel.* New York: Morrow, 1971.

"Negro Voting Power: How Strong?" *U.S. News & World Report* (September 29, 1969), 67:36–37.

"New South Notes." *New South* (Winter 1967), 22:86.

Noble, Gaile Patricia. "The Delta Ministry: Black Power, Poverty, and Politics in the Mississippi Delta." Masters thesis, Cornell University, 1969.

Note. "At-Large Electoral Schemes and Vote Diluton." *Harvard Law Review* (November 1980), 94:138–49.

Note. "*Chavis v. Whitcomb:* Apportionment, Gerrymandering, and Black Voting Rights." *Rutgers Law Review* (Spring 1970), 24:521–50.

Note. "The Constitutional Significance of Discriminatory Effects of At-Large Elections." *Yale Law Journal* (April 1982), 91:974–99.

Note. "Equal Protection of the Laws—Reapportionment—Multimember Districting of County Governing Bodies May Work Unconstitutional Dilution of Minority Voting Strength—*Zimmer v. McKeithen.*" *Harvard Law Review* (June 1974), 87:1851–60.

Note. "Racial Vote Dilution in Multimember Districts: The Constitutional Standard After *Washington v. Davis.*" *Michigan Law Review* (March 1978), 76:694–732.

Oberdorfer, Don. "Daily Dilemmas of the Attorney General." *New York Times Magazine*, March 7, 1965, pp. 28 ff.

O'Neill, William L. *Coming Apart: An Informal History of America in the 1960s.* New York: Quadrangle, 1975.

Orfield, Gary. *Congressional Power: Congress and Social Change.* New York: Harcourt Brace Jovanovich, 1975.

—— *The Reconstruction of Southern Education: The Schools and the 1964 Civil Rights Act.* New York: Wiley, 1969.

Ozog, James W. "Judicial Review of Municipal Annexations Under Section 5 of the Voting Rights Act." *Urban Law Annual* (1976), 12:311–20.

Panetta, Leon E. and Peter Gall. *Bring Us Together: The Nixon Team and the Civil Rights Retreat.* Philadelphia: Lippincott, 1971.

Parker, Frank R. "County Redistricting in Mississippi: Case Studies in Racial Gerrymandering." *Mississippi Law Journal* (June 1973), 44:391–424.

—— "The Impact of *City of Mobile v. Bolden* and Strategies and Legal Arguments for Voting Rights Cases in its Wake." In *The Right to Vote: A Rockefeller Foundation Conference, April 22–23, 1981*, pp. 98–124. New York: The Rockefeller Foundation, 1981.

Parker, Frank R. and Barbara Phillips. "Justice Department Voting Rights Act Enforcement: Political Interference and Retreats." *Lawyers' Committee For Civil Rights Under Law Memorandum,* January 20, 1982.

Parmet, Herbert S. *The Democrats: The Years After FDR.* New York: MacMillan, 1976.

Peirce, Neal R. *The Deep South States of America: People, Politics, and Power in the Seven Deep South States.* New York: Norton, 1974.

Peters, Christopher. "At-Large Elections of Parish Officials." *Alabama Law Review* (Fall 1973), 26:163–76.

Philips, Kevin. *The Emerging Republican Majority*. New Rochelle, New York: Arlington House, 1969.

Piven, Frances Fox and Richard A. Cloward. *Poor People's Movements: Why They Succeed, How They Fail*. New York: Pantheon Books, 1977.

Pollak, Stephen J. "Effective Anti-Discrimination Legislation: An Analysis of the Voting Rights Act of 1965." Paper, Department of Justice Office Files, May 1, 1974.

Powers, Brian A. "Annexations and the Voting Rights Act." *North Carolina Law Review* (January 1976), 54:206–16.

Preston, Michael B., Lenneal J. Henderson, and Paul Puryear, eds. *The New Black Politics: The Search for Political Power*. New York: Longman, 1982.

Prince, Vinton M., Jr. "Black Voting Strength in Mississippi: The Case of the Unreal Advantage." Paper, Symposium on Southern Politics, The Citadel, 1978.

Radosh, Ronald. "From Protest to Black Power: The Failure of Coalition Politics." In Marvin E. Gettleman and David Mermelstein, eds., *The Great Society Reader: The Failure of American Liberalism*, pp. 278–93. New York: Random House, 1967.

Rainwater, Lee and William L. Yancey. *The Moynihan Report and the Politics of Controversy*. Cambridge: MIT Press, 1967.

Ramundo, Clifford J. "Voting Rights—Voting Rights Act of 1965 Section 5— Federal Preclearance of Local Election Laws—*United States v. Board of Commissioners*." *New York Law School Law Review* (1979), 25:167–86.

Ranney, Austin. *Curing the Mischiefs of Faction: Party Reform in America*. Berkeley: University of California Press, 1975.

Read, Frank T. and Lucy S. McGough. *Let Them Be Judged: The Judicial Integration of the Deep South*. Metuchen, New Jersey: Scarecrow Press, 1978.

Rice, Bradley Robert. *Progressive Cities: The Commission Government Movement in America, 1901–1920*. Austin: University of Texas Press, 1977.

Roberts, Gene. "A Kind of Black Power in Macon County, Alabama." *New York Times Magazine*. February 26, 1967, pp. 32 ff.

—— "A Remarkable Thing Is Happening in Wilcox County, Alabama." *New York Times Magazine,* April 17, 1966, pp. 26 ff.

Rodgers, Harrell R., Jr., and Charles S. Bullock III. *Law and Social Change: Civil Rights Laws and Their Consequences*. New York: McGraw-Hill, 1972.

Roman, John J. "Section 5 of the Voting Rights Act: The Formation of an Extraordinary Remedy." *American University Law Review* (Fall 1972), 22:111–33.

Ross, David F. "Black Power: Alabama: First Steps." *New Republic* (September 27, 1969), 161:14–15.

Rovere, Richard. "Letter From Washington." *New Yorker* (June 18, 1966), 42:118–43.

Rowan, Carl. "The Consequences of Decision." In C. Eric Lincoln, ed., *Martin Luther King, Jr.: A Profile*, pp. 212–18. New York: Hill & Wang, 1970.

Rozier, John. *Black Boss: Political Revolution in a Georgia County.* Athens: University of Georgia Press, 1982.

Rozman, Stephen L. "The Political Attitudes of the Black Community in Canton, Mississippi." Paper, in possession of author, c. 1973.

Rudwick, Elliott and August Meier. "Integration vs. Separatism: The NAACP and CORE Face Challenge from Within." In August Meier and Elliott Rudwick, *Along the Color Line,* pp. 238–64. Urbana: University of Illinois Press, 1976.

Rustin, Bayard. "Black Power and Coalition Politics." *Commentary* (September 1966), 42:35–40.

—— *Down the Line.* Chicago: Quadrangle Books, 1971.

—— "From Protest to Politics: The Future of the Civil Rights Movement." *Commentary* (February 1965), 39:25–31.

—— "The Southern Negro Vote and the 1968 Elections." *New South* (Fall 1967), 22:48–53.

Safire, William. *Before the Fall: An Inside View of the Pre-Watergate White House.* Garden City, New York: Doubleday, 1975.

St. John, Jeffrey. *Jimmy Carter's Betrayal of the South.* Ottawa, Illinois: Hill, 1976.

Salamon, Lester M. "Leadership and Modernization: The Emerging Black Political Elite in the American South." *Journal of Politics* (August 1973), 35:615–46.

—— "Mississippi Post-Mortem: The 1971 Elections." *New South* (Winter 1972), 27:43–47.

—— "Protest, Politics, and Modernization in the American South: Mississippi as a 'Developing Society.' " Doctoral dissertation, Harvard University, 1971.

Salamon, Lester M. and Stephen Van Evera. "Fear, Apathy, and Discrimination: A Test of Three Explanations of Political Participation." *American Political Science Review* (December 1973), 67:1288–1306.

—— "Fear Revisited: Rejoinder to 'Comment' by Sam Kernell." *American Political Science Reivew* (December 1973), 67:1319–26.

Schell, Jonathan. *The Time of Illusion.* New York: Vintage, 1976.

Scher, Richard K. and James W. Button. "Voting Rights Act: Implementation and Impact." In Charles S. Bullock III and Charles M. Lamb, eds., *Implementation of Civil Rights Policy,* pp. 20–54. Monterey, California: Brooks/Cole, 1984.

"Securing a Valid Annexation in Virginia: State and Federal Requirements." *University of Richmond Law Review* (Spring 1976), 10:557–96.

Seess, Thomas J. "Federal Power to Combat Private Racial Violence in the Aftermath of *Price, Guest,* and the Civil Rights Act of 1968." Doctoral Dissertation, Georgetown University Law School, 1972.

Sellers, Cleveland with Robert Terrell. *The River of No Return: The Autobiography of a Black Militant and the Life and Death of SNCC.* New York: Morrow, 1973.

Sentell, R. Perry, Jr. "Federalizing Through the Franchise: The Supreme Court and Local Government." *Georgia Law Review* (Fall 1971), 6:34–73.

Shafer, Byron E. *Quiet Revolution: The Struggle for the Democratic Party and the Shaping of Post-Reform Politics.* New York: Russell Sage Foundation, 1983.

Sherrill, Robert. *The Accidental President.* New York: Grossman, 1967.

—— "Bubble of Unreality." *Nation* (June 20, 1966), 202:734–37.

Simpson, William M. "The 'Loyalist' Democrats of Mississippi: Challenge to a White Majority, 1965–1972." Doctoral dissertation, Mississippi State University, 1974.

Sitkoff, Harvard. *The Struggle for Black Equality 1954–1980.* New York: Hill & Wang, 1981.

Sloan, Lee. " 'Good Government' and the Politics of Race." *Social Problems* (Fall 1969), 17:161–74.

Smith, George Bundy. "The Failure of Reapportionment: The Effect of Reapportionment on the Election of Blacks to Legislative Bodies." *Howard Law Journal* (1975), 29:639–84.

Smith, Stanley H. "A Case Study of Socio-Political Change." *Phylon* (Winter 1968), 29:380–87.

Snyder, David M. "Voting Rights: Stuck Inside of Mobile with the Voting Blues Again: Vote Dilution Claims Confined." *Stetson Law Review* (1981), 10:363–76.

Steed, Robert P., Laurence W. Moreland, and Tod A. Baker, eds. *Party Politics in the South.* New York: Praeger, 1980.

Stern, Mark. "Southern Congressional Civil Rights Voting and the New Southern Demography." Paper, American Political Science Association, 1979.

Stern, Mark and John Baker. "Civil Rights Voting in the United States Senate: The South and the Nation." Paper, in possession of the author, c. 1979.

Stone, Chuck. *Black Political Power in America.* Revised edition. New York: Dell, 1970.

Stoper, Emily. "The Student Nonviolent Coordinating Committee: Rise and Fall of a Redemptive Organization." *Journal of Black Studies* (September 1977), 8:13–34.

Straud, Kandy. *How Jimmy Won: The Victory Campaign from Plains to the White House.* New York: Morrow, 1977.

Stronach, Corey E. "Anatomy of a Black Victory." *Nation* (August 26, 1973), 217:146–48.

Strong, Donald. "Alabama Transition and Alienation." In William C. Havard, ed., *The Changing Politics in the South,* pp. 427–71. Baton Rouge: Louisiana State University Press, 1972.

Stuart, Reginald. "Once Again, a Clash Over Voting Rights." *New York Times Magazine,* September 27, 1981, pp. 100 ff.

Suitts, Steve. "Blacks in the Political Arithmetic After *Mobile*: A Case Study of North Carolina." In *The Right to Vote: A Rockefeller Foundation Conference, April 22–23, 1981,* pp. 47–93. New York: The Rockefeller Foundation, 1981.

Sundquist, James L. *Politics and Policy: The Eisenhower, Kennedy, and Johnson Years.* Washington, D.C.: The Brookings Institution, 1968.

Terchek, Ronald J. "Political Participation and Political Structures: The Voting Rights Act of 1965." *Phylon* (March 1980), 41:25–35.

The Right to Vote: A Rockefeller Foundation Conference April 22–23, 1981. New York: The Rockefeller Foundation, 1981.

Thernstrom, Abigail M. "The Odd Evolution of the Voting Rights Act." *Public Interest* (Spring 1979), 55:49–76.

Thomas, William R., David V. Lee, and Raymond Brown. "Form of Government and Black Representation in Georgia Counties: Exploring Conventional Wisdom." Paper, Southern Political Science Association, 1982.

Thompson, Kenneth H. *The Voting Rights Act and Black Electoral Participation.* Washington, D.C.: Joint Center for Political Studies, 1982.

Tucker, David M. *Memphis Since Crump: Bossism, Blacks, and Civic Reformers 1948–1968.* Knoxville: University of Tennessee Press, 1980.

Vocino, Thomas, John H. Morris, and Steve D. Gill. "The Population Apportionment Principle: Its Development and Application to Mississippi State and Local Legislative Bodies." *Mississippi Law Journal* (November 1979), 47:943–78.

"Voting Rights—Or Wrongs?" *Newsweek* (December 22, 1969), 74:19–20.

Wall, Dennis J. "Multi Member Legislative Districts: Requiem for a Constitutional Burial." *University of Florida Law Review* (Summer 1977), 29:703–27.

Wall, Marvin. "New South Notes." *New South* (Winter 1969), 24:82.

Walters, Ronald. "Democratic Panel Decision Causes Stir." *Focus* (February 1975), 3:7.

—— "Democratic Party Guidelines: Full Role for Blacks." *Focus* (March 1974), 2:2–5.

Walton, Hanes, Jr. *Black Political Parties: An Historical and Political Analysis.* New York: The Free Press, 1972.

Wasby, Stephen. *Vote Dilution, Minority Voting Rights, and the Courts.* Washington, D.C.: Joint Center for Political Studies, 1982.

Washington Research Project. *The Shameful Blight: The Survival of Racial Discrimination in the South.* Washington, D.C.: Washington Research Project, 1972.

Washington, Robert B., Jr. "Fair and Effective Representation Revisited—The Shades of *Chavis v. Whitcomb.*" *Howard Law Journal* (1972), 17:382–400.

Wasserman, Lee. "The Voting Rights Act: There's No Time Like the Present." *Albany Law Review* (Spring 1982), 46:1045–68.

Watters, Pat. "South Carolina." *The Atlantic* (September 1968), 222:20–28.

Watters, Pat and Reese Cleghorn. *Climbing Jacob's Ladder: The Arrival of Negroes in Southern Politics.* New York, Harcourt, Brace & World, 1967.

Watts, Brian J. "*City of Mobile v. Bolden:* The Requirement of Discriminatory Intent in Vote Dilution Claims." *Baylor Law Review* (Fall 1980), 32:639–46.

Wells, Janet. "Voting Rights in 1975." *Civil Rights Digest* (Summer 1975), 7:13–19.

Wernz, William J. " 'Discriminatory Purpose,' 'Changes,' and 'Dilution,': Recent Judicial Interpretations of Section 5 of the Voting Rights Act." *Notre Dame Lawyer* (December 1975), 51:333–51.

White, Theodore H. *The Making of the President 1972.* New York: Atheneum, 1973.

Whittemore, L.H. *Together: A Reporter's Journey into the New Black Politics.* New York: Morrow, 1971.

Wiebe, Robert H. "White Attitudes and Black Rights from *Brown* to *Bakke.*" In Michael V. Namorato, ed., *Have We Overcome? Race Relations Since Brown,* pp. 147–71. Jackson: University Press of Mississippi, 1979.

Wieck, Paul R. "Southern Democrats: Not What They Used To Be." *New Republic* (August 3, 1968), 159:13–15.

Williams, Eddie N. "Black Voter Participation." *Focus* (November 1978), 6:4–5.

—— "Perspective," *Focus* (July 1982), 10:2.

Wilson, C.J. "Voices From Mississippi." *New South* (Spring 1973), 28:62–71.

Wirt, Frederick. *Politics of Southern Equality.* Chicago: Aldine, 1970.

Witcover, Jules. *Marathon: The Pursuit of the Presidency 1972–1976.* New York: Viking, 1977.

Wofford, Harris. *Of Kennedy and Kings: Making Sense of the Sixties.* New York: Farrar-Straus-Giroux, 1980.

Wolfson, Howard. *"City of Mobile v. Bolden:* A Setback in the Fight Against Discrimination." *Brooklyn Law Review* (Fall 1980), 47:169–201.

Wolk, Allan. *The Presidency and Black Civil Rights: Eisenhower to Nixon.* East Rutherford, New Jersey: Fairleigh Dickinson University Press, 1971.

Wooten, James. *Dasher: The Roots and the Rising of Jimmy Carter.* New York: Summit Books, 1978.

Yoste, H.M., Jr. "Section 5: Growth or Demise of Statutory Voting Rights?" *Mississippi Law Journal* (September 1977), 48:818–51.

Zimmerman, Joseph F. "The Federal Voting Rights Act: Its Impact on Annexation." *National Civic Review* (June 1977), 66:278–83.

Interviews and Oral Histories

Amerson, Lucius. Oral History. Howard University, Washington, D.C.

Arrington, Richard. Oral History. University of North Carolina, Chapel Hill, North Carolina.

Brown, Ben. Oral History. University of North Carolina, Chapel Hill, North Carolina.

Carter, Hodding, III. Oral History. Mississippi State University, Starkville, Mississippi.

Carter, Jimmy. Oral History. University of North Carolina, Chapel Hill, North Carolina.

Clemon, U.C. Oral History. University of North Carolina, Chapel Hill, North Carolina.

Evers, Charles. Oral History. University of Southern Mississippi, Hattiesburg, Mississippi.

Ford, Johnny. Oral History. University of North Carolina, Chapel Hill, North Carolina.

Gray, Fred. Interview. March 24, 1970. Tuskegee, Alabama.

Hamer, Fannie Lou. Oral History. University of Southern Mississippi, Hattiesburg, Mississippi.

Heineman, Ben. Oral History. Lyndon B. Johnson Library, Austin, Texas.

Henry, Aaron. Interview. February 14, 1979. Clarksdale, Mississippi.

Henry, Aaron, Oral History. Lyndon B. Johnson Library, Austin, Texas.

Hulett, John. Oral History. Howard University, Washington, D.C.

Jones, Gerald. Interview. July 26, 1979. Washington, D.C.

Jordan, Vernon E., Jr. Oral History. Howard University, Washington, D.C.

Katzenbach, Nicholas deB. Oral History. Lyndon B. Johnson Library, Austin, Texas.

King, Ed. Interview. February 11, 1979. Jackson, Mississippi.

Kirksey, Henry. Interview. February 18, 1979. Jackson, Mississippi.

Leonard, Jerris. Interview. July 31, 1979. Washington, D.C.

Lewis, John. Oral History. University of North Carolina, Chapel Hill, North Carolina.

Magee, Ruby. Oral History. University of Southern Mississippi, Hattiesburg, Mississippi.

McGhee, Silas. Oral History. Howard University, Washington, D.C.

McGill, Lillian. Oral History. Howard University, Washington, D.C.

McPherson, Harry. Oral History. Lyndon B. Johnson Library, Austin, Texas.

Nimetz, Matthew. Oral History. Lyndon B. Johnson Library, Austin, Texas.

Rauh, Joseph. Interview. July 16, 1979. Washington, D.C.

Rauh, Joseph. Oral History. Howard University, Washington, D.C.

Rauh, Joseph. Oral History. Lyndon B. Johnson Library, Austin, Texas.

Reed, Joe. Oral History. University of North Carolina, Chapel Hill, North Carolina.

Sanders, Barefoot. Oral History. Lyndon B. Johnson Library, Austin, Texas.

Shores, Arthur. Oral History. University of North Carolina, Chapel Hill, North Carolina.

Taylor, Hobart. Oral History. Lyndon B. Johnson Library, Austin, Texas.

Vance, Robert. Oral History. University of North Carolina, Chapel Hill, North Carolina.

Young, Andrew. Oral History. University of North Carolina, Chapel Hill, North Carolina.

Young, Whitney. Oral History. Lyndon B. Johnson Library, Austin, Texas.

Index

Abernathy, Ralph David, 55

Affirmative action, xiv, 288-89; and Democratic party reform, 194, 195, 201-3; and Justice Department, 22-23, 300; and Lyndon Johnson, 24; and "reverse discrimination," 221, 289; and Voting Rights Act, 22, 32, 33

AFL-CIO, 96, 114, 285

Alabama: and black political parties, 104-10; and Democratic party reform, 115-16, 200-1; and election of (1966), 34-35, 107-8, 109; and election of (1971), 270; and election of (1974), 270-71; and election of (1982), ix; and section five, 209; and voter registration, 35

Alabama Democratic Conference, 106, 109

Alabama Independent Democrats (AID), 116, 325n85

Alexander, Clifford, 47, 48, 72

Allen, James, 151, 158, 249, 252

Allen v. State Board of Elections, 133, 160, 161, 162, 163, 206

Amerson, Lucius, 107-8

Anderson, John B., 87

Andrews, George, 293

Annexation, 172, 212-15, 259; *see also* Section five

Aronson, Arnold, 26, 28, 76, 78

Arrington, Richard, 274

At-large elections, 172, 204, 209, 212-14, 217-23; *see also* Section five

Bail out, *see* Voting Rights Act (1965); Voting Rights Act (1970); Voting Rights Act (1975); Voting Rights Act (1982)

Baker, Howard, 85, 357n14

Baker, James, 255

Baker, Wilson, 35

Baker County (Ga.), 128

Barefield, Stone D., 243, 348n64

Barrett, St. John, 23

Bayh, Birch, 140-41, 148, 152, 194

Beer v. United States, 215-17, 259

Belzoni, Miss., 184

Berry, Jason, 180

Birmingham, Ala., 32-33, 35

Black, Earl, 270

Black, Hugo, 134

Black elected officials, ix, 107, 110, 275; assessment of, 11; and influence of, 267-69, 353n43; and problems of, 265-67; role of, 263-64; statistics on, 4, 39, 155, 186, 188, 230, 264, 265, 275-76, 293, 298, 359n40

Blackmun, Harry, 277, 278, 280

Black power, xiv, 12, 13, 64, 73, 90, 108, 295; criticism of, 5, 91-92, 94; and Meredith march, 52, 57, 62, 89; and suffrage, 57-58, 105; *see also* Carmichael, Stokely

Blacks, socioeconomic status of, 36-37, 127, 256, 272, 273, 302

Black suffrage, 191; benefits from, 12, 179, 181, 301; and civil rights protests, 263; and demographic changes, 188; and economic status, 273; and illiteracy, 102, 128, 231, 261, 352n22; limitations of, 272, 273-74, 301-2; problems of, 109, 204, 217-18, 232-33; and racial moderation, x, 4, 13, 149, 154-55, 189, 198, 224-25, 269-72, 274, 295-96, 301; and voter turnout, 273, 296, 355n70, 359n38; *see also* Voter registration

Bolden, Wiley L., 276

Bolivar County (Miss.), 41-42

Bond, Julian, 224, 258, 263; and black elected officials, 275; and black power, 90, 295; and Democratic convention chal-

Contemporary American History Series
WILLIAM E. LEUCHTENBURG, GENERAL EDITOR

(Continued from front flap)

renewal of the Voting Rights Act in 1970, 1975, and 1982. He also evaluates the extent to which black southerners have gained political power and influence from the right to vote. Of special interest is the relationship between blacks gaining the ballot and the decline in the use of protest tactics that were so effective for the civil rights movement before blacks had the vote. At the same time, Lawson notes the responses of southern politicians such as George Wallace to the expanded black electorate.

Lawson concludes that the ballot did improve the lives of southern blacks, but that black involvement in the political process has been hindered by continued economic deprivation and the vestiges of a century of discrimination. And he notes that while there have been many historic black "firsts" in electoral politics since the 1960s, blacks still "stand on the threshold of political power, waiting to participate more fully in their own governance." Drawn from a wide variety of original manuscript sources dealing with civil rights, *In Pursuit of Power* will be of significant interest and lasting importance to historians, political scientists, sociologists, legal scholars, and all interested in race relations.

Contemporary American History William E. Leuchtenburg, General Editor

Steven F. Lawson is Associate Professor of History at the University of South Florida in Tampa. He is the author of *Black Ballots*, also published by Columbia University Press, and numerous articles about the civil rights movement.